The Gospel according to
ST JOHN
1 - 10

CALVIN'S COMMENTARIES

CALVIN'S COMMENTARIES

The Gospel according to

ST JOHN

I — 10

Translator
T. H. L. PARKER

Editors
DAVID W. TORRANCE
THOMAS F. TORRANCE

WILLIAM B. EERDMANS PUBLISHING COMPANY
GRAND RAPIDS, MICHIGAN

THE PATERNOSTER PRESS
CARLISLE

Translation © 1961 Oliver and Boyd Ltd.

Published jointly in the United States
by Wm. B. Eerdmans Publishing Co.
255 Jefferson Ave. S.E., Grand Rapids, Michigan 49503
and in the U.K. by The Paternoster Press
P.O. Box 300, Carlisle, Cumbria CA3 0QS

First paperback edition published 1995

Printed in the United States of America

00 99 98 97 96 95   7 6 5 4 3 2 1

Eerdmans ISBN 0-8028-0804-2

British Library Cataloguing in Publication Data

Calvin, Jean
The Gospel according to St. John 1-10 - New ed.
(Calvin's New Testament Commentaries; Vol. 4)
I. Title   II. Parker, T. H. L.   III. Series
226.507

Paternoster ISBN 0-85364-683-X

INTRODUCTION

On November 19th, 1552, Calvin wrote to Blaurer, the Constance reformer: 'Robert Estienne has my Commentary on John in the press now,' and promised him a copy when it was published.[1] The book came out at the beginning of January, 1553, as a folio bearing the title:

> In Evangelium secundum Iohannem Commentarius
> Iohannis Calvini.
> Oliva Roberti Stephani. MDLIII.

and the colophon:

> Excudebat Robertus Stephanus in sua officina
> anno MDLIII Cal. Ian.

This commentary was dedicated to the Senate of Geneva, a copy being given them on January 9th, 1553. The gift is recorded in the Acts of the Senate: 'M. Calvin has given to the Seigneurie a commentary book on S. John's Gospel, of which the preface is addressed to the Seigneurie.'[2]

In the same year Calvin translated the work into French:

> Commentaire de M. Iean Calvin sur l'Evangile selon
> sainct Iean, Traduit du latin. 1553. 8º.

In its second edition it appeared in one volume with the commentary on the Harmony of the first three Gospels:

> Commentarius in quatuor Evangelia.
> Genevae. Rob. Stephanus. 1555.

This also had its French counterpart in the same year. Thereafter it ran into many editions and impressions, sometimes with the commentary on Acts as well as the other Gospels.

The Commentary was first translated into English by Christopher Fetherstone:

> The holy gospel of Iesus Christ, according to John, with the commentarie of M. Iohn Calvine: Faithfully translated out of latine into englishe by Christopher Fetherstone, student of divinitie.

It was printed in London by Thomas Dawson for G. Byshop in 1584, and was added to:

[1] C.R. xiv. 413. C.T.S. 2. 360. Blaurer's reply: C.R. xiv. 459. January 16th, 1553.
[2] C.R. xxi. 532.

INTRODUCTION

A Harmonie upon the three evangelists, Matthew, Mark and
Luke, with the commentarie of Iohn Calvine; translated by
E. P(aget)

Another edition of Fetherstone's translation appeared in 1610 printed
by Thomas Dawson for Thomas Adams.

The second rendering of the Commentary was for the Calvin
Translation Society:

Commentary on the Gospel According to John by John Calvin.
A new translation, from the original Latin. Translated by the
Rev. William Pringle. Edinburgh. 1847.

The present translation is a revision of Pringle's. How complete,
may be judged from a comparison of the two. With the best will in the
world, it cannot be said that Pringle's was a good attempt. His in-
ability to grasp the close coherence of Calvin's ideas, and his missing
many of the characteristic images, are the least of his faults. Far worse
is his carelessness in omitting negatives or even whole passages and
putting in the wrong word altogether. Nevertheless, he has provided
a basis.

In conclusion, my thanks are due to the editors for their help and
forbearance. And I cannot refrain from mentioning that the material
for this introduction was collected in the hospitable Bibliothèque
Publique et Universitaire de Genève, a stone's throw from where the
commentary was written.

Great Ponton,   T. H. L. PARKER
July 21st, 1958

THE DEDICATORY EPISTLE

TO THE
RIGHT HONOURABLE LORDS
THE SYNDICS AND SENATE OF GENEVA
AND HIS RESPECTED LORDS
JOHN CALVIN
PRAYS FROM THE LORD
THE SPIRIT OF WISDOM AND STRENGTH
AND SUCCESS IN GOVERNMENT

As often as I recall the saying of Christ in which He prizes the humane duty of receiving strangers so highly that He reckons it as done to Himself, I also remember that He has thought you worthy of a special honour; for it was His will that your city should be the guest-chamber, not of one or a few, but of His Church at large. Among the heathen hospitality was not only praised but regarded as one of the foremost virtues. Hence, when they wished to condemn in any peoples the lowest barbarism and the most savage manners, they called them ἀξένους or, what comes to the same thing, inhospitable. A far higher praise is due to you that in these troublesome and unhappy days the Lord has appointed you to supply safety and protection to the godly and innocent men whom the cruel and sacrilegious tyranny of Antichrist has banished and driven away from their native lands. And not only this, but He has also dedicated to His name a sacred dwelling place among you where He may be worshipped purely.

Whoever attempts to abolish openly, or to take away secretly, the smallest part of these two things is not only acting in a way that will deform your city by stripping it of its chiefest ornaments, but is also malignantly harming its safety. Although the godly kindnesses which are done here for Christ and His dispersed members provoke the barking of those ungodly dogs, yet it should be sufficient compensation to you that from heaven the angels, and from every region of the world the children of God, bless you. You may therefore boldly despise the disgusting abuse of those without religion or shame who vomit out what they please on God Himself even more than on you; nay! who, when they want to slander you, begin by blaspheming God. Even though this same cause inflames the hatred of many against you, you need not dread any danger from it, so long as He opposes their fury with His protecting hand, who has promised that He will be the faithful guard of cities where the preaching of His Gospel dwells, and in which godly men who are unbearable to the world are allowed to live. I say nothing about its being unnecessary to be careful to conciliate this sort of enemy, since none is hostile to you on account of the Gospel who would not wish to see you ruined or oppressed for other reasons. But even if there were no other cause for you to be hated by the avowed enemies of sound doctrine than because they see you defending it, yet you ought to disregard their schemes and threats, and resolutely defend those two impregnable bastions, the cultivation of pure religion and a godly care to cherish the Church which Christ has placed under the shelter of your wings.

The Pope's gang of mercenaries accuse us of apostasy from the Church, because we have separated from the see of Rome. I wish we could as well protest with complete confidence before God and the angels that we are at the greatest distance from that cess-pool, as we can easily and readily defend ourselves from the crime they are accustomed to accuse us of. They claim the title of Catholic Church, who leave no part of the universal teaching of the Law and the Gospel pure of foul corruptions, who have profaned the whole worship of God with the filth of their superstitions, who were not ashamed to adulterate all the ordinances of God with their inventions. Nay, so catholic is the mass of errors by which they have overturned the whole of religion, that it would be enough to destroy and swallow up the Church a hundred times. Therefore, we can never sufficiently extol the infinite goodness of God, by which we have wonderfully escaped from that deadly whirlpool and have fixed the anchor of our faith in the firm and eternal truth of God. And indeed I hope that this commentary will itself be a clear witness that the Papacy is nothing but a monstrosity produced from the innumerable deceptions of Satan, and that what they call the Church is more confused than Babel (*Babylone*).

Yet I will frankly confess the truth. We are not yet far enough away from that filthy pit, whose infection is widespread. Antichrist complains that we have fallen away from him. But we are forced to groan that too many of the vices with which he has infected the world remain among us. A genuine purity of doctrine, sound religion, the simple worship of God and the right administration of the Sacraments have been restored to us, as they were delivered by Christ. But the chief cause that prevents the correction of manners and life flourishing among us is, that a good part remember the unbridled licence in which the Papists wanton against God, and cannot get used to the yoke of Christ. Accordingly, when our enemies, to stir up an unfair dislike against us among the ignorant, offensively cry out that we have broken all discipline, their slander is abundantly refuted (even were we to be silent) by this one fact, that at home we have no contest more serious than about what many consider our excessive strictness. But you are the best witnesses for myself and my colleagues that we are no more severe or strict than the necessity of duty demands and even forces us to be. And as we freely submit to the decision of your conscience, so, on the other hand, you will easily judge how ridiculous is the impudence of our enemies in this matter.

Let me now say something about myself personally. Although I trust that my numerous writings will be a sufficient witness to the whole world how I have taught this Church, yet I thought it would be worth while if there were a special memorial of this inscribed with your name. For it is very necessary that the kind of doctrine which, as you know, I have taught, should be set before everybody. Now, although in my books published hitherto, it has been my care that you and the people committed to you should benefit from them even after my death, and though it would not be right that the teaching which has flowed from your city to foreign nations should bear much fruit far and wide but be neglected in its own home, yet I trust that this commentary, which is especially dedicated to you, will take an even firmer hold in your memory. Therefore I pray God to inscribe it so deeply with His own finger on your hearts, that it may never be erased by any trick of Satan. For it belongs to God to give success to my work, who has this long time given to me such a mind as to desire nothing more than faithfully to care for the salvation of you all. Moreover, as I frankly confess that I am very far from possessing the careful diligence and the other virtues which the greatness and excellence of the office require in a good pastor, and as I continually bewail before God the many sins that hinder my course, so I dare profess that I do not lack a faithful and sincere will. Meanwhile, if the wicked do not cease to trouble me, as it is for me to refute their slanders by well-doing, so it will be your parts to restrain them with the holy authority in which you are strong. Farewell, most excellent Lords, honourable to me in Christ, to whose protection I commit you.

GENEVA. January 1st, 1553

THE THEME OF THE GOSPEL OF JOHN

THE meaning of the Greek word for Gospel is well enough known. In Scripture is signifies κατ᾽ ἐξοχήν[1] the glad and joyful message of the grace revealed to us in Christ, to teach us to despise the world and its transient riches and pleasures, and to desire with all our heart and to embrace this incomparable blessing when it is offered to us. The immoderate delight of irreligious men in the empty enjoyments of the world, who are not at all, or little, touched by a feeling for spiritual blessings, is innate in nearly all of us. Therefore, to correct this fault, God specially calls by the name Gospel the message which He commands to be proclaimed about Christ. For in this way He tells us that nowhere else can true and substantial happiness be obtained and that in Him we have in perfection all the parts of a blessed life.

Some extend the word Gospel to all the free promises of God scattered even in the Law and the Prophets. And it cannot be denied that whenever God declares that He will be propitious to men and forgives their sins, He sets forth Christ at the same time, whose property it is to shed abroad the rays of joy wherever He shines. I admit therefore that the fathers partook of the same Gospel as ourselves, so far as the faith of free salvation is concerned. But because the Spirit is wont to say in the Scriptures that the Gospel was first proclaimed when Christ came, let us keep to this manner of expression. Let us also hold to the definition of the Gospel that I have given, that it is a solemn proclamation of the grace revealed in Christ. For this reason, the Gospel is called the power of God unto salvation to everyone that believes; because in it God manifests His righteousness. It is also called an embassy, by which He reconciles men to himself. Moreover, as Christ is the pledge of the divine mercy and fatherly love towards us, so He is properly the subject of the Gospel.

Hence it came about that the histories which narrate that Christ appeared in the flesh, and died, and was raised from the dead, and at length was taken up into heaven, have particularly received the name of Gospel. For although, for the reasons we have given, the word denotes the New Testament, yet the practice has obtained that by synecdoche[2] it is used for that part of it which declares that Christ was manifested to us in the flesh, and died, and rose again from the dead. But since the bare history would not be sufficient, and indeed, would be of no use for salvation, the Evangelists do not simply relate that

[1] Pre-eminently.   [2] A part for the whole.

5

Christ was born, and died, and conquered death, but also explain to what end He was born, and died, and rose again, and what benefit we derive from this.

Yet there is also this difference between them, that the other three narrate the life and death of Christ more fully, whereas our present one emphasizes more the doctrine in which Christ's office and the power of His death and resurrection are explained. The others are certainly not silent on Christ's coming into the world to bring salvation, to atone for the sins of the world by the sacrifice of His death and, in short, to perform all the duties of a Mediator; just as John also devotes part of his work to historical narration. But the doctrine which points out to us the power and fruit of Christ's coming appears far more clearly in him than in the others. And since they all had the same object, to show Christ, the first three exhibit His body, if I may be permitted to put it like that, but John shows His soul. For this reason I am accustomed to say that this Gospel is a key to open the door to the understanding of the others. For whoever grasps the power of Christ as it is here graphically portrayed, will afterwards read with advantage what the others relate about the manifested Redeemer.

John is believed to have written chiefly with the intention of maintaining Christ's divinity against the ungodly blasphemies of Ebion and Cerinthus. Eusebius and Jerome relate this from the common opinion of the ancients. But whatever might be the contemporary reason for his writing, there can be no doubt that God intended far more for His Church. He therefore so dictated to the four Evangelists what they should write that, while each had his own part, the whole formed one complete body. It is for us now to blend the four in a mutual connexion, that we may let ourselves be taught as by the one mouth. As to John being put fourth in order, it was done because of his order in time. In reading them, a different order will be better. When we want to read in Matthew and the rest that Christ was given to us by the Father, we should first learn from John to what end He was manifested.

CHAPTER ONE

In the beginning was the Word, and the Word was with God, and the Word was God. The same was in the beginning with God. All things were made by him; and without him was not anything made that hath been made. In him was life; and the life was the light of men. And the light shineth in the darkness; and the darkness comprehendeth it not. (1-5)

1. *In the beginning was the Word.* In this prologue he declares Christ's eternal divinity, to teach us that He is the eternal God, manifest in the flesh. His object is to show that the restoration of mankind had to be accomplished by the Son of God, because by His power all things were created and He alone breathes life and energy into all creatures, so that they remain *in statu*, and because in man himself He has given unique proof of His power and grace and even after Adam's fall and failure has never ceased to show liberality and kindness to his descendants. Now, the knowledge of this doctrine is of the first importance. For since we should on no account seek life and salvation outside God, how can our faith rest in Christ if the certainty of this teaching is not established? In these words, therefore, the Evangelist asserts that we do not forsake the one, eternal God when we believe in Christ, and also that life is now restored to the dead through the kindness of Him who was the source and cause of life when nature was yet sound. I think he calls the Son of God 'the Word' (*Sermo*) simply because, first, He is the eternal wisdom and will of God, and secondly, because He is the express image of His purpose. For just as in men speech is called the expression of the thoughts, so it is not inappropriate to apply this to God and say that He expresses Himself to us by His Speech or Word. The other meanings of ὁ λόγος are not so apt. The Greek certainly means *definition* or *reason* or *calculation*; but I refuse to philosophize beyond the grasp of my faith. And we see that the Spirit of God is so far from approving such subtleties that in prattling with us His very silence proclaims how sober should be our intellectual approach in such high mysteries. Moreover, since God, in creating the world, revealed Himself by the Word, He formerly had Him within Himself, hidden. Thus the Word has a twofold relation, to God and to men. Servetus, that most arrogant and worthless Spaniard, imagines that the eternal Word came into being only when He was exercised in the creation of the world. As if He was not before His power was made known by His outward operation! The Evangelist teaches quite differ-

ently here, for he does not ascribe a temporal beginning to the Word
but, by saying that He was from the beginning, transcends all times.
I know well how this dog barks and what quibbles were once raised
by the Arians—that in the beginning God created heaven and earth
which, however, are not eternal, for beginning refers to order and does
not indicate eternity. But the Evangelist forestalls this calumny when
he says that He was with God. If the Word had a temporal beginning,
they must discover some time-series in God. And, indeed, by this
clause John wanted to distinguish Him from all creatures. For many
questions could arise: Where actually was this Word? How did He
exercise His power? What was His nature? Whence could He be
known? Therefore he denies that Christ was fixed in the world and
created things, since He was always united with God before the world
existed. Now, do not those who refer the beginning to the creation of
heaven and earth reduce Christ to the common order of the world,
from which He is here expressly excluded? By doing this they horribly
insult not only the Son of God but also His eternal Father, whom they
deprive of His Wisdom. If it is wrong to picture God apart from His
Wisdom, we must also confess that the origin of the Word is not to be
sought anywhere but in the eternal Wisdom of God. Servetus objects
that the Word cannot be conceived of before God is represented by
Moses as speaking. As if, because He was not yet openly manifest, He
did not subsist in God! As if He had no inner existence before He began
to show Himself outwardly! But the Evangelist destroys every loop-
hole for such drivelling nonsense when he affirms unconditionally that
the Word was with God. For he clearly calls us away from all tem-
poralness. Those who infer a continuing state from the imperfect
tense of the verb are in rather a weak position. They say that the word
'was being' (erat) better expresses a continuous series than if John had
said 'He was' (fuit). But such matters demand weightier reasons. What
I have brought forward should suffice—that the Evangelist sends us to
the eternal sanctuary of God and teaches us that the Word was, as it
were, hidden there before He revealed Himself in the outward work-
manship of the world. Augustine is therefore right when he reminds
us that the beginning mentioned here has in fact no beginning. For
although the Father is prior to His Wisdom in order, yet they who
imagine any point of time when He preceded His Wisdom despoil Him
of His glory. And this is the eternal Son (generatio) who, infinitely
before the foundation of the world, was concealed in God (if I may
put it like that), and who, after being obscurely outlined to the patriarchs under the Law for many succeeding years, was at length more
fully manifested in the flesh. I am surprised that the Latin versions put
verbum (word) for ὁ λόγος, for that is rather the translation of τὸ ῥῆμα.

But even if we allow that it is a possibility, it cannot be denied that *sermo* (Speech) is far more appropriate. This shows up the barbarous tyranny of those theologasters who harrassed Erasmus so fiercely because he changed a single word for the better.

And the Word was with God. We have already said that the Son of God is thus placed above the world and all creatures and before all ages. But at the same time this expression attributes to Him an *hypostasis* distinct from the Father. For it would have been absurd if the Evangelist had said that He was always with God or in the presence of God unless He had a certain subsistence of His own in God. This verse serves, therefore, to refute the error of Sabellius, since it shows the Son to be distinct from the Father. I have already said that such profound mysteries demand sober thinking. But the early Church writers were excusable when, because they could not in any other way defend true and pure doctrine against the ambiguous quibbles of the heretics, they were forced to coin certain words which yet said nothing but what is taught in the Scriptures in another way. They said that there are three *hypostases* or Persons in the one and simple essence of God. The word *hypostasis* has this sense in Heb. 1 and corresponds to the Latin *substantia*, as it is used by Hilary. They termed τὰ πρόσωπα or Persons, discrete properties (*proprietates*) in God which present themselves to our contemplation. As Gregory of Nazianzus says: 'I cannot think of the One without the Three forthwith shining around me.'

And the Word was God. Lest any doubt should remain as to Christ's divine essence, he clearly declares that He is God. Now, since God is one, it follows that Christ is of the same essence with the Father and yet in some way different. But we have already spoken about the second clause. Arius was extremely wicked in regard to the unity of the essence; to avoid being forced to confess the eternal divinity of Christ, he prated that God was some kind of creature. But when we hear that the Word was God, what right have we any longer to question His eternal essence?

2. *The same was in the beginning.* To drive more deeply into our minds what had already been said, the Evangelist summarizes the two preceding clauses into a short epilogue: He always was; and He was with God—so that you may understand that this beginning was before all time.

3. *All things were made by him.* Having declared that the Word is God and proclaimed His divine essence, he goes on to prove His divinity from His works. And it is in this practical knowledge that we ought especially to be trained. For the mere attribution of the name of God to Christ will leave us cold unless our faith feels Him to

be such indeed. But he rightly declares of the Son of God what properly accords with His person. Sometimes, indeed, Paul simply says that 'all things are of God' (Rom. 11.36). But when the Son is compared with the Father He is usually distinguished by this mark. Accordingly the ordinary manner of speaking is used here—the Father made all things by the Son, and all things are by God through the Son. Now, as I have said, the Evangelist's plan is to show that the Word of God came forth to outward action immediately from the creation of the world. For having previously been incomprehensible in His essence, He was then openly known by the effect of His power. Even some philosophers set up God as the architect of the world in such a way as to make Him the intelligence behind the building of this work. In this they are right, for they agree with Scripture; but as they soon fade off into paltry meditations, there is no reason why we should desire their witness at all eagerly; rather should we be satisfied with this heavenly oracle, knowing that it says much more than our minds can take in.

And without him was not anything made that hath been made. Although this verse has been variously interpreted, I have no hesitation in taking it as a single thought—*was not anything made that hath been made.* Nearly all the Greek manuscripts (or at least those with the best authority) agree in this. Moreover, the sense undoubtedly demands it. Those who separate the phrase *that hath been made* from the preceding clause, so as to connect it to the following sentence, force the sense into *that which hath been made was life in him*—i.e. 'lived', or 'was sustained in life'. But they cannot show that this manner of speaking is ever applied to creatures. Augustine, who is in his way an extreme Platonist, is addicted to the concept of the idea: before God built the world He had as a concept in His mind the form of the whole work; and, since the creation of the world was ordered in Christ, the life of those things which did not yet exist in Him. But how far this is from the thought of the Evangelist we shall soon see. I now return to the former clause. This is no faulty περιττολογία or redundancy, as it seems to be at first sight. For since Satan exerts all his strength to detract from Christ, the Evangelist wished to declare expressly that nothing at all is to be excepted from those things which have been made.

4. *In him was life.* So far, he has taught us that all things were created by the Word of God. He now likewise attributes to Him the preservation of what had been created; as if he were saying that in the creation of the world His power did not simply suddenly appear only to pass away, but that it is visible in the permanence of the stable and settled order of nature—just as Heb. 1.3 says that He upholds all things by the Word or command of His power. Moreover, this life can either be

referred at large to inanimate creatures, which do live in their own way though they lack feeling, or expounded only of the animate. It matters little which you choose, for the simple meaning is that the Word of God was not only the fount of life to all creatures, so that those which had not yet existed began to be, but that His life-giving power makes them remain in their state. For did not His continued inspiration quicken the world, whatsoever flourishes would without doubt immediately decay or be reduced to nothing. In short, what Paul ascribes to God, that in Him we have our being and move and live (Acts 17.28), John declares to be accomplished by the blessing of the Word. It is God, therefore, who gives us life; but He does so by the eternal Word.

The life was the light of men. I deliberately disregard some other interpretations which disagree with the evangelist's meaning. I think that this is a reference to that part of life in which men surpass the other animate creatures. It is as if he were saying that the life given to men was not life in general but life united with the light of reason. Moreover, he separates men from the others, because we are more aware of God's power by feeling it in us than by looking at it from a distance. Thus, in Acts 17.27 Paul tells us not to seek God afar off, since He reveals Himself within us. And so, when the Evangelist has put forward a general consideration of the grace of Christ, to persuade men to give it closer attention, he shows what was given to them in particular— that is, that they were not created in the likeness of the beasts but, endowed with reason, they held a higher rank. Furthermore, since God effectually illuminates their minds with His light, it follows that they were created to the end they might know that He is the author of such a unique blessing. And since this light streamed forth to us from the Word its source, it should be as a mirror in which we may see clearly the divine power of the Word.

5. *And the light shineth in the darkness.* The objection could be raised that men are called blind in many passages of Scripture and that the blindness for which they are condemned is but too well known. For in all their reasoning they peter out miserably. For whence come so many labyrinths of errors in the world but because men are led by their own understanding only into vanity and falsehood? Yet if no light is visible in men this witness of the Evanglist to the divinity of Christ is destroyed. For, as I have said, the third step was that in the life of men there is a something far more excellent than movement and breathing. The Evangelist forestalls this question by warning us at once that the light given to men in the beginning must not be assessed by their present state, since in this marred and degenerate nature light has been turned to darkness. And yet he denies that the light of reason

is completely put out; for in the darkling gloom of the human mind there still shine some sparks of that brightness. The reader will now understand that there are two ideas in this sentence. He says that men are now very different from that sound nature with which they were endowed in the beginning; their mind, which should have been radiant in every part, is sunk in the shades of unhappy blindness. And so, in this corruption of nature, the glory of Christ is as it were darkened over. But on the other hand, the Evangelist maintains that in the midst of the darkness certain remnants yet exist which show in some degree Christ's divine power. The Evangelist shows, therefore, that man's mind is quite blinded; so that it may fairly be regarded as overwhelmed with darkness. For he could have used a milder word and said that the light was gloomy or murky; but he wanted to express more clearly how wretched is our condition since the fall of the first man. His statement that the light shines in the darkness is not at all meant as praise of corrupt nature but rather to deprive ignorance of excuse.

And the darkness comprehended it not. Although the Son of God has always called men to Himself by this poor light still left in us, the Evangelist says that it was ineffectual, because 'seeing, they did not see'. For after man was estranged from God, such ignorance held sway over his mind that whatever light remains in it lies choked and ineffectual. Experience also proves this daily. For even those who are not regenerate by the Spirit of God still exercise a certain reason, so that we are plainly taught that man was made not only to breathe but to have understanding. Yet led by their reason they do not reach or even approach God; and so all their intelligence is in the end nothing but vanity. Whence it follows that there is no hope for men's salvation unless God shall help with a new help. For though the Son of God sheds His light upon them, they are so dull that they do not comprehend the source of that light; carried away by doting and perverse fancies they end up in madness. There are two main parts in that light which yet remains in corrupt nature. Some seed of religion is sown in all: and also, the distinction between good and evil is engraven in their consciences. But what is the fruition at last, save that religion comes to monstrous birth in a thousand superstitions, and conscience corrupts all judgment, confounding vice with virtue? In short, natural reason will never direct men to Christ. The fact that they are furnished with wisdom for ruling their lives and are formed for the humanities and sciences disappears without effect. Moreover, we must remember that the evangelist is speaking only of natural gifts and is not yet dealing with the grace of regeneration. For there are two distinct powers of the Son of God. The first appears in the architecture of the world and in the order of nature. By the second He renews and restores fallen nature. He is the eternal Word of God: and so by Him the world was made; by His power all things keep the life they once received; in particular, man was adorned with the unique gift of understanding, and though by his fall he lost the light of understanding, he still sees and understands, since what he naturally possesses from the grace of the Son of God is not entirely destroyed. But because by his dullness and perversity he darkens the light he still has, it remains for the Son of God to assume a new office, that of mediator, and re-form lost man by the Spirit of regeneration. Therefore, they put the cart before the horse who refer the light which the Evangelist mentions to the Gospel and the preaching of salvation.

There was a man, sent from God, whose name was John. The same came for witness, that he might bear witness of the light, that all might believe through him. He was not that light, but came that he might bear witness of the light. There was the true light, which lighteth every man coming into the world. He was in the world, and the world was made by him, and the world knew him not. He came unto his own, and they that were his own received him not. But as many as received him, to them gave he power to become the sons of God, even to them that believe on his name: which were born, not of blood, nor of the will of the flesh, nor of the will of man, but of God. (6-13)

6. *There was a man.* The Evangelist now begins to discuss the way in which the Word of God was manifested in the flesh. And lest any should doubt that Christ is the eternal Son of God, he tells how He was publicly proclaimed by a herald, John the Baptist. For Christ did not only show Himself to men but wished also to be made known by the witness and preaching of John. Or rather, God the Father sent this witness before His Christ that they might all the more readily receive the salvation He offered. But at first sight it might seem absurd that another should bear witness to Christ as if He were in need of it. For He declares that He does not seek witness from man. The answer is easy and obvious: this witness was ordained, not for Christ's sake but for ours. If any object that the witness of man is too weak to prove that Christ is the Son of God, the solution is again easy: the Baptist is not cited as a private witness, but as one who, endowed with divine authority, appeared in the role rather of an angel than of a man. And so he is not praised for his own abilities, but just because he was the ambassador of God. Nor does it contradict the self-witness of Christ in the preaching of the Gospel committed to Him. For the *raison d'être* of John as a herald was to draw his hearers' attention to Christ's teaching and miracles.

13

Sent from God. He does not confirm John's calling, but only mentions it in passing. This assurance is not sufficient for many people who push themselves forward and boast that they are sent by God. But the Evangelist, intending to say more later about this witness, thought the one word was enough for now—he had come at God's commission. We shall see afterwards how John claims that God is the author of his ministry. What we have to grasp now is (as I mentioned before) that what is said about John is required in all Church teachers: they must be called by God, so that the authority of teaching may have no other basis than God alone. He names John, not only to identify the man, but because the meaning of the name was attached to him. For there is no doubt that the Lord was referring to the office for which He intended him when through His angel He commanded that he should be called John; so that all might recognize from this that he was the herald of divine grace. For although יוֹחָנָן may be taken as passive and thus referred to him personally, that John would be pleasing to God, yet I unhesitatingly extend it to the fruit which others would gather from him.

7. *The same came for witness.* He glances briefly at the purpose of John's calling: that he should prepare the Church for Christ. For when he invites all to Christ, he shows plainly enough that he did not come to further his own cause. John had so little need of recommendation that the Evangelist emphasizes that he was not the light, in case an immoderate brightness ascribed to him should darken the glory of Christ. For some clung so tightly to him that they disregarded Christ. Just as a man, overcome at the sight of dawn, would not deign to look at the sun. Now we shall see what meaning the Evangelist gives to the word light. All the godly are 'light in the Lord' (Eph. 5.8) in that, enlightened by His Spirit, not only do they themselves see, but also by their example direct others to the way of salvation. The apostles are called light (Matt. 5.14) because they are the special Gospel torch-bearers, scattering the world's darkness. But here the Evangelist is discussing the unique and eternal fount of illumination, as he at once shows more clearly.

9. *There was the true light.* The Evangelist was not contrasting the true light with a false; he wanted to differentiate Christ from all others lest any should think that He has what is called light in common with angels or men. The difference is that heavenly and earthly light has only a derivative brightness; but Christ is light, reflecting from Himself and through Himself and thence shining brightly upon the whole world. There is no other source or cause of its brightness anywhere. And so he calls Him the true light whose own nature is to be light.

Which lighteth every man. The Evangelist emphasizes this that we

14

may learn that Christ is the light from the effect which each of us feels in himself. He could have argued more subtly that inasmuch as Christ is eternal light, He has a native and underived brightness. But instead, he recalls us to the experience we all have. For, since Christ makes us all partakers of His brightness, it must be acknowledged that to Him alone accords strictly the dignity of being called light. For the rest, this verse is commonly explained in one of two ways. Some limit the universal term to those who, begotten again by the Spirit of God, are made partakers of the life-giving light. Augustine uses the simile of a schoolmaster who, if his is the only school in the town, will be called the master of all even though many do not attend his school. There-fore, they regard this phrase relatively: all are enlightened by Christ, since none can boast that he has obtained the light of life otherwise than through His grace. But as the Evangelist mentions in general 'every man coming into the world', I prefer the other meaning—that beams from this light are shed upon the whole race of men, as I said before. For we know that men have this unique quality above the other animals, that they are endowed with reason and intelligence and that they bear the distinction between right and wrong engraven in their conscience. Thus there is no man to whom some awareness of the eternal light does not penetrate. But, since fanatics eagerly seize on this verse and twist it into saying that the grace of illumination is offered to all without distinction, let us remember that it is only referring to the common light of nature, a far lowlier thing than faith. For no man will penetrate into the kingdom of God by the cleverness and perspicuity of his own mind; the Spirit of God alone opens the gate of heaven to His elect. Moreover, we must remember that the light of reason which God imparted to men has been so darkened by sin that scarcely a few meagre sparks still shine unquenched in this intense darkness or rather dreadful ignorance and abyss of errors.

10. *He was in the world.* He accuses men of ingratitude, in that they were, so to say, voluntarily blinded; blinded in such a way that they did not know how the light they enjoyed was caused. And this is true of every age. Even before Christ was manifest in the flesh He revealed His power everywhere. Therefore those daily effects ought to correct men's sluggishness; for what could be more unreasonable than to draw water from a running stream and never think of the spring it flows from? Accordingly, the world cannot plead ignorance as a legitimate excuse for not knowing Christ before He was manifest in the flesh. For it came from slackness and a sort of malignant dulness in those who always had Him present in His power. The sum of it is that Christ was never so absent from the world that men ought not to have been

awakened by His rays and to have looked up to Him. Whence it follows that they are guilty.

11. *He came unto his own.* Here he shows man's utterly pitiable perversity and vice, their more than accursed ungodliness, in that, when the Son of God revealed Himself visibly in the flesh (and that to the Jews, whom God had separated to Himself from the other nations as His own) He was not acknowledged or received. This verse too is expounded in different ways. Some think the Evangelist is speaking of the whole world in general; for there is certainly no part of the world which the Son of God may not rightly claim as His own. Thus, according to them the meaning is: When Christ came to earth He did not enter a foreign country, for the whole human race was His own inheritance. But I think they are nearer the mark who refer it to the Jews only. The Evangelist heightens men's ingratitude by an implied comparison. The Son of God had chosen a dwelling place for Himself in one nation; when He appeared there, He was rejected. And this shows clearly how vicious is men's blindness. But the Evangelist must have said this simply to remove the offence which the Jews' unbelief might put in many people's way. For who would reckon Him to be the Redeemer of the whole world when He was despised and rejected by that nation to which He had been especially promised? This is why we see Paul struggling so hard with this same problem. For the rest, the emphasis lies on both the verb and the noun. The Evangelist says the Son of God came to where He was formerly. He therefore intends a new and extraordinary mode of presence by which the Son of God manifested Himself that men might behold Him closer at hand. When he says 'unto his own' he is comparing the Jews with other nations; for by a unique privilege they had been elected into the family of God. Christ therefore first offered Himself to them as if they were His own household and belonged to His Kingdom in their own right. The complaint of God in Isa. 1.3 is in the same tenor: 'The ox knoweth his owner, and the ass his master's crib: but Israel doth not know me.' For although He has dominion over the whole earth He becomes the Lord especially belonging to Israel, whom He had gathered, as it were, into a sacred fold.

12. *But as many.* In case anyone should be hindered by the stumbling-block that the Jews despised and rejected Christ, the Evangelist exalts above heaven the godly who believe in Him. He says that the result of their faith is the glory of being esteemed the sons of God. The universal term 'as many' implies an antithesis: the Jews were carried away by a blind glorying, as if God were restricted to them alone. So the Evangelist declares that their lot has changed; the Gentiles have succeeded to the place left empty by the disinherited Jews. It is just as

if he transferred the rights of adoption to strangers. As Paul says, the downfall of one nation was the life of the whole world (Rom. 11.12); for when the Gospel was, as it were, driven out from them, it began to be dispersed far and wide throughout the whole world. Thus they were despoiled of their surpassing favour. But their ungodliness did Christ no harm; for He set up the throne of His kingdom elsewhere and without discrimination called to the hope of salvation all peoples who formerly seemed to be rejected by God.

To them he gave power. I take the word ἐξουσία here to mean an honour (*dignitatem*) and it would be better to translate it so, to refute the Papist fiction. Their evil corruption of this verse is that we are given only a freedom of choice, a privilege we may see fit to make use of. To read free will from this word, as they do, is like getting fire out of water. At first sight there is some excuse for it; for the Evangelist does not say that Christ makes them sons of God, but gives them the power to become so. Hence they infer that this grace is only offered to us and that the capacity to make use of it or reject it lies with us. But the context overthrows this paltry quibbling over one word, for the Evangelist goes on to say that they become the sons of God, not by the will of the flesh but by being born of God. For if faith regenerates us so that we are the sons of God, and if God breathes faith into us from heaven, the grace of adoption offered to us by Christ is obviously not only potential but actual, as they say. And indeed in Greek ἐξουσία ἀντὶ ἀξιώσεως—i.e. ἐξουσία is occasionally taken as ἀξίωσις, or being reckoned worthy: which meaning squares best with this passage. The circumlocution which the Evangelist has used is better calculated to commend the excellence of grace than if he had said in a word that all who believe in Christ are made sons of God by Him. For here he is speaking of the unclean and profane who, condemned to perpetual disgrace, lay cast in death's darkness. And so Christ revealed a wonderful example of His grace by conferring this honour on such men, so that they suddenly began to be sons of God. The Evangelist rightly exalts the greatness of this blessing, and so does Paul in Eph. 2.4. But even if anyone prefers the common meaning of the word, yet as used here by the evangelist, 'power' does not stand for any sort of half-way faculty which does not include the full and complete effect. Rather it means that Christ gave what seemed to be impossible to the unclean and uncircumcised. For this was an incredible change—that Christ raised up children to God out of stones. Power is therefore the ἱκανότης that Paul speaks of in Col. 1.12 when he gives thanks to God 'who hath made us meet to be partakers of the inheritance of the saints'.

That believe on his name. He indicates briefly how Christ is to be received—that is, by believing on Him. Implanted into Christ by faith, we attain the right of adoption as the sons of God. And inasmuch as He is the only Son of God, this honour does not belong to us at all except so far as we are members. This again refutes the fiction about 'power'. The Evangelist declares that this power is given to those who already believe, and it is certain that they are indeed already the sons of God. Those who say that by believing a man only gets so far as becoming a son of God if he wishes greatly underestimate faith. They replace a present result by an undecided capability. The contradiction is shown to be even stupider |by the next words. The Evangelist says that they are already born of God who believe. It is not, therefore only the faculty of choice that is offered, for they obtain the very thing itself. Although in Hebrew 'name' is often used for 'power', it is here a reference to the preaching of the Gospel. For we believe in Christ when He is preached to us. I speak of the usual way by which the Lord leads us to faith. And this must be carefully noticed, since many foolishly invent for themselves a faith confused and without any understanding of the Gospel. No word is more commonplace among the Papists than 'believe', but it is said without the knowledge of Christ gained from hearing the Gospel. So Christ offers Himself to us through the Gospel and we receive Him by faith.

13. *Which were born.* I readily agree with those who think that this refers indirectly to the wicked presumption of the Jews. The worthiness of their line was always on their lips, as if they were naturally holy because they were born of a holy descent. They might justly have been proud that they were descended from Abraham if they had been true sons and not degenerate; but the glorying of faith claims nothing at all for fleshly begetting but declares that it has received all that is good from the grace of God alone. John therefore says that those previously unclean Gentiles who believe in Christ are not sons of God from the womb but are re-created by God that they may begin to be His sons. 'Bloods' seems to have been put in the plural to bring out the idea of the long succession of the line. For a part of the Jews' boasting was that they could trace their descent by an uninterrupted line back to the patriarchs.

The will of the flesh and *the will of man,* I think mean the same thing. For I do not see why 'flesh' should be taken for 'woman' (as many, following Augustine, suppose). The Evangelist is rather repeating the same thing in different words, so as to impress and fix it more deeply on our minds. And although he is thinking specifically of the Jews, who gloried in the flesh, a general doctrine can be gathered from this verse: we are reckoned the sons of God, not on account of our own nature, nor from our initiative, but because the Lord begat us voluntarily, that is, from spontaneous love. Hence it follows, first, that faith is not of our production, but is the fruit of spiritual regeneration. For the Evangelist says that none can believe save he who is begotten of God. Therefore faith is a heavenly gift. Moreover, faith is not a cold and bare knowledge, for none can believe except he be re-formed by the Spirit of God. It seems as if the Evangelist puts things back to front by making regeneration prior to faith, since it is rather the result of faith and therefore follows it. I reply, that the two orders are in perfect agreement: by faith we conceive the incorruptible seed by which we are born again to new and divine life; and also, faith is itself the work of the Holy Spirit, who dwells in none but the children of God. Thus, in many respects, faith is a part of our regeneration, an entering into the Kingdom of God, that He may number us among His children. The enlightening of our minds by the Holy Spirit belongs to our renewal. So faith flows from its source, regeneration. But since by this same faith we receive Christ, who sanctifies us by His Spirit, it is called the beginning of our adoption. Of course, another distinction can be advanced which is clearer and more straightforward. When the Lord breathes faith into us He regenerates us in a hidden and secret way that is unknown to us. But when faith has been given, we grasp with a lively awareness not only the grace of adoption but also newness of life and the other gifts of the Holy Spirit. For since, as we have said, faith receives Christ, it leads us in a sense to the possession of all His blessings. Thus so far as our attitude is concerned, we begin to be the sons of God only after we believe. For since the inheritance of eternal life is the result of adoption, we see that the Evangelist ascribes the whole of our salvation to the grace of Christ alone. And indeed, however closely men examine themselves, they will find nothing worthy of the children of God except what Christ has bestowed upon them.

And the Word became flesh, and dwelt among us, and we beheld his glory, glory as of the only begotten from the Father, full of grace and truth. (14)

14. *And the Word became flesh.* He now teaches the nature of the coming of Christ which he had spoken of—that, clothed in our flesh, He showed Himself openly to the world. Although the Evangelist touches only briefly upon the ineffable mystery of the Son of God putting on human nature, this brevity is wonderfully clear. Here some crackbrains play and fool about with paltry sophistries, such as: the Word is said to have become flesh, in that God sent His Son as a mental concept into the world to become man—as if the Word were I know not what shadowy idea. But we have shown that this expresses a genuine *hypostasis* in the essence of God.

Flesh. This word expresses his meaning more forcibly than if he

had said that He was made man. He wanted to show to what a low
and abject state the Son of God descended from the height of His
heavenly glory for our sake. When Scripture speaks of man derogatorily it calls him 'flesh'. How great is the distance between the spiritual
glory of the Word of God and the stinking filth of our flesh! Yet the
Son of God stooped so low as to take to Himself that flesh addicted to
so many wretchednesses. 'Flesh' here is not used for corrupt nature (as
in Paul), but for mortal man. It denotes derogatorily his frail and
almost transient nature: 'all flesh is grass' (Isa. 40.6) and similar verses.
But we must notice at the same time that this is the rhetorical synechdoche—the lower part embraces the whole man. Apollinaris was
therefore foolish to imagine that Christ was clothed with a human body
without a soul. For it is easy to gather from innumerable statements
that He was endowed no less with a soul than with a body. Nor, when
Scripture calls men flesh does it thereby make them soulless. The plain
sense therefore is that the Word begotten of God before all ages, and
ever dwelling with the Father, became man. Here there are two chief
articles of belief: First, in Christ two natures were united in one person
in such a way that one and the same Christ is true God and man.
Secondly, the unity of His person does not prevent His natures from
remaining distinct, so that the divinity retains whatever is proper to it
and the humanity likewise has separately what belongs to it. And so,
when Satan has tried through heretics to overturn sane theology with
this or that madness, he has always dragged in one or other of these two
errors: either that Christ was the Son of God and of man confusedly,
so that neither His divinity remained intact nor was He compassed
about by the true nature of man; or that He was clothed with flesh so
as to be as it were double and have two distinct persons. Thus Nestorius expressly acknowledged each nature but imagined one Christ
who was God and another who was man. Eutyches, on the other hand,
acknowledged that the one Christ is the Son of God and of man, but
left Him neither of the two natures, imagining they were mingled.
Today, Servetus and the Anabaptists invent a Christ who is a confused
compound of the twofold nature, as if He were a divine man. He
certainly declares in words that Christ is God, but if you allow his
insane imaginations, the Divinity was temporarily changed into human
nature and now the human nature has again been absorbed into the
Divinity. The Evangelist's words are apposite for refuting both these
blasphemies. When he says that the Word became flesh, we can plainly
infer the unity of His person. For it does not make sense that He who
is now man should be other than He who was always very God, since
it is God who is said to have become man. Again, since he distinctly
attributes the name of the Word to the man Christ, it follows that

when He became man Christ did not cease to be what He was before and that nothing was changed in that eternal essence of God which assumed flesh. In short, the Son of God began to be man in such a way that He is still that eternal Word who had no temporal beginning.

And dwelt among us. Those who say that the flesh was like a home to Christ have not grasped the Evangelist's thought. He does not ascribe a permanent residence among us to Christ, but says that He stayed for a time, as a guest. For the word he uses, ἐσκήνωσεν, is derived from 'tabernacles'. Hence he simply means that on earth Christ discharged His appointed office; in other words, that He did not only appear for one moment but lived among men while He was fulfilling the course of His office. It is doubtful whether the phrase 'among us' refers to men in general or only to John himself and the other disciples who were eye-witnesses of the events he narrates. I prefer the latter explanation, for the Evangelist immediately adds:

And we beheld his glory. For though the glory of Christ could have been seen by all, it was unknown to the most because of their blindness; only a few, whose eyes the Holy Spirit had opened, saw this manifestation of glory. The gist of it is that Christ was recognized as a man who showed in Himself something far greater and more sublime. Hence it follows that the majesty of God was not annihilated though clothed in flesh. It was indeed hidden under the lowliness of the flesh, yet so that it still sent forth its glory.

As of. In this verse this does not denote an improper comparison but rather a true and strong proof. Just as, when Paul says in Eph. 5.8, 'Walk as children of light', he wants us really to bear witness by our works to this very thing that we are—children of light. The Evangelist therefore means that in Christ there was to be seen a glory consistent with the Son of God and witnessing certainly to His divinity.

The only begotten. He calls Christ this because He is the only Son of God by nature. It is as if he wants to place Him above men and angels and claim for Him alone that which belongs to no creature.

Full of grace. This is a confirmation of the last clause. The majesty of Christ certainly appeared also in other respects, but the Evangelist chose this example instead of others to train us in the practical rather than the speculative knowledge of Him—a fact to be carefully observed. When Christ walked with dry feet upon the waters, when He put devils to flight and revealed His power in other miracles, He could indeed be recognized as the only begotten Son of God. But the Evangelist puts at the centre that part of the proof from which faith receives the sweet fruit of Christ, declaring that He is in very truth the inexhaustible fount of grace and truth. Stephen also was said to have been 'full of grace' (Acts 7.55), but in another sense. For the fulness of

grace in Christ is the well from which we all must draw, as will shortly
be said more fully. It can be expounded, by way of hypallage, as 'true
grace'. Or as an explanation: 'He was full of grace, which is truth or
perfection.' But since he immediately repeats the same form of words,
I consider the meaning to be the same in both places. This grace and
truth he afterwards contrasts with the Law; and therefore I simply
understand it as meaning that Christ was to be acknowledged the Son
of God by the apostles because He had in Himself the fullness of all
things belonging to the spiritual Kingdom of God. In short, that in all
things He truly showed Himself to be the Redeemer and Messiah,
which is the most important characteristic by which He ought to be
distinguished from all others.

*John beareth witness of him, and crieth, saying, This is he of whom I
said, He that cometh after me is preferred before me, for he surpassed me.
And of his fulness we all received, and grace for grace. For the law was
given through Moses; grace and truth came through Jesus Christ. No
man hath seen God at any time; the only begotten Son, which is in the
bosom of the Father, he hath declared him.* (15-18)

15. *John beareth witness.* He now describes John's proclamation. By
using the present tense he denotes a continued activity. And indeed,
this preaching must continually flourish, as if John's voice were continually sounding in men's ears. For the same reason, he then uses the
word 'crieth' to indicate that John's preaching was not at all obscure
or involved in ambiguities or murmured among the few. Publicly he
preached Christ in a loud voice. The first sentence refers to his being
sent on Christ's account, so that it would have been senseless for him
to be exalted while Christ was humbled.

This is he of whom I said. By these words he means that from the very
first his purpose was to make Christ known, and this was the aim of
his preaching; for in no other way could he carry out his duties as
ambassador than by calling his disciples to Christ.

He that cometh after me. It is true he was some months older than
Christ, but age is not what he is dealing with now. As he had performed the office of prophet for some time before Christ appeared in
public, he puts himself first in time. Therefore Christ followed John
so far as public appearance goes.

What follows might be literally rendered: *He became before me, for he
was my chief* (*primus meus*). But the meaning is that Christ was justly
preferred to John because He was more excellent. He therefore yields
to Christ and, as the proverb puts it, hands the torch on to Him. But
as Christ came later in time, he warns us that this is no bar to His being
preferred for the worthiness of His position. Thus, all who excel,

22

either in the gifts of God or in any degree of honour, must remain in
their own station, below Christ.

16. *And of his fulness.* He now begins to preach about Christ's office,
which contains such an abundance of all blessings that no part of
salvation is to be sought elsewhere. In God, indeed, is the fountain of
life, righteousness, power and wisdom; but this fountain is hidden and
inaccessible to us. Yet in Christ the wealth of all these things is laid
before us that we may seek them in Him. Of His own will He is ready
to flow to us, if only we make way for Him by faith. He declares
briefly that we should not seek any blessing at all outside Christ. But
this sentence consists of several clauses. First he shows that we are all
utterly destitute and empty of spiritual blessings. For Christ is rich
that He may help our failure, support our poverty and satisfy our
hunger and thirst. Secondly, he warns us that so soon as we forsake
Christ we seek in vain the slightest morsel of good, since God has
willed that whatever is good shall dwell in Him alone. Therefore, we
shall find angels and men dry, heaven empty, the earth barren and all
things worthless if we want to partake of God's gifts otherwise than
through Christ. Thirdly, he reminds us that we need not fear that we
shall lack anything if only we draw from the fulness of Christ, which
is in every way so perfect that we shall find it to be an inexhaustible
fountain indeed. John classes himself with the rest, not from modesty,
but to make it plainer that no man at all is excepted. It is uncertain
whether he is speaking of the whole human race in general or only of
those who, since Christ has been manifest in the flesh, have partaken
more fully of His blessings. It is true that all the godly who lived under
the Law drew from this same fulness; but since John shortly makes a
distinction between the ages, it is more probable that he is here specially
praising that plentiful wealth of blessings which Christ revealed when
He came. For we know that under the Law they had a more scanty
taste of the benefits of God; and when Christ was revealed in the flesh,
the blessings were poured out, as it were, with a full hand, even to
satisfaction. Not that any of us abounds in a richer grace of the Spirit
than Abraham, but I am speaking of God's ordinary dispensation and
of its manner and method. And therefore John the Baptist, the better
to attract his disciples to Christ, declares that in Him is offered for all
the wealth of the blessings which they lack. But it would not be
absurd if anyone chose to press the meaning further—or rather, it is
not at all against the drift of the argument. From the beginning of
the world all the patriarchs drew whatever gifts they had from
Christ. For although the Law was given by Moses, it was not from
him that they obtained grace. But I have already shown what explanation I prefer—that John here compares us with the patriarchs that

he may thereby bring into prominence what has been given to us.

And grace for grace. Augustine's interpretation of this verse is well known: all the blessings continually given to us by God, and at length everlasting life, are not a payment for our merits, as if they were wages owing to us, but it is of pure kindness that God thus rewards prior grace and crowns His own gifts in us. This is a godly and wise observation, but it does not fit in with the present verse. The meaning would be more simple if you took the preposition ἀντί comparatively, as if he said that whatever graces God heaps upon us flow equally from this source. It could also be taken as indicating the final purpose—we receive grace now that God may at last finish the work of our salvation, which will be the completion of grace. But I subscribe rather to the opinion of those who say that we are watered with the graces which were poured out on Christ. For not only as God does Christ bestow upon us what we receive from Him, but the Father conferred upon Him what would flow to us as through a channel. This is the anointing which was liberally poured upon Him that He might anoint us all along with Him. It is for this reason, too, that He is called Christ, and we, Christians.

17. *For the law was given through Moses.* He speaks proleptically, to forestall a hostile objection. For Moses stood so high with the Jews that they would hardly allow anything that differed from him. The Evangelist therefore teaches us how humble was Moses' ministry compared with the dominion of Christ. This comparison also brings out clearly Christ's power; for the Evangelist warns the Jews, who paid the utmost deference to Moses, that his contribution was extremely scanty compared to the grace of Christ. For it would have been a great stumbling-block to expect from the Law what we can only obtain through Christ.

But we must notice the antithesis in his contrasting of the law to grace and truth; for he means that the Law lacked both these. To my mind, the word truth denotes a firm and solid stability in things. By the word grace I understand the spiritual fulfilment of those things of which the bare letter was contained in the Law. Or the two words can be referred to the same thing by hypallage, as if he had said that grace, in which the truth of the Law consists, was at last revealed in Christ. But as the sense remains the same, it does not matter whether you connect or distinguish them. What is certain is that the Evangelist means that in the Law there was merely the outlined image of spiritual blessings, but that they are shown in their wholeness in Christ. Whence it follows that if you separate the Law from Christ nothing remains in it save empty shapes. This is why Paul says in Col. 2.17 that in the Law is the shadow, but the body is in Christ. But it must not be sup-

posed that anything false was shown in the Law; for Christ is the soul
which quickens what would otherwise have been dead in the Law.
But here we are dealing with a different question—the validity of the
Law in itself and apart from Christ. And the Evangelist denies that
anything substantial is to be found in it until we come to Christ.
Moreover, the truth consists in our obtaining through Christ the grace
which the Law could not give. Therefore I take the word grace
generally, as both the free forgiveness of sins and the renewal of the
heart. For when the Evangelist briefly indicates the difference between
the Old and New Testaments (which is more fully described in Jer.
31.31) he includes in this word everything that relates to spiritual
righteousness. Now there are two parts to this: God freely reconciles
Himself to us by not imputing our sins; and also, He has engraven His
Law in our hearts and reforms men inwardly by His Spirit unto
obedience to it. It is clear from this that the Law is expounded incorrectly and falsely if it binds men to itself or prevents them from
coming to Christ.

18. *No man hath seen God at any time.* This addition confirms very
aptly what goes before. For the knowledge of God is the door by
which we enter into the enjoyment of all blessings. Since, therefore,
God reveals Himself to us by Christ alone, it follows that we should
seek all things from Christ. This doctrinal sequence should be carefully observed. Nothing seems more obvious than that we each take
what God offers us according to the measure of our faith. But only a
few realize that the vessel of faith and of the knowledge of God has to
be brought to draw with.

When he says that none has seen God, it is not to be understood of
the outward seeing of the physical eye. He means generally that, since
God dwells in inaccessible light, He cannot be known except in Christ,
His lively image. Moreover, they usually expound this verse thus:
since the naked majesty of God is hidden within Himself, He could
never be comprehended except in that He has revealed Himself in
Christ. Hence God was known to the patriarchs of old only in Christ.
But I reckon rather that the Evangelist is here dwelling on the comparison already made—how much better our state is than the patriarchs', in
that God, who was then concealed in His secret glory, has now in a
sense made Himself visible. For certainly, when Christ is called 'the
express image of God', it refers to the special blessing of the New
Testament. So also in this verse the Evangelist points to something
new and strange when he says that the only begotten, who was in the
bosom of the Father, has displayed to us what was otherwise hidden.
He therefore praises the revelation of God, brought to us by the
Gospel, by which he distinguishes us from the patriarchs as superior to

them. Paul treats this more fully in II Cor. 3 and 4, declaring that
there is no longer any veil, as under the Law, but that God is openly
beheld in the face of Christ. If it seems ridiculous that the fathers
should be deprived of the knowledge of God, when their prophets
hand on the torch to us today, I reply that what is allotted to us is not
simply or absolutely denied to them, but (as they say) a comparison is
made between the minor and major; for they had nothing more than
little sparks of that light of life whose full brightness lightens us today.
If any object that even then God was seen face to face, I say that that
sight was not at all comparable to ours; but since God used at that time
to show Himself obscurely and as it were from afar, those to whom He
appeared more clearly said that they saw Him face to face. They speak
relatively to their own time. They only saw God wrapped up in many
coverings. The vision that Moses obtained on the mountain (Exod.
33.23) was unique and excelled almost all the others; and yet God
expressly declares: 'thou shalt not be able to see my face, thou shalt
see only my back.' By this metaphor He means that the time for the
full and clear revelation had not yet come. We must also note that,
when even the fathers wanted to behold God, they always turned their
eyes to Christ. I do not only mean that they contemplated God in His
eternal Word, but also that they stretched single-mindedly and whole-
heartedly towards the promised manifestation of Christ. For this reason
Christ will say in chapter 8: 'Abraham saw my day.' And succession
does not mean contradiction. This therefore is certain—that God,
who was formerly invisible, has now appeared in Christ.

When he says that the Son was *in the bosom of the father*, he uses a
human metaphor. Men are said to admit to their bosom those to
whom they communicate all their secrets. The breast is the seat of
counsel. He therefore teaches that the Son knew the most hidden
secrets of His Father, so that we may know that we have, so to say,
the breast of God laid open to us in the Gospel.

And this is the witness of John, when the Jews sent unto him from
Jerusalem priests and Levites, to ask him, Who art thou? And he
confessed, and denied not; and he confessed, I am not the Christ. And
they asked him, What then? Art thou Elijah? And he saith, I am not.
Art thou a prophet? And he answered, No. They said therefore unto
him, Who art thou? that we may give an answer to them that sent us.
What sayest thou of thyself? He said, I am the voice of one crying in
the wilderness, Make straight the way of the Lord, as said Isaiah the
prophet. (19-23)

19. *And this is the witness.* Hitherto the Evangelist has related John's
customary preaching about Christ. He now comes down to a more

outstanding example of this, which was delivered to the ambassadors of the priests to carry back to Jerusalem. So he says that John openly confessed why he was sent by God. But we may first ask what the priest's purpose was in questioning him. The common supposition is that they gave John a false honour out of hatred to Christ. But at that time Christ was not yet known to them. Others say that John was more *persona grata* with them because he came of the priestly line and order. But this is also improbable; for why should they invent a false Christ for themselves when they looked for all prosperity from Christ? I think that they were moved by another cause. For a long time they had been without prophets. John suddenly and unexpectedly appeared, and everyone's mind was excited and expectant. Besides, they all believed the Messiah's coming was nigh. Lest they should seem careless of their duty by neglecting or disguising such an important matter, the priests ask John who he is. At first, then, they did not act from malice, but, on the contrary, moved by a desire for redemption, they want to know whether John is the Christ, for he is beginning to change the usual order of the Church. And yet I do not deny that a desire to cling on to their rights was powerful in them; but nothing was farther from their minds than to transfer Christ's honour to another. Nor are they acting inconsistently with their office. For since they bore the government of the Church of God they had to take care that none should rashly put himself forward, that no founder of a new sect should arise, that the unity of the faith should not be broken among the people and that none should introduce new and foreign ceremonies. It is evident, therefore, that talk about John was common and excited everybody's mind. But this was ordered by the wonderful providence of God, that the witness might be the more conspicuous.

20. *And he confessed.* That is, he confessed openly and without any evasion or hypocrisy. The first 'confess' means in general that he stated the fact as it was. The second is a repetition to express the form of the confession. So he replied definitely that he was not the Christ.

21. *Art thou Elijah?* Why do they mention Elijah rather than Moses? Because they learned from the prophecy in Mal. 4.5 that when the Messiah should rise, Elijah would be as His morning star. But they ask this from a false presupposition. For, believing as they did in the transmigration of souls, they imagined that when the prophet Malachi announced that Elijah would be sent, he meant the same Elijah who lived under Ahab. John therefore replies fairly and properly that he is not Elijah, using the word in their sense. But Christ affirms that he is Elijah, from a true interpretation of the prophet (Matt. 11.14).

Art thou a prophet? Erasmus incorrectly restricts this to Christ, for the addition of the article has no weight in this verse; and the messengers

afterwards declare plainly enough that they meant a different prophet
from Christ, when they summarize it all by saying: 'If thou art neither
Christ, nor Elijah, nor a Prophet.' Thus we see that different persons
are meant. Others think that they were asking whether he was one of
the prophets of old. But I do not like that exposition either. Rather,
by this term they are referring to John's office, as to whether he was a
prophet appointed by God. When he denies this, he is not lying out
of modesty but honestly and sincerely separating himself from the
number of the prophets. And yet this reply is not contrary to Christ's
description of him. Christ bestows on John the title of prophet and
even adds that he is 'more than a prophet' (Matt. 11.9). But by these
words He only purchases credit and authority for John's teaching, at
the same time extolling the excellence of the office committed to him.
But in this passage John has a different aim—to show that he has no
personal commission, as was usual with the prophets, but was appointed
only to be the herald of Christ. This will become clearer by a metaphor.
Even ambassadors who are sent on matters of no great moment receive
the name and authority of ambassadors, if indeed they hold personal
commissions. Such were all the prophets who, provided with definite
prophecies, discharged the prophetic office. But suppose a matter of
great weight comes up and two ambassadors are sent, one of whom
announces that another will soon come to negotiate the whole affair
and with a commission to carry the business through. Will not the
former be reckoned a part and appendix of the principal one? So it was
with John, to whom God had enjoined nothing other than the preparation of disciples for Christ. And this meaning is easily drawn out
from the whole context of the passage; for we must consider the
opposing clause immediately following. He says: 'I am not a prophet,
but a voice crying in the wilderness.' The distinction lies in the fact
that the voice crying, that a way may be prepared for the Lord, is not
a prophet, with a distinct function peculiar to himself, but only, so to
say, an assistant minister, and his preaching only a sort of preparation
for listening to another teacher. In this way John, though more excellent than all the prophets, is nevertheless not a prophet himself.

23. *The voice of one crying.* Since he would have been rash in assum-
ing the teaching office unless he had been given a ministry, he shows
what his function was and confirms it with the testimony of Isa. 40.3.
Whence it follows that he did nothing but what God commanded.
Isaiah is not there speaking only of John; but, promising the restoration
of the Church, he foretells that joyful voices will be heard commanding
a way to be levelled for the Lord. Now although he means God's
coming in bringing back the people from the Babylonian captivity,
yet the true fulfilment was the manifestation of Christ in the flesh.

Therefore, among the heralds who announced that the Lord was nigh, John was chief.

It is trifling to philosophize subtly, as some do, about the word 'voice'. John is called a voice because the duty laid upon him was to cry out. Isaiah allegorically calls the wretched waste of the Church a desert which seemed to preclude the people's return; as if he said that the way out for the captive people was blocked, but that the Lord would find a way through the trackless land. But that visible wilderness in which John preached was a figure or image of the lonely waste where was no hope of deliverance. If you think about this comparison, you will soon see that the prophet's words have not been twisted. God arranged everything in such a way as to set a mirror of this prophecy before the eyes of His people, bewildered by their miseries.

And they had been sent from the Pharisees. And they asked him, and said unto him, Why then baptizest thou, if thou art not the Christ, neither Elijah, neither a prophet? John answered them, saying, I baptize with water: in the midst of you standeth one whom ye know not: he it is who coming after me is preferred before me, the latchet of whose shoe I am not worthy to unloose. These things were done in Bethabara beyond Jordan, where John was baptizing. (24-28)

24. *Were from the Pharisees.* He says that they were Pharisees, who held then the highest place in the Church, to teach us that they were not some minor figures of the Levitical order but men endowed with authority. This is why they ask about his Baptism. Ordinary ministers would have been satisfied with any kind of answer; but these men, because they cannot get the reply they want, accuse John of rashness for daring to introduce a new ceremony.

25. *Why then baptizest thou?* They seem to argue acutely when they lay down these three degrees—'if thou art not Christ, neither Elijah, neither a prophet'; for it is not for everyone to institute the practice of Baptism. All authority was to be in the hands of the Messiah. Of the Elijah who was to come they had formed the opinion that he would begin the restoration of both the Kingdom and the Church. They also grant that the prophets of God ought to discharge the office committed to them. They conclude, therefore, that for John to baptize is an unlawful innovation, since he had received no public office from God. But even though he denies that he is the Elijah of whom they were dreaming, they are at fault in that they do not acknowledge him to be the Elijah mentioned in Mal. 4.5.

26. *I baptize with water.* This should have been sufficient to correct their mistake; but however clear teaching may be, it is no use to the deaf. When he sends them to Christ and declares that He is already

present it is plain, not only that he was divinely appointed to be Christ's minister, but that he is the true Elijah sent to testify to the restoration of the Church. The full antithesis is not expressed here; for the spiritual Baptism of Christ is not distinctly contrasted with the external Baptism of John, but that latter clause about the Baptism of the Spirit might well be supplied. Indeed, shortly afterwards the Evangelist puts them both down.

There are two points in this answer: John claims nothing beyond what is right for him, for the author of his Baptism is Christ, in whom consists the truth of the sign. Secondly, he has no more than the administration of the outward sign, while all the power and efficacy is in the hands of Christ alone. So he defends his Baptism, inasmuch as its truth depends on another. But yet, by disclaiming the power of the Spirit, he praises the worthiness of Christ, that men may look to Him alone. The best self-restraint is when a minister so borrows from Christ whatever authority he claims for himself that he gives Him the credit, ascribing it all to Him alone. But the very silly mistake has been made of supposing that John's Baptism was different from ours. John is not here arguing about the usefulness and profitableness of his Baptism, but is merely comparing his role with that of Christ. Just as today, if it were asked what is our part in Baptism and what is Christ's, we have to acknowledge that Christ alone performs what Baptism represents, and we have nothing beyond the bare administration of the sign. Scripture speaks in a twofold way about the Sacraments. Sometimes it tells us that they are 'the laver of regeneration' (Titus 3.5), that there our sins are washed away, that we are grafted into the body of Christ, that our old man is crucified and that we rise again in newness of life. And in these instances it unites the power of Christ with the ministry of man, so that the minister is nothing but the hand of Christ. Such modes of expression show, not what the man can accomplish of himself, but what Christ effects by the man and the sign as His instruments. But since men tend to fall into superstition and from their innate pride to snatch from God His honour and keep it for themselves, Scripture, to curb this blasphemous arrogance, occasionally distinguishes the ministers from Christ, as in this passage, that we may learn that ministers are and can do nothing.

In the midst of you standeth one. He indirectly censures their stupidity in not knowing Christ, whom they ought to have been taking particular notice of. And he always carefully insists that nothing can be known of his ministry until men have come to its author. He says that Christ stands in their midst, so that he may make them eager to know Him. The sum of it is that he wants to abase himself as much as he can lest any degree of honour wrongly given to him should obscure the

superiority of Christ. It is probable that these sentences were frequently
on his tongue when he saw himself immoderately praised by the
distorted opinions of men.

27. *Who coming after me.* Here he says two things: that Christ
followed him in time; but that in degree of dignity He was far before
him. For the Father preferred Him before all. Soon after he will add
a third point—that why Christ was preferred to all others was because
He excelled all others by right.

28. *These things were done in Bethabara.* The place is mentioned, not
only to authenticate the account, but also to inform us that this reply
was given in a crowded assembly. For many came to John's Baptism,
and this was his ordinary place for baptizing. It is also thought to have
been a passage across the Jordan; and they derive the name from this,
for they interpret it as 'the house of passage'. Some, perhaps, may
prefer the opinion of those who refer it to the memorable passage of
the people, when God opened up a way for them through the midst
of the waters, under Joshua (Joshua 3.13). Others consider it should be
read Betharaba. The name Bethany, put here by some, is a mistake;
for we shall see later how close Bethany was to Jerusalem. The site of
Bethabara which the topographers describe agrees best with the
Evangelist's words. But I do not dispute about the pronunciation of
the word.

> *On the morrow, John seeth Jesus coming unto him, and saith, Behold, the*
> *Lamb of God, which taketh away the sin of the world! This is he of whom*
> *I said, After me cometh a man which was preferred to me: for he was*
> *more excellent than I. And I knew him not; but that he should be made*
> *manifest to Israel, for this cause came I baptizing with water. And*
> *John bare witness, saying, I have beheld the Spirit descending as a dove*
> *out of heaven; and it abode upon him. And I knew him not: but he that*
> *sent me to baptize with water, he said unto me, Upon whomsoever thou*
> *shalt see the Spirit descending, and abiding on him, the same is he that*
> *baptizest with the Holy Spirit. And I have seen, and have borne witness,*
> *that this is the Son of God. (29-34)*

29. *On the morrow.* There is no doubt that John had previously
spoken of the manifestation of the Messiah; but when Christ came
forth, he wanted his proclamation to be known quickly: and the time
was now at hand when Christ would bring John's ministry to an end,
just as the dawn suddenly disappears at sunrise. Therefore, when he
had borne witness to the embassy of priests that He from whom they
ought to seek the truth and power of his Baptism was already present
and living in the midst of the people, the next day he makes Him
known openly. For these two acts will have more force in moving

their minds because of their temporal conjunction. This, too, is why
Christ showed Himself in his presence.

Behold, the Lamb of God. The chief office of Christ is explained
briefly but clearly. By taking away the sins of the world by the sacrifice of His death, He reconciles men to God. Christ certainly bestows
other blessings upon us, but the chief one, on which all the others
depend, is that by appeasing the wrath of God He brings it to pass that
we are reckoned righteous and pure. The source of all the streams of
blessings is that by not imputing our sins, God receives us into favour.
Accordingly John, that he may lead us to Christ, begins with the free
pardon of sins which we obtain through Him.

The Lamb is an allusion to the ancient sacrifices of the Law. He was
dealing with the Jews, who were used to sacrifices and could not be
taught about satisfaction in any other way than by having a sacrifice
set in their midst. But as there were various kinds, he uses synechdoche.
Probably John is thinking of the Paschal Lamb. The main point is that
John used a mode of expression which was more apt and forceful for
teaching the Jews. Just as today, because of the rite of Baptism we
understand better what the forgiveness of sins through the blood of
Christ means when we hear that we are washed and cleansed by it from
our pollutions. At the same time, as the Jews commonly held superstitious notions about sacrifices, he corrects the fault in passing by
reminding them of the object they all pointed to. It was a very bad
abuse of sacrifice to fix their trust in the outward signs. Therefore
John, putting Christ forward, bears witness that He is the Lamb of
God; by which he means that whatever sacrificial victims the Jews
used to offer under the Law had no power at all to atone for sins, but
were only figures whose reality was revealed in Christ Himself.

Sin. He puts it in the singular, as any kind of iniquity; as if he said
that every sort of unrighteousness which alienates God from men is
taken away by Christ. And when he says *the sin of the world* he extends
this kindness indiscriminately to the whole human race, that the Jews
might not think the Redeemer has been sent to them alone. From this
we infer that the whole world is bound in the same condemnation;
and that since all men without exception are guilty of unrighteousness
before God, they have need of reconciliation. John, therefore, by
speaking of the sin of the world in general, wanted to make us feel our
own misery and exhort us to seek the remedy. Now it is for us to
embrace the blessing offered to all, that each may make up his mind
that there is nothing to hinder him from finding reconciliation in
Christ if only, led by faith, he comes to Him.

Besides, he proclaims one way only of taking away sins. We know that
from the beginning of the world, when their consciences convicted

them, all men laboured anxiously to earn pardon. Hence so many kinds of propitiatory offerings, by which they wrongly imagined they appeased God. I confess, indeed, that all the spurious propitiatory rites originated in a holy beginning; which was that God had ordained the sacrifices which directed men to Christ. But yet everyone made up his own way of appeasing God. But John calls us back to Christ alone and teaches us that God is only reconciled to us through His blessing, since He alone takes away sins. He therefore leaves no other course for sinners than to flee to Christ. In this way he excludes all human satisfactions, expiations and redemptions, since they are nothing but ungodly inventions framed by the craft of the devil.

Taketh away can be expounded in two ways. Either that Christ took upon Himself the burden under which we were crushed, as it is said in I Pet. 2.24 that He 'carried our sins on the tree'; and Isa. 53.5 says that the correction of our peace was put on Him; or that He absolves our sins. But since the latter depends on the former, I willingly accept both—that Christ, by bearing our sins, takes them away. Although, therefore, sin continually stays in us, yet in the judgment of God it is nothing, for as it is abolished by the grace of Christ, it is not imputed to us. Nor do I dislike Chrysostom's point that the present tense of the verb denotes a continuing action; for the satisfaction which was once completed flourishes for ever. But he tells us, not merely that Christ takes away sin, but also the method—that He has reconciled the Father to us by the good deed of His death; for this is what he means by the word Lamb. Let us therefore learn that we are reconciled to God by the grace of Christ if we go straight to His death and believe that He who was nailed to the cross is the only sacrificial victim by whom all our guilt is removed.

30. *This is he of whom I said.* He comprehends everything in a summary when he declares that it is Christ whom he had said would be preferred before him. For it follows that John is nothing but a herald sent on His account. And from this again it is established that Christ is the Messiah. Three things are mentioned here. When he says that a man is coming after him, he means that he himself was before Christ in time, to prepare the way for Him, according to the testimony of Malachi, 'Behold, I send my messenger before my face.' When he says that He was preferred to himself, this refers to the glory with which God adorned His Son when He came into the world to perform the office of Redeemer. Finally, the reason is added—that Christ is far above John the Baptist in dignity. The honour, therefore, which the Father bestowed upon Him was not adventitious but was the due of His eternal majesty. But I have already touched upon this expression, 'He was preferred to me, because He was before me.'

31. *And I knew him not.* That his testimony may not be suspected of having been given from friendship or favour, he forestalls the doubt, denying that he had any other knowledge of Christ than what came to him from God. The sum of it therefore is that John does not speak from his own understanding, nor to please man, but at the instigation of the Spirit and by the command of God.

I came baptizing with water, he says. That is, I was called and ordained to this office, that I might manifest Him to Israel. The Evangelist afterwards explains this more fully and confirms it when he represents him as testifying that he had known Christ by a divine oracle. In place of what we have here ('I came to baptize') he there declares expressly that he was sent. For it is only the calling of God that makes regular ministers of the Church. Whoever pushes himself forward unasked, whatever learning or eloquence he may possess, is not entitled to any authority, for he has not come from God. Now since John, to baptize regularly, had to be sent by God, you must understand that no man has any right to institute Sacraments. This right belongs to God alone. Just as Christ on another occasion, to prove the Baptism of John, asks whether it was from heaven or from men (Matt. 21.25).

32. *I have beheld the Spirit descending as a dove.* This is an unliteral and figurative expression; for with what eyes could he see the Spirit? But as the dove was a sure and infallible sign of the presence of the Spirit, it is called the Spirit by metonymy; not that it is really the Spirit, but it shows Him in a way man can grasp. And this symbolism is usual in the Sacraments; for why does Christ call the bread His body but because the name of the thing is suitably transferred to the sign— especially when the sign is at the same time a true and efficacious pledge by which we are assured that the thing itself which is signified is bestowed on us? Yet you must not think that the Spirit who fills heaven and earth was included under the dove, but that He was present by His power, so that John might know that such a sight was not put before his eyes in vain. In like manner we know that the body of Christ is not bound to the bread, but yet we enjoy participation in Him.

And now, why did the Spirit appear under the form of a dove? We must always hold that here is an analogy between the sign and the reality. When the Spirit was given to the apostles, they saw fiery and cloven tongues (Acts 2.3) because the preaching of the Gospel was to be spread abroad throughout all tongues and was to have the power of fire. But in this verse God wished to represent openly that gentleness of Christ which Isa. 42.3 praises: 'The smoking flax shall he not quench, and a bruised reed shall he not break.' This was the first time that the Spirit was seen descending upon Him. Not that before this He had been empty of the Spirit, but now He is, as it were, consecrated with a solemn ceremony. For we know that He remained hidden like a private individual for thirty years, because the time of His manifestation was not yet come. But when He wished to make Himself known to the world, He began with Baptism. He therefore received the Spirit on that occasion not so much for Himself as for His people. And the Spirit descended visibly that we may know that in Christ dwells the abundance of all gifts of which we are destitute and empty. This may easily be gathered from the words of the Baptist. For when he says: 'Upon whom thou shalt see the Spirit descending, and abiding upon him, he it is who baptizeth with the Spirit,' it is just as if he had said that the Spirit was seen under a visible form, and rested on Christ to the end that He might water all His people with His fulness. What it is to baptize with the Spirit I have briefly touched on above—that Christ gives Baptism its effect, so that it shall not be vain and invalid, and this He does by the power of His Spirit.

33. *Upon whom thou shalt see.* Here a difficult question arises: If John did not know Christ, why does he refuse to admit Him to Baptism? He would certainly not say to someone he did not know: 'I ought rather to be baptized by thee' (Matt. 3.14). Some reply that he knew Him so far that, although he reverenced Him as a distinguished prophet, he did not know that He was the Son of God. But this is a dull solution, for everyone should obey the calling of God without any respect of persons. No dignity or excellence of man ought to stop us doing our duty. Therefore John would have wronged God and his Baptism if he had spoken like this to any person other than the Son of God. Therefore he must have known Christ previously. First, we must note that this refers to a knowledge arising from intimate and reciprocal familiarity. Although he recognizes Christ as soon as he sees Him, it is still true that they were not known to each other in the ordinary way of human friendship, for the beginning of his knowledge came from God. But the question is not yet fully resolved, for he says that the sight of the Holy Spirit was the mark of recognition. But he had not yet seen the Spirit when he addressed Christ as the Son of God. I willingly agree with the opinion of those who think that this sign was added for confirmation, and that it was not so much for John's sake as for us all. Certainly, John alone saw it, but for others rather than for himself. Bucer aptly quotes Moses in Exod. 3.12: 'This shall be the token unto thee, that after three days' journey, you shall sacrifice to me upon this mountain.' Undoubtedly, when they were going out they already knew that God would lead and direct their liberation; but this was an *a posteriori* confirmation, as they say. Similarly, it came as an addition to the former revelation which had been given to John.

34. *And I have seen and have borne witness.* He means that he is not putting forward anything doubtful; for God was pleased to give him thorough and profound knowledge of those things of which he was to be a witness to the world. And it is noteworthy that he testified that Christ was the Son of God, for the giver of the Holy Spirit must be the Christ, since the honour and office of reconciling men to God belongs to no other.

Again on the morrow John was standing, and two of his disciples; and he looked upon Jesus as he walked, and saith, Behold, the Lamb of God! And the two disciples heard him speak, and they followed Jesus. And Jesus turned, and beheld them following, and saith unto them, What seek ye? And they said unto him, Rabbi, (which is to say, being interpreted, Master), where abidest thou? He saith unto them, Come, and ye shall see. They came therefore and saw where he abode, and they abode with him that day: it was about the tenth hour. (35-39)

36. *Behold, the Lamb of God!* In this appears more clearly what I have already said, that when John felt that he was reaching the end of his course, he kept pressing on incessantly to hand on the torch to Christ. His persistence gives greater weight to his witness. But by insisting so earnestly day after day on repeating his praise of Christ, he shows that his own course was now finished. Moreover, we see here how weak and low the beginning of the Church was. John indeed had prepared disciples for Christ, but not until now had Christ begun to collect a Church. He has just the two obscure and insignificant men, but even this makes His glory shine forth, that within a short time, unhelped by man's power or a strong company, He extends His Kingdom in a wonderful and unbelievable way. We ought also to observe where especially he leads men to—to find in Christ the forgiveness of sins. And even as Christ had expressly presented Himself to the disciples that they might come to Him, so now, when they do come, He kindly encourages and exhorts them; for He does not wait for them to speak first, but asks them, 'What seek ye?' This winning and friendly invitation, once made to two men, now belongs to all. Therefore, we must not be afraid that Christ will hold back from us or deny us easy access, if only He sees us striving towards Him. No, indeed! He will stretch out His hand to help our exertions. And will He not hasten to those who come to Him, He who seeks afar off the wandering and astray, to bring them back into the right road?

38. *Rabbi.* This name was commonly given to men of high rank or with any kind of honour. But here the Evangelist records another contemporary use of it: by this name they addressed teachers and expounders of the Word of God. Although, therefore, they do not

yet know that Christ is the only teacher of the Church, nevertheless, moved by John's record of Him, they regard Him as a prophet and teacher, which is the first step towards teachableness.

Where abidest thou? From this example we are taught by the very beginnings of the Church to acquire such a taste for Christ as shall kindle our desire to progress. Nor should we be satisfied with a bare passing look, but must seek His dwelling place, that He may receive us as His guests. For there are very many who merely sniff at the Gospel from a distance, and thus let Christ suddenly disappear, and whatever they have learned about Him slip away. Although they did not then become His full-time disciples, there is no doubt that He taught them more fully that night, that He might have them entirely devoted to Him soon afterwards.

39. *It was about the tenth hour.* That is, the evening was coming on, for it was only two hours to sunset. At that time the day was divided into twelve hours, which were longer in summer and shorter in winter. And from this matter of the time we gather that those two disciples were so eager to hear Christ and to know him more intimately, that they were not concerned about their night's lodging. But we, for the most part, are very different from them, for we procrastinate endlessly, because it is never convenient for us to follow Christ.

One of the two that heard John speak, and followed him, was Andrew, Simon Peter's brother. He findeth first his own brother Simon, and saith unto him, We have found the Messiah (which is, being interpreted, Christ). He brought him unto Jesus. Jesus looked upon him and said, Thou art Simon the son of John: thou shalt be called Cephas (which is by interpretation, Peter). (40-42)

40. *One of the two was Andrew.* The Evangelist's aim, down to the end of the chapter, is to inform us how little by little the disciples were led to Christ. Here he relates about Peter, and afterwards he will add Philip and Nathanael. That Andrew immediately brings his brother expresses the nature of faith, which does not keep the light hidden within or quench it, but rather spreads it in every direction. Andrew has scarcely one spark; and yet by it he enlightens his brother. Woe to our apathy, if we, more fully enlightened than he, do not try to make others partakers of the same grace! We may indeed notice two things in Andrew that Isaiah requires of the children of God (Isa. 2.3)—that each should take his neighbour by the hand, and also that he should say, 'Come ye, and let us go up to the mountain of the Lord, and he will teach us.' For Andrew holds out his hand to his brother, with just this object, that he may become a school-fellow with him in the school of Christ. Moreover, we ought to notice God's design. He wanted

37

Peter, who was to be far the more eminent, to be led to the knowledge of Christ by Andrew's agency and ministry, so that none of us, however excellent, may refuse to be taught by an inferior. For He will severely punish that fastidious, or rather arrogant, person who, from contempt of a man, will not deign to come to Christ.

41. *We have found the Messiah.* The Evangelist has translated this word into Greek, so as to publish to the whole world what had been a Jewish mystery. It was the ordinary title of kings, as anointing was the practice with them. But yet they were aware that one King would be divinely anointed under whom they hoped for perfect and eternal happiness, especially when they learned that David's earthly kingdom would not last. Then as God stirred them up, overcome and burdened with various tribulations, to look for the Messiah, so He showed them more clearly that His coming was at hand. Daniel's prophecy is clearer than the rest, so far as relates to the name of *Christ* (Dan. 9). For he does not, like the earlier prophets, ascribe it to kings, but makes it peculiar to the Redeemer alone. Thus, this way of speaking prevailed, that whenever the Messiah or Christ was mentioned they understood by it none other than the Redeemer. And so in chapter 4 the woman of Samaria says, 'the Messiah will come', which makes it the more amazing that He who was so eagerly longed for and spoken about by all should be accepted by so few.

42. *Thou art Simon.* Christ gives Simon a name, not, as is usual, because of some past event, or from what He sees in him, but because He was going to make him Peter. First, He says, 'Thou art Simon, the son of Jonas.' He puts the name of his father in its abridged form, a common enough custom when names are translated into foreign languages. It will be clear from the final chapter that he was the son of Johanna or John. But all this amounts to His saying that he will be very different from what he is now. For He does not mention his father because he was of high repute, but since Peter was born of an obscure family and of no esteem among men, He declares that this will not prevent Him making Simon a man of unconquerable resolution. The Evangelist therefore records it as a prediction, that a new surname was given to Simon. I understand it as a prediction, not only in that Christ foresaw the future steadfastness of faith in Peter, but also that He foretold what He was going to give him. So now, in a sort of aphorism, He praises the grace which He had determined to give him later on; and therefore He does not say that this is his present name, but postpones it to the future.

Thou shalt be called Cephas, He says. It belongs to all the godly, indeed, to be Peters who are grounded in Christ that they may be fitted for building the temple of God. But in his singular excellence he alone is called this. But the Papists are ridiculous when they put him in Christ's place as the foundation of the Church, as if he, too, were not founded on Christ like the others. And they are doubly ridiculous when they make a head out of a stone. A silly canon stands under the name of Anacletus, among Gratian's rhapsodies, which, by changing a Hebrew word for a Greek and so muddling up κεφαλή with *Cepha*, suggests that by this name Peter was appointed Head of the Church. Moreover, *Cepha* is Aramaic rather than Hebrew, but that was the usual post-exilic pronunciation of it. There is, then, no ambiguity in Christ's words. He promises Peter what he would never have expected, and thus magnifies in him His grace to all ages, that his former state may not tell against him, since this remarkable title proclaims that he has been made a new man.

> *On the morrow Jesus was minded to go forth into Galilee, and he findeth Philip: and he saith unto him, Follow me. Now Philip was from Bethsaida, of the city of Andrew and Peter. Philip findeth Nathanael, and saith unto him, We have found Jesus, the son of Joseph of Nazareth, of whom Moses in the law, and the prophets did write. And Nathanael said unto him, Can any good thing come out of Nazareth? Philip saith unto him, Come and see. (43-46)*

43. *Follow me.* Philip's mind was set afire to follow Christ by this one word; and hence we infer how great is the efficacy of the Word, though it is not evident in all indiscriminately. For God urges many without any effect; just as if He were beating upon their ears with an empty sound. Therefore, the external preaching of the Word is of itself unfruitful, except that it mortally wounds the reprobate, so as to render them inexcusable before God. But when the secret grace of the Spirit quickens it, all the senses will inevitably be so affected that men will be prepared to follow whithersoever God calls them. We must therefore pray Christ to put forth the same power of the Gospel in us. It is true that Philip's following of Christ was special, for he was commanded to follow, not only like any of us, but as an intimate companion (*contubernalis*) and an inseparable comrade. All the same, this is a pattern of calling in general.

44. *Was of Bethsaida.* The name of the city seems to have been mentioned to show more clearly God's goodness to the three apostles. We learn from other passages how sternly Christ threatens and curses that city. Accordingly, that some from such an ungodly and wicked race should be received into God's favour ought to be regarded as their being brought out of hell. And that Christ should deem those rescued from the bottomless abyss worthy of such honour as to be appointed apostles is a magnificent and memorable blessing.

45. *Philip findeth Nathanael.* However much the proud may despise these beginnings of the Church, we ought to see in them a greater glory of God than if the condition of the Kingdom of Chri. had been noble from the start and grand in every way. For we know to how great a harvest this little seed by and by grew. Again, we are shown in Philip the same eagerness to build which was seen in Andrew. There is also pointed out his modesty, in desiring and caring only to get others to learn along with him from the common Master of all.

We have found Jesus. How small was Philip's faith appears from the fact that he cannot say four things about Christ without including two stupid mistakes. He calls Him the son of Joseph, and wrongly makes Nazareth His native town. And yet, because he really wants to help his brother and make Christ known, God approves his earnestness and makes it successful. Everyman, indeed, needs to keep soberly within his own limits; and the Evangelist certainly does not mention it as praiseworthy of Philip to dishonour Christ twice, but just relates that his teaching, though faulty and involved in error, was useful because in spite of everything it pursued the aim of making Christ truly known. He foolishly calls Jesus the son of Joseph and ignorantly makes Him a Nazarene, but all the same, he leads Nathanael to none other than the Son of God who was born in Bethlehem. He does not forge a counterfeit Christ, but only wants Him to be known as He was propounded by Moses and the prophets. Thus we see that the chief thing in preaching is that those who hear us should somehow or other come to Christ.

Many argue acutely about Christ, but so obscure and wrap Him up with their subtleties that He can never be found. In this way, the Papists will not say that Christ is the son of Joseph, for they know precisely what His name is; but yet they empty Him of His power and so exhibit a phantom in His place. Would it not be better to stammer foolishly with Philip and yet keep the true Christ than to introduce a fiction in clever and impressive language? Nay, many a poor common man today, awkward and unskilled in speaking, proclaims Christ more faithfully than all the Pope's theologians with their lofty speculations. This passage, therefore, warns us not to reject disdainfully anything about Christ put badly by the simple and unlearned, provided they do direct us to Christ. But lest we should be drawn away from Christ by the false imaginings of men, let us always keep the remedy at hand of seeking the pure knowledge of Him from the Law and the prophets.

46. *Can any good thing come out of Nazareth?* At first Nathanael, put off by Christ's birthplace as described by Philip, backs away. But he is deceived by Philip's thoughtless word. What Philip foolishly thought, Nathanael took as certain. To this is added an unreasonable criticism arising from hatred or contempt of the place. We should observe both

these points carefully. This holy man was not far from shutting the
door to Christ in his own face. Why was this? Because he is too quick
to believe Philip's incorrect statement about Him, and also because his
mind was full of the preconceived opinion that nothing good was to be
expected from Nazareth. Unless we take great care, we shall be in the
same danger. By similar obstacles Satan daily strives to prevent us
coming to Christ. For he takes care to spread very many falsehoods,
which make the Gospel detestable or suspect to us, so that we do not
venture to sample it. Moreover, there is another stone he does not
leave unturned to make Christ contemptible to us. For we see what a
stumbling-block to many is the lowliness of the cross, both in Christ
the Head and also in His members. But as we can hardly be so careful
as not to be assailed by those tricks of Satan, let us at least remember
the words 'Come and see'. Nathanael allowed his twofold error to be
corrected by what Philip said. And so, following his example, let us
first show ourselves teachable and compliant; and next, let us not
shrink from seeking when Christ Himself is ready to remove the doubts
which harass us. Those who take this sentence as an affirmation are
greatly mistaken. How trite this would be! And again, we know that
the city of Nazareth was not thought much of then; and Philip's reply
plainly betrays hesitation and mistrust.

*Jesus saw Nathanael coming to him, and saith of him, Behold, an
Israelite indeed, in whom is no guile. Nathanael saith unto him, Whence
knowest thou me? Jesus answered and said unto him, Before Philip called
thee, when thou wast under the fig tree, I saw thee. Nathanael answered,
and said unto him, Rabbi, thou art the Son of God; thou art King of
Israel. Jesus answered and said unto him, Because I said unto thee, I saw
thee underneath the fig tree, thou believest; thou shalt see greater things
than these. And he saith unto him, Verily, verily, I say unto you,
Hereafter ye shall see the heaven opened, and the angels of God ascending
and descending upon the Son of man. (47-51)*

47. *Behold, an Israelite indeed.* Christ does not praise Nathanael on
his own account, but under his person gives a general lesson. For since
many who call themselves believers are anything but believers in fact,
it is important to have some mark to distinguish the true and upright
from the false. We know how proudly the Jews gloried in their father
Abraham, how boldly they boasted the holiness of their descent. And
yet scarcely one in a hundred was not utterly degenerate and a stranger
to the faith of the patriarchs. Therefore Christ, to tear the mask from
hypocrites, says briefly what a true Israelite is, and at the same time
removes the offence which was soon to arise from the ungodly hard-
heartedness of the people. For those who wished to be accounted the

children of Abraham and the holy people of God were shortly afterwards to become the implacable enemies of the Gospel. And so, lest
the ungodliness common in nearly all ranks should dishearten or worry
anyone, He gives a timely warning that there are only a few true
Israelites among those who claim the name of Israelite.

Moreover, since this passage is also a definition of Christianity, we
must not pass it by hastily. Now, to sum up Christ's meaning in a few
words, we must observe that 'deceit' is contrasted to sincerity. Hence
He calls those deceitful who elsewhere in Scripture are said to have a
double heart. Nor does this refer only to that gross hypocrisy when
those who know they are wicked pretend to be good, but also to
another inward hypocrisy when men are so blinded by their sins that
they deceive not only others but themselves as well. Integrity of heart
in the eyes of God and uprightness before men make a Christian. What
Christ is chiefly pointing to is the deceit that Ps. 32.2 speaks of. 'Aληθῶs
here means something more than *certainly*. The Greek word is often
used as a simple affirmation; but as we must supply an antithesis
between the thing and the bare title, he is said to be 'indeed' who is in
reality what he is supposed to be.

48. *Whence knowest thou me?* Although He did not intend to flatter
him, He wanted to gain a hearing to elicit a new question, by replying
to which He would prove Himself to be the Son of God. Nor is it
without reason that Nathanael asks whence Christ knew him, for a
man so sincere as to be free from all deceit is a rare specimen and the
knowledge of that purity of heart belongs to God alone. Christ's reply,
however, seems off the point. Seeing Nathanael under the fig tree
does not enable Him to penetrate into the profound coverts of the
heart. The reason is quite different. As it belongs to God to know men
that were never seen, so also to see what is not visible to the eyes.
Nathanael knew that Christ saw in a way not human, but by a seeing
truly divine, and so he could gather that Christ did not now speak as
a man. The proof therefore is taken from things that are alike; for God
is no less qualified to see what lies out of sight than to judge purity of
heart. We should also gather from this passage a useful lesson, that
when we are not even thinking of Christ we are observed by Him; and
this must needs be so, that He may bring us back when we have with-
drawn from Him.

49. *Thou art the Son of God.* That he acknowledges Him to be the
Son of God from His divine power is not surprising. But why does he
call Him King of Israel? The two things do not seem connected; but
Nathanael looks higher. He had already heard that He was the
Messiah, and to this belief he adds the confirmation which had been
given him. He holds also another principle: that the Son of God will

not come without showing Himself as King over the people of God. He therefore justly confesses the Son of God to be also the King of Israel. And indeed, faith should not cling only to the essence of Christ, so to say, but should pay heed to His power and office. For it would be of little advantage to know who Christ is unless the second point is added of what He wishes to be towards us and for what purpose He was sent by the Father. Hence it has come about that the Papists have nothing but an esoteric Christ, for all their care has been to apprehend His naked essence; His Kingdom, which consists in the power to save, they have neglected.

Again, when Nathanael declares He is King of Israel, it is a confession limited to the measure of his faith, for His Kingdom extends to the utmost limits of the earth. For he had not yet advanced so far as to know that He was appointed to be King over the whole world; or rather, that from every quarter the children of Abraham would be gathered in, so that the whole world would be the Israel of God. We to whom the extent of Christ's Kingdom has been revealed should exceed those narrow limits. But all the same, let us follow Nathanael's example and employ our faith in hearing the Word and strengthen it by whatever means we can; allowing it not to stay buried but to break forth into confession.

50. *Jesus answered.* He does not reprove Nathanael as if he had been too credulous, but rather by His assent approving his faith, promises to him and all others greater proofs of confirmation. Besides, it was peculiar to one man that he was seen under a fig tree by Christ when absent and far away; but now Christ brings forward a proof which would be common to all, and thus, as if breaking off His discourse, He turns from one to all.

51. *Ye shall see the heaven opened, etc.,* He says. To my way of thinking, those who anxiously inquire into the place where and the time when Nathanael and the others saw the heavens opened are much at fault; for He is rather pointing to something continuous which was always to exist in His Kingdom. I acknowledge, of course, that the disciples sometimes saw angels, who are not seen today. I acknowledge that the manifestation of the heavenly glory, when Christ ascended to heaven, was different from what is so now for us. But if we think it over carefully, we see that what happened then is perpetually living. For the Kingdom of God, once closed to us, has in Christ indeed been opened. A visible example of this was shown to Stephen, and to the three disciples on the mountain, and also to the other disciples at Christ's ascension. But all the signs by which God shows Himself present with us relate to this opening of heaven, especially when God communicates Himself to us to be our life.

43

A second clause follows, on angels. They are said to 'ascend and descend' that they may be ministers of the divine kindness towards us. Thus by this expression the reciprocal communication between God and men is noted. Now we must acknowledge that this benefit was received in Christ, because without Him the angels have rather a deadly enmity against us than a friendly care to help us. They are said to 'ascend and descend' on Him not because they minister to Him alone, but because for His sake and in His honour, they include the whole body of the Church in their care. Nor do I doubt that He alludes to the ladder which was shown to the patriarch Jacob in a dream (Gen. 28.12), for what that vision sketched out is really fulfilled in Christ. Finally, the sum of this passage is that though the whole human race was outside the Kingdom of God, the gate of heaven is now open to us, so that we are fellow-citizens of the saints and companions of the angels, and that they, the appointed guardians of our salvation, descend from that blessed calm to relieve our miseries.

CHAPTER TWO

And the third day there was a marriage in Cana of Galilee; and the mother of Jesus was there. And Jesus also was bidden, and his disciples, to the marriage. And when the wine failed, the mother of Jesus saith unto him, They have no wine. And Jesus saith unto her, Woman, what have I to do with thee? mine hour is not yet come. His mother saith unto the servants, Whatsoever he saith unto you, do it. Now there were six waterpots of stone set there after the Jew's manner of purifying, containing two or three firkins apiece. Jesus saith unto them, Fill the waterpots with water. And they filled them up to the brim. And he saith unto them, Draw out now, and bear unto the ruler of the feast. And they bare it. And when the ruler of the feast tasted the water now become wine, and knew not whence it was (but the servants which had drawn the water knew) the ruler of the feast calleth the bridegroom, and saith unto him, Every man setteth on first the good wine; and when men have drunk freely, then that which is worse: thou hast kept the good wine until now. This beginning of his signs did Jesus in Cana of Galilee, and manifested his glory; and his disciples believed on him. (1-11)

1. *There was a marriage in Cana of Galilee.* The fact that this story relates the first miracle performed by Christ is sufficient reason to consider it extremely carefully, though, as we shall see later, there are other reasons which compel our attention. But its manifold usefulness will be shown more clearly as we go along. The Evangelist first names the place, Cana of Galilee; not the one situated towards Sarepta, between Tyre and Sidon, and called 'the greater' in comparison with this other Cana, which some place in the country of the tribe of Zebulon and others assign to the tribe of Asher. For Jerome also declares that even in his time there existed a little town of this name. It is likely that it was near the town of Nazareth, since the mother of Jesus came to attend the marriage. From Chapter Four it will be seen that it was within a day's journey of Capernaum. Its proximity also to the city of Bethsaida can be inferred from the fact that the Evangelist tells us the marriage was celebrated three days after Christ had been in that district. It is possible there was also a third Cana, not far from Jerusalem, though outside Galilee; but I leave this undetermined, because I do not know.

And the mother of Jesus was there. It was probably some kinsman of Christ's who was being married, for Jesus is mentioned as having accompanied His mother. From the fact that the disciples are also

45

invited we can gather how simple and frugal was His way of living, since He lived in common with them. It might be thought incongruous that a man not at all rich or well supplied (as will appear from the failure of the wine) invites four or five others for Christ's sake. But the poor are readier and more open in their invitations; for, unlike the rich, they are not afraid of being disgraced if they do not treat their guests sumptuously and magnificently. It is the poor who keep up the old-fashioned custom of mutual hospitality.

Again, it seems uncivil that the bridegroom should let his guests go short of wine in the middle of the dinner. For he is an inconsiderate man who does not have enough wine for his feast. I reply, what is related here often happens, especially when wine is not in daily use. Besides, the context shows that the wine began to fail towards the end of the feast when it is usual to have had enough already. The ruler of the feast says as much: 'Other men place inferior wine before the drunken, but thou hast saved the best till now.' Moreover, I have no doubt that all this was arranged by divine providence, that there might be an opportunity for the miracle.

3. *The mother of Jesus saith unto him.* It may be doubted whether she hoped or asked anything from her son, since He had not yet performed any miracle. And it is possible that without expecting any such help, she advised Him to allay the guests' annoyance with some godly exhortations, at the same time relieving the embarrassment of the bridegroom. Moreover, I consider her words as συμπάθεια or solicitude. For when the holy woman saw that the feast might be disturbed from the guests' thinking themselves treated with discourtesy and grumbling at the bridegroom, she wanted to find some way of relieving the situation. Chrysostom suspects her of being moved by her feminine instincts to seek after some sort of favour for herself and her Son. This conjecture is baseless.

But why does Christ repulse her so sternly? I reply that although neither ambition nor any other carnal affection motivated her, she yet sinned by going beyond her proper bounds. Her solicitude about the inconvenience of others and her desire to remedy it in some way came from kindliness and should be given its credit; all the same, by putting herself forward, she could have obscured the glory of Christ. But we also ought to notice that Christ spoke like this not so much for her sake as for others. Her modesty and goodness were too great to need so severe a reproof. Again, she was not sinning knowingly and willingly; but Christ just meets the danger of His mother's words being misconstrued, as if it were at her behest that He afterwards performed the miracle.

4. *Woman, what have I to do with thee?* The Greek literally means,

What to me and thee? But this expression in Greek comes to the same thing as the Latin: *Quid tibi mecum?* (What hast thou to do with me?) The old translator led many astray by saying that Christ regarded the failure of the wine as no concern of His or of His mother. But from the second clause we may easily conclude how far this is from Christ's meaning; for He takes upon Himself this care and declares it is His concern when He adds that His hour had not yet come. These two things should be joined—that Christ understands what He must do and yet that He will do nothing in this matter at His mother's suggestion.

This is indeed a remarkable passage. For why does He positively refuse to His mother what He afterwards freely granted so often to all sorts of people? Again, why is He not satisfied with a bare refusal, but puts her in the common order of 'women', not even honouring her with the name of mother? It is certain that this saying of Christ openly warns men not to transfer to Mary what belongs to God, by superstitiously exalting the honour of the maternal name in Mary. Christ therefore addresses His mother like this so as to transmit a perpetual and general lesson to all ages, lest an extravagant honour paid to His mother should obscure His divine glory.

How necessary this warning became, in consequence of the gross and abominable superstitions which followed later, is known well enough. For Mary has been made Queen of Heaven, the Hope, the Life and the Salvation of the world; and in fact, their insane raving went so far that they just about stripped Christ and adorned her with the spoils. And when we condemn those accursed blasphemies against the Son of God, the Papists call us malicious and envious. Nay, they spread the wicked slander that we are deadly foes to the honour of the holy Virgin. As if she had not all the honour that belongs to her without being made a goddess! As if it were honouring her to adorn her with sacrilegious titles and put her in Christ's place! It is they who do Mary a cruel injury when they snatch from God what belongs to Him that they may deform her with false praises.

Mine hour is not yet come. He means that He has not been inactive from carelessness or laziness, and at the same time hints that He will take care of the matter when the right time comes. And so He not only charges His mother with unseasonable zeal, but also gives her hope of a miracle. The holy Virgin recognizes both these thoughts, for she does not press Him further. And when she tells the servants to do whatever He commands, she shows that she is expecting something new to happen. But this lesson has a wider application: whenever the Lord keeps us in suspense and delays His aid, it does not mean that He is inactive, but rather that He regulates His works so that He acts only at the right time. Those who have applied this passage to the ordering of time by Fate are too ridiculous to need a single word wasted on refuting them.

The 'hour' of Christ sometimes means the hour appointed for Him by the Father; and He will afterwards call His time what was convenient and suitable for carrying out the Father's commands. But in this place He claims the right of taking and choosing the time to work.

5. *His mother saith unto the servants.* Here the holy Virgin shows an example of the true obedience she owed to her Son in matters, not of human duties but of His divine power. Therefore she modestly acquiesces in Christ's reply, and exhorts others to obey His will. I acknowledge that the Virgin spoke about that present situation as if she were denying to herself any jurisdiction in the matter and saying that Christ would follow His own will and do whatever He pleased. But if you look into her intention, her statement has a wider application. For she first disclaims and lays aside the power she might seem to have usurped, and then she ascribes all power to Christ alone when she tells them to follow His command. Hence, we are taught here in general that if we desire anything from Christ we shall not obtain our prayers unless we depend entirely on Him, look to Him and in short do whatever He commands. But He does not send us away to His mother but invites us to Himself.

6. *Now there were six waterpots of stone.* According to Budaeus' reckoning, we gather that these waterpots were very large; for as one *metreta* equals twenty *congii*, each contained at least one *sextarius* in our Savoy measure. Christ supplied them therefore with a great abundance of wine; enough indeed for more than a hundred and fifty people at a merry feast. Besides, both the number and the size of the waterpots serve to confirm the truth of the miracle. If they held only two or three *congii* many might have suspected that the wine had been brought from elsewhere. If the water had been changed into wine in one vessel only, the certainty of the miracle would not have been so clear and indisputable. It is not, therefore, without a good reason that the Evangelist mentions their number and says how much they held.

The presence of so many large vessels came from superstition. They received the ceremony of cleansing from the Law of God; but as the world is prone to excess in externals, the Jews, not satisfied with the simplicity enjoined by God, amused themselves with continual sprinklings; and since superstition is ambitious, it undoubtedly led to ostentation. In the same way, we see in the Papacy today that everything said to belong to the worship of God is arranged for pure display. There was, then, a twofold error: without any command from God they engaged rashly in an unnecessary ceremony of their own invention;

and also, under pretence of religion, ambition ruled in that pomp.

Now, certain scamps in the Papacy had the astounding wickedness to dare to put forward some waterpots as being these very ones; but, first, they are too small, and also they are unequal in size. Even today they are not ashamed in the broad light of the Gospel to palm off such shoddy goods. This is certainly not deception by juggling but insolently making fun of the blind. The world must be bewitched by Satan not to perceive such obvious derision.

7. *Fill the waterpots with water.* This command may have seemed absurd to the servants, for they already had more than enough water. But this is the way the Lord is wont to act towards us, so that an unexpected result may make His power shine forth the more brightly. This detail is put in to emphasize the miraculousness; for when the servants drew wine from vessels that had been filled with water, no suspicion can remain.

8. *Bear unto the ruler of the feast.* For the same reason Christ wanted the wine to be tasted by the ruler of the feast before He himself or any other of the guests had drunk any. From the quiet way that the servants obey Him in everything we can see His great authority and reputation. The man whom the Evangelist calls the ruler of the feast superintended the preparation of the feast and the arrangement of the tables—not that the feast was very grand and magnificent, but because poor weddings borrowed high-flown titles from the grandeur and magnificence of the rich. But it is surprising that Christ, a teacher of self-control, should supply a large quantity of wine and that of the very best. I reply, when God daily provides us with plenty of wine it is our own fault if His kindness is an incitement to luxury; but it is an undoubted proof of our temperance if we are sparing and moderate in the midst of plenty. Just as Paul rejoices that he had learned both to be filled and to be hungry (Phil. 4.11).

11. *This beginning of signs.* The meaning is that this was Christ's first miracle. For although the angel's proclamation to the shepherds that He was born in Bethlehem and the star appearing to the Magi and the Holy Spirit descending upon Him in the likeness of a dove were miracles, yet strictly speaking they were not performed by Himself. It is here talking about miracles of which He Himself was the author. For that is a trifling and absurd interpretation which some give, that this is numbered first among the miracles which Christ did in Cana of Galilee; as if He chose a place to manifest His power where we read He only went to twice. The Evangelist's purpose was rather to note the order of time which Christ followed in exercising His power. For until He was thirty he stayed at home like any private person. His Baptism was an admission into the exercise of His duties, after which

He began to appear in public and show openly by clear proofs to what
end He had been sent by the Father. We need not be surprised, therefore, if He postponed the first proof of His divinity until now. Marriage is greatly glorified that Christ not only honoured a wedding feast
with His presence but also adorned it with His first miracle. Certain
ancient canons exist in which the clergy are forbidden to attend
weddings. The reason for the prohibition was that their being spectators of the customary licentiousness might perhaps be construed as
approbation. But it would have been far better for them to have taken
with them a seriousness that would curb the wantonness which shameless and dissolute men indulge in when there is no one to keep an eye
on them. Rather let Christ's example be our rule; and let us not
suppose that anything can do more good than what we read of Him
doing.

And manifested his glory—by giving this remarkable and glorious
evidence from which it could be established that He was the son of
God. For all the miracles which He showed to the world were so many
testimonies to His divine power. And now the proper time for manifesting forth His glory had come, when at the Father's behest He willed
to be known. Moreover, from this we learn the purpose of miracles,
for the expression amounts to a declaration that Christ performed this
miracle to reveal His glory. But what are we to think of those miracles
which obscure the glory of Christ?

And his disciples believed on him. If they were disciples they must
already have had some tinge of faith. But whereas they had hitherto
followed Him with an uncertain and cloudy faith, they now began to
dedicate themselves to Him, acknowledging Him to be the Messiah,
as He had already been proclaimed to them. But Christ is very kind
to accept as His disciples those whose faith was so weak. And indeed,
this doctrine has a universal application. For any adult faith was once
in its infancy; nor is it so perfect in any man that he does not need to
progress in believing. So they who were already believers begin to
believe inasmuch as they daily make further progress towards the mark.
Therefore let those who have arrived at the beginnings of faith strive
always to progress. Here is shown also the fruit of miracles—that they
ought to be related to the confirmation and progress of faith. Whoever
twists them to any other purpose corrupts and debases their whole use.
Just as we see the Papists boasting of their fictitious miracles for no
other purpose than to bury faith and turn men's minds away from
Christ to creatures.

*After this he went down to Capernaum, he, and his mother, and his
brethren, and his disciples: and there he abode not many days. And the*

passover of the Jews was at hand, and Jesus went up to Jerusalem. And
he found in the temple those that sold oxen and sheep and doves and the
changers of money sitting: and he made a scourge of cords and cast them
all out of the temple, with the sheep and the oxen; and he poured out the
changers' money, and overthrew their tables; and to them that sold the doves
he said, Take these things hence; make not my Father's house a house of
merchandise. His disciples remembered that it was written, The zeal of
thine house hath eaten me up. (12-17)

12. *He went down to Capernaum.* The Evangelist passes to a quite
new story. He had resolved to collect a few things worthy of remembrance which the other three had omitted and he states the time when
what he is about to tell us took place. For the others also relate what we
here read of Christ doing, but the difference of time shows it was a
similar but not the same event. Christ therefore twice cleansed the
Temple from base and secular financial business: first, near the beginning of His mission and the other time when He was about to depart
from the world to His Father.

To get a general view of the passage we must examine the details in
order. There was a good reason for oxen, sheep and doves being
offered for sale in the Temple and for money-changers sitting there.
For they could claim that their transactions were not at all secular, but
on the contrary were connected with the sacred worship of God, so
that anyone could easily obtain something to present to the Lord. And
certainly it was very convenient for religious people to find the various
oblations on the spot and so be spared the trouble of looking for them.
Therefore, it is surprising that Christ should be so angry. But two
reasons must be noted. The priests misused this merchandise for their
own gain and avarice, and such a mockery of God was unendurable.
Again, whatever excuse men may plead, so soon as they depart, however slightly, from God's command they are blameworthy and need
correcting. And this is the chief reason why Christ took it upon Him
to cleanse the Temple, for He clearly declares that the Temple of God
is not a place of merchandise.

But it may be asked why He did not begin by teaching them. It
seems a disorderly and inverted procedure to use force to correct abuses
before the remedy of teaching has been tried. But Christ had a different
aim. For since the time had come for Him to discharge in public the
office committed to Him by the Father, He wanted in some way to
enter into possession of the Temple and set forth evidence of His divine
authority. And that all might pay heed to His teaching, their sluggish
and drowsy minds had to be aroused by something new and strange.
Now the Temple was the shrine of heavenly doctrine and religion.

Since He wanted to restore purity of doctrine it was of great importance to establish Himself as the Lord of the Temple. Besides, there was no other way to bring the sacrifices and other religious exercises back to their spiritual purpose than by removing abuses of them. What he did at that time was therefore a sort of prelude to the reformation the Father had sent Him to accomplish. In a word, it was proper that the Jews should be aroused by this example to expect something strange and uncommon from Christ; and it was also necessary to remind them powerfully of the corruption and perversion of the worship of God, that they might not object to its correction.

And his brethren. Why His brethren accompanied Christ is uncertain, unless they just happened to be going to Jerusalem at the same time. Further, by the word 'brethren' the Hebrew language, as is well known, signifies all sorts of male relatives.

13. *And the passover was at hand; and so he went.* The Greek is literally 'and he went', but the Evangelist puts the copulative 'and' in place of the causal conjunction. For he means that He went up then to keep the passover at Jerusalem. He had a twofold object: since the Son of God was subject to the Law for our sake, He wished, by observing precisely all the Law's commands, to show in Himself a type of complete submission and obedience. Again, as He could do more good among a multitude of people He almost always made use of such an opportunity. Whenever, therefore, it is said afterwards that Christ came to Jerusalem for the feast days, let the reader observe that He did so, first, that along with the rest He might perform the exercises of religion instituted by God and, next, that He might proclaim His teaching to a larger concourse of people.

16. *Make not my Father's house.* At the second cleansing of the Temple the other Evangelists mention His harsher and severer language —that they had made the Temple of God a den of thieves, and this was proper when a milder reproof was of no avail. He simply warns them now not to profane the Temple of God by perverting it to alien uses. The Temple was called the House of God because God willed to be invoked there in particular, because there He exercised His power and because He had set it apart for spiritual and holy ceremonies.

Christ declares that He is the Son of God so as to claim the right and authority to cleanse the Temple. Moreover, since He here gives a reason for what he did, anyone who wishes to derive advantage from it must concentrate chiefly on this sentence. Why then does He cast the buyers and sellers out of the Temple? To restore the worship of God to its integrity, which had been corrupted by the wickedness of men and in this way to renew and defend the holiness of the Temple. Now that Temple, as we know, was made to be the shadow of those things whose lively image is in Christ. That it might remain sacred to God, it had to be applied exclusively to spiritual uses. For this reason He declares it unlawful that it should be turned into a market-place. He founds His statement on God's institution, which we ought always to hold. By whatever illusions Satan may deceive, let us know that whatever (however small) turns us aside from God's command is perverse. It was a specious and misleading deceit that the worship of God was aided and promoted if sacrifices were conveniently at hand for believers. But since God had ordained His Temple to other uses, Christ disregards the objections that could be offered against the order set up by God.

This cannot be applied to our Church buildings today, but what is said of the ancient Temple applies justly and properly to the Church, which is the heavenly shrine of God on earth. Wherefore the majesty of God which dwells in the Church should always be set before our eyes, that it may not be defiled by any impurities. But its holiness will remain sound only if nothing foreign to the World of God is admitted into it.

17. *His disciples remembered.* Some people waste their time asking how the disciples remembered Scripture which was hitherto unknown and strange to them. We must not think that this passage of Scripture came into their minds at this time; but afterwards, when, taught by God, they considered among themselves what this action of Christ's might mean, this passage of Scripture occurred to them under the direction of the Holy Spirit. And indeed the cause of God's works is not always plain to us at once; but afterwards in the course of time He makes His purpose known to us. And this is a bridle well-fitted to curb our restiveness, lest we should be troublesome to God when our judgment does not approve His actions. We are reminded at the same time that when God holds us in suspense we must wait patiently for the time of fuller knowledge and curb our innate overhastiness. For God delays the full manifestation of His works to keep us humble.

The meaning is that the disciples at length grasped that Christ was impelled by a burning zeal for God's house to drive these profanations out of it. Without doubt David by synechdoche designates under the Temple the whole worship of God. For the complete verse runs thus: 'The zeal of thine house hath eaten me up; and the reproaches of them that reproach thee are fallen on me.' The second clause balances the first, or rather is simply an explanatory repetition. The sum of both clauses is that David was so anxious to defend God's glory that he willingly accepted on his own head all the reproaches that the wicked cast at God; and that he burned with such zeal that this one feeling swallowed up all others. He tells us that he himself felt like this; but

53

there can be no doubt that in his own person he was describing what properly pertained to the Messiah.

Accordingly the Evangelist says that this was one of the marks by which Jesus was known to the disciples as the avenger and restorer of the Kingdom of God. Now observe that they followed the guidance of Scripture to understand Christ aright. And indeed none will ever learn what Christ is, or the purpose of His actions and sufferings, save by the guiding and teaching of the Scriptures. So far, then, as each of us desires to advance in the knowledge of Christ we shall need to meditate industriously and continually on Scripture. Nor does David mention the House of God heedlessly when he speaks of His glory. For although God is sufficient to Himself and can be satisfied with Himself alone, He yet wishes His glory to be revealed in the Church. In this He shows a remarkable proof of His love towards us, because He joins as by an indissoluble bond His glory with our salvation. Now it remains that each individual shall apply himself to the imitation of Christ, since in the example of the Head is set forth a general lesson for the whole body, as Paul teaches in Rom. 15.3. So far as we can, let us not allow the sacred Temple of God to be polluted in any way. At the same time we must all beware of transgressing the bounds of our calling. In common with the Son of God we should all be zealous; but it is not for all of us to take a whip and forcibly correct vices. For the same power has not been given to us nor the same office laid upon us.

The Jews therefore answered and said unto him, What sign shewest thou unto us, seeing that thou doest these things? Jesus answered and said unto them, Destroy this temple, and in three days I will raise it up. The Jews therefore said, Forty and six years was this temple in building, and wilt thou raise it up in three days? But he spake of the temple of his body. When therefore he was raised from the dead, his disciples remembered that he spake this; and they believed the scripture, and the word which Jesus had said. (18-22)

18. *What sign showest thou?* From the fact that in such a big crowd no one laid hands on Christ and none of the cattle dealers or money-changers drove Him away by violence we may conclude that they were all beaten down and stunned by God and were just petrified. Hence, if they had not been utterly blind this miracle would have been obvious enough, that one man should dare so much, one man against many, an unarmed man against the strong, an unknown man against great rulers. Since they were far the stronger, why did they not prevent Him, save because their strength was loosened and as it were broken?

Yet they have some cause for questioning Him; for it is not for everyone to change at once anything faulty or displeasing in God's Temple. All are certainly at liberty to condemn corruptions; but if a private man sets out to remove them, he will be blamed for his temerity. As the custom of selling in the Temple was accepted, Christ undertook something new and unusual; and so they quite rightly ask Him to prove that He was sent by God; for they base their argument on the principle that in public administration it is not lawful to change anything without a definite calling and command of God. But where they went wrong was in refusing to admit the calling of Christ unless He performed a miracle; for it was not a general principle that the prophets and other ministers of God had to perform miracles, nor had God bound Himself to this necessity. They are therefore wrong to impose a law on God by demanding a sign. When the Evangelist says that the Jews asked Him, he undoubtedly means the multitude standing by and, as it were, the whole body of the Church; as if he were saying that it was not the word of one or two but of the people.

19. *Destroy this temple.* This is an allegorical expression. Christ deliberately spoke so obscurely because He reckoned them unworthy of a direct reply—just as elsewhere He declares that He speaks to them in parables because they cannot grasp the mysteries of the Kingdom of Heaven (Matt. 13.13). But first He refuses them the sign they asked for, either because it would have done no good or because He knew it was not the right time. He occasionally made some concessions even to their unsuitable requests; so there must have been some strong reason why He refused now. But in case they seize on this as an excuse for themselves, He declares that His power will be proved and confirmed by an uncommon sign. For no greater proof of the divine power in Christ could be desired than His resurrection from the dead. But He hints this figuratively because He does not judge them worthy of a clear promise. In short, He treats unbelievers as they deserve and at the same time frees Himself from all contempt. They are, indeed, not yet confirmed as obstinate, but Christ well knew what their attitude was.

But since He performed so many and various miracles, it may be asked why He now mentions only one. I reply, He was silent about all the other miracles because His resurrection alone was sufficient to shut their mouths; and also He did not want to expose the power of God to their mocking. For He spoke allegorically even about the glory of His resurrection. Thirdly, I say that He mentioned what was appropriate to the case; for by these words He shows that all authority over the Temple belongs to Him, since His power is so great in building the true Temple of God. But although He uses the word Temple in accommodation to the present situation, yet the body of Christ is justly and congruently called a Temple. Each of our bodies is called a tabernacle (II Cor. 5.4) because the soul dwells in it; but the body of Christ was the abode of His divinity. For we know that the Son of God so clothed Himself with our nature that in the flesh which He assumed the eternal majesty of God dwelt as in His Sanctuary.

Nestorius' misuse of this passage to prove that one and the same Christ is not both God and man is easily refuted. He reasoned thus: The Son of God dwelt in the flesh as in a temple; therefore the natures are divided so that the same one was not God and man. But this argument might be applied to men; for it will follow that it is not one man whose soul dwells in the body as in a tabernacle; and therefore it is folly to twist this form of expression to take away the unity of person in Christ. Moreover, it ought to be observed that our bodies also are called temples of God (I Cor. 6.19), but in a different sense, namely, because God dwells in us by the power and grace of His Spirit; but in Christ the fulness of the Godhead dwells bodily, so that He is truly God manifested in the flesh.

I will raise it up. Here Christ claims for Himself the glory of His resurrection, though generally in Scripture it is declared to be the work of God the Father. But these two statements are thoroughly accordant. For to commend God's power to us Scripture expressly ascribes it to the Father that He raised His Son from the dead; but here Christ particularly proclaims His own divinity. And Paul reconciles the two in Rom. 8.11, for the Spirit whom he makes the author of the resurrection he calls indiscriminately sometimes the Spirit of Christ, sometimes the Spirit of the Father.

Forty and six years. Daniel's reckoning agrees with this passage (Dan. 9.25), for he calls it seven weeks, which makes forty-nine years; but before the last of these weeks had ended the Temple was complete. It seems contradictory that the time mentioned in the history of Ezra is far shorter, but in fact it does not conflict with the prophet's words. For when the Sanctuary had been set up, before the edifice of the Temple was complete, they began to offer sacrifices. Afterwards there was a long interruption in the work due to the people's laziness, as is clear from the complaints of the prophet Haggai (1.4) who reproves the Jews severely for being too busy building their private houses the while they left the Temple of God unfinished. But why does He mention the Temple that had been demolished by Herod forty years or so earlier? The present Temple, though built very magnificently and at vast expense, had been completed by Herod in eight years, contrary to expectation, as Josephus relates (*Antiq.*, Bk. xv, ch. 11). I think it likely that this new building of the Temple was regarded as if it were the ancient Temple always remaining *in statu*, that it might be held in greater veneration. And so speaking in the common and usual way they said that the Temple was hardly and with the greatest difficulty built by the fathers in forty-six years.

Their reply shows plainly in what spirit they sought a sign; for if they had been ready to obey reverently a prophet sent by God, they would not have rejected so arrogantly what He had said in confirmation of His office. They want some testimony of divine power and yet they will not receive anything that does not answer to man's little capacity. In the same way the Papists today demand miracles, not that they would give way to the power of God (for they are determined to prefer men to God and not to shift a hair's breadth from what they have received by usage and custom); but that they may not seem to rebel against God without a cause, they make this excuse a cloak for their obstinacy. So do the minds of unbelievers rage blindly and desire to have the hand of God exhibited to them and yet do not want it to be divine.

When therefore he was raised from the dead. This remembering was similar to the other that the Evangelist has just mentioned. The disciples did not understand Christ's saying; but the teaching which seemed to have vanished uselessly into thin air later produced fruit in its own time. Although therefore many of our Lord's actions and sayings are obscure at the time, we must not give up in despair or despise what we do not understand at once. The context should be noted here: 'they believed the scripture and the word of Christ.' By comparing the Scripture with the word of Christ they were helped to progress in faith.

Now when he was in Jerusalem at the passover, during the feast, many believed on his name, beholding his signs which he did. But Jesus did not trust himself unto them, for that he knew all men, and because he needed not that any one should bear witness concerning man; for he himself knew what was in man. (23-25)

23. *Many believed, etc.* He appropriately connects this narrative with the former. Christ had not given such a sign as the Jews sought. Now since He had made no progress among them by many miracles, except that they conceived a cold and abstract faith, the present event shows that they did not deserve Him to fall in with their wishes. There was indeed some result of the signs in that many believed in Christ and in His name so as to profess their readiness to follow His teaching—for 'name' is used here for authority. This was some sort of a semblance of faith and hitherto was evanescent, but it might become true faith in the end and be a useful preparation for proclaiming the faith of Christ to others. Yet what we have said is true, that they were far from the right attitude to progress in the divine works as they should have done.

Theirs was not however a pretended faith to commend themselves to men. For they were convinced that Christ was some great prophet, and perhaps they even ascribed to Him the office of Messiah, who was then widely expected. But since they did not grasp the Messiah's special office, their faith was absurd, clinging as it did to the world and earthly things. It was also a cold belief, a persuasion empty of any serious attitude of heart. For hypocrites assent to the Gospel, not that they may devote themselves to the allegiance of Christ, nor that with sincere religion they may follow God's call, but because they do not dare to reject outright acknowledged truth, especially when there is no reason to oppose it. For just as they do not voluntarily or gratuitously wage war against God, so also when they see that His teaching is against their flesh and perverse desires they are at once upset or at least withdraw from the faith they had adopted.

So when the Evangelist says that those men believed, I do not take it as a pretended and non-existent faith, but that they were in some way constrained to enlist on Christ's side: and yet that it was not a true and genuine faith is shown by Christ excluding them from the number of those whose conviction could be relied on. Besides their faith depended only on miracles and hitherto had no root in the Gospel, so that it could not be steady and permanent. The children of God are indeed helped by miracles to reach faith; but that is not yet a true believing when they are amazed at God's power in such a way as merely to believe that the teaching is true without subjecting themselves to it wholly. And therefore, when we treat of faith in general let us realize that there is a certain faith which is apprehended by the understanding only, and afterwards quickly disappears because it is not fixed in the heart; and that is the faith which James calls dead, whereas true faith always depends on the Spirit of regeneration (Jas. 2.17, 26). Observe that the works of God do not profit all men equally; for by them some are led to God while others are only driven by a blind impulse, so that although they perceive the power of God they do not cease to wander in their own imaginations.

24. *But Christ did not trust.* Those who expound it as Christ being on His guard against them because He knew they were not honest and faithful, do not seem to me to express the meaning of the Evangelist well enough. Even less apt is what Augustine brings in about catechumens. The Evangelist means rather, in my opinion, that they were not regarded by Christ as genuine disciples but despised as light and trifling. This passage should be observed carefully; not all who profess to be Christ's are such in His estimation. But the reason which immediately follows must be added:

For that he knew all men. Nothing is more dangerous than hypocrisy;

for this among other reasons, that it is an exceedingly common fault. There is scarcely a man who is not pleased with himself; and while we deceive ourselves with empty flatteries we think God is blind like ourselves. But here we are warned how widely His judgment differs from ours. For He sees clearly the things that escape our notice because they are hidden in masks; and He estimates according to their hidden source, that is, according to the most secret attitude of the heart, the things which dazzle our eyes with their false brilliance. This is the same as Solomon says in Prov. 21.2: 'Every way of a man is right in his own eyes: but the Lord weigheth the hearts.' Let us remember therefore that they only are the true disciples of Christ who are approved by Him, because He alone is the proper arbiter and judge of this matter.

Where the Evangelist says that Christ knew all men, it may be asked whether he means only those of whom he had just spoken or whether it refers to the whole human race. Many extend it to man's common nature and think that the whole world is here condemned for ungodly and faithless hypocrisy. And it is certainly a true judgment that nothing can be found in men why Christ should accept them in the number of His own. But I do not see that this squares with the context and therefore I limit it to those who had been mentioned.

As it might be doubted where Christ obtained this knowledge, the Evangelist anticipates the question and replies that everything in men concealed from us is seen by Christ, so that He could of His own right distinguish between men. Christ therefore who knows the hearts had no need of a teacher to learn what sort of men they were. But he knew them to be imbued with such a nature and attitude that He justly regarded them as foreign to Him.

Some ask whether we too, after Christ's example, may suspect those who have not given us proof of their probity; but this has nothing to do with the present passage. Our judgment is far different from His. Christ knew the very roots of the trees; but we can only know the nature of any individual tree from the outward fruits. Besides, as Paul says, love is not distrustful (I Cor. 13.5) and we have no right to suspect without good reason men who are unknown to us. But that we may not always be deceived by hypocrites and that the Church may not be too much exposed to their wicked frauds, it belongs to Christ to furnish us with the Spirit of criticism.

CHAPTER THREE

Now there was a man of the Pharisees, named Nicodemus, a ruler of the Jews. The same came unto him by night, and said to him, Rabbi, we know that thou art a teacher come from God: for no man can do these signs that thou doest, except God be with him. Jesus answered and said unto him, Verily, verily, I say unto thee, Except a man be born again, he cannot see the kingdom of God. Nicodemus saith unto him, How can a man be born when he is old? Can he enter again into his mother's womb, and be born? Jesus answered, Verily, verily, I say unto thee, Except a man be born of water and the Spirit, he cannot enter into the kingdom of God. That which is born of the flesh is flesh; and that which is born of the Spirit is spirit. (1-6)

1. *Now there was a man.* In the person of Nicodemus the Evangelist now shows us how transient and frail was the faith of those who had been moved by Christ's miracles and hastily joined His side. For this man was of the order of Pharisees and held the rank of a ruler in his nation and should therefore have been far in advance of the rest. The common people for the most part are swayed by levity. But who would not have thought that a man strong in learning and experience was also serious and wise? Yet from Christ's reply it is plain that nothing was further from his purpose in coming than a desire to learn the rudiments of religion. If a ruler among men is less than a boy, what are we to think of the public in general? Now, although the Evangelist's aim was to show us as in a mirror how few in Jerusalem were properly disposed to receive the Gospel, yet this story is extremely useful on other counts as well. Particularly because in it we are taught about the corrupt nature of the human race, what is the right entrance into the school of Christ, by what beginnings we must be formed for making progress in heavenly doctrine. For the sum of Christ's discourse is that to be His true disciples we must become new men. But before we go any further, we must, from the details narrated by the Evangelist, consider the obstacles which kept Nicodemus from giving himself entirely to Christ.

Of the Pharisees. This was of course a title of honour for Nicodemus among his countrymen; but the Evangelist does not give it him for the sake of honour but, on the contrary, marks it out as an obstacle to his coming boldly and freely to Christ. Hence we are reminded that the lofty ones of this earth are mostly caught in the worst snares; indeed

60

we see many of them so firmly trapped that they do not breathe even the slightest prayer to Heaven in their whole life. We have explained elsewhere why they were called Pharisees, for they boasted they were the only interpreters of the Law, as if they possessed the marrow and hidden meaning of Scripture; and for that reason they called themselves *Perushim*.[1] Although the Essenes won a reputation for holiness by their more austere life, they were like hermits and forsook the common life and custom of men; and therefore the sect of the Pharisees was held in the higher estimation. Besides, the Evangelist mentions not only that Nicodemus was of the order of the Pharisees but that he was one of the rulers of his nation.

2. *He came unto Jesus by night.* From his coming by night we infer that he was very faint-hearted; his eyes were dazzled as it were by his own distinction. Perhaps, too, he was hindered by shame, for ambitious men think that their reputation is ruined if they once descend from the elevation of master to the rank of scholar. There is no doubt he was puffed up with a foolish opinion of his learning. In short, as he had a high idea of himself he did not want to resign it at all. And yet some seed of piety appears in him; for hearing that a prophet of God had come he does not despise or neglect the teaching brought from heaven and is moved by a certain desire for it—a wish sprung simply from the fear and reverence of God. Many are titillated by an idle curiosity to inquire eagerly after novelties, but there is no doubt that religion and a perception of conscience impelled Nicodemus to desire to know the teaching of Christ more intimately. And although that seed long lay hidden and dead, after the death of Christ it yielded such fruit as no one would ever have expected (19.39).

Rabbi, we know. These words amount to his saying, 'Master, we know that thou art come as a teacher.' But as learned men were then commonly called 'Master', Nicodemus first salutes Christ in the usual way, giving Him the ordinary title, and afterwards declares that he who performs the office of a master was sent by God. And on this principle depends all the authority of teachers in the Church. For from the Word of God alone must we learn wisdom, and therefore no others should be listened to save those by whose mouth God speaks. And we must observe that although religion was greatly corrupted and almost overthrown among the Jews they always kept to the principle that no man was a lawful teacher unless he had come from God. But since none boast more arrogantly and definitely of their divine title than

---

[1] *Comm. on Harm. of Gospels*, on Matt. 5.20 and 23.2; cf. also *Comm. on Phil.* 3.5. Calvin derives 'Pharisee' from *Parash* (פרש) meaning to divide, separate, or to declare distinctly. Calvin chooses the latter meaning, whereas modern scholars usually prefer the former, and so describe them as 'the separated ones'.

false prophets, they need to be tried by the spirit of discernment. Accordingly Nicodemus adds that it is certain that Christ has been sent by God, for God displays His power in Him so strongly that it cannot be denied that God is with Him. He takes it for granted that God is not accustomed to work but through His ministers, that thus He may set His seal to the office He has entrusted to them. And he is right, for God always intended miracles to be the seals of His doctrine. He is also right in making God the sole author of miracles, when he says that no man can do these signs unless God be with him. It is as if he said that they are not human acts, but that the power of God reigns and stands out plainly in them. In a word, miracles have the twofold result of preparing us for faith and then of further strengthening what has been conceived by the Word; and so Nicodemus profited aright in the former part, since from the miracles he recognizes Christ as a true prophet of God.

Yet this seems inconclusive. For since prophets may deceive the ignorant with their deceits as fully as if they had by true signs proved themselves the ministers of God, what difference will there be between truth and falsehood if faith depends on miracles? Indeed Moses expressly declares that in this way we are tested as to whether we love God (Deut. 13.3). We know also Christ's warning, and Paul's, that believers should beware of lying signs by which Antichrist dazzles many eyes (Matt. 22.24). I answer, this is done by the righteous permission of God, that those who deserve it may be deceived by the trickery of Satan. But I say that this does not stop the power of God being manifested to the elect in miracles, which may be a valuable confirmation of true and sound doctrine to them. Thus Paul glories that his apostleship was confirmed by signs and wonders (II Cor. 12.12). Therefore however Satan may strut about aping God in the dark, yet when eyes are opened and the light of spiritual wisdom shines, miracles are a strong enough attestation of the presence of God, as Nicodemus here declares.

3. *Verily, verily, I say unto thee.* Christ repeats the word 'verily' (*amen*) to catch his attention. For when He was going to speak of the most important and weighty of all subjects He needed to make Nicodemus more attentive; otherwise he might have passed over this whole discourse carelessly and lightly. Such then is the purpose of the double affirmation.

Although this discourse seems far-fetched and almost untimely, yet it was most apt for Christ to begin like this. For as it is useless to sow seed in an uncultivated field, so the doctrine of the Gospel is thrown heedlessly away unless the hearer has first been broken in and duly prepared to be obedient and teachable. Christ saw that Nicodemus' mind was so full of thorns and choked with many noxious weeds that there was scarcely room for spiritual teaching. This exhortation was therefore like a ploughing to clean him, that nothing should make the teaching unfruitful. Let us therefore remember that this was spoken to just one man, so that the Son of God may address us all daily in the same tenor. For which of us will say that he is so free from corrupt affections that he does not need such a cleansing? If therefore we want to progress well and usefully in the school of Christ let us learn to start out from here.

Except a man be born again. In other words, so long as you lack the most important thing in the Kingdom of God I do not think much of your acknowledging me as Master; for your first step into the Kingdom of God is to become a new man. But as this is an outstanding passage, every part of it must be examined in detail.

To see the Kindgom of God comes to the same thing as entering into the Kingdom of God, as soon appears from the context. But they are mistaken who think the Kingdom of God means Heaven. It is rather the spiritual life, which is begun by faith in this world and daily increases according to the continual progress of faith. So the meaning is that no man can be truly gathered into the Church and be reckoned among the children of God until he has first been renewed. And thus this shows briefly what is the beginning of the Christian life. At the same time we are taught by this expression that at birth we are exiles and complete strangers to the Kingdom of God, and that there is perpetual opposition between God and us until He changes us by a second birth. For the statement is general and comprehends the whole human race. If Christ had said just to one man or to a few that they could not enter into heaven except first they had been born again, we might have supposed that it was only certain sorts of people who were meant; but He is speaking of all without exception. For the language is unlimited and has the same import as such a universal expression as 'Whosoever will not be born again', etc.

Moreover, by the term *born again* He means not the amendment of a part but the renewal of the whole nature. Hence it follows that there is nothing in us that is not defective; for if reformation is necessary in the whole and in each part, corruption must be spread everywhere. We shall shortly speak about this more fully. Erasmus, following Cyril's opinion, has incorrectly translated the adverb ἄνωθεν as 'from above'. I own that the meaning is ambiguous in Greek, but we know that Christ spoke to Nicodemus in Hebrew. In that case there would have been no ambiguity to mislead Nicodemus into his childish hesitation over a second birth of the flesh. Hence he took Christ's words in no other sense than that a man must be born *again* before he is deemed to be in the Kingdom of God.

4. *How can a man be born?* Although Christ's form of speech does not expressly occur in the Law and the prophets, yet as renewal is everywhere mentioned in Scripture and is one of the first principles of the faith, it is plain how imperfectly learned the Scribes then were in the reading of the Scriptures. This man was certainly not the only one at fault in not knowing what the grace of regeneration was. The chief thing in the teaching of godliness was neglected because almost all of them were preoccupied with empty subtleties. The Papacy today shows us a similar instance in her theologians. For they wear out their whole lives in recondite speculations but know no more about all that belongs to the worship of God, to the assurance of our salvation or to the practice of godliness than a cobbler or a ploughman knows about astronomy. And what is more, delighting in exotic mysteries, they openly despise the true teaching of Scripture as unworthy of the rank of teachers. We need not be surprised, then, that Nicodèmus trips over a straw, so to speak; for it is a just vengeance of God that those who think themselves the most excellent and eminent teachers and to whom the ordinary simplicity of doctrine is vile and low are amazed at little things.

5. *Except a man be born of water*. This passage has been explained in various ways. Some have thought that two parts of regeneration are distinctly expressed and that by the word *water* is meant the denial of the old man, while they take the *Spirit* as the new life. Others think there is an implied antithesis, as if Christ contrasted water and Spirit —i.e. pure and liquid elements—with man's earthly and gross nature. Thus they take this saying as allegorical, that Christ was commanding us to put off our heavy and burdensome mass of flesh and become like water and air so as to move upwards or at least not be so much weighed down to earth. But both opinions seem to me alien to Christ's meaning.

Chrysostom, with whom the greater part agree, relates the word *water* to Baptism. The meaning would then be that by Baptism we enter into the Kingdom of God because God's Spirit regenerates us then. Hence arose the belief in the absolute necessity of Baptism for the hope of eternal life. But even were we to grant that Christ is speaking of Baptism here, we ought not to press His words so as to make Him confine salvation to the outward sign. On the contrary, He connects water with the Spirit because under that visible sign He testifies and seals the newness of life which by His Spirit God alone effects in us. It is true indeed that we are excluded from salvation if we neglect Baptism; and in this sense I confess it is necessary. But it is absurd to confine assurance of salvation to the sign. So far as this passage is concerned, I cannot at all bring myself to believe that Christ is speaking of Baptism, for it would have been inopportune. And we must always keep Christ's purpose in mind, which we have already explained as a wish to urge Nicodemus to newness of life, because he was not capable of receiving the Gospel until he began to be another man.

That to be the children of God we must be born anew and that the Holy Spirit is the author of this second birth is therefore one single and simple statement. For while Nicodemus was dreaming of some Pythagorean *palingenesis* Christ, to liberate him from this error, added by way of explanation that it does not happen naturally that men are born a second time and that they do not have to put on a new body but are born when they are renewed in mind and heart by the grace of the Spirit. Accordingly He used the words *Spirit* and *water* to mean the same thing, and this ought not to be regarded as harsh or forced. It is a frequent and common way of speaking in Scripture, when the Spirit is mentioned, to add the word *water* or *fire* to express His power. We sometimes hear of Christ baptizing with the Holy Spirit and with fire, where fire does not mean something different from the Spirit but only shows what is His power in us. It matters little that He puts the word *water* first. This phrase just flows more easily than the other, since a plain and straightforward statement follows the metaphor. It is as if Christ had said that no one is a son of God until he has been renewed by water and that this water is the Spirit who cleanses us anew and who, by His power poured upon us, imparts to us the energy of the heavenly life when by nature we are utterly barren. And to reprove Nicodemus for his ignorance Christ very properly uses a form of speech common in Scripture. For Nicodemus ought at length to have acknowledged that what Christ had said was taken from the ordinary teaching of the prophets. By water therefore is meant simply the inward cleansing and quickening of the Holy Spirit. Nor is it unusual to employ the word *and* explanatorily when the latter clause is an explanation of the former. And the context supports me too; for when Christ at once adds the reason why we must be born again He shows without mentioning water how the newness of life which He requires comes from the Spirit alone. Whence it follows that *water* must not be separated from *the Spirit*.

6. *That which is born of the flesh.* He shows by a contrast that the Kingdom of God is closed to us unless an entrance be opened to us by a new birth. For He takes it for granted that we cannot enter into the Kingdom of God unless we are spiritual. But we bring nothing from the womb but a carnal nature. Therefore it follows that we are all naturally banished from the Kingdom of God, deprived of heavenly life and in slavery to death. Besides, when Christ argues here that men

E

must be born again because they are only flesh He undoubtedly comprehends all mankind under the word *flesh*. Flesh means in this place not the body but the soul and consequently every part of it. The Popish theologasters are stupid to restrict it to that part which they call sensual, for Christ's argument must in that case have been the inept one that we need a second birth because a part of us is corrupt. But if flesh is contrasted to the Spirit as something corrupt to what is sound, the crooked to what is straight, the defiled to the holy, the polluted to the pure, we may readily conclude that the whole of man's nature is condemned in one word. Christ is therefore saying that our understanding and reason are corrupted because they are carnal and that all the affections of the heart are depraved and wicked because they too are carnal.

But here the difficulty might be raised that, since the soul is not begotten by human generation, we are not in our chief part born of the flesh. This has led many to think that not only does our body derive its origin from our parents but that our souls are also passed on by propagation. For it was thought absurd that original sin, which properly is seated in the soul, should be spread from one man to all his posterity, unless all souls flowed from his soul as from a spring. And indeed at first sight, Christ's words seem to suggest that we are flesh just because we are born of flesh. I reply that Christ's words mean nothing but that we are all carnal when we are born: and that inasmuch as we come into this world as mortal men our nature has no taste for anything but what is flesh. He is simply distinguishing between nature and a supernatural gift. For the corruption of all mankind in the person of Adam alone did not proceed from generation but from the ordinance of God. As in one man He adorned us all, so He has also in him deprived us of His gifts. Therefore, we do not draw our individual vice and corruption from our parents but are all alike corrupted in Adam alone, because immediately after his fall God took away from human nature what He had given to it.

Here another difficulty arises. It is certain that in this degenerate and vitiated nature some remnant of God's gifts still remains; whence it follows that we are not perverted in every part. The solution is easy: The gifts which the Lord left to us after the Fall are certainly worthy of praise judged in themselves. But since the contagion of evil has run riot through every part, nothing pure and free from all defilement will be found in us. That some knowledge of God is innate in us, that some distinction between good and evil is engraven on our consciences, that we have the capacity to cope with supporting our present life, that, in short, we excel the brute beasts in so many ways, is excellent in itself, inasmuch as it proceeds from God. But all these things are polluted in us, just as wine which has been completely spoilt and tainted by the stench of its leather bottle loses the pleasantness of its flavour and has a bitter and horrible taste. For the knowledge of God as it now remains in men is nothing but a dreadful fountain of idolatry and all superstitions; the judgment of choosing and distinguishing things is partly blind and foolish, partly imperfect and confused; whatever industry we have is wasted on vanity and trifles; and the will itself rushes with raging impetus headlong into evil. Thus in the whole of our nature there remains not a speck of uprightness. And so it is plain that we must be formed for the Kingdom of God by a second birth. And the meaning of Christ's words is that, since a man is born from his mother's womb only carnal, he must be fashioned anew by the Spirit that he may begin to be spiritual. And the word *Spirit* is used here in two senses —for grace, and for the effect of grace. In the first place Christ is teaching us that the Spirit of God is the only author of a pure and upright nature and afterwards He says that we are spiritual because we are renewed by His power.

Marvel not that I said unto thee, Ye must be born again. The wind bloweth where it listeth, and thou hearest the voice thereof, but knoweth not whence it cometh, and whither it goeth: so is everyone that is born of the Spirit. Nicodemus answered and said unto him, How can these things be? Jesus answered and said unto him, Art thou a teacher of Israel, and understandest not these things? Verily, verily, I say unto thee, We speak that we do know, and bear witness of that we have seen; and ye receive not our witness. If I told you earthly things, and ye believe not, how shall ye believe, if I tell you heavenly things? (7-12)

7. *Marvel not.* Commentators have twisted this passage in various ways. Some think that it attacks the stupidity of Nicodemus and his like; as if Christ were saying that there is nothing surprising in that they do not grasp the mystery of heavenly regeneration, since even in the order of nature they do not attain the reason for sensible things. Others work out a meaning which is ingenious but much too forced: that even as the wind blows freely so we are set at liberty by the begetting of the Spirit and, freed from the yoke of sin, may run voluntarily to God. Also foreign to Christ's meaning is Augustine's suggestion that the Spirit of God works at His own pleasure. Chrysostom and Cyril are better, when they say that the comparison is taken from the wind and apply it to this passage thus: though its power is felt, its origin and cause are hidden. While I do not dissent much from their opinion, I shall try to explain Christ's meaning more clearly and surely.

My starting point is that Christ borrows a comparison from the order of nature. Nicodemus reckoned what he had heard about regeneration and a new life incredible; for the manner of this regeneration exceeded his grasp. To get rid of this sort of difficulty for him, Christ teaches him that even in the bodily life there appears a marvellous power of God whose principle is hidden. For all draw their vital breath from the air; even the movement of the air is perceptible, but where it comes from and where it goes to we do not know. If in this frail and transitory life God acts so powerfully that we have to marvel at His power, how absurd it is to want to measure by the apprehension of our own mind His secret work in the heavenly and supernatural life and believe no more than we can see! Thus when Paul breaks out in indignation against those who reject the doctrine of the resurrection on the grounds that it seems impossible for the body which is now subject to putrefaction, to be clothed, after it has been reduced to dust and nothing, with a blessed immortality, he reproaches them for stupidity in not considering the similar power of God in a grain of wheat. For the seed does not germinate until it has been putrefied (I Cor. 15.36, 37). This is the marvellous wisdom of which David exclaims in Ps. 104.24. They are therefore extremely stupid who, at the prompting of the common order of nature, do not rise higher and acknowledge that the hand of God is far more powerful in Christ's spiritual Kingdom. Again, when Christ tells him to marvel not, it should not be understood as if He meant us to despise so splendid a work of God, one so worthy of the highest admiration. But He means that we ought not to be gripped by such an amazement as will hinder our faith. For many reject as fabulous what they think too lofty and difficult. In a word, let us not doubt that by the Spirit of God we are re-fashioned and made new men, though the way He does this is hidden from us.

8. *The wind bloweth where it listeth.* Not that, strictly speaking, the blowing is voluntary, but because the movement is free and vagrant and changeable; for the air is carried sometimes in this direction and sometimes in that. And this is relevant, for if it flowed in a uniform direction, like water, it would be less marvellous.

So is everyone. Christ means that the movement and operation of God's Spirit is no less perceptible in the renewal of man than the movement of the air in this earthly and outward life, but its mode is hidden. And we, therefore, are ungrateful and niggardly if we do not adore the incomprehensible power of God in the heavenly life, of which He shows us so outstanding an example in this world, and if we ascribe to Him less in restoring the salvation of our souls than in preserving the estate of our bodies. The application will be a little clearer if you put the sentence like this: Such is the power and efficacy of the Holy Spirit in the renewed man.

9. *How can these things be?* We see what Nicodemus' main difficulty was. Everything that he hears seems extravagant, because he does not understand its mode. There is no worse obstacle to us than our own pride; for we always want to be wiser than is proper, and therefore we reject with devilish pride everything that is not explained to our reason, as if it were fair to limit God's infinite power to our poor capacity. We may indeed inquire into the manner and reason of God's works to a certain extent, with sobriety and reverence. But Nicodemus rejects it as a fable with the objection that he does not think it possible. We shall treat this subject more fully in Chapter Six.

10. *Art thou a teacher of Israel?* Because Christ sees that He is wasting His time and energy in teaching this proud man, He now rebukes him. And certainly with such people no teaching will ever make progress until the perverse confidence with which they are puffed up is destroyed. Moreover, this is a very apposite objection to subdue his pride, for Christ criticizes his ignorance in the very matter on which he thinks he is most acute and wise. He thought it weighty and shrewd not to allow the impossible, because a man who accepts something on the word of another before going into it well is foolishly credulous. But yet it is Nicodemus, with his magisterial arrogance, who is ridiculous, because he is more at a loss about the first principles than any schoolboy. Such a doubt is indeed base and shameful. For what religion have we, what knowledge of God, what rule for right conduct, what hope of eternal life, if we do not believe that a man is renewed by the Spirit of God? There is an emphasis, therefore, on the word *these*; for since Scripture repeatedly insists on this part of doctrine, it should not be unknown even to the veriest tyro. Hence it is quite unbearable that a man who professes to be a teacher in the Church of God should be ignorant and unskilled in it.

11. *We speak that we do know.* Some refer this to Christ and John the Baptist; others say that the plural is used for the singular. But I have no doubt that Christ is joining Himself with all the prophets of God and speaking for them all. For philosophers and other conceited teachers often put forward trifles which they have invented. But Christ claims it as peculiar to Himself and all God's servants that they deliver no doctrine but what is certain. God does not send them to chatter of things unknown or doubtful, but trains them in His school to pass on to others what they have learned from Himself. Moreover, since Christ in this testimony commends to us the certainty of His doctrine, He enjoins on all His ministers a rule of modesty, that they shall not put forward their own dreams or conjectures nor publish human inventions which have no solidity, but shall give a faithful and pure witness to God. Let every man therefore regard what the Lord

has revealed to him, so that none goes beyond the limits of his faith. And finally let none allow himself to speak anything save what he has heard from the Lord. It ought also to be observed that Christ here confirms His teaching by an oath, that it may have complete authority over us.

Ye receive not our witness. This is added that the Gospel may not suffer from the ingratitude of men. For since God's truth encounters few who believe it and is everywhere rejected by the world, we should free it from contempt lest its majesty be the less esteemed by nearly the whole world despising it and obscuring it by ungodliness. Now though the meaning of the words is simple and straightforward, a twofold lesson is to be gathered from the passage. The first is that faith in the Gospel must not waver among us if it has few disciples on earth; as if Christ had said, 'Though you do not receive my teaching, it still remains certain and lasting; for men's unbelief will never prevent God from remaining always faithful.' The other is, that those who in our own day refuse to believe the Gospel will not escape unpunished, for the truth of God is inviolable. We must be armed with this shield so that we can persevere in obedience to the Gospel in opposition to men's disobedience. This principle must indeed be held, so that our faith may be founded on God. But when we have God as our founder we should, as if we were raised above the heavens, boldly tread the whole world down and not be confounded by the unbelief of anyone whatsoever. We learn from Christ's complaint that His testimony is not received, that the fate, as it were, of God's Word has in all ages been that it won belief among only a few. For the phrase *ye receive not* relates to the majority, almost to the whole body of the people. There is no reason therefore why the fewness of believers today should cast us down.

12. *If I told you earthly things.* Christ concludes that Nicodemus and his like must be blamed if they do not advance in the doctrine of the Gospel; for He shows that it is not His fault that all are not trained properly, since He comes right down to earth to raise us up to heaven. It is a very common fault that men want to be taught subtly and scholastically; and this is why such a large part like lofty and abstruse speculations, and why the most underprize the Gospel, since they do not find grand language in it to fill their ears. And so they do not deign to give themselves to the study of a common and low doctrine. But how very wicked it is for us to yield less reverence to God's speaking because He lowers Himself to our ignorance! Let us know that it is for our sakes that the Lord prattles with us in Scripture in an awkward and common style. Whoever says that he is offended at such meanness or pleads it as an excuse for not subjecting himself to the Word of God is a liar. For

he who cannot bear to embrace God when He is near him will certainly not fly away to Him above the clouds.

Earthly things. Some expound this as the rudiments of spiritual doctrine; for denial of ourselves is a sort of first stage of training in godliness. But I rather agree with those who refer this to the form of teaching. For though the whole of Christ's discourse was heavenly, yet He spoke in such a homely way that His style might have seemed in a certain sense earthly. Moreover, these words ought not to be restricted to a single discourse, for Christ's ordinary method of teaching —that is, with common simplicity—is here contrasted with the display and brilliance to which ambitious men are so addicted.

And no man hath ascended into heaven, but he that descended out of heaven, even the Son of man, which is in heaven. And as Moses lifted up the serpent in the wilderness, even so must the Son of man be lifted up: that whosoever believeth in him may not perish, but have eternal life. For God so loved the world, that he gave his only begotten Son, that whosoever believeth on him should not perish, but have eternal life. For God sent not his Son into the world to judge the world; but that the world should be saved through him. He that believeth on him is not judged: he that believeth not hath been judged already, because he hath not believed on the name of the only begotten Son of God. (13-18)

13. *No man hath ascended into heaven.* He again exhorts Nicodemus not to trust in himself and his own perspicacity; for no mortal man can penetrate by his own industry into heaven, but only he who tends towards it by the guidance of the Son of God. For an ascent into heaven entails a pure knowledge of the mysteries of God and the light of spiritual understanding. Here Christ is teaching the same thing as Paul, who says that 'the natural man graspeth not the things which are of God' (I Cor. 2.14), and therefore he excludes all the acuteness of man's understanding from divine things, because it lies far below God.

But we must observe that it says that Christ alone, who is heavenly, *ascends into heaven,* while the entrance is closed to all others. In the former clause He humbles us by keeping the whole world out of heaven. Paul tells those who want to be wise with God to be fools with themselves (I Cor. 3.18). There is nothing we less like to do. Therefore we must believe that all our senses fade away and fail when we have to do with God. But after Christ has shut heaven against us, He at once puts forward the remedy by adding that what was denied to all others was given to the Son of man. For He did not ascend into heaven to benefit Himself personally and alone, but to be our Leader and Guide. And He calls Himself the Son of man so that we shall not doubt that we have an entrance in common with Him who clothed Himself with our

71

flesh to make us participants in all blessings. Since, therefore, He is the
only interpreter of the Father, He admits us into those secrets which
would otherwise have lain hidden. It might seem absurd that He says
He *is in heaven* while He is dwelling on earth. If you reply that it is
true of His Divinity, then the expression means something else—that
while He was man He was in heaven. It might be said that there is no
mention of a place here, but that Christ is only distinguished from the
rest in status, in that He is the Heir of the Kingdom of God from which
the whole human race is banished. But since, for the sake of the unity
of person in Christ, it is frequent and common to transfer the property
of the one nature to the other, we need not look for another solution.
Hence Christ, who is in heaven, put on our flesh that, by stretching out
a brotherly hand to us, He might raise us to heaven along with Himself.

14. *And as Moses.* He explains more clearly why He said that heaven
is open to Him alone—that He may take there all who are willing to
follow Him as their Leader. For He declares that He will be publicly
and openly revealed to all so that He may pour out His power upon
them.

Lifted up means to be set in an outstanding and eminent place so as to
be open to everybody's view. This happened in the preaching of the
Gospel. The explanation which some give of it as referring to the
cross does not agree with the context and is foreign to His argument.
The simple meaning of the words is that by the preaching of the Gospel
Christ would be raised like a standard which all would look at, as
Isaiah foretold (Isa. 2.2f). As a type of this lifting up He chooses the
brazen serpent set up by Moses, the sight of which was a remedy to
save those who had been wounded by the deadly bite of the serpents.
The story as told in Num. 21.9 is well known. In this passage Christ
introduces it to teach us that He has to be set before all eyes in the
teaching of the Gospel, that whosoever looks upon Him by faith will
receive salvation. Hence we must infer that Christ is clearly set before
us in the Gospel and no one can complain it is obscure, and that this
revelation is common to all, and that there is a looking of faith which
perceives Him as present—just as Paul tells us that Christ is vividly
portrayed with His cross when He is truly preached (Gal. 3.1).

The similitude is not inappropriate or far-fetched. Even as it was
only a serpent in outward appearance and had no infection of poison,
so Christ put on the form of sinful flesh which was nevertheless pure
and free from sin, to cure in us the deadly wound of sin. It was not in
vain that when the Jews were bitten by serpents the Lord countered it
with this sort of antidote; and this confirms Christ's discourse. For
when He saw that he was despised as an obscure and lowly man there
was nothing more appropriate than for Him to refer to the lifting up

of the serpent as if He were saying that it should not be thought absurd if, contrary to men's opinion, He were raised up from the lowest depths, as this had already been outlined under the Law in the type of the serpent. It may now be asked whether Christ compares Himself to the serpent because there was a resemblance between them, or that He means it was a sacrament in the same way that manna was. For although manna was bodily good, Paul declares it was a spiritual mystery (I Cor. 10.3). I think it was the same with the brazen serpent, both from this passage and also because it was preserved for posterity until it was changed into an idol by the people's superstition. If anyone thinks differently, I shall not argue the point.

16. *For God so loved.* Christ shows the first cause and as it were source of our salvation. And this He does that no doubt may be left. For there is no calm haven where our minds can rest until we come to God's free love. The whole substance of our salvation is not to be sought anywhere else than in Christ, and so we must see by what means Christ flows to us and why He was offered as our Saviour. Both points are clearly told us here—that faith in Christ quickens all and that Christ brought life because the heavenly Father does not wish the human race that He loves to perish. And this sequence should be carefully noticed. For such is the ungodly ambition innate to our nature that when we think of the origin of our salvation devilish imaginations about our own merits at once creep into our minds. Accordingly, we imagine that God is favourable to us because He has reckoned us worthy of His regard. But Scripture everywhere extols His pure and simple mercy which abolishes all merits.

And Christ's words mean nothing different when He says the cause lies in the love of God. For if we want to go any higher the Spirit prevents us with Paul's declaration that this love was founded on 'the good pleasure of his will' (Eph. 1.5). And it is plain that Christ spoke like this to divert men's eyes from themselves to the mercy of God alone. Nor does He state that God was moved to save us by seeing in us something deserving of such a blessing. He ascribes the glory for our salvation entirely to His love. And this becomes still clearer from the context, for He adds that the Son was given to men that they should not perish. It follows that until Christ vouchsafes to help the lost, all are appointed to eternal destruction. Paul also demonstrates this from the time sequence, for we were loved even when we were enemies through sin (Rom. 5.8, 10). And indeed, where sin reigns we shall find nothing but the wrath of God and the death it bears with it. Therefore it is mercy alone that reconciles us to God and at the same time restores us to life.

This way of speaking, however, may seem to conflict with many

testimonies of Scripture, which place the first foundation of the divine
love towards us in Christ and say that outside Him we are detested by
God. But we should remember, as I have already said, that the secret
love in which our heavenly Father embraced us to Himself is, since it
flows from His eternal good pleasure, precedent to all other causes; but
the grace which He wants to be testified to us and by which we are
stirred to the hope of salvation, begins with the reconciliation provided
through Christ. For since He necessarily hates sin, how shall we be
convinced that He loves us until those sins for which He is justly angry
with us have been expiated? Thus before we can have any feeling of
His fatherly kindness, the blood of Christ must intercede to reconcile
God to us. But because we first hear that God gave His Son to die for
us because He loved us, it is at once added that it is Christ alone to
whom, properly speaking, faith ought to look.

*He gave his only begotten Son, that whosoever believeth on him should not
perish.* The true looking of faith, I say, is placing Christ before one's
eyes and beholding in Him the heart of God poured out in love. Our
firm and substantial support is to rest on the death of Christ as its only
pledge. The word *only begotten* is emphasized, to praise the fervour of
the divine love towards us. For men are not easily convinced that God
loves them; and so, to remove all doubt, He has expressly stated that
we are so very dear to God that for our sakes He did not spare even
His only begotten Son. God has most abundantly declared His love
toward us and therefore whoever is still doubtful and unsatisfied by this
testimony does Christ a serious injury, as if He had been some ordinary
man who had died accidentally. We should rather consider that God's
love for His only begotten Son is a measure of how precious our
salvation was to Him, that He willed that the death of the Only Begotten Himself should be its price. Again, Christ possesses this name
by right, inasmuch as He is by nature the only Son of God. But He
shares this honour with us by adoption when we are ingrafted into
His body.

That whosoever believeth on him should not perish. The outstanding
thing about faith is that it delivers us from eternal destruction. For He
especially wanted to say that although we seem to have been born for
death sure deliverance is offered to us by the faith of Christ so that we
must not fear the death which otherwise threatens us. And He has used
a general term, both to invite indiscriminately all to share in life and to
cut off every excuse from unbelievers. Such is also the significance of
the term 'world' which He had used before. For although there is
nothing in the world deserving of God's favour, He nevertheless shows
He is favourable to the whole world when He calls all without exception to the faith of Christ, which is indeed an entry into life.

Moreover, let us remember that although life is promised generally to all who believe in Christ, faith is not common to all. Christ is open to all and displayed to all, but God opens the eyes only of the elect that they may seek Him by faith. The wonderful effect of faith is shown here too. By it we receive Christ as He is given to us by the Father—the one who has freed us from the condemnation of eternal death and made us heirs of eternal life by expiating our sins through the sacrifice of His death, so that nothing shall prevent God acknowledging us as His children. Therefore, since faith embraces Christ with the efficacy of His death and the fruit of His resurrection there is nothing surprising in our also obtaining by it the life of Christ.

But it is not yet clear enough why and how faith bestows life on us. Whether it is because Christ regenerates us by His Spirit, so that the righteousness of God may live and flourish in us; or because, cleansed by His blood, we are accounted righteous before God by a free pardon. It is indeed certain that these two aspects are always joined together. But since we are concerned now with assurance of salvation, the central idea is that we live because God freely loves us by not imputing our sins to us. This is why sacrifice is expressly mentioned, by which the curse and death are destroyed as well as sins. I have already explained the trend of these two clauses: they teach us that in Christ we recover the life which we lack in ourselves; for in this wretched state of mankind redemption precedes salvation.

17. *For God sent not.* This is confirmation of the former statement. For God's sending His Son to us was not fruitless. Yet He did not come to destroy; therefore it follows that the proper function of the Son of God is that whosoever believes may obtain salvation through Him. None need now wonder or worry how he can escape death, since we believe it was God's purpose that Christ should rescue us from it. The word *world* comes again so that no one at all may think he is excluded, if only he keeps to the road of faith.

The word *judge* is here used for 'condemn' as in many other passages. By saying that He did not come to condemn the world He points to the true purpose of His coming. For what need was there for Christ to come to destroy us who were already ruined over and over again? Therefore we should not regard anything else in Christ than that God out of His infinite goodness wished to help and save us who were lost. And whenever our sins press hard on us, whenever Satan would drive us to despair, we must hold up this shield, that God does not want us to be overwhelmed in everlasting destruction, for He has ordained His Son to be the salvation of the world.

When elsewhere Christ says that He is come for judgment, when He is called a stone of stumbling, when He is said to be set for the falling of many, it may be regarded as accidental, or so to say, foreign. For those who reject the grace offered in Him deserve to find Him the judge and avenger of such unworthy and shocking contempt. A striking example of this is to be seen in the Gospel, which, although it is strictly the power of God unto salvation to everyone who believes, is turned into death by the ingratitude of many. Paul expresses both aspects when he rejoices that he has vengeance at hand by which he will punish all the opponents of his preaching after the obedience of the godly has been fulfilled (II Cor. 10.6). It is as if he had said that the Gospel is especially and in the first place intended for believers, that it may be salvation for them; but that afterwards unbelievers will not escape unpunished when they despise the grace of Christ and would rather have Him as the author of death than of life.

18. *He that believeth on him is not condemned.* Since He so often and so earnestly emphasizes that all believers are out of danger of death, we can deduce how necessary is assurance and steadfastness of trust, that our consciences may not be continually agitated and perplexed. He therefore again declares that no condemnation remains when we believe; and He will explain this more fully in Chapter Five. The present tense is here used instead of the future according to the custom in Hebrew. He means that believers are safe from the fear of condemnation.

The next sentence, *he that believeth not hath been condemned already,* means that there is no other remedy by which any man can escape death: in other words, that nothing but death remains for all who reject the life in Christ, since life consists only in faith. He uses the past tense of the verb emphatically, the better to express that all unbelievers are completely ruined. But it should be observed that Christ is speaking especially of those whose ungodliness will be shown in open contempt of the Gospel. It is true that there was never any other way to escape death than for men to flee to Christ. But as Christ is here speaking of the preaching of the Gospel which was to be spread throughout the whole world, He directs His discourse against those who deliberately and maliciously extinguish the light kindled by God.

And this is the judgement, that the light is come into the world, and men loved the darkness rather than the light; for their works were evil. For everyone that doeth ill hateth the light, and cometh not to the light, lest his works should be reproved. But he that doeth the truth cometh to the light, that his works may be made manifest, that they have been wrought in God. (19-21)

19. *And this is the judgement.* He meets the murmurs and complaints with which ungodly men are very much wont to censure what they

regard as the rigour of God when He is more severe towards them than they like. All think it harsh that those who do not believe in Christ should be given up to destruction. And so lest anyone should ascribe his condemnation to Christ, He tells us that everyman should put the blame on himself. The reason is that unbelief bears witness to a bad conscience. And hence it is plain that it is their own perversity that prevents unbelievers from coming to Christ. Some think that this is merely an indication of the sign of condemnation; but Christ's purpose is to restrain the wickedness of men, that they may not, according to their custom, dare to dispute or argue with God as if He treated them unfairly when He punishes unbelief with eternal death. He shows therefore that such a condemnation is just and is not open to any criticisms—not only because those men act wickedly who prefer dark-ness to light and flee from the light freely offered to them, but because hatred of the light is born only in a wicked mind, conscious of its evil. A beautiful appearance of holiness may indeed shine in many who nevertheless oppose the Gospel; but although they seem holier than angels, they are without doubt hypocrites, who reject Christ's teaching simply because they love their dens where their vileness can be hidden. Since therefore hypocrisy alone makes men offensive to God, all are held convicted because, did they not in the blindness of their pride delight in their vices, they would be ready and willing to receive the doctrine of the Gospel.

20. *For everyone that doeth ill.* The meaning is that the light is hateful to them because they are evil and desire to hide their sins as far as they can. Whence it follows that they may be said to cherish the cause of their condemnation purposely by driving away the remedy. We are greatly mistaken, therefore, if we think that those who rage against the Gospel are moved by godly zeal. On the contrary, they abhor the light, that they may the more freely flatter themselves in darkness.

21. *But he that doeth the truth.* This seems an incorrect and absurd remark unless you are willing to admit that some are upright and true before they are regenerated by the Spirit of God, which does not at all fit in with the general teaching of Scripture, for we know that faith is the root from which good works spring. Augustine tries to solve this difficulty by expounding *doeth the truth* as 'acknowledging how wretched we are and destitute of all power of well-doing'. And it is indeed a true preparation for faith when a sense of our poverty compels us to flee to the grace of God. But all this is quite foreign to Christ's meaning; for He simply wanted to say that those who act sincerely desire nothing more than light, that their works may be proved. By such a trial it becomes clearer that in God's sight they are true and free from all deceit. But someone may incorrectly and ignorantly infer

from this that men have a good conscience before they have faith. Christ does not say that the elect believe so that they win praise for their good works, but only what unbelievers would do if they had not a bad conscience. Christ used the word *truth* because, when we are deceived by the outward beauty of works, we do not think of what lies hidden within. And so He says that men who are sound and not at all false, willingly go into the presence of God, who alone is the proper judge of our works. For *works* are here said to be *wrought in God* which are approved by Him and are good according to His criterion. Hence, let us learn that we must not judge of works except by bringing them to the light of the Gospel, since our reason is completely blind.

After these things came Jesus and his disciples into the land of Judaea; and there he tarried with them, and baptized. And John also was baptizing in Aenon near to Salim, because there was much water there: and they came and were baptized. For John was not yet cast into prison. There arose therefore a questioning on the part of John's disciples with the Jews about purifying. And they came unto John, and said to him, Rabbi, he that was with thee beyond Jordan, to whom thou hast borne witness, behold, the same baptizeth, and all men come to him. John answered and said, A man can receive nothing, except it have been given him from heaven. Ye yourselves bear me witness, that I said, I am not the Christ, but that I am sent before him. (22-28)

22. *After these thing came Jesus.* When the feast day was over Christ probably came into that part of Judaea near the town Aenon, which was situated in the tribe of Manasseh. The Evangelist says that there was much *water* there, and Judaea was not so well supplied with rivers. Geographers tell us that these two towns of Aenon and Salim were not far from where the Jabbok ran into the Jordan; and they put Scytho-polis near them. Moreover, from these words we may infer that John and Christ administered Baptism by total immersion, though we must not worry overmuch about the outward rite so long as it accords with the spiritual truth and the Lord's institution and rule. So far as we can conjecture, their proximity caused various rumours to spread and many discussions to arise everywhere about the Law, the worship of God and the state of the Church, because two new baptizers arose at the same time. For where the Evangelist says that Christ baptized, I refer it to the first beginnings, when He took up publicly the office appointed Him by the Father. And though Christ did this through His disciples, He is here named as the author of the Baptism and His ministers are left out, for they did nothing save in His name and at His command. On this subject we shall say something further at the be-ginning of the next chapter.

25. *There arose therefore a questioning* etc. Not without cause does
the Evangelist here relate that an argument arose on the part of John's
disciples; for their self-confidence in starting an argument was as great
as their theological learning was little—ignorance is always reckless.
They might be excusable if others had attacked them first; but for them,
unequal as they were to maintaining the dispute, to challenge the Jews
unprovoked, was just rash and wrong. The words mean that the
argument was started by them. So not only were they at fault in discussing something they did not understand and recklessly going beyond
the limits of their learning; but they also erred in another way just as
bad, that they were not so much concerned to assert the legitimate use
of Baptism as to defend their master's cause and buttress his authority.
They were blameworthy in both respects, because by not understanding the true nature of Baptism they exposed God's holy ordinance
to ridicule and by sinful ambition they set up their master's cause in
opposition to Christ.

And so they were clearly upset and crushed by one word when they
met the reply that Christ was also baptizing. For they were taken up
with the person of a man and so were the less concerned with his
teaching. By their example we are shown what men are reduced to
who are moved by perverse enthusiasms for men rather than by zeal
for God; and we are consequently warned that the one thing to be
kept in mind and attended to in every way is that Christ alone may be
prominent.

About purifying. The question was about purifying. The Law appointed various baptisms for the Jews; but, not satisfied with those in
the Law, they meticulously observed many more which they had
received from their ancestors. When a new rite of purifying is introduced by Christ and by John in addition to the many and various
already in existence, they think it absurd.

26. *To whom thou hast borne witness.* By this argument they try
either to make Christ inferior to John or to put Him under an obliga-
tion to him for the honour John had done Him. For they consider it
a privilege that John invested Christ with such honouring testimonies.
As if it were not his duty towards Christ to proclaim Him! Nay, as if
it were not his highest dignity to be the herald of the Son of God!
It was utterly wrong to make Christ inferior to John, for He had
been praised by his witness. For we know what John's witness
had been. Their remark, *all men come to Christ,* is the voice of perverse
rivalry; they are afraid that their master will soon be forsaken by the
crowd.

27. *A man can receive nothing.* Some refer this to Christ, as if John
were accusing his disciples of wicked presumption against God by

trying to take from Christ what had been given Him by the Father.
Thus, they think the meaning is: 'It is God's work that in this short
while he has risen to so great honour; and therefore it is in vain for you
to strive to degrade him whom God has with His own hand exalted.'
For others it is an exclamation which he indignantly voices because his
disciples had so far made such poor progress. And certainly it was very
foolish to want to confine the one whom they had so often heard was
the Christ to the rank and file, so that He should not rise above His
own ministers. And so John could justly say that it is a waste of time
to teach people, for they are dull and stupid until their minds are
renewed. But I rather agree with the opinion of those who expound
it of John—that he denies it is in his power or theirs to make him great,
because the stature of us all is that we are what God wanted us to be.
For if even the Son of God took not that honour to Himself, who of
His flock shall dare to desire more than the Lord has given him? If this
one thought were deeply rooted in everyone's mind, it would be more
than sufficient to restrain their ambition. And if ambition were corrected and destroyed, the plague of contentions would be removed at
the same time. For why is it that everyone exalts himself more than he
ought, and that we do not depend on the Lord, satisfied with the rank
He assigns us?

28. *Ye yourselves bear me witness.* John expostulates with his disciples
that they did not believe his words. He had often told them he was
not the Christ. Therefore the only alternative was that he was a
servant, subject to the Son of God like all the rest. And this passage is
noteworthy, for by affirming that he is not the Christ he leaves himself
nothing but to be subject to the Head and to serve in the Church as
one of the rest and not be so highly exalted as to obscure the honour
of the Head. He says that *he was sent before* to prepare the way for
Christ as attendants used to do for kings.

> *He that hath the bride is the bridegroom: but the friend of the bridegroom,*
> *who standeth and heareth him, rejoiceth greatly because of the bridegroom's*
> *voice: this my joy therefore is fulfilled. He must increase, but I must*
> *decrease. He that cometh from above is above all: he that is of the earth*
> *is of the earth, and of the earth he speaketh: he that cometh from heaven*
> *is above all. What he hath seen and heard, of that he beareth witness;*
> *and no man receiveth his witness. He that hath received his witness hath*
> *set his seal to this, that God is true. For he whom God hath sent speaketh*
> *the words of God: for God giveth not the Spirit by measure.* (29-34)

29. *He that hath the bride.* By this comparison he gives a stronger
confirmation that Christ alone is outside the ordinary number of men.
He who marries a wife does not invite and call his friends to the

wedding that he may prostitute his bride to them or by giving up his own rights allow them to share the bridal bed, but rather that the wedding may be honoured by them and made the more holy. Similarly, Christ does not call His ministers to the teaching office that they may subdue the Church and dominate it but that He may make use of their faithful labours to unite it to Himself. It is a great and splendid thing for men to be put in authority over the Church to represent the person of the Son of God. They are like the friends attached to the bridegroom to celebrate the wedding with him, though they must observe the difference between them and remember their position lest they should appropriate to themselves what belongs to the bridegroom. It all comes to this, that whatever excellence teachers may have should not stand in the way of Christ alone having the dominion in His Church or ruling it alone by His Word.

This comparison often occurs in Scripture, when the Lord wants to express the holy bond of adoption by which He unites us with Himself. For as He offers Himself to be truly enjoyed by us and to be ours, so He justly demands of us the mutual fidelity and love that a wife owes her husband. Moreover, this marriage was in every respect fulfilled in Christ, whose flesh and bones we are, as Paul teaches (Eph. 5.30 A.V. and Vulg.). The chastity which He demands consists particularly in obedience to the Gospel and not letting ourselves be seduced from its pure simplicity, as he also says in II Cor. 11.2, 3. We must therefore submit to Christ alone; He must be our only Head; we must not turn aside a hair's breadth from the simple teaching of the Gospel; He alone must be pre-eminent in glory that He may retain a bridegroom's right and place among us.

But what of the ministers? The Son of God summons them to carry out their duty to Him in administering the holy wedding. Therefore, it is for them to make all the arrangements for the bride who is committed to their charge being presented as a chaste virgin to her husband —a thing that Paul rejoices he had done, in the passage already quoted. Those who win the Church over to themselves rather than to Christ faithlessly violate the marriage which they ought to honour. And the greater the honour that Christ confers on us when He puts His bride in our charge, the more wicked is our faithlessness if we do not study to defend His rights.

This my joy therefore is fulfilled. He means that he has obtained the height of his wishes and that he has nothing further to desire, for he sees Christ reigning and people listening to Him as He deserves. Whoever has the attitude of setting aside all thought of himself and extolling Christ and being satisfied that He is honoured, will be faithful and successful in presiding over the Church. But whoever swerves from that aim in the slightest degree is an impure adulterer and can do nothing but corrupt the bride of Christ.

30. *He must increase.* He goes further. Earlier he had been raised by the Lord to the highest dignity; but he says that this was only temporary and now that the Sun of righteousness had risen, he must give place. And so he not only drives away and dispels the empty mist of honour with which he had been surrounded by men's thoughtlessness and error, but also is very careful that the true and legitimate honour that the Lord had bestowed on him should not obscure the brightness of Christ. For this reason he says that he had been reckoned a great prophet only inasmuch as he was temporarily placed in his lofty position until Christ came, to whom he had to hand over the torch. Meanwhile he declares that he will willingly endure to be reduced to nothing, providing Christ fills the whole world with His beams and possesses it. And every pastor of the Church ought to imitate John's zeal and humble himself to exalt Christ.

31. *He that cometh from above.* He uses another comparison to show how much Christ differs from all others and how far He is above them. He compares Him to a king or a ruler who should be heard with reverence for his authority when he speaks from his high throne. But he says that for himself it is enough if he speaks from a lowly bench. He says that Christ came from above, not only inasmuch as He is God, but because in Him there is nothing but the heavenly and kingly to be seen. The usual translation has 'is of the earth' only once; but the Greek manuscripts agree in the other reading. I conjecture that this was erased by unlearned men who thought it redundant. But the meaning is that he who is of the earth smacks of his origin and remains on an earthly level in accordance with the state of his nature. He asserts that it is peculiar to Christ alone to speak from above because He came down from heaven.

But it may be asked whether John did not also come from heaven so far as his calling and office were concerned, so that the Lord ought to have been heard speaking from his mouth. For he seems unjust to the heavenly teaching he delivers. I reply that this is not a straightforward statement, but a comparison. If ministers be considered in themselves, they speak with the highest authority as from heaven what God has commanded them; but as soon as they begin to be contrasted with Christ, they must be nothing. Thus, the Apostle, comparing the Law with the Gospel in Heb. 12.25, says: 'If they escaped not, when they refused him that warned them on earth, see that ye refuse not him who is from heaven.' Hence, Christ wants to be acknowledged in His ministers, but so that He alone may remain the Lord and that they may be content to be servants. And especially when a comparison is made does He wish to be so differentiated that He alone may be exalted.

32. *What he hath seen and heard.* John proceeds in his duty. So that he may prepare disciples for Christ, he commends His doctrine as being certain, in that He utters nothing but what He has received from the Father. Seeing and hearing are contrasted to doubtful opinions, empty rumours and all kinds of fictions. He means that Christ teaches nothing that He does not know fully. But it may be said that little credit is due to one who has nothing but what he has heard. I reply, this word means that Christ has been taught by the Father, so that He puts forward nothing but what is divine, inasmuch as it was revealed to Him by God. And this agrees completely with the person of Christ as He was sent into the world as the Father's ambassador and interpreter.

He then accuses the world of ingratitude in rebelliously and wickedly rejecting such a sure and faithful witness of God. He forestalls the offence that might turn many aside from the faith and hinder or delay the progress of others. For as we are used to depend too much on men's judgment, the most part judge the Gospel by the world's contempt of it; or at least, where they see it everywhere rejected they are prejudiced and become more loth and slow to believe. Consequently, whenever we see such obstinacy in the world let this warning keep us constantly obedient to Him, that He is the truth come forth from God. When he says that *no man* receives Him, he means that compared with the vast crowd of unbelievers there are very few, almost no, believers.

33. *But he who received his witness.* He now exhorts and encourages the godly to embrace the teaching of the Gospel boldly, as if to say that there was no reason for them to be ashamed and worried because of their fewness, since they have God as the author of their faith, who alone is abundantly sufficient to be everything for us. And so, though the whole world should refuse or withhold faith in the Gospel, it should not prevent good men from agreeing with God. When they know that to believe the Gospel is simply to assent to the oracles of God, they have something safe to rest on. Moreover, we gather that it is the property of faith to rest upon God and to be established in His Word. For there can be no assent unless God takes the initiative by speaking. In this teaching faith is not only distinguished from all human inventions but also from doubtful and uncertain opinions. For it must correspond to the truth of God, which is free from all doubt. And so, even as God cannot lie, it would be inconsistent that faith should waver. Let Satan try to disturb and shake us with whatever stratagems he likes, we shall always stand victorious if we are armed with this defence.

This also tells us how acceptable and precious a sacrifice faith is in the eyes of God. For as nothing is dearer to Him than His truth, we can

83

offer Him no worship more acceptable than the faithful confession that
He is true, for then we give Him His real honour. On the other hand,
no worse injury can be done to Him than not to believe the Gospel.
For He cannot be despoiled of His truth without all His glory and
majesty being destroyed. There is a sense in which His truth is enclosed
in the Gospel; and there He wishes to be known. Hence, unbelievers,
so far as lies in them, leave God nothing at all. Not that their wickedness
overthrows the faithfulness of God, but because they do not hesitate to
accuse God of untrustworthiness. This noble title that adorns faith
ought, if we are not harder than stones, to kindle in our minds a
burning enthusiasm for it. How great is the honour that God confers
on wretched manikins that they, by nature nothing but falsehood and
vanity, are yet thought worthy of approving by their assent the sacred
truth of God!

34. *For he whom God hath sent.* He confirms his preceding statement
by showing that we are indeed concerned with God when we receive
Christ's teaching. For Christ proceeded from none other than the
heavenly Father. Hence it is God alone who speaks by Him. We
attribute less to Christ's teaching than we should, if we do not acknowledge it to be divine.

For God giveth not the Spirit by measure. This passage is expounded in
two ways. Some extend it to the ordinary dispensation in that God,
the inexhaustible fount of all good, does not at all exhaust Himself
when He bountifully and plentifully pours out His gifts on men.
Those who draw out of any vessel what they distribute to others come
at last to the bottom. But there is no danger of anything like this
happening with God; nor will the abundance of His gifts ever be so
bountiful that He will not often be pleased to surpass it with a new
liberality. This exposition seems to have something to be said for it,
since the language is indefinite.

I would rather follow Augustine, however. He interprets it as said
of Christ. Nor is it valid to object that Christ is not expressly mentioned in this clause, for the next one removes all ambiguity, where
what might appear to have been said indiscriminately about many is
restricted to Christ. For these words, 'the Father hath given all things
into the hand of his Son, because he loveth him', were certainly added
as an explanation. They are therefore to be read in the same context.
The verb in the present tense denotes a continued action. For although
He was given the Spirit in the highest perfection once, yet as He continually flows from a source, so to speak, it is not out of place to say
that Christ now receives Him from the Father. If anyone prefers to
interpret it more simply, it is not unusual to have a change of tenses in
such verbs.

The meaning is now clear. The Spirit was not given to Christ by measure, as if the resources of grace which He possesses were in some way limited—just as Paul teaches in I Cor. 12.7 and Eph. 4.7 that to everyone is distributed according to the measure of the gift, so that none may possess the fulness on his own. For whereas it is a mutual bond of brotherly fellowship between us that none is sufficient in himself but all need one another, Christ is different in that the Father has poured out upon Him an unlimited wealth of His Spirit. And indeed it is right that the Spirit should dwell in Him without measure, that we may all draw from His fulness, as we have seen in Chapter One. What follows is also related to this, that the Father has given all things into His hand. For in these words John not only proclaims Christ's excellence but also shows the purpose and use of the riches with which He is endued. Because He has been appointed by the Father as His administrator, He distributes to everyone as He thinks best and it is expedient; as Paul explains more fully in the fourth chapter of Ephesians which I quoted above. Although, therefore, God enriches His people diversely, it is peculiar to Christ alone to have all things in His hand.

The Father loveth the Son, and hath given all things into his hand. He that believeth on the Son hath eternal life; but he that believeth[1] not on the Son shall not see life, but the wrath of God abideth on him. (35-36)

35. *The Father loveth the Son.* But what is the significance of this explanation? Does He hate all others? The answer is easy: He is not speaking of the common love which God has to all men whom He has created or to His other works, but of that unique love which begins at the Son and flows from Him to all creatures. For this love wherewith, loving the Son, He embraces us also in Him is the cause of His communicating all His benefits to us by Christ's hand.

36. *He that believeth on the Son.* This was added not only to teach us that we must seek all good things from Christ but also that we may grasp the way in which they are enjoyed. He tells us that this enjoying consists in faith, since by it Christ is possessed, who brings with Himself both righteousness and faith, the fruit of righteousness. We gather from faith in Christ being called the cause of life that life is contained in Christ alone and that we become partakers of it only by the grace of Christ. But all do not agree on the way in which the life of Christ comes to us. Some understand it thus: Since by believing we receive the Spirit who regenerates us into righteousness, we also obtain salvation by that same regeneration. For my own part, although I admit it

[1] French: *ou, qui desobeit au Fils*—or, who disobeyeth the Son. Vide R.V. and margin.

is true that we are renewed by faith as the Spirit of God rules us, yet I
say that the first thing to consider is the free forgiveness of sins, through
which it comes to pass that we are accepted by God. Moreover, I say
that on this alone is founded and consists the whole confidence of our
salvation. For righteousness cannot be imputed to us before God in
any other way than by His not imputing our sins to us.

But he that believeth not on the Son. Just as he had proclaimed life in
Christ to invite us by its sweetness, so now he adjudges to eternal
death all who do not believe in Christ. And thus he magnifies God's
kindness by warning us that there is no other escape from death but by
Christ delivering us. This sentence depends on the fact that in Adam
we are all lost. But if it is Christ's office to save the lost, those who
reject the salvation offered in Him deservedly remain in death. We
have just said that this belongs peculiarly to those who reject the Gospel
which has been made known to them. For although the whole human
race is involved in the same destruction, a heavier and double vengeance
awaits those who refuse to have the Son of God as their Deliverer. And
indeed there is no doubt that the Baptist, by threatening unbelievers
with death, wanted the terror of it to stir us up to faith in Christ.
Moreover, it is plain that all the righteousness which the world thinks
it has outside Christ is condemned and annihilated. Nor can anyone
object that it is unfair for those who are otherwise godly and holy to
perish simply because they do not believe; for it is vain to imagine that
there is any holiness in men unless it has been given them by Christ.

To see life is put here for 'enjoying life'. But to express more clearly
that no hope remains for us unless we are delivered by Christ he says
that *the wrath of God abideth* on unbelievers. Yet I am not dissatisfied
with Augustine's idea that the word *abideth* is used to teach us that we
were appointed to death from the womb in that we are all born the
children of wrath. At any rate, I willingly admit a suggestion of this
sort, so long as we hold the genuine and simple meaning to be what I
have said—that death burdens all unbelievers and holds them oppressed
and overwhelmed in such a way that they can never escape. And
indeed, although the reprobate are already naturally condemned, they
bring on themselves a new death by their unbelief. And it is for this
purpose that the power of binding was given to the ministers of the
Gospel. For it is a just punishment on men's obstinacy that those who
shake off the saving yoke of God should fetter themselves with the
chains of death.

CHAPTER FOUR

When therefore the Lord knew how that the Pharisees had heard that Jesus was making and baptizing more disciples than John (although Jesus himself baptized not, but his disciples), he left Judaea, and departed again into Galilee. And he must needs pass through Samaria. So he cometh to a city of Samaria, called Sychar, near to the parcel of ground that Jacob gave to his son Joseph: and Jacob's well was there. Jesus, being wearied with his journey, sat thus by the well. It was about the sixth hour. There cometh a woman of Samaria to draw water: Jesus saith unto her, Give me to drink. For his disciples were gone away into the city to buy food. The Samaritan woman therefore saith unto him, How is it that thou, being a Jew, askest drink of me, which am a Samaritan woman? (For the Jews have no dealings with Samaritans.) (1-9)

1. *When therefore the Lord knew.* The Evangelist is now going to speak about the conversation Christ had with a Samaritan woman, and begins by explaining the cause of His journey. Knowing that the Pharisees were ill-disposed towards Him, He did not want to expose Himself to their anger before the time. This was His reason for leaving Judaea. So the Evangelist tells us that He did not go to Samaria to dwell there, but because He had to pass through it on the way to Galilee. For until a door should be opened for the Gospel by His resurrection it behoved Him to be employed in gathering the sheep of Israel, for whom He was sent. His honouring of the Samaritans with His teaching was extraordinary and as it were accidental, if I may put it like that.

But why does He seek retirement and concealment in Galilee, as if He did not want to be known, which was most desirable? I reply that He knew how He should act and made such use of His time that He did not waste a moment. So He wanted to run His course in the right order and steadily, as He should. And this teaches us also that our minds should be so settled that no fear ought to deter us from going ahead with our duty and yet that we should not be over rash in seeking dangers. All who are zealous in their calling will cultivate this middle way. For although they will steadfastly follow the Lord through the midst of deaths, they will not rush in headlong, but will walk in His ways. Let us therefore remember to go no further than our calling demands.

The Pharisees alone are mentioned by the Evangelist as being hostile to Christ. Not that the other scribes were friendly, but this sect was in the ascendant then and also they were most mad with rage, or righteous indignation, as they would have called it. It may be asked whether they envied Christ because He had more disciples; for their leaning towards John made them studious of his honour and reputation. But the words do not mean this. For whereas at first they took it badly that John collected disciples, they were still more annoyed when they saw that even more came to Christ. And from the time that John confessed that he was nothing but the herald of the Son of God, greater crowds began to flock to Christ and John had already nearly finished his ministry. So he gradually resigned to Christ his office of teaching and Baptism.

2. *Although Jesus himself baptized not.* He calls Christ's Baptism that which He administered by the hands of others, to teach us that Baptism is not to be valued from the person of the minister, but that its whole force depends on its author, in whose name and by whose command it is administered. Hence we receive a special strengthening when we know that our Baptism has no less efficacy to cleanse and renew us than if it had been given directly by the Son of God. And there is no doubt that He deliberately abstained from the outward administration of the sign while He was in the world so as to bear witness to all ages that nothing is lost from the power of Baptism when it is administered by a mortal man. In short, not only does Christ baptize inwardly by His Spirit, but the very symbol that we receive from a mortal man should be regarded in the same light as if Christ Himself had put forth His hand from heaven and stretched it out to us. Now, if the Baptism administered by man is Christ's Baptism, it will not cease to be Christ's whoever the minister may be. And this suffices to refute the Anabaptists, who maintain that Baptism is vitiated by the vice of the minister and disturb the Church with this madness. Augustine has aptly used this argument against the Donatists.

5. *Called Sychar.* Jerome in his epitaph on Paula thinks this is an incorrect reading and that it should have been written Sichem. And that was certainly the ancient and true name. But by the time of the Evangelist the word Sychar was probably used. As to the place, it is generally agreed that it was a town situated on the side of Mount Gerizim, whose inhabitants were treacherously slain by Simeon and Levi (Gen. 34.25) and which Abimelech, a native of the place, afterwards razed to the ground. But it was a convenient site and a third town was built there, which they called Neapolis in Jerome's time. By accumulating all these details the Evangelist takes away any controversy. For it is certain enough from Moses where the field was which Jacob gave to the sons of Joseph. Everyone admits, too, that Mount Gerizim

was near Sichem. We shall see later on that a temple was built there. And there can be no doubt that Jacob lived there with his family for a long time.

And Jesus being wearied with his journey. He was not pretending to be tired, but was weary in very truth. For He took our weaknesses upon Him, the more to sympathize and suffer with us, as the Apostle says in Heb. 4.15. The time factor comes in here too; for it is not surprising that He should rest at the well when He was thirsty and tired about mid-day (for the sixth hour was noon, as their day from sunrise to sunset had twelve hours). When he says that He sat *thus* he is expressing the attitude of a tired man.

7. *There cometh a woman of Samaria.* When He asks the woman for water, He does so not simply with the intention of engineering an opportunity to teach her. His thirst made Him want something to drink. But this cannot stop Him utilizing the occasion to teach which has turned up, for He puts the woman's salvation before His own needs. So His thirst is forgotten, as if leisure and the chance of talking to her were enough for Him, if He might instruct her in true godliness. He draws an analogy between the visible and the spiritual water, and with the heavenly Gospel He waters the mind of her who had denied Him water.

9. *How is it that thou, being a Jew.* This reproach is a retaliation for the usual contempt shown by His nation. The Samaritans are known to have been the off-scourings of foreign peoples. They corrupted the worship of God and cultivated many perverse and false ceremonies and were deservedly detested by the Jews. Yet there is no doubt that the Jews for the most part made zeal for the Law a pretext for carnal hatred. Many were moved more by ambition and envy and by indignation that the land given to them should be occupied by the Samaritans than by grief and sorrow that the worship of God had been so outraged. There was just ground for the separation so long as their attitude was pure and well disposed. This is why Christ, when He first sends the Apostles to preach the Gospel, forbids them to turn aside to the Samaritans (Matt. 10.5).

But this woman does what is natural to nearly all of us. We want to be esteemed and take it very ill if we are despised. This disease is so common in human nature that everyone wants his vices to meet with approval. If anyone disapproves of us or our actions we are at once uncritically angry. Let any man examine himself and he will find this seed of pride in his mind until it has been eradicated by God's Spirit. And so this woman knew that the superstitions of her people were condemned by the Jews and she now insults them in the person of Christ.

For the Jews have no dealings with Samaritans. I think the woman spoke these words. Others take them as an interpolation by the Evangelist in explanation. It is of little importance which meaning you choose, but it seems to me to fit in best that the woman is jeering at Christ like this: 'Oh! You're sure it's all right to ask me for a drink, when you think we are so irreligious?' If any prefer the other interpretation, I shall not argue about it. Besides, it may mean that the Jews cut themselves off from the Samaritans beyond all reason. For as we have said that they misused their false pretence of zeal, so they easily went to extremes, as happens with all those who give way to sinful dispositions.

Jesus answered and said unto her, If thou knewest the gift of God, and who it is that saith to thee, Give me to drink; thou wouldest have asked of him, and he would have given thee living water. The woman saith unto him, Sir, thou hast nothing to draw with, and the well is deep: from whence then hast thou that living water? Art thou greater than our father Jacob, which gave us the well, and drank thereof himself, and his sons, and his cattle? Jesus answered and said unto her, Everyone that drinketh of this water shall thirst again: but whosoever drinketh of the water that I shall give him shall never thirst; but the water that I shall give him shall become in him a well of water springing up into eternal life. The woman saith unto him, Sir, give me this water, that I thirst not, neither come all the way hither to draw. (10-15)

10. *Jesus answered.* Christ now takes the opportunity to preach about the grace and power of His Spirit, and that to a hussy who did not deserve Him to speak to her at all. A wonderful example of His goodness indeed! For what was there in this unhappy woman, that suddenly from a prostitute she became a disciple of the Son of God? Yet in all of us He has shown the same proof of His mercy. Obviously, all women are not prostitutes; nor are all men marked by some terrible crime; but what excellence can any of us put forward as deserving of the heavenly Gospel and the honour of adoption? Nor did this talk with such a person happen by chance. For the Lord was showing us, as under a type, that He does not choose from worthiness those to whom He imparts the preaching of salvation. And it is at first sight astonishing that He should pass over so many great men in Judaea and yet talk familiarly with this woman. But in His person there had to be expressed the truth of that saying of the Prophet: 'I am found of them that sought me not; I am made manifest to them that asked not for me. I said to those that sought me not, Behold, I am here' (Isa. 65.1).

If thou knewest the gift of God. These two clauses, *If thou knewest the gift of God,* and, *Who it is that speaketh with thee,* I read separately and take the latter as an interpretation of the other. For it was through God's wonderful kindness that she had Christ with her, who also brought eternal life. The meaning will be plainer if, instead of the copula, we supply an explanatory word, thus: 'If thou knewest the gift of God, that is to say, who it is that speaketh with thee.' We are taught by these words that we know what Christ is only when we understand what the Father has given us in Him and what blessings He brings us. But that knowledge begins with a sense of our poverty. For to desire a remedy one must first be conscious of one's ills. And so the Lord invites to eat and drink not those who have drunk enough but the thirsty, not those who are full but the hungry. And why should Christ be sent to us with the fulness of the Spirit unless we are empty?

Moreover, as the man who feels his failure and already acknowledges how much he needs outside help has made good progress, so it would not be enough if he groaned under his evils unless the expectation of speedy help were at hand. In this way, we should merely waste away in sorrow or like the Papists rush about everywhere and exhaust ourselves with useless and superfluous weariness. But when Christ appears, we no longer wander in vain, seeking a remedy where none can be found, but go straight to Him. This is the only true and useful knowledge of God's grace—when we know that it is displayed to us in Christ and held out to us in His hand. Moreover, Christ reminds us how efficacious the knowledge of His blessings is, since it stirs us up to seek them and inflames our minds. 'If you knew,' He says, 'you would have asked.' The purpose of these words is not at all obscure. He wanted to sharpen the woman's longing so that she should not reject contemptuously the life He offered her.

He would have given thee living water. With these words Christ testifies that if our prayers are addressed to Him they will not be in vain. Without this confidence the earnestness of asking would certainly cool off entirely. But when Christ meets those who come to Him and is ready to satisfy them all, there is no place left for disinclination or delay. Only a man's unbelief stops him feeling that this is said to us all.

Although He took the word 'water' from the circumstances and applied it to the Spirit, this metaphor is usual enough in the Scriptures and has the best warrant. For we are like a dry and barren soil; there is no moisture, no activity in us, until the Lord water us with His Spirit. Elsewhere the Spirit is called 'pure water', but in the different sense that He washes and cleanses us from the filthiness that covers us. But here and in similar passages it is talking about the secret quickening by which He restores, maintains and perfects life in us. Some explain this of the preaching of the Gospel, with which I admit this title agrees.

But I think that here Christ is including the whole grace of renewal. For we know that He was sent to bring us new life. To my mind therefore He was contrasting water with the emptiness of all blessings with which mankind is afflicted and depressed. Moreover, He calls it living water, not from its effect as life-giving, but in reference to different kinds of water. This is called living because it flows from a living fountain.

11. *Sir, thou hast nothing to draw with.* As the Jews despised the Samaritans, so the Samaritans in their turn regarded the Jews with contempt. Hence this woman at first not only despises Christ, but even jeers at Him. She knows perfectly well that Christ is speaking figuratively, but she counters Him with another figure, as if to say that He is promising more than He can perform. Then she accuses Him of arrogance in exalting Himself above the holy patriarch Jacob. 'Jacob was satisfied with this well for the use of himself and his family,' she says, 'and have you got better water than this?' The faultiness of this comparison is plain enough from the fact that she compares the servant to the master and a dead man to the living God. But how many today make the same mistake? We should be the more careful not to exalt the persons of men in such a way as to obscure God's glory. We ought indeed to honour reverently the gifts of God wherever they appear; and therefore it is right to honour men outstanding in godliness or endowed with other rare gifts—yet in such a way that God may always stand out above them all and that Christ may shine clearly; for to Him must all the brightness of the world give place.

We must also note that the Samaritans falsely boasted of being descended from the holy fathers. So today the Papists, though illegitimate and an adulterous seed, most arrogantly boast of the fathers and look down on the true children of God. Even if the Samaritans had been descended from Jacob after the flesh, yet as they were altogether fallen away and estranged from true godliness, this boasting would have been ridiculous. But though they are Cutheans in origin, or at least gathered out of the unconsecrated gentiles, they still do not give up their claim to the holy patriarch as their own. But this is no advantage to them, for like all who wrongly exult in the glory of men, they deprive themselves of the light of God and have nothing in common with the holy fathers whose name they have misused.

13. *Everyone that drinketh of this water.* Although Christ sees that He is doing little good and that His teaching even meets with derision, He goes on to explain more clearly what He had said. He distinguishes between the use of the two kinds of water. The one is for the body temporarily, and the virtue of the other is to quicken the soul for ever. For as the body is corruptible, so the aids that support it must needs be

perishable and transitory. But that which quickens the soul cannot but be eternal. Christ's words do not contradict the fact that believers to the very end of their lives ardently desire more abundant grace. For He does not mean that we drink so that we are fully satisfied from the very first day, but only that the Holy Spirit is a constantly flowing well. So there is no danger of those who are renewed by spiritual grace becoming dry. And therefore, although we thirst throughout our life, it is nevertheless certain that we have not drunk of the Spirit just for one day or for any short time, but as of a perennial fountain that will never fail us. Thus believers thirst, and that keenly throughout their life; and yet they abound with quickening moisture. For however little grace they have received, it quickens them continually, so that they are never completely dry. Therefore, He is contrasting that satisfaction, not with desire, but only with dryness.

Shall become a well of water springing up unto eternal life. These next words express more clearly what has been said already. They indicate a continual watering which sustains in believers a heavenly eternity during this mortal and perishing life. Christ's grace therefore does not flow to us only for a little while but pours on into a blessed immortality; for it does not cease to flow until the incorruptible life that it commences is completely perfected.

15. *Give me this water.* There is no doubt the woman knows perfectly well that Christ is speaking of spiritual water; but because she despises Him, she cares nothing for His promises. So long as we allow no authority to the one who speaks, we block the way of his teaching. Indirectly therefore the woman taunted Christ, as if to say, 'You've got a lot to say for yourself, but I can't see anything; put it into action if you can.'

Jesus saith unto her, Go, call thy husband, and come hither. The woman answered and said unto him, I have no husband. Jesus said unto her, Thou saidst well, I have no husband; for thou hast had five husbands; and he whom thou now hast is not thy husband: this hast thou said truly. The woman saith unto him, Sir, I perceive that thou art a prophet. Our fathers worshipped in this mountain; and ye say that in Jerusalem is the place where men ought to worship. Jesus saith unto her, Woman, believe me, the hour cometh when neither in this mountain, nor in Jerusalem, shall ye worship the Father. (16-21)

16. *Call thy husband.* This seems to be quite irrelevant. Or rather we might think that Christ was disheartened and confused by the woman's impudence and so changes the conversation. But this is not so; for when He saw that His words were received with jeers, He applied an appropriate remedy to the disease. He struck the woman's

conscience with a conviction of her sin. And this again is a remarkable
example of His compassion—when she would not come to Him
voluntarily he draws her almost unwillingly. But we ought especially
to notice something I have mentioned; that those who are quite careless, almost deadened, have to be wounded with a sense of sin. For
Christ's Gospel will seem like a fable to them until they are summoned
to the judgment seat of God and made to dread Him as a judge whom
before they had despised. All who do not hesitate to rise against the
Gospel of Christ with their scurrilous wit must be treated like this, so
that they may feel they will not go unpunished. Many, too, are so
obstinate that they will never listen to Him until they have been fiercely
subdued. So whenever we see that the oil of Christ is flavourless we
must mix vinegar with it, that it may begin to taste. And indeed this
is necessary for us all; for we are not seriously affected by Christ's
speaking unless we have been aroused to repentance. To profit aright
in His school, a man's hardness must be subdued or ploughed by the
sight of his own wretchedness. For it is this knowledge alone that takes
away all our delight, so that we no longer dare mock God. Whenever
neglect of the Word of God overcomes us, no remedy will be more
appropriate than for each of us to consider his sins that he may be
ashamed of himself, and in terror at the judgment of God may be
humbled to obey Him he had wantonly despised.

17. *I have no husband.* The woman does not yet understand this
warning by which Christ wanted to pierce her heart unto repentance.
And indeed, our self love so intoxicates, or rather stupefies, us that we
are not at all moved by the first pricks. But Christ has the right cure for
this slowness too. He presses the ulcer harder, for He openly accuses
her of her wickedness. I do not think He is referring to one act of
adultery, for when He says that she has had five husbands, we may
suppose it happened because she drove her husbands to divorce her
with her wanton and stubborn ways. I interpret the words like this:
Though God joined you to lawful husbands, you never stopped sinning,
and at last your divorces cost you your reputation and you gave
yourself up to prostitution.

19. *Sir, I perceive that thou art a prophet.* Now the rebuke is bearing
fruit. Not only does the woman modestly acknowledge her fault but
she is ready and prepared to listen to Christ's teaching which she had
rejected before, and desires and demands it of her own accord. Repentance, as I have already said, is the beginning of true teachableness
and opens the entrance gate into the school of Christ. The woman
teaches us by her example that when any teacher is given to us we
must buy up the opportunity; otherwise we shall be ungrateful to God,
who never sends prophets to us without as it were inviting us to

94

Himself with outstretched hand. And we must remember that Paul says that those who have the faculty of teaching are sent to us by God (Rom. 10.15).

20. *Our fathers.* Some have the mistaken idea that the woman finds the rebukes disagreeable and hateful and cunningly changes the conversation. On the contrary, she passes from the particular to the general, and having been informed about her sin wants to be taught generally about the pure worship of God. Here she acts properly and regularly in consulting a prophet lest she should make mistakes in worshipping God. It is as if she inquired of God Himself how He wishes to be worshipped—for nothing is more perverted than to invent various ways of worship for ourselves apart from the Word of God.

As is well known, there was continual friction between the Jews and the Samaritans about the true pattern of worship. Although the Cutheans and other foreigners who had been brought into Samaria when the ten tribes were led into captivity, were constrained by plagues to adopt the ceremonies of the Law and to profess the worship of the God of Israel (as we read in II Kings 17.24f), religion was defective and corrupted in many ways among them. This was intolerable to the Jews. The dispute became still more inflamed after Manasseh, son of the high priest John and brother of Jaddus, had built the temple on Mount Gerizim. This happened when Darius the last king of the Persians held Judaea through Sanballat his governor. Manasseh married a daughter of this satrap, so as not to be inferior to his brother, and made himself priest there and purchased by bribery as many renegades as he could, as Josephus relates in *Ant.* XI.

Our fathers. We may infer from what the woman said that the Samaritans acted as deserters from true godliness usually do. They sought to appeal to the fathers for precedents. It is certain that this was not the cause of their offering sacrifices there; but when they had once set up a perverted worship their obstinacy was ingenious in inventing excuses. I acknowledge indeed that light and thoughtless men sometimes get bitten by a bug and in their foolish haste, as soon as they learn that something has been done by the saints, instantly and uncritically seize on it as a precedent. But the other fault is still more common of using the deeds of the fathers as a cloak for error—a thing readily discernible in the Papacy. But this passage is a remarkable warning of how pervertedly they act who neglect God's command to conform to the examples of the fathers, and we ought to observe that the world falls into this sin in many ways. For it often happens that the majority uncritically follow as fathers those who are least entitled to be called fathers. Thus today we see that the Papists keep on trumpeting about the fathers and have no time for the prophets and apostles. When they have mentioned a few who are worthy of honour, they collect a huge mob of men like themselves, or at any rate, come down to the more corrupt ages in which, although such a gross barbarism did not yet prevail, religion and purity of doctrine had nevertheless greatly declined. We should therefore keep carefully to the distinction that none are to be reckoned fathers but those who were certainly the sons of God; and then those who by their outstanding piety deserved this honourable title. Men also frequently err in that they rashly establish a common law from the actions of the fathers. For the multitude thinks it is not conferring sufficient honour on the fathers unless it makes them superhuman. And when we forget that they were fallible men we uncritically mix up their vices with their virtues and rise to the worst confusion in the conduct of life. For whereas all human deeds ought to be tried by the rule of the Law, we subordinate the scales themselves to what is weighed. In short, where the imitation of the fathers is all-important, the world thinks it can sin guiltlessly in following their example.

A third fault is perverted imitation; as for example, when we who are not endowed with the same Spirit or supplied with the same command, drag in as a precedent for us what any of the fathers did. For instance, if any private person wanted to avenge with the sword the injuries done to his brothers because Moses did so (Ex. 2.12), or if anyone were to execute fornicators because this was done by Phinehas (Num. 25.7). Many think that the inhuman insanity of sacrificing their own children originated in the Jews wanting to be like their father Abraham; as if the command 'Offer up thy son Isaac' (Gen. 22.2) were general and not just a unique testing of one man. Such a κακοζηλία or mischievous emulation is mostly bred of pride and over-confidence, when men claim far too much for themselves and are not content with their own limits. And so none of these truly imitate the fathers, but many ape them. Those who examine the writings of the ancients intelligently will acknowledge that a good deal of old monachism flowed from the same source. And therefore, unless we want to err deliberately, we must always pay attention to the spirit each father was given, what his calling demanded of him, what was individually proper to him and what he was individually commanded to do.

Closely allied to this third fault is another, the confusing of different ages. Later generations devote themselves to the examples of the fathers, not thinking that a different law of action has been enjoined on them by the Lord. We can ascribe to this ignorance the huge mass of ceremonies with which the Church under the Papacy has been buried. Immediately after the beginning of the Church they began to sin in this way from a foolish and undue affectation of Judaism. The Jews had their sacrifices; and therefore, that Christians also might not be without a show, the rite of sacrificing Christ was invented. As if the state of the Christian Church would be any the worse if all the shadows should pass away that obscure the brightness of Christ! This madness later broke out more strongly and spread beyond all bounds.

Therefore, that we may not fall into this error, we must always heed the following rule: Incense, lights, sacred vestments, altar, vessels and ceremonies of this kind were formerly pleasing to God; and the reason was that nothing is more acceptable or precious to Him than obedience. But since the coming of Christ the order has been changed. We must therefore regard what He enjoins us in the Gospel, so that we may not unthinkingly follow what the fathers observed under the Law. For what was then a sacred observing of the worship of God would now be a wicked sacrilege.

Where the Samaritans went wrong was that they did not take into account how much the manner of their own time differed from that of Jacob. The patriarchs were allowed to erect altars everywhere because the place which the Lord afterwards chose had not yet been appointed. But from the time that God ordered the Temple to be built on Mount Zion their former freedom ceased. This is why Moses said, 'Hereafter you shall not each one do what seems right to him, but only what I command you' (Deut. 12.8, 14). From the time the Lord gave the Law He restricted the true worship of Himself to the tenets of the Law, when previously more freedom was used. A similar excuse was offered by the worshippers at Bethel. Jacob had offered a solemn sacrifice to God there; but after the Lord had fixed the place of sacrifice at Jerusalem it was no longer *Bethel* but *Bethaven*.

We can now see what lay behind the woman's question. The Samaritans took the example of the fathers as a precedent; the Jews were grounded on the commandment of God. Although the woman had hitherto followed the custom of her people, she was not satisfied with it. By worship, understand not any kind of worship (for daily prayers can be offered anywhere) but that which was connected with sacrifices and was the public and solemn profession of religion.

21. *Woman, believe me.* The first part of His reply curtly abolishes the ceremonial worship instituted under the Law. For when He says that the hour is at hand when there shall be no particular and special place of worship, He means that what Moses handed down was only temporary and that the time was coming when the wall of partition would be demolished. In this way He extends the worship of God far beyond its earlier narrowness, so that the Samaritans might also share in it.

The hour cometh. He here uses the present tense instead of the future;

but it means that the repeal of the Law is already near at hand so far as the Temple and priesthood and other outward ceremonies are concerned. By calling God Father, He seems to be contrasting Him indirectly to the fathers whom the woman had mentioned, as if to say that God is going to be a Father common to all and will be worshipped in common without distinction of place or nation.

Ye worship that which ye know not: we worship that which we know: for salvation is from the Jews. But the hour cometh, and now is, when the true worshippers shall worship the Father in Spirit and truth: for such doth the Father seek to be his worshippers. God is Spirit, and they that worship him must worship in Spirit and in truth. The woman saith unto him, I know that Messiah will come (which is called Christ): when he is come, he will declare unto us all things. Jesus saith unto her, I that speak unto thee am he. (22-26)

He now explains more fully what He had touched on before about the abolition of the Law. He divides the subject into two parts. First, He condemns the form of worshipping God which the Samaritans used as superstitious and false, and declares that the acceptable and lawful form was with the Jews. And He puts as the reason for the difference that the Jews received assurance from the Word of God about His worship, whereas the Samaritans had no certainty from God's lips. Secondly, He declares that the ceremonies observed by the Jews hitherto would soon be ended.

22. *Ye worship.* This is a sentence worth remembering. By it we are taught that we are not to essay anything in religion rashly or unthinkingly. For unless there is knowledge present, it is not God that we worship but a spectre or ghost. Hence all so-called good intentions are struck by this thunderbolt, which tells us that men can do nothing but err when they are guided by their own opinion without the Word or command of God. Christ takes the side of His own nation and says that the Jews are far different from the Samaritans. And why?

For salvation is from the Jews. He means by these words that they are superior in this one respect—that with them God had made a covenant of eternal salvation. Some restrict it to Christ, who was sprung from the Jews; and indeed, since all the promises of God were ratified and confirmed in Him (II Cor. 1.20) there is no salvation but in Him. But since there can be no doubt that Christ gives the preference to the Jews because they do not worship some unknown deity but only the God who revealed Himself to them and by whom they were adopted as His people, we ought to understand by the word 'salvation' the saving manifestation which they had in the heavenly doctrine.

But why does He say that it was from the Jews, when rather it was entrusted to them that they alone might enjoy it? In my judgment, He is alluding to what was foretold by the prophets, that the Law should go forth out of Zion (Isa. 2.3). They were separated from the rest of the nations on the condition that the pure knowledge of God should in the end flow out from them to the whole world. What it all comes to is that God is only worshipped properly in the certainty of faith, which is necessarily born of the Word of God; and hence it follows that all who forsake the Word fall into idolatry. For Christ plainly declares than an idol or an empty image is put in God's place when men are ignorant of the true God; and He accuses of ignorance all to whom God has not revealed Himself. As soon as we are deprived of the light of His Word, darkness and blindness reign in us.

And we must notice that when the Jews in their faithlessness annulled the covenant of eternal life made with the fathers, they were deprived of the treasure which they had possessed until then; for they had not yet been rejected from God's Church. But now that they deny the Son, they have nothing in common with the Father. The same is true of all who have left the pure faith of the Gospel for their own and other men's inventions. However much in their obstinacy those who worship God from their own notions or men's traditions flatter and praise themselves, this one Word thundering from heaven overthrows every divine and holy thing they think they possess: *Ye worship that which ye know not*. And so, if our religion is to be approved by God, it must needs rest on knowledge conceived of His Word.

23. *But the hour cometh*. Now follows the latter clause on the repealing of the worship of the Law. When He says that the hour cometh or will come, He teaches that the order handed down by Moses is not for everlasting; when He says that the hour is now come, He puts an end to the ceremonies and so declares that 'the time of reformation' has been fulfilled. Meanwhile He approves of the Temple and the priesthood and all the ceremonies pertaining to them, so far as their past use is concerned (Heb. 9.10). Moreover, to show that God does not wish to be worshipped either in Jerusalem or in Mount Gerizim, He takes up a higher principle—that the true worship of Him lies in the Spirit. Whence it follows that He may be worshipped properly in all places.

But here we must ask first, why and in what sense the worship of God may be called spiritual. To understand this we must note the antithesis between the Spirit and external figures, as between the shadow and the substance. The worship of God is said to consist in the Spirit because it is only the inward faith of the heart that produces prayer and purity of conscience and denial of ourselves, that we may be given up to obedience of God as holy sacrifices.

This gives rise to another question: Did not the fathers worship Him spiritually under the Law? I reply, since God is always true to Himself He did not, from the beginning of the world, approve any other worship than the spiritual, which is consistent with His nature. This is abundantly attested by Moses himself. He declares in many places that the only aim of the Law is that the people shall cleave to God in faith and with a pure conscience. The prophets express it still more clearly when they harshly attack the people's hypocrisy in that they thought they had satisfied God when they had performed the sacrifices and the outward display. There is no need here to cite the many testimonies which come everywhere, but the most remarkable passages are Ps. 50, Isa. 1, 58, 66, Mic. 6, Amos 5. But although the worship of God under the Law was spiritual it was wrapped up in so many outward cere-monies that it had a flavour of carnality and earthliness. This is why in Gal. 4.9 Paul calls the ceremonies 'flesh' and 'the beggarly elements of the world'. Similarly, the author of the Epistle to the Hebrews says that the old Sanctuary with all that belonged to it was earthly (Heb. 9.1). Hence we may well say that the worship of the Law was spiritual in its substance but something carnal and earthly in its form. For that whole economy whose reality is now openly manifested was shadowy.

We now see what the Jews had in common with us and in what way they were different. In all ages God wanted to be worshipped by faith, prayer, thanksgiving, purity of heart and innocency of life. And never did He delight in any other sacrifices, though in the Law there were various additions so that the Spirit and truth were concealed under coverings. But now that the veil of the Temple has been rent, there is nothing obscure or hidden. There are indeed among us today certain outward exercises of godliness which our childishness needs. But they are moderate and sober enough not to obscure the naked truth of Christ. In short, what was sketchily outlined to the fathers is now openly displayed to us.

But under the Papacy this distinction is not only confused but alto-gether overturned. For there the shadows are no less dense than they used to be under Judaism. It cannot be denied that here Christ is making a plain distinction between us and the Jews. By whatever subterfuges the Papists may try to get out of it, it is certain that we differ from the fathers only in the outward form, because in their spiritual worship of God they were bound to ceremonies which were abolished by the coming of Christ. Therefore all who burden the Church with an excessive host of ceremonies despoil her of the presence of Christ, so far as lies in them. I think nothing of the weak excuse that many ordinary folk in our day need those aids as much as the Jews did of old. For we must always pay attention to the way the Lord wished His Church to be governed, for He alone knows best what is advantageous for us. But it is sure that nothing is more contrary to the divine ordinance than the gross and doubly carnal show which prevails in the Papacy. The shadows of the Law certainly hid the Spirit, but these masks of the Papacy disfigure Him altogether. Therefore we must on no account connive at such horrible and unworthy corruptions. However cleverly men or those too timid to correct abuses may argue that these things are indifferent and should be regarded as neither good nor bad, it is simply unbearable that the rule laid down by Christ should be violated.

The true worshippers. Christ seems in passing to reprove the obstinacy which later broke forth in many. For we know how obstinate and contentious the Jews were in defending the ceremonies they were used to when the Gospel was revealed. The statement has, however, a wider significance. He knows that the world will never be free from superstitions, and therefore He separates the godly and true worshippers from the perverted and hypocritical. Armed with this testimony, let us not hesitate to condemn the Papists in all their inventions and despise their reproaches. For why should we fear when we hear that God is pleased with this bare and simple worship, which is disdained by the Papists because it is not swollen with a mass of ceremonies? And what good does the empty show of the flesh do them, which Christ says quenches the Spirit? What it is to worship God in Spirit and truth appears plainly from what has already been said. It is to remove the coverings of the ancient ceremonies and retain simply what is spiritual in the worship of God. For the truth of the worship of God rests in the Spirit, and ceremonies are so to say adventitious. And here again it must be observed that truth is not contrasted to falsehood but to the outward addition of the figures; so that it is, as they say, the pure and simple substance of spiritual worship.

24. *God is Spirit.* Here is confirmation from the very nature of God. Since men are flesh, it is not surprising that they delight in what corresponds to their natures. This is why they invent many things in the worship of God which are full of insubstantial display. They should first consider that they are dealing with God, who no more agrees with the flesh than fire does with water. When we are concerned with the worship of God it ought to suffice in restraining the wantonness of our mind if we just think that God is so unlike us that those things which please us most are to Him disgusting and boring. What if hypocrites are so blinded by their pride that they are not afraid to subject God to their will, or rather lust? Let us know that modesty does not hold the lowest place in the true worship of God and regard with

suspicion whatever is pleasing to the flesh. And as we cannot ascend to His height let us remember that we must seek from His Word the rule that shall direct us. This passage is often cited by the fathers against the Arians to prove the divinity of the Spirit, but this is really twisting it; for Christ is simply saying here that His Father is of a spiritual nature and therefore unmoved by trifles, as men in their levity are wont to be.

25. *The Messiah will come.* Although among the Samaritans religion was impure and mixed with many errors, some principles taken from the Law were nevertheless fixed in their minds, like that about the Messiah. And when the woman gathered from Christ's discourse that an unusual change was about to take place in the Church of God, she probably at once remembered the Christ, under whom she hoped all things would be completely restored. When she says that the Messiah will come she seems to be speaking of a time close at hand, And indeed there is plenty of evidence that everywhere people were excited by the expectation of the Messiah who would remedy what was so wretchedly ruined, or rather utterly destroyed.

What is beyond all controversy is that the woman puts Christ before Moses and all the prophets as a teacher. For in a few words she sums up three things. First that the teaching of the Law was not complete in every detail but only rudiments were delivered in it. For unless there had been some farther advance to be made, she would not have said that the Messiah would tell them everything. A contrast between Him and the prophets is implied, in that it is His proper office to bring His disciples to the finishing post whereas the prophets had only as it were entered them and started them off. Secondly, the woman says that she expects a Christ who will be the interpreter of the Father and the teacher and master of all the godly. Finally she declares that we must not desire anything better or more perfect than His Gospel, for this is the furthest bourne of wisdom, beyond which it is unlawful to proceed.

Would that those who now boast of being pillars of the Christian Church at least imitated this poor woman and were satisfied with the simple teaching of Christ rather than claiming I know not what authority for intruding their inventions! For where was the religion of the Pope and Mohammed fabricated but from the distorted additions by which they imagined they filled out the teaching of the Gospel? As if it would have been incomplete without such drivel! But whoever is properly taught in the school of Christ will neither ask nor allow any other master.

26. *I that speak with thee am he.* When He acknowledges to the woman that He is the Messiah, He unquestionably presents Himself as her teacher in correspondence with the hope she had conceived. And so I think it probable that He went on to give her fuller instruction to

satisfy her thirst. He wanted such an example of His grace to be visible in the case of this poor woman that He might testify to all that He never fails in His duty when we want Him to be our teacher. There is no danger of His disappointing one of these whom He finds ready to be His disciple. But those who disdain to submit to Him, as we see with many proud and irreligious men, or who look elsewhere for a more perfect wisdom, as the Turks and Papists do, deserve to be dragged about by endless delusions and plunged in a labyrinth of errors. Again, by these words, 'I that speak with thee am the Messiah, the Son of God', He sets the name of Messiah as a seal to ratify the teaching of His Gospel; for we must remember that He was anointed by the Father, and the Spirit of God rested on Him, that He might bring us the message of salvation, as Isaiah says (Isa. 61.1).

And upon this came his disciples; and they marvelled that he was speaking with a woman; yet no man said, What seekest thou? or, why speakest thou with her? So the woman left her waterpot and went away into the city, and saith to the men, Come, see a man which told me all things that ever I did: is not this the Christ? they went out of the city and were coming to him. In the meanwhile the disciples prayed him, saying, Rabbi, eat. But he said unto them, I have meat to eat that ye know not. The disciples therefore said one to another, Hath any man brought him aught to eat? Jesus saith unto them, My meat is to do the will of him that sent me, and to accomplish his work. (27-34)

27. *And they marvelled.* The disciples' surprise which the Evangelist records could have come from two causes. Either they were scandalized by the woman's lowness, or they thought Jews were polluted if they conversed with Samaritans. But although both these feelings arose from a devout reverence for their Master, they are wrong to marvel as if it were discordant that He should honour so highly such a common woman. Why do they not look at themselves? They would certainly have found no less cause for surprise that they, worthless fellows and as it were the dregs of the people, should be raised to the highest rank of honour. And yet we must notice that they did not dare question Him. We are taught by their example that if now and then anything in the works or words of God and Christ shock us, we must not take the bit between our teeth and grumble audaciously, but rather modestly keep quiet until what is hidden from us is revealed from heaven. The basis of such a modesty is in the fear of God and the reverence of Christ.

28. *So the woman left.* The Evangelist relates this to express her burning enthusiasm. It is a sign of haste that she leaves her waterpot

when she returns to the city. And it is the nature of faith that we want to bring others to share eternal life with us when we have become partakers of it. The knowledge of God cannot lie buried and inactive in our hearts and not be made known to men. For that word must be true: 'I believed, and therefore will I speak' (Ps. 116.10). We should note the woman's earnestness and eagerness all the more, in that it was only a small spark of faith that kindled them. She had scarcely tasted Christ when she broadcast His fame throughout the whole city. On the other hand, she might seem blameworthy in that while she is still ignorant and imperfectly taught, she goes beyond the bounds of her faith. I reply, she would have acted recklessly if she had assumed the office of a teacher; but when she was desiring nothing more than to stir up her fellow-citizens to hear Christ speak, we will not say that she forgot herself and went too far; for she was only being, as it were, a trumpet or a bell to invite others to Christ.

29. *See a man.* It seems as if she is speaking doubtfully and so was not much moved by Christ's authority. I reply, since she was not qualified to preach about such mysteries, she gets busy in her own small way, persuading her townsfolk to be taught by Christ. Moreover, her knowledge by means of a clear and unambiguous sign that He was a prophet was a very strong incitement to them. For since they could not judge from His teaching, this inferior preparation was useful and apt for them. And so, when they learned that hidden things had been revealed to the woman, they inferred that He was a prophet of God. This settled, they begin to pay heed to His teaching. And yet the woman goes further. She tells them to consider if He may not be the Messiah. She was satisfied if they would only seek by themselves what she had already found in Christ; for she knew that they would find more than she promised.

Why does she lie and say that Christ told her *all things*? I have already pointed out that Christ did not reprove her for her fornication alone, but put before her in a few words the many sins in her life. The Evangelist has not recorded every sentence in detail, but only states in summary that, to curb the woman's banter, Christ laid bare her past and present life. Yet we see that in her godly enthusiasm, she does not at all spare herself or her reputation to magnify the name of Christ, for she does not hesitate to relate her infamy.

32. *I have meat.* It is amazing that He should refuse food when He is tired and hungry. If it be said that He does this to teach us by His example to endure hunger, why did He not always do so? But He had another object than to say that food ought to be refused. The important thing to notice is that His anxiety about the present business so presses upon Him and absorbs all His attention that it does not at all irk Him

to neglect His food. He is not, however, professing to be so eager to obey His Father's commands that He neither eats nor drinks. He is only pointing out what comes first and what is secondary. And so by His example He shows that the Kingdom of God is to be put before all bodily comforts. God certainly lets us eat and drink, provided we are not drawn away from what comes first—that is, that every man shall be occupied in His own vocation.

Someone may say that eating and drinking cannot fail to be distractions that steal some of our time from a better use of it. This I allow to be true. But since the Lord of His kindness lets us care for our bodies so far as necessity demands, he who looks after his body frugally and soberly does not fail to give due preference to his obedience to God. At the same time we must take care not to keep so rigidly to fixed hours as not to be ready to go without food when God offers some opportunity and, as it were, arranges our time for us. Christ now has in His hands an opportunity that might slip away and He embraces it with open arms and holds it fast. Therefore, because the duty enjoined on Him by the Father is so urgent that He has to lay aside everything else, He does not hesitate to postpone His meal. And indeed, it would have been all wrong for Christ to show less zeal when the woman left her waterpot and ran to call the people. Finally, if we are determined not to lose the purpose of living for the sake of life, it will not be hard to maintain a proper proportion. For the man who regards the aim of life as serving the Lord, from which it is not right for us to turn aside even in the imminent peril of death, will certainly look upon it as more important than eating and drinking. The metaphor of eating and drinking is the more graceful in that it was opportunely taken from the present discourse.

34. *My meat is.* He means not only that it takes the first place with Him, but that there is nothing He likes better or in which He is more cheerfully or eagerly employed. Just as David, to magnify God's Law, says not only that it was precious to Him but sweeter than honey (Ps. 19.10). To follow Christ, therefore, we must both give ourselves up diligently to God and be so willing to obey His commands that the labour is not at all irksome or grievous.

To do his will. By adding these words, Christ explains fully what is the will of the Father to which He is devoted. It is that He shall fulfil the office laid upon Him. Thus, every man should pay heed to his calling, so that he may not think God has laid it on him when he has undertaken it rashly and from self-will. Moreover the nature of Christ's office is well known—to advance the Kingdom of God, to restore lost souls to life, to spread the light of the Gospel and in short to bring salvation to the world. The importance of these things made

Him forget meat and drink when He was tired and hungry. From this we receive no common comfort. It tells us that Christ was so anxious for men's salvation that the height of pleasure for Him was to attend to it; for we cannot doubt that He has the same attitude towards us today.

Say not ye, There are yet four months, and then cometh the harvest? behold, I say unto you, Lift up your eyes, and look on the fields, that they are white already unto harvest. He that reapeth receiveth wages, and gathereth fruit unto life eternal; that he that soweth and he that reapeth may rejoice together. For herein is the saying true, One soweth, and another reapeth. I sent you to reap that whereon ye have not laboured: others have laboured, and ye are entered into their labour. (35-38)

35. *Say not ye?* He goes on from what He has just said. He had declared that nothing was more important to Him than to finish the Father's work; and now He shows how ripe it is by comparing it to the harvest. For just as the harvest cannot be delayed when the corn is ripe, or the grain would drop, so now that the spiritual corn is ripe He says that there must be no tarrying, for delay will ruin it. We see that the comparison is used to explain the cause of His haste. By this clause, *Say not ye?* He wanted to hint at how much more careful men's minds are for earthly things than for heavenly. For they are so consumed with looking for harvest that they carefully count up the months and days. But it is surprising how lazy they are in reaping the wheat of heaven. And daily experience confirms that this depravity is not only inborn in us but can hardly be torn out of our hearts. Whereas all provide for their earthly futures, how careless we are in thinking of heavenly things! Elsewhere Christ Himself says: 'Hypocrites, you discern from the look of the heaven what sort of day tomorrow will be, but you do not acknowledge the time of my visitation' (Luke 12.56).

36. *He that reapeth receiveth wages.* He shows by another argument how diligently we ought to devote ourselves to God's work, in that a large and splendid reward is laid up for our labour. He promises there will be fruit, and fruit incorruptible and imperishable at that. But what He says about fruit may be expounded in two ways—either as an announcement of the reward, so that He would be saying the same thing again in different words; or He is praising the labours of those who enrich the Kingdom of God, as He later repeats in 15.16: 'I chose you, that you should go and bear fruit, and that your fruit should abide.' And both ought certainly to encourage ministers of the Word and uphold them in their toil when they hear that a crown of glory is laid

up for them in heaven and know that the fruit of their harvest will be both precious in the sight of God and eternal. It is to this end that the Scripture everywhere speaks of reward, and not that we shall assess the merits of works from it. For if it comes to a reckoning, who will not be found more deserving of punishment for laziness than of reward for diligence? Therefore, there will be nothing left for even the best workmen but humbly to turn to God with the prayer of forgiveness. But the Lord who acts in a fatherly way towards us to correct our laziness and encourage us who would otherwise be downhearted, deigns to bestow on us a free reward.

Moreover, this is so far from overturning justification by faith that it rather establishes it. For how does it come about that God finds aught in us to reward but because He has given it to us by His Spirit? And we know that the Spirit is the earnest and pledge of adoption. Secondly, how does it come about that God gives so much honour to imperfect and sinful works but in that, when He has freely reconciled us to Himself, He accepts our works apart from any merit by not imputing the sins which adhere to them? The sum of this passage is that the labour the Apostles spent on teaching was not to be regarded as hard and unpleasant, since they knew it was so useful to Christ and the Church.

That he that soweth. By these words Christ shows there is no cause for complaint that the Apostles will gather fruit from the husbandry of others. And this amplification must be noted. For if in the world the groans of those who grumble that the fruit of their labour has been given to another does not stop the new possessor from cheerfully reaping what another has sown, how much more cheerful should the reapers be when there is mutual accord and mutual joy and thanksgiving?

But to understand this passage properly we must grasp the antithesis between sowing and reaping. The sowing was the teaching of the Law and the Prophets, for the seed then cast on the soil remained, as it were, in the blade; but the teaching of the Gospel which brings men to perfect maturity is aptly compared to the harvest. For the Law was far from the perfection at length revealed in Christ. The well-known comparison between childhood and manhood which Paul uses in Gal. 4.1 is on the same lines. In short, since Christ's coming brought with it present salvation, it is not surprising if the Gospel in which the door of the Kingdom of Heaven is opened is called the harvesting of the teaching of the prophets. Yet this does not stop the fathers under the Law being gathered into God's granary. But the method must be referred to the mode of teaching. As the childhood of the Church lasted to the end of the Law and reached manhood as soon as the Gospel had been preached, so the salvation began then to ripen which the prophets had only sown.

But as Christ delivered this discourse in Samaria He seems to extend the sowing beyond the Law and the Prophets. And there are some who expound these words equally of the Gentiles and the Jews. I acknowledge that some grains of piety were always scattered throughout the whole world and there can be no doubt at all that God sowed, so to say, by the hand of philosophers and secular authors the noble statements that exist in their writings. But since that seed was defiled from the very root and since the corn which might have sprung from it (although it was neither good nor natural) was choked by a huge mass of errors, it is ridiculous for such harmful corruption to be compared to sowing. Besides, what is said here about common rejoicing does not at all fit in with philosophers or their ilk.

But the knot is not yet untied, for Christ is referring especially to the Samaritans. I reply, although everything among them was infected with corruptions, yet some seed of godliness was still hidden there. For why, as soon as they hear a word about Christ, are they so quick to seek Him but because they had learned from the Law and the Prophets that the Redeemer would come? Judaea was the Lord's peculiar field which He had cultivated by His prophets. But as some small portion of seed had been carried into Samaria, Christ had good reason to say that the seed ripened there too. If it be objected that the apostles were chosen to proclaim the Gospel throughout the whole world, the reply is easy: Christ spoke as His age could bear; save that because they looked for the fruit which was already nearly ripe He commends in the Samaritans the seed of prophetic teaching, mixed and muddled though it was with much darnel.

37. *For herein is the saying true.* This was a common proverb which indicated that men often receive the fruit of another's labours. But there was this difference, that he who has laboured is annoyed that the fruit is borne away by another, whereas the prophets shared in the apostles' gladness. And yet it cannot be inferred from this that the prophets themselves witness or are aware of what is now going on in the Church. Christ only means that in their lifetime the prophets taught with the attitude that they already rejoiced for the fruit which it was not given to them to gather. The comparison which Peter uses in the first chapter of his epistle (I Pet. 1.12) is not dissimilar, except that he exhorts all believers in general whereas Christ is addressing only the disciples, and in their person the ministers of the Gospel. With these words He commands them to contribute their work to the common store, so that there shall be no wicked envy among them. Those who are sent first to the work are to be so attentive to the cultivation they

are doing that they shall not envy a greater blessing to those who will follow them; and those who are sent, as it were, to gather the ripe fruit are to be about their work with a like cheerfulness. For the comparison which is made here between the teachers of the Law and the Gospel may also be applied to the latter in relationship to one another.

And from that city many of the Samaritans believed on him because of the word of the woman, who testified, He told me all things that ever I did. So when the Samaritans came unto him, they besought him to abide with them: and he abode there two days. And many more believed because of his word; and they said to the woman, Now we believe, not because of thy speaking: for we have heard for ourselves and know that this is indeed the Christ, the Saviour of the world. And after two days he went forth from thence into Galilee. For Jesus himself testified, that a prophet hath no honour in his own country. So when he came into Galilee, the Galilaeans received him, having seen all the things that he did in Jerusalem at the feast: for they also went unto the feast. (39-45)

39. *They believed because of the word of the woman.* The Evangelist here relates how powerful the woman's proclamation to her townsfolk was. And from this it is evident that there was a strong expectation and desire among them for the Messiah. The word *believe* is used loosely here and means that they were moved by the woman's word to acknowledge that Christ was a prophet. It is in a way the beginning of faith when minds are prepared to receive teaching. Such an entrance to faith is here dignified as faith, that we may learn how highly God esteems reverence for His Word when He confers so great an honour on the teachableness of those who had not yet been instructed. And their faith is shown by their being seized with a desire to advance, and for that reason they want Christ to stay with them.

41. *And many more believed.* It is plain from what followed that Christ's consent was not too facile. For we see that the two days He granted to their request were fruitful. By this example we are taught never to stop, when we can extend the Kingdom of God. And therefore if we are afraid that our readiness may be open to slander or may often prove useless, let us seek from Christ the Spirit of counsel to guide us. The word *believe* is now used in a different sense, as meaning not only that they were prepared for faith but were actually filled with true faith.

42. *Because of thy speaking.* Though I have followed Erasmus in his rendering, because *loquela* which the old translator uses[1] is a barbarous term, the reader must remember that the Greek word is equivalent to the Latin *loquentia*, that is talk or gossip. And the Samaritans seem to

[1] Vulgate.

be claiming that they now have a stronger support than a woman's tongue—which is usually untrustworthy.

We believe. This expresses better the nature of their faith, that it is conceived of the very Word of God, so that they can glory in having the Son of God as their teacher. And indeed it is only on His authority that we can safely rely. He is not, indeed, visibly present now so as to speak with us face to face, but whoever it may be through whom we happen to hear Him, our faith can rest only on Him. Nor does the knowledge that is mentioned come from any other. For the speech which proceeds from a mortal man can certainly fill and satisfy the ears; but it will never establish the soul in calm confidence of salvation, so that he who has heard may justly claim that he knows. Therefore, the first thing in faith is to know that it is Christ who speaks by His ministers. The next is to render Him the honour that is His—that is, not to doubt that He is faithful and true, so that trusting such a sure authority we may rest safely on His teaching.

Again, when they proclaim that Jesus is the Saviour of the world and the Christ, they have undoubtedly learned this from hearing Him. From this we infer that in two days Christ taught the sum of the Gospel more plainly there than He had so far done in Jerusalem. And He declared that the salvation He had brought was common to the whole world, so that they should understand more easily that it belonged to them also. He did not call them as lawful heirs, but taught them that He had come to admit strangers into the family of God and to bring peace to them that were far off.

44. *For Jesus himself testified.* The seeming contradiction that appears here at first sight has given rise to various interpretations. Augustine's explanation is too subtle, that Christ lacked honour among His own people because He had done more good in a couple of days among the Samaritans than in a long time among the Galilaeans, and because He had gained more disciples in Samaria without miracles than a great many miracles had won for Him in Galilee. Nor do I like Chrysostom's understanding of Christ's country as Capernaum, because He lived there more often than anywhere else. And so I agree rather with Cyril who says that when He had left the city of Nazareth He went into a different part of Galilee; for the other three Evangelists mention Nazareth when they relate this testimony of Christ. The meaning could well be that since the time of full manifestation was not yet come He wished to remain concealed in His native land, which was a more obscure retreat. Some explain it to mean that He remained two days in Samaria because there was no reason for Him to hurry to a place where contempt awaited Him. Others think He went straight to Nazareth and then left again at once; but since John says nothing like

this, I do not venture to take up the guess. Thus, it is more true to say that when He saw Himself despised in His native town of Nazareth He preferred to go elsewhere. And therefore it immediately goes on that He came into the town of Cana. And what is also added, that He was received by the Galilaeans because of His miracles, was a sign of reverence, not of contempt.

A prophet in his own country. I have no doubt that this was a proverb; and we know that proverbs are repeated because they serve a frequent and ἐπὶ τὸ πολύ use. In such cases precise truth is not always to be looked for, as if what is said were necessarily true. It is certain that prophets are admired rather elsewhere than in their own country. But it may sometimes happen, and in fact does happen, that a prophet is not less honoured by His countrymen than by foreigners. But the proverb states what is usual and common—that prophets more readily receive honour anywhere but among their own people.

Now this proverb and its meaning may have a twofold origin. It is a universal fault that those we saw wailing in the cradle and playing the fool in their boyhood are despised by us throughout their whole life as if they had made no progress since childhood. To this is added another evil, envy, which is prevalent more among acquaintances. But I think the proverb probably arose from the prophets being so ill-treated by their own nation. For when good and holy men saw in Judaea such ingratitude towards God, such contempt of His Word and such obstinacy they could justly cry out and complain that nowhere were the prophets of God less honoured than in their own country. If the former meaning is preferred, the name of prophet is to be taken generally for any teacher, just as Paul calls Epimenides a prophet of the Cretans (Titus 1.12).

45. *They received him.* How long this honour lasted we cannot say, for there is nothing more prevalent than forgetfulness of God's gifts. Nor does John relate this with any other aim than to teach us that Christ performed the miracles before many witnesses, so that they were proclaimed far and wide. Again, this points out one usefulness of signs, in that they smooth the way for the Gospel by procuring reverence for Christ.

Jesus came therefore again into Cana of Galilee, where he made the water wine. And there was a certain nobleman, whose son was sick at Capernaum. When he heard that Jesus was come out of Judaea into Galilee, he went unto him, and besought him that he would come down and heal his son; for he was at the point of death. Jesus therefore said unto him, Except ye see signs and wonders, ye will in no wise believe. The nobleman saith unto him, Sir, come down ere my child die. Jesus

saith unto him, Go thy way; thy son liveth. The man believed the word
that Jesus spake unto him, and he went his way. And as he was now
going down, his servants met him, saying, Thy son liveth. So he
inquired of them the hour when he began to amend. They said therefore
unto him, Yesterday at the seventh hour the fever left him. So the
father knew that it was at that hour in which Jesus said unto him, Thy
son liveth: and himself believed, and his whole house. This is again the
second sign that Jesus did, having come out of Judaea into Galilee. (46-54)

46. *And there was a certain nobleman.* This is the truer rendering,
though Erasmus thinks otherwise. I acknowledge of course that at that
time what are now called dukes or barons or earls were styled minor
kings. But the constitution of Galilee was such that there could be no
one of that rank living in Capernaum. Moreover, I think he was
someone from Herod's court; for those who think he was sent from
Caesar have no evidence at all. And the Evangelist expressly mentions
this, because the miracle was the more striking in the case of such a man.

47. *When he heard that Jesus was come.* It is some sign of faith that
he seeks help from Christ; but when he limits the way in which Christ
may help him he shows how ignorant he is. He binds Christ's power
to His bodily presence, so that he had no other idea of Christ than that
He was a prophet sent by God with the authority and power of proving that He was God's minister by performing miracles. But Christ
overlooked this fault, much as it deserved censure, and rebukes him
severely, and indeed all the Jews, for the other reason that they were
too eager for miracles.

But why is Christ now so harsh, who usually kindly receives others
who desire a miracle? There must certainly have been some special
reason which is unknown to us, why He treated this man more
severely than His wont. Perhaps He regarded not so much the person
as the whole nation. He saw that His teaching had little authority and
was not only neglected but despised outright; and moreover, that they
were all set on miracles and all their senses were overcome by stupidity
rather than admiration. Hence that wicked contempt of the Word,
so common then, wrung this complaint from Him. It is true that some
of the saints occasionally wished for confirmation by signs that they
might not doubt the truth of the promises. And we see that God by
kindly agreeing to their requests was not offended at them. But Christ
is here pointing to a far greater wickedness. The Jews depended so
much on miracles that they left no place for the Word. First, it was
extremely perverse that in their stupidness and carnality they had no
reverence for the teaching unless they were roused by miracles. For
they must have been quite familiar with the Word of God in which

they had been brought up. Then, when miracles were performed, they were so far from profiting by them that they were just stupid and amazed. Thus, there was no religion, no knowledge of God, no practice of godliness among them, except in miracles.

On the same lines was Paul's reproach that the Jews seek a sign. He means that they were unreasonably and immoderately attached to signs and cared little for the grace of Christ, or the promises of eternal life, or the secret power of the Spirit, but, on the contrary, rejected the Gospel disdainfully because they had no taste for anything but miracles. I wish there were not so many today suffering from the same disease. But nothing is commoner than the saying, 'Let the miracles come first and then we will give ear to their teaching.' As if the truth of Christ should be so vile to us unless it has another support. But even if God were to overwhelm them with a huge heap of wonders, they are lying when they say that they would believe. There would be some outward surprise, but no more attention would be paid to the teaching.

49. *Sir, come down.* As he perseveres in asking and at last gets what he wants, you can infer that Christ did not reprove him as if He were going to reject him altogether and refuse his prayer, but that He did it to correct the fault which was obstructing his way into true faith. We ought to remember what I said before—that this was a reproof common to the whole people rather than peculiar to one man. And so what is perverse or distorted or superfluous in our prayers must be corrected or removed, so that harmful obstructions may be taken away. Now, since courtiers are usually grand and haughty and do not cheerfully put up with harsh treatment, it is worth noticing that this man, humbled by his need and the fear of bereavement, does not burst into a passion or grumble when Christ takes him up roughly, but overlooks the reproof and keeps quiet. We find the same thing in ourselves. For we are amazingly spoilt, amazingly impatient and fretful, until we are subdued by adversities and forced to lay aside our pride and disdain.

50. *Thy son liveth.* Here primarily shines forth the humanity and kindness of Christ in pardoning the man's ignorance and stretching forth His power beyond what he had hoped. He asked that Christ would come and heal his son. He thought it was possible that he who was sick could be freed from disease, but not that he could be raised up when he was dead. And therefore he begs Him to make haste lest death should get there first. Therefore, when Christ pardons both these errors, we can see how much He values even a weak faith. It is also worth noticing that although Christ does not grant his desire, He gives him far more than he asked. For he receives the assurance that his son is even now well. So our heavenly Father often does not

H 113

comply with our prayers in every detail but goes to work in an unexpected way to help us, so that we may learn not to dictate to Him in anything. When Christ says that his son is alive, He means that he has been delivered from the danger of death.

The man believed the word. He was the more ready to believe because he had come with the conviction that Christ was a prophet of God. And so, as soon as he had grasped one word he fixed it in his heart. Although he did not honour Christ's power as he ought to have done, a little promise suddenly begot a new trust in his mind and he believed his son's life was enclosed in a single word of Christ. The Word of God should indeed be received with this readiness, but it is very far from always having such an immediate effect on its hearers. How few profit as much from a number of sermons as this half-heathen man did from hearing a single word? We must labour the more zealously to stir up our slowness, and above all to pray that God would so touch our hearts that we may be no less ready to believe than He is gracious and kind to promise.

51. *And as he was going down.* Here the effect of faith and the efficacy of the Word are described. As Christ restores to life this dying child by a word, so in a moment the father by his faith regains his son once more healthy. Let us therefore understand that whenever the Lord offers His benefits to us, His power will always be ready to perform whatever He promises, so long as our unbelief does not shut the door against Him. I acknowledge it does not happen continually and is not even frequent or common, that the Lord instantly puts forth His hand to give us help. But whenever He delays, He has His reasons and it is for our good. And it is certain that He Himself never delays, but rather fights against the obstacles we put up. And so, when His help does not at once appear, let us think how much mistrust lies in us, or at least how small and limited our faith is. And we must not be surprised if He does not want His benefits to be lost or scatters them at random on the earth, but chooses to bestow them on those who open the heart of their faith and are ready to receive them. And although He does not always help His people in the same way, never will the faith of anyone be fruitless, but we shall experience the truth of what the prophet says, that God's promises, even when they seem to delay, are really making great haste.

So he inquired of them. It was from a secret impulse from God that he asked his servants when his son began to get better. And this, that the truth of the miracle might come out more plainly. For by nature we have a very malicious desire to extinguish the light of God's power, and Satan labours by various artifices to hide His works from our sight. Therefore, that they may win from us their due praise, they must be made so clear to us that no room is left for doubt. So however ungrateful men may be, this detail will not let such an outstanding work of Christ be ascribed to chance.

53. *And himself believed, and his whole house.* It may seem absurd that the Evangelist should mention this as the beginning of faith in a man whose faith he had already commended. Nor can the word *believe* refer (at any rate in this passage) to the progress of faith. But we must understand that this man, as a Jew and one brought up in the teaching of the Law, had already been given some taste of faith when he came to Christ. That he afterwards believed the Word of Christ was a special faith referring no further than to his son's life. But now he begins to believe in a different way, in that having embraced Christ's teaching, he professed openly that he was one of His disciples. Thus he now not only believes his son will be cured by Christ's blessing, but he acknowledges Christ to be the Son of God and takes his stand on the side of the Gospel. He has his whole family for company, who witnessed the miracle. Nor can it be doubted that he did his utmost to bring others with him into Christianity.

CHAPTER FIVE

After these things there was a feast of the Jews; and Jesus went up to Jerusalem. Now there is in Jerusalem by the sheep gate a pool, which is called in Hebrew Bethesda, having five porches. In these lay a multitude of them that were sick, blind, halt, withered, waiting for the moving of the water. For an angel went down at intervals into the pool, and troubled the water: whosoever then first after the troubling of the water stepped in was made whole of whatever disease he had. And a certain man was there which had been thirty and eight years in his infirmity. When Jesus saw him lying, and knew that he had been now a long time in that case, he saith unto him, Wouldest thou be made whole? The sick man answered him, Sir, I have no man when the water is troubled to put me into the pool; but while I am coming, another steppeth down before me. Jesus saith unto him, Arise, take up thy bed, and walk. And straightway the man was made whole, and took up his bed, and walked. Now it was the Sabbath on that day. (1-9)

1. *There was a feast.* Although the Evangelist does not definitely say what feast this was, the probability is that he means Pentecost—that is, if what is related here happened immediately after Christ had come into Galilee. Soon after the Passover He had set out from Jerusalem; as He was passing through Samaria He reckoned four months to the harvest; then when He entered Galilee He healed the nobleman's son. The Evangelist adds that the feast followed this, and so the order of time leads us to understand it as Pentecost, though I will not argue the point. Christ came to Jerusalem for the feast, partly because there would be a large assembly of people at that time and so He would have a greater opportunity of spreading the Gospel; and partly because it was necessary that He should be subject to the Law, to redeem us all from its bondage, as we have already explained elsewhere.

2. *By the sheep gate a pool.* He adds where it happened, and from this we gather that the miracle was not secret or known only to a few. The five porches suggest that the place was well frequented; and this is borne out by its proximity to the Temple. Besides, the Evangelist expressly says that many sick people lay there. As to the meaning of the name, the learned justly reject Jerome's conjecture, which makes it Betheder instead of Bethesda and translates it as the house of the flock. For a pool is mentioned here which was near the sheep market. Those who read it Bethseda, a place of fishing, have no grounds for it. There

is greater probability in the opinion of those who explain it as a place of pouring out, for the Hebrew אֶשֶׁד (*eshed*) means flowing out. But the Evangelist used the Aramaic pronunciation *Esda*, as was then customary. For I think the water was conveyed to it by conduits, so that the priests could draw from it. Unless perhaps the place was so called because the water was poured in through pipes. It was called the sheep gate, in my opinion, because the beasts which were to be offered in sacrifice were taken there.

3. *In these lay a multitude.* It may be that the sick lay in the porches to ask alms when people who were going into the Temple to worship passed by. There, too, it was usual to buy the animals that were to be sacrificed. At each feast God healed a certain number, so that in this way He might commend the worship prescribed in the Law and the holiness of the Temple. But it might seem out of place when we do not read of any such thing being done at a time when religion was at its peak, and when even in the age of the prophets miracles were not ordinarily performed, that God's power and grace should be displayed more strikingly than usual in miracles when things were so decayed and almost ruined. I reply that I think there were two reasons. Because the Holy Spirit who dwelt in the prophets was a completely sufficient witness of the divine presence, religion needed no other confirmation then. For the Law had been confirmed by perfectly suitable signs, and God did not cease to approve by innumerable testimonies the worship He had commanded. But at the time of Christ's advent, they were without prophets and their condition was most wretched. And since various temptations pressed on them from every side they needed this extraordinary aid, lest they should think God had entirely deserted them and so be discouraged and fall away. We know that Malachi was the last of the prophets, and therefore he ends his teaching by telling the Jews to remember the Law delivered by Moses (Mal. 4.4) until the Christ shall appear. For God saw it was best to deprive them of the prophets and keep them in suspense for a time that they might burn with a stronger desire for Christ and receive Him with the greater reverence when He was revealed. Yet as a witness to the Temple and the sacrifices and the whole of that worship from which salvation was to appear for the world, the Lord retained among the Jews this gift of healing so that they might be aware that God had not separated them from the other nations in vain. By healing the sick God showed openly, as by a hand stretched out from heaven, that He approved the kind of worship that they received from the commands of the Law. Secondly, I have no doubt that God was warning them by such signs that the time of redemption was at hand and that Christ the author of salvation was already near, so as to arouse all their minds.

I think there was a double purpose for signs in that age: that the Jews might know that God was with them, and thus might stand fast in obedience to the Law; and secondly, that they might earnestly look for a new and unusual state.

Of halt, blind, withered. To teach us that these were no ordinary diseases healed by the Lord, the Evangelist tells us what some of them were. For human remedies could not help the halt, blind and withered. It was indeed a sad sight to see in such a crowd of men all these many kinds of deformities. Nevertheless, the glory of God shone there more brightly than in a large and well arranged army. For there is nothing more magnificent than when an unusual power of God corrects and restores the defects of nature. Nor is anything lovelier and pleasanter than when in His infinite goodness He relieves men's afflictions. Therefore the Lord wanted this place to be a famous theatre in which not only natives, but foreigners also, might see His majesty. And as I have already hinted, it was no small adornment and glory of the Temple that God should show clearly His presence by stretching forth His hand.

4. *For an angel.* The healing of the sick was indeed God's own work. But He was accustomed to use the hand and work of angels, and so commanded an angel to perform this duty. This is why angels are called potencies or powers. It is not as if God surrenders His power to them and sits idle in heaven Himself, but by His acting powerfully in them He magnifies and proclaims His power to us. They are wicked and perverse therefore, who imagine the angels possess anything of their own or who make them mediators between us and God, so as to obscure the glory of God, as if it were far from us, when in fact it reveals its presence in them. We must beware of Plato's silly speculations, for the distance between us and God is too great for us to go to the angels that they may procure grace for us. On the contrary, we must come straight to Christ, that by His guidance, protection and command we may have the angels as helpers and ministers of our salvation.

At intervals. God could have healed them all, at once and in a moment. But as His miracles have their purpose, they must also have a limit. Just as Christ also reminds them that although many died in the time of Elisha, only the one child was raised (II Kings 4.32f), and that although many widows went hungry in the time of drought, only one had her poverty relieved by Elijah (I Kings 17.9, Luke 4.25f). Thus the Lord reckoned it was enough to give a proof of His presence in regard to a few sick people. But the healing method described here shows plainly that there is nothing more unreasonable than for men to subject the works of God to their own judgment. For I ask you, what help or remedy could be expected from troubled water? But it is in this way, by taking from us our own attitude of mind, that the

Lord accustoms us to the obedience of faith. We are too quick to follow what pleases our reason, even though it be contrary to God's Word. Therefore, to make us obedient to Him, He often sets before us things that contradict our reason. And we only show our teachableness when we follow the bare Word with our eyes shut, though it does not seem worth our while. We have an example of this in Naaman the Syrian (II Kings 5.10). The prophet sends him to Jordan to be healed of his leprosy. At first he despises this as tomfoolery, but later he sees that God acts contrary to human reason in such a way that He never disappoints or plays with us.

The troubling of the water was a clear proof that God freely uses the elements for His own will and that He claims for Himself the result of the work. It is a very common fault to ascribe to creatures what belongs to God alone. It would be utterly silly to seek in the troubled waters the cause of the cure. He therefore so commends the external symbol that, by seeing the symbol, the sick have to look to the only author of grace Himself.

5. *And a certain man was there.* The Evangelist collects various details which show that the miracle is authentic. The long duration of the disease had taken away all hope of cure. The man complains that he is deprived of the healing water. He had frequently tried to throw himself into the water, but without success, for there was none to help him; hence Christ's power shines the more brightly. This, too, was the significance of the command to take up his bed, that it might be plain to all that he was only cured by the blessing of Christ. For when he gets up suddenly, healthy and strong in all his formerly impotent members, so sharp a change will the more rouse and strike the minds of the spectators.

6. *Wouldest thou be made whole?* He asks the question, not as if it were doubtful, but partly to kindle a desire for the grace He was offering him and partly to catch the attention of the onlookers, who might have missed the miracle if their minds had been elsewhere—a thing that often happens in sudden actions. The preparation was necessary, then, for these two reasons.

7. *I have no man.* This sick man does what we nearly all do. He limits God's help to his own ideas and does not dare promise himself more than he conceives in his mind. But in Christ forgiving his weakness we have a mirror of the kindness which each of us daily experiences when we keep concentrated on the means at hand. When against all hope He stretches forth His hand from hidden places. He shows how far His goodness exceeds the narrowness of our faith. Moreover, this example ought to teach us patience. Thirty-eight years was a long time for God to delay His blessing and aid from this poor man, which

yet He had from the beginning determined to bestow on him. However long He keeps us in suspense therefore, let us so groan in anguish under our afflictions that we may never be worn out by the irksomeness of the time. For though there seems no end to our protracted troubles, we ought always to believe that God is a wonderful deliverer who easily shatters every obstacle by His power.

9. *Now it was the Sabbath.* Christ was well aware that great offence would be taken when they saw a man marching along carrying a burden; for the Law expressly forbids the carrying of any burden at all on the Sabbath (Jer. 17.21). But Christ disregarded this danger and caused such a spectacle for two reasons. First, that the miracle might be more widely known. And secondly, that He might make occasion and, so to say, open up the way for the wonderful sermon which He soon preached. Moreover, the knowledge of that miracle was so important that it was His duty to set aside boldly the people's being offended, especially when He had a just defence ready, by which, although it was not accepted by the wicked, He abundantly refuted their calumnies. We should therefore observe the rule that even if the whole world should boil over in rage, we must proclaim God's glory and declare His works so far as His glory requires them to be known. Nor must we be worried or discouraged if our work turns out badly, so long as we keep to the object I have mentioned and do not go beyond the limits of our office.

So the Jews said unto him that was cured. It is the sabbath, it is not lawful for thee to take up thy bed. But he answered them, He that made me whole, the same said unto me, Take up thy bed, and walk. They asked him, who is the man that said unto thee, Take up thy bed, and walk? But he that was healed wist not who it was: for Jesus had conveyed himself away, a multitude being in that place. Afterward Jesus findeth him in the Temple, and said unto him, Behold, thou art made whole: sin no more, lest a worse thing befall thee. The man went away, and told the Jews that it was Jesus which had made him whole. And for this cause did the Jews persecute Jesus, and sought to slay him, because he did these things on the sabbath. (10-16)

10. *It is the sabbath.* Since the observance of the sabbath had to be upheld by everyone, they accuse the man properly and justly. But when the excuse he offers does not satisfy them, they themselves begin to err, for when the reason was known he should have been acquitted. As we have said, it was a violation of the sabbath to carry a burden. But Christ laid the burden on his shoulders and supports him with His own authority. We are therefore taught by this example to beware of hasty judgments and wait for the reason for each action to be fully

known. Whatever contradicts the Word of God deserves to be condemned unhesitatingly. But since there is a good deal of thoughtless talk about this, our inquiry should be reserved and calm, our decision sound and sober. The Jews were prejudiced by a wicked outlook and had no patience for inquiry; and so they shut the door on judgment and moderation. If they had let themselves be taught, not only would the offence have been taken away, but they would have been led further into the knowledge of the Gospel to their own good.

We now see how far the Jews were at fault in that they did not admit a reasonable defence. The defence is that the man who was healed replies that he does nothing but at the command of Him who had the authority and power to command. For although he did not yet know who Christ was, he was convinced that He had been sent by God, because he had experienced His divine power and learned from it that Christ is endowed with authority, so that He must of necessity be obeyed. But it also seems blameworthy that a miracle should separate him from obedience to the Law. I certainly confess that he does not use strong enough arguments against them. But they also are wrong on two accounts, in that they neither consider that this is an extraordinary work of God nor suspend their judgment until they shall have heard a prophet of God equipped with the Word.

13. *But he wist not who it was.* Christ certainly did not want the glory of so great a work to vanish away. But He did want it to be generally known before He acknowledged He was its author. He therefore withdrew for a little, to give the Jews a chance of judging the fact itself without respect of person. From this we gather that the healing cannot be ascribed to the man's faith, since even after he was healed he did not know his physician. And yet he carried his bed when he was told to and this seems to have been done under the guidance of faith. For myself, although I do not deny there was some secret movement of faith in him, yet I say that it is clear from the context that he had no solid doctrine or clear light to rely on.

14. *Afterwards Jesus findeth him.* These words show still more clearly that Christ did not hide Himself for a time that the memory of His kindness might perish, for He now appears in public of His own accord. It was just that He intended the work to be known first and then that He should be its avowed author. Now this passage contains a very useful lesson; for when Christ says, *Behold, thou art made whole,* He means that we wickedly abuse God's gifts unless we are stirred to gratitude. For Christ does not bring up against him what He had given him but only reminds him that he had been healed to remember the grace he had received and worship God his Saviour all his life. Therefore, as God teaches and spurs us on to repentence by stripes, so He

also invites us to it by His goodness and forbearance. And indeed the general purpose both of our redemption and of all God's gifts is to keep us entirely devoted to Him. But this cannot be done, unless the remembrance of past punishment is fixed in our minds, and unless he who has obtained pardon practises this meditation all his life.

This admonition also teaches us that all the ills we suffer should be imputed to our sins. The afflictions of men are not accidental but are so many stripes to chastise us. First, then, we must acknowledge that it is God's hand that strikes us and not imagine that our ills come from blind fortune. Next, we should ascribe this honour to God, that as He is indeed a good Father He has no pleasure in our sufferings and therefore does not treat us harshly unless He is displeased with our sins. When He commands him to *sin no more*, He is not demanding complete freedom from all sin, but only in comparison with his previous life. Christ tells him to come to his senses and not to remain like he was before.

Lest a worse thing. If God does not make progress with us by the stripes with which as a most kind father He gently chastises us, His tender and delicate children, He is forced to assume a new and so to say foreign character. He seizes the whip to tame our wildness, as He threatens in the Law (Lev. 26.14f, Deut. 28.15f, Ps. 32.9f), and indeed throughout the Scriptures passages of the same kind occur. Thus when we are incessantly pressed down by affliction upon affliction we ought to blame it on our stubbornness. Not only are we like restive horses and mules but even untamed wild beasts. So it is not surprising if God, as it were, pulverizes us with fiercer punishments, when moderate punishment is of no avail. It is right that those who will not suffer correction should be broken. In short, punishments are used to make us more careful in the future. If after the first and second strokes we keep up our obstinate hard-heartedness, He will strike us seven times more severely. If, when we have shown signs of repentance for a time, we return to our old nature He chastises our slothful and forgetful levity more sharply.

Again, it is worth noticing in the person of this man how kindly and gently the Lord bears with us. Let us suppose that he was approaching old age. In that case he must have been attacked by the disease in the prime of his life, perhaps even from his earliest infancy. Now think how grievous this punishment going on for years was to him. We certainly cannot accuse God of too much severity that He wore down this half dead man with such a long debility. And so when we are punished more lightly, let us learn that it is because the Lord in His infinite goodness tempers the full rigour of His punishments. Let us learn also that there is no punishment so savage and fierce that the Lord cannot intensify it whenever He pleases. Nor can we doubt that unhappy men often draw down upon themselves dreadful and incredible tortures by their wicked complainings when they say that their evils could not be worse. 'Are not these things hidden among my treasures?' says the Lord (Deut. 32.34). We should notice, moreover, how slow we are to benefit from God's chastisements. For if Christ's exhortation was not superfluous, it tells us that this man's soul was not yet fully cleansed from all sins. Indeed, the roots of vice are too deep in us to be torn out in a day or two, and the healing of diseases of the soul is far too difficult to be effected by short-term remedies.

15. *The man went away.* Nothing was further from his mind than to kindle ill feeling against Christ, and nothing was further from his expectation than their furious rage against Him. His intention therefore was good, for he wanted to give fair and due honour to his Physician. But the Jews show their venom, not only in accusing Christ of sabbath-breaking but in bursting out into extreme cruelty.

> *But Jesus answered them, My Father worketh even until now, and I work. For this cause therefore the Jews sought the more to kill him, because he not only brake the sabbath, but also called God his own Father, making himself equal with God. Jesus therefore answered and said unto them, Verily, verily, I say unto you, The Son can do nothing of himself, but what he seeth the Father doing: for what things soever he doeth, these also the Son doeth in like manner.* (17-19)

17. *My Father.* We must see what kind of defence Christ uses. He does not reply that the law on keeping the sabbath was temporary and ought now to be annulled, but rather denies that He has broken the Law, for He had done a divine work. It is true that Christ put an end to those shadowy ceremonies by His coming, as Paul teaches in Col. 2.16; but that has nothing to do with the present question. Men are commanded to rest only from their own works. Hence circumcision, which is God's work and not man's, is not against the sabbath.

What Christ insists on is that God's works do not disturb the holy rest commanded by the Law of Moses. And for this reason He excuses not only His own action but also the man's carrying his bed, which was a supplement, and as it were a part of the miracle, in that it was simply a proof of it. Moreover, if thanksgiving and the proclamation of His glory are reckoned among the works of God, it was no profanation of the Sabbath to bear witness to God's grace with feet and hands. But Christ is speaking chiefly of Himself, for the Jews were more hostile to Him. He says that the health He has restored to the sick man is a proof of His divine power. He declares that He is the Son of God and asserts that He acts in the same way as His Father.

I am not now discussing the use of the sabbath and the reasons why it was commanded. Enough for the present passage that the observance of the Sabbath, so far from interrupting or hindering the course of God's works, actually gives place to them alone. For why does the Law tell men to cease from their own works, but to keep all their senses empty and free for considering the works of God? Consequently, he who does not on the sabbath allow God's works a free sovereignty, wickedly subverts it and interprets it falsely.

If it be objected that God's example is set before men for them to rest on the seventh day, the answer is easy. Men are not conformed to God in that He kept a rest day, but from ceasing from the confused actions of this world and aspiring to the heavenly rest. Therefore the sabbath of God is not inactivity but substantial perfection, which carries with it a calm state of peace. And what Moses said is not inconsistent with this, that God finished His works (Gen. 2.2); for he means that when He had perfected the construction of the world, He hallowed that day, that men might spend it in meditating on His works. Yet He did not cease to uphold with His power the world which He had made, to govern it by His wisdom, to cherish it with His goodness and to regulate all things in heaven and earth by His will. The creating of the world was completed in six days, therefore, but its government is continual and God is incessantly at work guarding and preserving its order; just as Paul teaches that in Him we live and move and are (Acts 17.28). And David says that all things stand so long as God's Spirit animates them and fail so soon as they are deprived of His power (Ps. 104.29). Nor is it only by a general providence that the Lord maintains the nature He has created, for He orders and regulates every part of it. More especially, by His protection He keeps and guards believers, whom He has taken under His care and protection.

And I work. Christ now leaves His defence of this case and explains the purpose and use of the miracle as a means whereby He might be known as the Son of God. For in all His deeds and words His purpose was to show that He was the author of salvation. What He claims for Himself now pertains to His divinity—in the words of the apostle, 'he upholds all things by his powerful will' (Heb. 1.3). And the reason why He declares He is God is that He, manifested in the flesh, might execute the office of the Christ. Thus He affirms that He came from heaven, chiefly because He wants it known why He came down to earth.

18. *For this cause therefore.* His defence irritated rather than calmed their fury. He was not unaware of the malignity of their wickedness and iron obstinacy, but His first aim was to help those few of His own who were there and after that to bring the Jews' incurable malice out

into the open. By His example He taught us never to yield to the fury
of the wicked but to try to defend the truth of God when need arises,
though the whole world should contradict us and shout us down. And
there is no reason why the servants of Christ should take it amiss that
they do not benefit all men as they would wish, for even Christ Himself did not succeed in this. And there is nothing to be surprised at if
Satan rages the more violently in His members and instruments, the
more God reveals His glory.

When in the first clause the Evangelist says that they were hostile to
Christ because He had broken the sabbath, he is speaking from their
point of view. For I have already shown that this was not the case.
The chief cause of their anger was that He called God His Father. And
Christ certainly wanted it to be understood that God was His Father
in a particular sense, that He might be distinguished from the ordinary
rank of other men. He made Himself equal with God when He
ascribed continual working to Himself. And Christ not only does not
deny this but confirms it the more clearly. This refutes the madness
of the Arians, who confessed that Christ is God in such a way that they
did not regard Him as equal to the Father, as if inequality could exist
in the one and simple essence of God.

19. *Jesus therefore answered.* We see what I have said, that Christ, so
far from clearing Himself of the Jews' accusation, misrepresentation
though it was, maintained more openly that it was true. First He
insisted that the work which the Jews cavilled at was divine, to make
them understand that they would have to fight against God Himself if
they persisted in condemning what must necessarily be ascribed to
Him. In the old days this passage was thrashed out in various ways
between the orthodox fathers and the Arians. Arius inferred from it
that the Son is inferior to the Father, in that He can do nothing of
Himself. The fathers objected that in these words there is denoted only
a distinction of person, to make it known that Christ is from the
Father and yet that He is not deprived of intrinsic power of action. But
both sides were wrong. For this discourse is not concerned with the
naked divinity of Christ, and the statements we are shortly to hear do
not simply and of themselves refer to the eternal Word of God at all,
but accord only with the Son of God as He was manifested in the
flesh. Therefore let us keep our eyes on Christ as He was sent into the
world to be our Redeemer. The Jews saw nothing higher than human
nature in Him. And so He insists that it was not His humanity which
healed the sick man but His divine power hidden under His visible
flesh. The issue revolved around this: They fixed on the sight of the
flesh and despised Christ; and so He commands them to rise higher
and look at God. The whole discourse turns on the contrast that those

who think they are dealing with a mortal man go far astray in accusing
Christ of truly divine works. This is why He affirms so strongly that
in this work He differs nothing from His Father.

*For the Father loveth the Son, and sheweth him all things that himself
doeth: and greater works than these will he shew him, that ye may marvel.
For as the Father raiseth the dead and quickeneth them, even so the Son
also quickeneth whom he will. For neither doth the Father judge any
man, but he hath given all judgement unto the Son; that all may honour
the Son, even as they honour the Father. He that honoureth not the Son
honoureth not the Father which sent him. Verily, verily, I say unto
you, He that heareth my word, and believeth in him that sent me, hath
eternal life, and cometh not into judgement, but hath passed out of death
into life. (20-24)*

20. *For the Father loveth the Son.* Everyone can see how harsh and
forced the exposition of the old writers is here. They say that God
loves Himself in the Son. But it accords beautifully with Christ
clothed in flesh that He is loved by the Father. Nay, we know that it
is by this pre-eminent title that He is distinguished from both angels
and men: 'This is my beloved Son' (Matt. 3.17). And we know that
Christ was chosen that the whole love of God might dwell in Him, so
as to flow from Him to us as from a full fountain. Christ is loved by
the Father in that He is the Head of the Church. He shows that this
love is the cause of the Father's doing all things by His hand, for when
He says that 'He sheweth to Him' the word must be taken as implying
communication, as if He had said, 'As the Father has poured out His
mind on Me, so also His power, that in my works the divine glory
may shine; yea, so that men cannot seek anything divine which they
may not find in Me.' And indeed, out of Christ the power of God is
sought in vain.

Greater works than these will he shew him. By these words He means
that the miracle which He had performed in healing the man was not
the greatest of the works commanded Him by the Father. For in it
He had given only a faint taste of that grace of which He is properly
both minister and author—i.e. of restoring life to the world.

When He goes on, *that ye may marvel,* He indirectly accuses them of
ingratitude in despising such a shining demonstration of God's power,
as if He were saying, 'Though you are dull and stupid, what God shall
perform by me later on will ravish you with admiration, however
reluctant.' Yet this does not seem to have been fulfilled, for we know
that 'seeing they saw not', as Isaiah says of the reprobate being blind to
God's light (Isa. 6.9). I reply, Christ was not speaking here about their

attitude, but only recorded how magnificently He would soon after prove that He was the Son of God.

21. *For as the Father.* Here He summarizes the nature of the office given Him by the Father. For though He seems to single out one aspect, this is in fact a general doctrine, in which He declares that He is the Author of life. But life contains righteousness and all the gifts of the Holy Spirit and all the parts of our salvation. And indeed this miracle had to be such a special proof of Christ's power as to yield this general fruit—that is, to open a door to the Gospel. Moreover, we must note the way in which Christ bestows life on us. Because He found us all dead, it was necessary to begin with the resurrection. Yet it is not superfluous that He joins the two words, for it would not have been sufficient for us to be rescued from death without Christ fully and substantially restoring life to us. Again, He does not make this life common to all, but says that He gives life to whom He will. By which He means that He specially honours only certain men, the elect, with this grace.

22. *For neither doth the Father.* He now expresses more clearly the general truth that the Father governs the world in the person of the Son and exercises His dominion by His hand. The Evangelist takes the word 'judgment' for dominion and power, according to the Hebrew idiom. We can now grasp the tenor of this: the Kingdom was delivered to the Son by the Father, that He might govern heaven and earth according to His will. But it might seem very absurd that the Father should surrender His right to govern, and be idle in heaven like a private person. The answer is easy. This is said both in regard to God and to men. No change took place in the Father when He appointed Christ supreme King and Lord of heaven and earth, for He Himself is in the Son and works in Him. But since all our senses fail as soon as we wish to rise to God, Christ is set before our eyes as the visible image of the invisible God. There is no reason therefore why we should vainly toil, probing into the secrets of heaven, when God provides for our weakness by showing Himself near in the person of Christ. Rather, since all power is placed in Christ, let us learn to look to Him alone whenever we are concerned with the government of the world or our own state, or the heavenly protection of our salvation. For in His face God the Father, otherwise hidden far away, appears to us, so that the naked majesty of God shall not engulf us with its infinite brightness.

23. *That all men may honour.* This clause sufficiently confirms what I mentioned above—that God does not rule in the person of Christ in such a way that He Himself reposes in heaven like a lazy king, but in that He proclaims His power and shows Himself to be present in

Christ. For what else do the words, 'that all men may honour the Son', mean, except that the Father wants to be known and worshipped in the Son? Therefore, it is for us to seek God the Father in Christ, to behold His power in Him and to worship Him in Him. For as it goes on to say at once, *he that honoureth not the Son* deprives God of His proper honour. All admit that we should worship God, and this sentiment, naturally inborn in us, has deep roots in our hearts, so that none dares absolutely to deny honour to God. Yet men's minds fade away in seeking God out of the way. Hence so many pretended deities; hence so much perverse worship. Therefore we shall not find the true God save in Christ, nor shall we worship Him aright save by 'kissing the Son' as David puts it (Ps. 2.12); for as John elsewhere declares, 'He that has not the Son has not the Father' (I John 2.23).

Turks and Jews certainly adorn the god they worship with beautiful and fine titles. But we must hold that the name of God is nothing but an empty imagination when it is separated from Christ. Therefore, whoever wants to have his worship approved by the true God, let him not turn aside from Christ. Nor was the state of the fathers under the Law any different; for though they beheld Christ obscurely under shadows, God never revealed Himself without Christ. But now since Christ has been manifested in the flesh and appointed King over us, the whole world must bow to Him in order to obey God. For the Father has commanded Him to sit at His right hand, and therefore he who imagines God without Christ takes away the half of Him.

24. *He that heareth my word.* This describes the way and method by which He is to be honoured, lest any should think it consists merely in some external rite and trifling ceremonies. For the teaching of the Gospel is like Christ's sceptre with which He governs believers, whom the Father has submitted unto Him. And this definition is particularly noteworthy. Nothing is commoner than a false profession of Christianity. Even the Papists, who are most hostile enemies to Christ, boast that they are His most presumptuously. But here Christ is claiming from us no other honour than that we obey His Gospel. Whence it follows that all the honour that hypocrites give Christ is but the traitor's kiss of Judas, by which he betrayed his Lord. Though they proclaim Him King a hundred times, they despoil Him of His Kingdom and all power by not having faith in the Gospel.

He also commends the fruit of obedience when He says *hath eternal life*—so that we may be more willing to practise it. For who would be so hardened as not to submit willingly to Christ when the reward of eternal life is offered him? And yet we see how few are won by such great goodness. It is our depravity that we would rather perish voluntarily than surrender in obedience to the Son of God and be saved by His goodness. Christ here includes both the rule of godly and sincere worship which He demands of us and the way by which He restores us to life. For it would not be enough to hold what He had taught before—that He came to raise the dead—without also knowing how He restores us to life. Now He declares that life is obtained by hearing His teaching. By *hearing* He means faith, as He soon says. But faith is situated, not in the ears, but in the heart. The source of faith's great power we have pointed out elsewhere. We must always consider what the Gospel offers us. For it is not surprising that he who receives Christ with all His merits is reconciled to God and acquitted from the condemnation of death, and that he who has been given the Holy Spirit is clothed with heavenly righteousness that he may walk in newness of life (Rom. 6.4).

The subjoined clause *believeth him that sent him* serves to establish the authority of the Gospel. Christ declares that it proceeded from God and was not a human fabrication. Just as He affirms elsewhere that what He says is not from Himself but was commanded Him by the Father (14.10).

And cometh not into judgement. There is an implied contrast here between the guilt to which we are all naturally liable and the free acquittal we have through Christ. For if condemnation did not await all, what is the point of excepting those who believe in Christ? The meaning therefore is that we are out of death's danger because we are acquitted through the benefit of Christ. Therefore, although Christ sanctifies and regenerates us by His Spirit unto newness of life, yet what is here especially mentioned is the free forgiveness of sins, in which alone consists men's happiness. For a man begins to live when He has God gracious to him. And how should God love us without pardoning our sins?

Hath passed. Some Latin versions have this in the future, 'will pass'. But this has arisen from someone's ignorance and thoughtlessness in not grasping the Evangelist's meaning and taking more liberty than he should have done. For there is no ambiguity at all in the Greek word. There is nothing wrong in saying that the transition from death has already taken place, for the incorruptible seed of life is in the children of God from the time they are called, by hope they already sit in the heavenly glory with Christ and they have the Kingdom of God already established within them (Luke 17.21; Col. 3.3). For the fact that their life is hidden does not stop them possessing it by faith; and that they are besieged on every side by death does not prevent them having peace, since they know that they are safe enough through Christ's protection. Yet let us remember that believers are now in life in such a way that they always bear about with them the substance of death. The Spirit who dwells in them, however, is life, and He will at last destroy the remnants of death. Paul's words are true—the last enemy that shall be destroyed is death (I Cor. 15.26). And indeed, this passage does not refer to the complete destruction of death or to the substantial revelation of life, But though life has only made a start in us, Christ says that believers are so sure to obtain it that they must not fear death—and this is not surprising, for they are incorporated in Him who is the inexhaustible fount of life.

> *Verily, verily, I say unto you, the hour cometh, and now is, when the dead shall hear the voice of the Son of God; and they that hear shall live. For as the Father hath life in himself, even so gave he to the Son also to have life in himself: and he gave him authority to execute judgement, because he is the Son of man. Marvel not at this: for the hour cometh in which all that are in the tombs shall hear his voice, and they shall come forth; they that have done good unto the resurrection of life; and they that have done ill, unto the resurrection of judgement.* (25-29)

25. *Verily, verily.* We can see from the Evangelist's showing the Son of God solemnly swearing so often in reference to our salvation, first, how eager is His care for us, and secondly, how important it is that the faith of the Gospel should be thoroughly and deeply fixed and confirmed. What is related here certainly seems incredible when it relates the effect of the faith that Christ is speaking of. He therefore confirms by an oath that the voice of His Gospel is so quickening that it is powerful to raise the dead. It makes sense to take Him as speaking of spiritual death, and those who refer it to Lazarus and the widow's son at Nain and the like are refuted by the context itself. Christ first tells us that we are all dead before He quickens us. Hence it is clear what man's whole nature can contribute to salvation. The Papists, when they want to set up their freewill, compare it to the Samaritan whom the robbers had left half dead on the road. As if it were right to obscure a clear statement, by which Christ plainly adjudges us to death, by the smoke-screen of an allegory! And indeed, because we have from the fall of the first man been alienated from God by sin, all who do not acknowledge that they are under the threat of eternal destruction are simply deceiving themselves with empty flatteries.

I readily allow that a certain remnant of life remains in man's soul, for understanding and judgment and will and all the senses are so many parts of life. But since there is no part which aspires to the heavenly life, it is not surprising if the whole man is accounted dead so far as the Kingdom of God is concerned. Paul explains this death more fully in Eph. 2.1 and 4.17 when he says that we are divorced from the pure and sound reason of the understanding, that we are enemies to God and opposed to His righteousness in the complete attitude of our hearts, that we wander blindly in darkness and are given up to wicked lusts. If such a corrupted nature has no power to desire righteousness, it follows that the life of God is extinguished in us. So the grace of Christ is a true resurrection from the dead.

Moreover, this grace is conferred on us by the Gospel. Not that the external voice has such an energy, for it mostly sounds in the ear in vain; but because Christ inwardly addresses our hearts by His Spirit so that by faith we receive the life which is offered us. He is not here concerned with all the dead indiscriminately, but means only the elect, whose ears God pierces and opens so that they may catch the voice of His Son which restores them to life. By His words Christ expressly commends to us this twofold grace when He says, *The dead shall hear the voice of the Son of God; and they that hear shall live.* For it is no less contrary to nature that the dead should hear than that they should be brought back to the life they had left. Therefore both come from the secret power of God.

When He says *the hour cometh, and now is,* He is speaking of it as a thing hitherto rare. And indeed, the publication of the Gospel was a new and sudden resurrection of the world. But if any ask, Did not the Word of God always give life to men? the reply is easy. When the preaching of the Law and Prophets was addressed to God's people, it had the purpose of preserving the children of God in life rather than of bringing them back from death. It was otherwise with the Gospel, by which peoples who were formerly foreigners to God's Kingdom and separated from God and deprived of all hope of salvation, were summoned to the fellowship of life.

26. *For as the Father hath life.* He shows the source of the efficacy of His voice—that He is the fountain of life and by His voice pours it forth on men. For life would not flow to us from His mouth unless its cause and source were in Himself. For God is said to have life in Himself, not only because He alone lives by His own inherent power, but because He contains the fulness of life in Himself and quickens all things. And this is peculiar to God; as it is said, 'With thee is the fountain of life' (Ps. 36.9). But because God's majesty, which is far removed from us, would be like a secret and hidden spring, He has revealed Himself in Christ. And so we have an open fountain at hand to draw from. The words mean that God did not want to have life hidden and as it were buried within Himself, and therefore He transfused it into His Son that it might flow to us. Hence we conclude that this title is to be applied properly to Christ, inasmuch as He was manifested in the flesh.

27. *And he gave him authority.* He repeats that the Father has given

Him dominion to have complete power over everything in heaven and earth. The word ἐξουσία here means 'honour'. And *judgment* is taken for rule and government—as if He were saying that the Father had appointed the Son as the King who should govern the world and exercise the Father's own authority.

Because he is the Son of man. This reason, immediately added, is particularly noteworthy, for it means that He comes to men adorned with such a full authority that He may communicate to them what He receives from the Father. Some think that this passage says nothing different from what Paul declares in Phil. 2.7, that Christ, when He was in the form of God, emptied Himself by taking the form of a servant, and humbled Himself even to the death of the cross. And therefore the Father exalted Him and gave Him a name above every name, that every knee should bow before Him, etc. But I would make it more extensive: that Christ, inasmuch as He is man, was appointed by the Father to be the Author of life, that we should not have to seek it afar off. For Christ did not receive it for Himself, as if He needed it, but to enrich us with His wealth. To summarize: What had been hidden in God is revealed in Christ the man, and life, formerly inaccessible, is now close at hand. Some tear this argument from its context and join it to the following clause; but this is forced and against Christ's meaning.

28. *Marvel not at this,* His argument does not seem at all apposite, when He takes the last resurrection as confirmation of what He had said. For it is no greater to raise up bodies than souls. I reply that His comparison between the greater and the less relates not to the real state of things but to what men think of it. For they are carnal and admire nothing but what is outward and visible. Hence it happens that they carelessly pass over the resurrection of the soul, but the resurrection of the body wins their greater admiration. Another effect of this our gross stupidity is that the things perceived by the eyes are far more powerful in producing faith than those which can be conceived by faith alone. Since He is referring to the last day He does not again add the limitation *and now is,* but simply says that the time will come one day.

Now we meet with another objection. Although believers look for the resurrection of their bodies, they cannot rely on this knowledge to conclude that, because bodies will one day rise from their graves, souls are now delivered from death. And among the ungodly what is more ridiculous than to use a common phrase to prove something more unknown? I reply, Christ here proclaims His power over the reprobate so as to bear witness that the full restoration of all things is committed to Him by the Father—as if He were saying, 'What I now say

I have started, I will one day complete before your eyes.' And indeed when, by the voice of His Gospel, Christ now quickens souls buried in perdition it is a sort of prelude of the last resurrection. Moreover, since this embraces the whole human race He goes on to distinguish between the elect and the reprobate. This distinction shows that the reprobate, just as they are now summoned to judgment by the voice of Christ, will by the same voice also be dragged and presented at His judgment seat.

But why does He mention only those who are in their graves, as if others would not be partakers of the resurrection, whether they perished in shipwreck or were devoured by wild beasts or were reduced to ashes? But since the dead are usually buried, He intends by synecdoche all who are already dead. It is more emphatic than if He had merely said 'the dead'. For those whom death has already deprived of the spirit and light, the grave, so to say, removes from the world.

The voice of the Son means the sound of the trumpet which will sound forth by the command and power of Christ (Matt. 24.31, I Cor. 15.52, I Thess. 4.16). For although an angel will be the herald or deputy, that does not prevent what is done by the authority of the Judge and, as it were, in His own person, being ascribed to Himself.

29. *They that have done good.* He marks out believers by their good works, just as elsewhere He says that a tree is known by its fruit (Matt. 7.16). He praises their good works, which began when they were called. The thief to whom Christ on the cross promised life and who had been given up to crime all his life, desires to do good at his last breath. And as he is born again a new man, and from the slave of sin begins to be the servant of righteousness, the whole course of his past life is not taken into account before God. Moreover, the sins themselves of which believers are daily guilty and damnable are not imputed to them. For without pardon no man ever lived who can be regarded as living well. Nor is there one work that will be reckoned entirely good unless God pardons its sinfulness, since all are imperfect and corrupted. Therefore those are here called doers of good works whom Paul calls studious or zealous of them (Titus 2.14). But this estimate depends on the Fatherly kindness of God, who freely approves what deserved to be rejected.

The Papists' inference from these passages, that eternal life repays the merits of works, may be refuted without any difficulty. For Christ is not here treating of the cause of salvation, but only distinguishing the elect from the reprobate by their own mark. And this He does to invite and exhort His own people to holiness and innocence. And indeed we do not deny that the faith which justifies us is joined to a

133

desire to live well and righteously. Only, we teach that our confidence can be placed nowhere but in the mercy of God alone.

I can of myself do nothing: as I hear, I judge: and my judgement is righteous; because I seek not mine own will, but the will of my Father that sent me. If I bear witness of myself, my witness is not true. It is another that beareth witness of me; and I know that the witness which he witnesseth of me is true. (30-31)

30. *I can of myself do nothing.* It would be superfluous to reason subtly here whether or not the Son of God can do anything of Himself so far as His eternal divinity is concerned; for He did not want to busy us with such sophistries. Consequently, there was no reason why the old writers should have worried so anxiously about refuting the misrepresentations of Arius. That worthless fellow gave out that the Son is not equal to the Father, because He can do nothing of Himself. The holy men reply that the Son justly ascribes all that He has received to the Father, from whom He takes His beginning in respect of person. But first, Christ is not here speaking of His naked divinity, but teaches us that as He is clothed with our flesh He is not to be judged from the outward appearance, for He possesses something higher than man. Again, we ought to consider with whom He is dealing. He had to refute the Jews, who were trying to make a contrast between Him and God. He therefore affirms that He does nothing humanly, since He has as His Guide and Director the God who dwells in Him. We must always remember that whenever Christ speaks about Himself He claims only what is proper to man; for He has an eye to the Jews, who wickedly said that He was merely one of the common rank of men. For the same reason He ascribes to the Father whatever is higher than man.

Judging refers strictly to His teaching; but He intends it to cover the whole of His administration—as if He were saying that He has the Father behind Him in everything, that the Father's will is His rule, and that therefore He will uphold Him.

And my judgement is righteous. He concludes that His deeds and words stand beyond the risk of blame, because He does not allow Himself to undertake anything but by the Father's direction and command. For it must be regarded as beyond all controversy that whatever comes from God is right. The first principle of godliness for us ought to be the modesty of feeling such reverence for the Word and works of God that the name of God alone shall suffice to prove their righteousness and rectitude. But how few there are who will acknowledge willingly that God is just! I confess indeed that God demonstrates His righteousness to us by experience. But to restrict it to the perception of our flesh, so that we merely think of it what our own mind suggests, is most wicked impiety. Let it therefore be a certain and undoubted consequence that whatever is from God is right and true, and that it is impossible for God not to be true in all His words, just and right in all His actions. We are also reminded that the only rule for right conduct is to undertake nothing but by God's direction and oversight. And if after this the whole world should rise against us, let this invincible defence be sufficient, that he who follows God does not go astray.

Because I seek not mine own will. He is not at all making His own will and His Father's clash, as if they were contraries, but only refutes what they falsely imagined—that He was motivated by human presumption rather than ruled by the authority of God. He affirms therefore that He has no disposition peculiar to Himself and separate from the Father's command.

31. *If I bear witness.* He is not detracting from the authority of His witness, which elsewhere He strongly asserts, but is making a concession. For since Christ was most abundantly armed in another way, He concedes that they should not believe Him. 'If,' He says, 'my witness about myself is suspected by you in the ordinary way of men, let it go for nothing.' We know what any man says about himself is not taken as true and authentic, even though in other respects he speaks the truth, for no man is a fit witness in his own cause. And although it would be unjust to reduce the Son of God to this level, He prefers to give up His right, so that He may convince His enemies by God's authority.

Ye have sent unto John, and he hath borne witness unto the truth. But I receive not witness from man: howbeit I say these things that ye may be saved. He was a burning and a shining lamp: and ye were willing to rejoice for a season in his light. But I have greater witness than that of John: for the works which the Father hath given me to accomplish, the very works that I do, bear witness of me, that the Father hath sent me. (33-36)

33. *Ye have sent unto John.* Before putting forward the witness of God, He presses them with John's reply, from which they could not sincerely withhold their belief. For what was the point of sending to him unless they were ready to accept what he said? For they send to him as a prophet of God, and so pretend that his word will be like an oracle to them. Now, though this implies another concession, Christ openly accuses them that only their malice stops them believing. And therefore we see that the fact that they sent to John and, as if they really wanted to learn, inquired of him who the Messiah was, and yet paid no heed to his reply, is very much to the point.

34. *I receive not witness from man.* Yet God did not choose John to be a witness to Him for nothing and Christ Himself says elsewhere that the disciples will be His witnesses (Acts 1.8). I reply that Christ uses John's testimony, not because He needs it, but inasmuch as it is good for us to receive confirmation from it. Men accept testimony from one another because they cannot do without such help. It is different with God and Christ. For if philosophers assert that virtue needs no outside aid, what is there in man to strengthen the truth of God? And Christ at once adds that He puts forward John's witness for their sake; by which He means that it is not so much from a regard for Himself as for men's good that He raises up the heralds of His Gospel, by whom He witnesses to us concerning His will. In this there shines His wonderful goodness, that He accommodates all things to our salvation. It is therefore for us on our side to endeavour that His care in saving us may not be in vain.

35. *He was a burning and a shining lamp.* By calling John a burning lamp, He shows up their ingratitude. For it follows that they are blind only of their own will, since the lamp of God burned before their eyes. The words therefore mean, 'God did not want you to go astray, for He appointed John as a lamp to guide you with His brightness. There-fore it is a voluntary error that you do not acknowledge Me to be the Son of God.' Another reproach follows, that not only did they neglect the light offered to them by shutting their eyes, but they deliberately misused it to oppress Christ. That they were ready to applaud John above his rightful rank arose from a malicious and treacherous plan to deny a place to the Son of God.

Christ gracefully compares this wicked abuse of heavenly light to wantonness; as if the head of the household were to light a lamp for his servants at night for them to perform the duties he had ordered, but they use it instead for revelry and every kind of wantonness. Moreover, in these words Christ both accuses the Jews, and also warns all of us in general, not to misuse the faithful teachers whom God ordains to guide us in the true paths, by wandering hither and thither. The experience of all ages shows how useful this warning is. God under-takes to direct men through the whole course of their lives to the final goal and sends His prophets to be their guides. Yet such is men's wildness that they would rather dance saucily around in one place than go walking forward. So, inconstant and frivolous are they, that they despise and reject His continual guidance and are carried away by their sudden passions.

Therefore He says, *for a season,* or, for an hour. By this term He reproves their folly in thinking that transient and short-lived wicked-ness could extinguish God's eternal light. Thus today the Papists put to the opposite use those godly teachers whom God has given to His Church as burning lamps; as if they intended to dazzle their eyes by looking at the light. And not only do they misuse the lamps to extinguish the light of God, but also they often rejoice in the darkness, as when they glorify the absurd fictions of their noisy advocates against the pure doctrine of the Gospel. What Christ here declares of John, Paul says is common to all believers. They have the Word of life and ought to shine like lights in the world (Phil. 2.15). But Christ tells us that it belongs properly to the apostles and ministers of the Gospel to be the leading guides for the rest. For though we all dwell blindly in darkness, God shines upon us with the light of His Word. But here He specially adorns John with his title, because by his ministry God shone much more brightly upon His Church.

36. *I have greater witness.* After He has shown that in John the Jews had wickedly corrupted the gift of God, He now repeats for the second time what He had said, that He has no need of man's testimony, as if He were not self-sufficient. Yet, seeing that they despised Him, He recalled them to His Father, as was His wont.

For the works which the Father hath given me. He sets forward two things which proved Him to be the Son of God. 'The Father,' He says, 'bears witness by miracles that I am His Son. Even before I came into the world He bore abundant witness to Me in the Holy Scriptures.' Let us always remember His object. He wants to be acknowledged as the Messiah promised by God, so that He may be heard. Hence He insists that He is now revealed to be such as the Scripture proclaims. It may be asked whether miracles have enough force to prove this, since similar miracles had been already performed by the prophets. I reply, those signs that God did by the hand of the prophets only answered the purpose they were intended for—namely, to show that they were the ministers of God who would not gain authority in any other way. But He wished to exalt His Son more highly. And this purpose of God should be regarded as the design in miracles. Therefore, if they had not been filled with malice and voluntarily shut their eyes, Christ could easily have made plain to them who and what He was by virtue of His miracles.

And the Father which sent me, he hath borne witness of me. Ye have neither heard his voice at any time, nor seen his form. And ye have not his word abiding in you: for whom he sent, him ye believe not. Search the Scriptures; because ye think that in them ye have eternal life; and these are they which bear witness of me; and ye will not come to me that ye might have life. (37-40)

37. *And the Father which sent me.* It is wrong to restrict this to the

voice which was heard at His Baptism; for He says, using the past tense, that the Father bore witness to Him to show that He did not come forward as one unknown, but the Father had long ago marked Him out in the Law and the Prophets, so that He might bring His distinguishing marks with Him and be recognized from them. So I interpret it as God bearing witness of His Son whenever He had held out to the ancient people the hope of salvation or promised the full restoration of the kingdom of Israel. Thus the Jews should have had an idea of Christ from the prophets before He was manifested in the flesh. By despising and consequently rejecting Him when He is with them, they show plainly that they have no taste for the Law; and Christ reproaches them for this. They boasted their knowledge of the Law as if they had been brought up in the bosom of God.

Ye have neither heard his voice. After He complains that He is not accepted, Christ attacks their blindness more sharply. 'They had never heard God's voice' and 'had never seen His form' are metaphorical expressions to teach them briefly that they are utterly estranged from the knowledge of God. Just as men are known by their appearance and speech, so God utters His voice to us by the voice of the prophets, and in the Sacraments puts on, as it were, a visible form, from which He can be known according to our small capacity. But he who does not recognize God in His lively image shows plainly by this very fact that the only deity he worships is one he has invented. This is why Paul says that they had a veil placed before their eyes, that they might not perceive the glory of God in the face of Christ (II Cor. 3.15).

38. *And ye have not his word.* We really profit when the Word of God takes root in us, so that it is fixed in our hearts and has a sure hold there. Christ says that heavenly doctrine has no place among the Jews because they do not receive the Son of God whom it everywhere proclaims, and His reproach is just. For God did not speak by Moses and the Prophets for nothing. But Moses' only intention was to call all men straight to Christ. Whence it is plain that those who repudiate Christ are not Moses' disciples. Besides, how can he have the Word of life abiding in him who drives away life itself? How can he keep the teaching of the Law who destroys the soul of the Law, so far as in him lies? Without Christ the Law is empty and insubstantial. Therefore the intimacy of a man's knowledge of Christ is the measure of his progress in the Word of God.

39. *Search the Scriptures.* Christ's saying that He has the Father as His witness in heaven refers, as we have said, to Moses and the Prophets. A clearer explanation follows, when He says that the witness stands in the Scriptures. But He again reproves their foolish boasting, because they professed they had life in the Scriptures but only seized on the

dead letter. He does not actually blame them for seeking life in the Scriptures, for they were ordained to that end and use. But the Jews thought that the Scriptures were in themselves life-giving, when they were in fact strangers to its real meaning and even quenched the light of life contained in them. For how can the Law bestow life without Christ, who alone quickens it?

Again, we are taught in this passage that the knowledge of Christ must be sought from the Scriptures. Those who imagine what they like about Christ will ultimately have nothing but a shadowy ghost in His place. First then, we must hold that Christ cannot be properly known from anywhere but the Scriptures. And if that is so, it follows that the Scriptures should be read with the aim of finding Christ in them. Whoever turns aside from this object, even though he wears himself out all his life in learning, will never reach the knowledge of the truth. For how can we be wise apart from the Wisdom of God? Moreover, as we are commanded to seek Christ in the Scriptures, so He declares in this passage that our work will not be fruitless, for there the Father bears witness to His Son in such a way that He will manifest Him to us beyond all doubt. But what hinders most men is that they look at them only carelessly and as it were in passing. But it needed the utmost application, and so Christ commanded them to search diligently for this hidden treasure. Accordingly, the abhorrence for Christ which the Jews feel, who have the Law constantly in their hands, must be imputed to their laziness. For the brightness of God's glory shines clearly in Moses, but they want to have a veil to obscure that brightness. By *the Scriptures*, of course, is here meant the Old Testament. For Christ did not first begin to be manifested in the Gospel; but the one to whom the Law and the Prophets bore witness was openly revealed in the Gospel.

40. *And ye will not.* Again He reproaches them that nothing but malice prevents them taking the life offered in the Scriptures. For when He says that they will not, He is imputing the cause of their ignorance and blindness to depravity and obstinacy. And indeed, since He offered Himself so kindly to them, they must have been wilfully blind. When they deliberately fled from the light and even wished to cover the sun with the darkness of their unbelief, Christ justly reproves them more severely.

I receive not glory from men. But I know you, that ye have not the love of God in yourselves. I am come in my Father's name, and ye receive me not: if another shall come in his own name, him will ye receive. How can ye believe, which receive glory one of another, and the glory that cometh from God alone ye seek not? Think not that I will accuse you

*to the Father: there is one that accuseth you, even Moses, on whom ye
have set your hope. For if ye believed Moses, ye would believe me; for
he wrote of me. But if ye believe not his writings, how shall ye believe
my words? (41-47)*

41. *Glory from men.* He goes on with His reproof. But lest He
should be suspected of pleading His own case, He forestalls them by
saying that the glory of men means nothing to Him, and that He is
neither worried nor sorry for Himself when He is despised. Indeed,
He is too great to depend on men's opinions, for the malignity of the
whole world can detract nothing from Him nor diminish one jot of
His greatness. But He is insistent to refute their calumny and exalts
Himself above men. After this, He attacks them freely and charges
them with contempt and hatred of God. And though we are far below
Christ in honour, we ought boldly to despise men's adverse opinions.
We should certainly take great care that contempt does not move us
to anger, and learn to get angry only when due honour is not paid to
God. Let this holy jealousy burn and torture us whenever we see the
world so ungrateful as to reject God.

42. *That ye have not the love of God.* The love of God is here put for
all godly dispositions. For none can love God without honouring and
submitting entirely to Him. And on the other hand, where the love
of God does not reign, there can be no desire to obey Him. This is
why Moses puts as the ἀνακεφαλαίωσις or recapitulation of the Law,
'thou shalt love God with all thy heart', etc.

43. *I am come in my Father's name.* Christ proves that the Jews neither
love nor revere God, by the argument that they receive false prophets
enthusiastically but refuse to submit to God. For He takes it as axio-
matic that it is a sign of a depraved and ungodly mind when men
willingly subscribe to lies and disregard the truth. If it is objected that
this usually comes from ignorance rather than malice, the reply is easy;
for none is subject to the wiles of Satan except in so far as he prefers
falsehood to the truth from some perverted disposition. How is it that
we are deaf when God speaks, whereas Satan finds us ready and willing,
save because we are turned from righteousness and of our own accord
desire iniquity. Yet we must note that Christ is speaking particularly
of those whom God had specially enlightened, even as He honoured
the Jews with the privilege of being taught by His Law, that they
might keep to the true way of salvation. It is certain that such people
listen to false teachers only because they want to be deceived. And so
Moses says that when false prophets arise, the people are being tested
and tried as to whether they love their God (Deut. 13.3). There seems,
indeed, in many to be an innocent simplicity. But their eyes are blinded

by the hypocrisy lurking in their minds. For it is certain that God never shuts the door against those who knock, never disappoints those who sincerely seek Him. And therefore Paul justly ascribes it to God's vengeance when the power to deceive is granted to Satan, 'that they who have rejected the truth, and had pleasure in unrighteousness, should believe a lie', and says that 'they perish who received not the love of the truth, that they might be saved' (II Thess. 2.9ff). In this way is uncovered the hypocrisy of many, who are given up to the impostures and ungodly superstitions of the Pope and burn with poisonous rage against the Gospel. For if their minds were disposed to the fear of God, that fear would also produce obedience.

In my Father's name. False prophets certainly boast of this title. In our own day the Pope shoots off his mouth that he is the vicar of Christ. And under the same disguise Satan has deceived many unhappy men from the very beginning. But here Christ points to the reality and not a pretence. For He testifies that He is come in the Father's name, both because the Father had sent Him and also because He is faithfully executing His commission. Moreover, by this mark He distinguishes lawful teachers of the Church from the spurious and frauds. Hence this passage teaches us to reject boldly all who exalt themselves and usurp for themselves authority over souls. For he who wants to be reckoned God's servant must have nothing apart from Him. But if all the teaching of the Pope is examined, even the blind can see that he has come in his own name.

44. *How can ye believe?* It might seem harsh that those who from childhood had been trained and at home in the Law and the Prophets should be condemned of such gross ignorance and declared enemies of the truth. And because it might even seem incredible, Christ shows what hinders them from believing—ambition has deprived them of a sound mind. He is really speaking to the priests and scribes, who could not submit to God, for they were so swollen with pride. This is a remarkable passage, teaching that the door of faith is shut against all whose minds are filled with a vain desire for earthly glory. For he who wants to be something in the world cannot help becoming wandering and transient, so that he will not move towards God. A man is only prepared to obey the heavenly teaching when he is convinced that the chief thing to be sought in all his life is God's approval.

But the perverse confidence by which hypocrites exalt themselves in the presence of God might seem a greater obstacle than worldly ambition; and we know that the scribes were suffering from this disease too. The answer is easy. Christ wanted to tear from them the false mask of sanctity by which they deceived the ignorant. And so He points as with a finger to the worse vice, which makes it plain that

what they wanted to be thought and what they were, were two quite
different things. Besides, although it is against God that hypocrisy
glorifies itself, yet in the world and before men it is always ambitious.
Indeed it is this vanity alone that swells us with false presumption, in
that we rely more on our own judgment and that of others than on
God's. He who really presents himself before God his Judge must of
necessity fall broken down and humbled. Thus, for any man to seek
glory from God alone, he must be overwhelmed with shame and fly
to the free mercy of God. Those who look to God see that they are
condemned and lost and that there is nothing left for them to glory in
but the grace of Christ. The desire for such glory will ever be joined
with humility.

But so far as this passage is concerned, Christ means that there is no
other way for men to be prepared for receiving the teaching of the
Gospel, than by withdrawing all their senses from the world and
turning them to God alone and seriously considering that it is with
Him that they have to do, so that they may forget their usual flatteries
for deceiving themselves and descend into their own consciences. No
wonder then if the Gospel today finds so few who are teachable, when
ambition sways them here and there. No wonder also if many default
from professing the Gospel, for they are carried away by their vanity
and fly off. We should the more earnestly seek this one thing; so that
while we are despised and lowly in the eyes of the world, and even
disordered inwardly, we may be reckoned among the children of God.

45. *Think not.* This is how the obstinate and hardened ought to be
dealt with, when they do not profit from teaching and friendly warnings—they must be summoned to the judgment seat of God. Few,
indeed, openly laugh at God, but very many imagine that God, whom
they actually oppose as enemies, is favourable to them and amuse
themselves securely with empty flatteries. Thus today our Titans who
wickedly trample down the whole teaching of Christ are as proud as
if they were God's dearest friends. For who can persuade the Papists
that Christianity exists anywhere else than among them? The scribes,
with whom Christ is here disputing, were like them. Though they
were the worst despisers of the Law, they boasted pompously of Moses
and did not hesitate to set him up as a shield against Christ. He knew
that if He had threatened that He would be a powerful and unbearable
enemy to them, it would have been completely despised. Therefore
He gives them notice that an accusation drawn up by Moses would be
preferred against them.

Those who think this is a distinction between the office of Christ and
of Moses are mistaken, for the property of the Law is to accuse unbelievers. Christ did not intend that; but was only shaking hypocrites

out of their confidence when they falsely boasted of their reverence for Moses. It is as if someone today retorted to the Papists that they will find no more hostile enemies than the holy doctors of the Church, whom they falsely claim on their side. Moreover, let us learn from this not to glory in the Scriptures for the wrong reason, for unless we worship the Son of God in the true obedience of faith, all whom God has moved to be His witnesses will rise up against us in accusation at the last day. When He says that they *set their hope on Moses*, He is not accusing them of superstition, but means that they are wrong to rely on Moses' help, as if with their wicked obstinacy they had him on their side.

46. *For if ye believed*. He shows why Moses will be their accuser—because they reject his teaching. We know that no greater insult can be offered to God's servants than when their teaching is despised or defamed. Those whom the Lord has ordained ministers of His Word should also be its defenders. Therefore He laid on all His prophets a twofold commission: to be teachers and instructors for the salvation of the godly; and at the last to pierce the reprobate with their testimony.

Christ's saying that Moses wrote of Him needs no long proof with those who acknowledge that Christ is the end and soul of the Law. But if anyone is not satisfied on this point and wants the passages pointed out to him, I would advise him first to read carefully the Epistle to the Hebrews, with which Stephen's sermon in Acts 7 agrees, and then to notice the quotations that Paul applies to his purpose. I allow, of course, that there are few places where Moses openly proclaims Christ; but what was the point of the tabernacle, the sacrifices and all the ceremonies, except as figures drawn in conformity to that first pattern which was shown him in the mountain? Therefore, without Christ the whole ministry of Moses vanishes. Again, we see how he continually recalls the people to the Covenant of the fathers which was confirmed in Christ, and even how he sets up Christ as the chief Head and foundation of the Covenant. And this was not unknown to the holy fathers, who were always directed towards the Mediator. A longer essay on this would be inconsistent with the brevity which is my aim.

47. *But if ye believe not his writings*. Christ seems to claim less authority for Himself than for Moses here. Yet we know that heaven and earth have been shaken by the voice of the Gospel. But Christ is accommodating His discourse to His hearers. To the Jews, the authority of the Law was sacred beyond controversy. Thus it was impossible for Christ to be inferior to Moses. To the same purpose is the contrast between *writings* and *words*. For He heightens their unbelief, in that the truth of God, recorded as it were on tables, has no authority with them.

CHAPTER SIX

After these things Jesus went away to the other side of the sea of Galilee,
which is the sea of Tiberias. And a great multitude followed him, because
they beheld the signs which he did on them that were sick. And Jesus
went up into the mountain, and there he sat with his disciples. Now the
passover, the feast of the Jews, was at hand. Jesus therefore lifting up his
eyes, and seeing that a great multitude cometh unto Him, saith unto
Philip, Whence are we to buy bread, that these may eat? And this he
said to prove him: for he himself knew what he would do. Philip
answered him, Two hundred pennyworth of bread is not sufficient for
them, that every one may take a little. One of his disciples, Andrew,
Simon Peter's brother, saith unto him, There is a lad here, which hath
five barley loaves, and two fishes: but what are these among so many?
Jesus said, Make the men sit down. Now there was much grass in the
place. So the men sat down, in number about five thousand. Jesus
therefore took the loaves; and having given thanks, he distributed them
to the disciples, and the disciples to them that were set down; likewise
also of the fishes as much as they would. And when they were filled, he
saith unto his disciples, Gather up the broken pieces which remain over,
that nothing be lost. So they gathered them up and filled twelve baskets
with the broken pieces of the five barley loaves, which remained over
unto them that had eaten. (1-13)

1. *After these things Jesus went away.* Although John usually collected
the actions and sayings of Christ omitted by the first three Evangelists,
in this passage, contrary to his custom, he narrates a miracle which they
had told. But he does so expressly to go on to the discourse Christ
delivered the next day at Capernaum, since the two were connected.
So this narrative, though common to the other three Evangelists as
well, is peculiar in being directed to another object, as we shall see.
The others say that this happened shortly after the death of John the
Baptist, by which detail of time they indicate the cause of Christ's
departing. For when tyrants are once stained with the blood of the
godly, they burn with still greater savagery, just as intemperate
drinking whets the thirst of drunkards. Christ therefore wanted to
calm Herod's rage by His absence. He puts 'sea of Galilee' for the lake
of Gennesareth. By adding that it was called 'of Tiberias' he explains
more fully what place Christ withdrew to, for the whole lake did not
have that name, only that part of it off the shore where Tiberias lay.

2. *And a great multitude followed him.* Such enthusiasm in following Christ arose from their seeing His power in miracles and being convinced that He was some great prophet, sent by God. But the Evangelist omits what the other three relate—that part of the day was spent in teaching and healing the sick, and that when the sun was setting, His disciples asked Him to send away the multitudes. He thought it was sufficient to mention the sum and substance of it, so that he might use it as an opportunity for leading on to the rest of the story which follows. We now see, first of all, how eagerly the people desired to hear Christ, since they are all unmindful of themselves and are not worried about a night in the desert. So much the less excusable is our sluggishness, or rather sloth, that we are so far from preferring Christ's heavenly teaching to the needs of hunger that the slightest interruptions immediately lead us away from meditating on the heavenly life. How rarely, indeed, does Christ find us free and unhampered of the obstructions of the world! Scarcely one in ten of us can bear to receive Him when He comes to us at home in the midst of comforts, let alone being ready to follow Him to a mountain in the desert. And although this disease is spread through nearly all the world, it is sure that none will be fit for the Kingdom of God until he has put aside such indulgence and learned to desire the good of the soul so earnestly that his belly shall not be a hindrance to him.

But as the flesh is always demanding attention, we also observe that of His own accord Christ cares for those who neglect themselves. He does not wait till they are famished and cry out that they are starving and have nothing to eat, but provides food for them without being asked. Someone may say that this does not always happen, and that we often see the godly exhausted and almost wasting with hunger, devoted to the Kingdom of God though they may be. I reply, although Christ wishes to try our faith and patience like this, He nevertheless beholds our need from heaven and takes care to relieve us, as far as is expedient for us. When He does not help us at once, it is for the best reason, even though that reason may be concealed from us.

3. *And Jesus went up into a mountain.* Christ undoubtedly sought retirement until the feast of the Passover. And so it is said that He sat down on a mountain with His disciples. This was His intention as a man; but God's counsel was different and He willingly obeyed it. Although, therefore, He fled from men's view, He let Himself be led by God's hand into a crowded theatre, as it were. For there was a bigger crowd in this desert mountain than in any populous city, and the miracle became better known than if it had taken place in the open market at Tiberias. Hence we are taught by this example to fit our plans in with the course of events; but so that, if they turn out differ-

K   145

ently from what we expected, we may not be grieved that God is above us and regulates all things according to His will.

5. *He saith unto Philip.* What we here read as being said to Philip alone, the others tell us was said to all. But there is no inconsistency in this. It is probable that Philip was spokesman for the common opinion, and so Christ replies to him in particular. Just as Andrew is then introduced as speaking, where the others assign what he said to all alike. In the person of Philip He tests the disciples as to whether they are looking for such a miracle as they shortly beheld. When He sees that they have no idea of an extraordinary remedy, He stirs up their sleepy minds so that they may at any rate have their eyes open to see what is going on. The aim of the disciples in all they say is to dissuade Christ from keeping the people. And perhaps they are thinking of themselves in this, lest they should come in for some of the inconvenience. Accordingly, Christ disregards their objections and goes forward with His purpose.

7. *Two hundred pennyworth.* As the *denarius*, according to Budaeus' reckoning, is equal to four *caroli* and two *deniers* of Tours, this sum comes to approximately thirty-five francs. If you divide this among five thousand men, each hundred of them will have fourteen Tours *sols*. If we now add about a thousand women and children, it will be found that Philip allots to each person a Tours *denier* and *maille* to buy a little bread. But as usually happens with a big crowd, he probably overestimated the number. And as the disciples were poor and impecunious, Andrew wanted to alarm Christ with the greatness of the sum—as if he were saying they were not rich enough to entertain all these people.

10. *Make the men sit down.* That the disciples were not quicker to grasp the hope their Master gave them and did not think of ascribing to His power all that was proper, was blameworthy stupidity. But their ready obedience deserves no small praise, in now obeying His command, although ignorant of His intention or what good it will do. The people showed the same readiness to obey; for although they were uncertain what was going to happen, they all sat down at a single word of command. And this is the proof of true faith, when God commands men to walk in darkness, as it were. And therefore, let us learn not to be wise in ourselves, but amid great confusion to hope still for a prosperous sequel when we follow as our Leader the God who never disappoints His own.

11. *And having given thanks.* Christ has more than once taught us by His example that we should begin our meals with prayer. For all those things that God has appointed for our use summon us to praise Him as symbols of His infinite goodness and fatherly love toward us.

And thanksgiving, as Paul tells us in I Tim. 4.4 is a kind of solemn sanctification, so that the use of them begins to be pure to us. It follows that those who swallow them down without thinking of God are sacrilegious profaners of God's gifts. And this teaching should be the more carefully noticed, because we still see a large part of the world stuffing themselves like animals. By Christ's wanting the bread given to the disciples to increase in their hands, we are taught that God blesses our labour when we serve one another.

Let us now summarize the meaning of the miracle as a whole. It has this in common with others, that in it Christ exercised His divine power in conjunction with His kindness. It is also confirmation to us of the statement in which He exhorts us to seek the Kingdom of God, promising that all the rest shall be added unto us. For if He took care of those who were led to Him just by a sudden impulse, how will He fail us if we seek Him with a firm purpose? It is true that He will sometimes let His people hunger, as I have said, but He will never leave them without His help. Meanwhile, He will have good reasons for not helping us except as a last resort.

Moreover, Christ made it plain that He not only bestows spiritual life on the world but was also commanded by His Father to nourish the body. Abundance of all blessings is committed to His hands, that He may, as a channel, convey it to us. Yet I am wrong to call Him a channel, for He is rather the living fountain flowing from the eternal Father. Accordingly, Paul prays that all blessings may come to us from the Father and from Him in common (1 Cor. 1.3). And in another place he tells us that in all things we ought to give thanks to God the Father through Him (Eph. 5.20). And not only is this an office proper to His eternal Divinity, but even in the flesh the Father has appointed Him the Steward, to feed us by His hand. Now, although we do not see miracles every day, yet Christ shows His power in feeding us no less liberally. And indeed, we do not read that whenever He wanted to give a supper to His friends, He used any novel means. Therefore it would be a perverse request for anyone to demand food and drink to be given him in some unusual way.

Again, Christ did not provide the people with rare delicacies. Those who saw His wonderful power in that meal had to be satisfied with barley bread and dry fish. And though He does not now satiate five thousand men with five loaves, He nevertheless does not cease to feed the whole world wonderfully. It seems contradictory to us that man does not live by bread only, but by the Word that proceeds out of the mouth of God (Deut. 8.3). For we are so attached to outward means that nothing is harder than to depend on God's providence. This is why there is such agitation as soon as we run short of food. If we

consider everything aright, we shall be forced to see God's blessing in
all food. But custom and familiarity make us undervalue the miracles
of nature. And yet in this respect, malignity is our hindrance rather
than stupidity. For how few there are who would not rather roam
around the earth a hundred times in the roving error of their minds,
than look to the God who offers Himself?

13. *And filled twelve baskets.* Matthew writes that when four thous-
and men were fed by seven loaves there were the same number of
baskets as loaves (Matt. 15.37). The smaller amount of food sufficient
for a greater number of men and almost twice as much left over, shows
us the more clearly how powerful is that blessing of God to which we
deliberately shut our eyes. We should also notice in passing that,
although it is to emphasize the miracle that Christ commands them to
fill the baskets, He is at the same time exhorting His disciples to frugality
when He says, *Gather it up that nothing be lost.* For God's greater bounty
ought not to incite us to luxury. Let those who abound, therefore,
remember that one day they will give account of their excessive
possessions if they do not carefully and faithfully apply their super-
fluity to a good purpose which God approves.

When therefore the people saw the sign which he did, they said, This is
of a truth the prophet that cometh into the world. Jesus therefore per-
ceiving that they were about to come and take him by force, to make him
king, withdrew again into the mountain himself alone. And when
evening came, his disciples went down unto the sea; and they entered into
a boat, and were going over the sea unto Capernaum. And it was now
dark, and Jesus had not yet come to them. And the sea was rising by
reason of a great wind that blew. When therefore they had rowed about
five and twenty or thirty furlongs, they behold Jesus walking on the sea,
and drawing nigh unto the boat: and they were afraid. But he saith unto
them, It is I; be not afraid. They were willing therefore to receive him
into the boat: and straightway the boat was at the land whither they
were going. (14-21)

14. *When therefore the people.* The miracle seems to have done some
good, in that they acknowledge its Author to be the Messiah. And
Christ had no other aim than this. But soon they misapply the knowledge they have conceived of Christ to a different end. And this fault
is more than common among men, that they corrupt and pervert His
truth with their falsehoods as soon as God has revealed Himself to
them. Even when they seem to have started on the right path, they
soon degenerate.

15. *To make him king.* These people had good reason to give Christ
the title and honour of king; but they greatly erred in taking to them-

selves the liberty of making a king. Scripture ascribes this to God alone; as Ps. 2.6 puts it, 'Yet I have set my king,' etc. Again, what sort of kingdom do they imagine for Him? An earthly one, which is utterly foreign to His person. Let us learn from this how dangerous it is in divine matters to forsake His Word and invent anything from our own reason. For there is nothing that the perverted cunning of our minds does not commit. And what good is the pretence of zeal when by our perverted worship we affront God worse than if someone were expressly and deliberately to attack His glory?

We know how previously His enemies tried to extinguish Christ's glory. And that violence reached its climax when He was crucified. But by this means salvation was won for the world and Christ Himself triumphed gloriously over death and Satan. If He had let Himself be made a king at this point, His spiritual Kingdom would have been destroyed, the Gospel stamped with everlasting infamy and the hope of salvation utterly wiped out. Counterfeit worship and rites rashly invented by men have no other result than to despoil God of His true honour and simply load Him with reproach.

We must also note the expression *take by force*. They wanted to take Christ by force, says the Evangelist; that is, with impetuous violence they wanted to make Him a king against His will. Therefore, if we want Him to approve the honour we render Him, we must always consider what He requires. And indeed, those who force their self-invented rites on God, attack Him and in a certain sense do Him violence; for the foundation of true worship is obedience. Let us also learn from this how reverently we should abide in the pure and simple Word of God. As soon as we turn even slightly aside, the truth is tainted by our leaven, so that it ceases to be like itself. They had learned from the Word of God that the promised Redeemer would be a king. But from their own minds they invent an earthly kingdom, and offer Him a kingdom apart from the Word of God. Whenever we mix up our opinions with the Word of God, faith degenerates into miserable guess-work. Let believers, therefore, train themselves in modesty, that Satan may not carry them away into a perverse enthusiasm of zeal, so that like the Titans, they violently attack God, who is only worshipped rightly when we embrace Him as He presents Himself to us.

It is amazing that five thousand men should have had the reckless audacity to make a new king without hesitating, and so provoke against themselves Pilate's forces and the power of the Roman empire. They would certainly never have gone so far if they had not trusted in the predictions of the Prophets and hoped that God would be on their side and that so they would win. But they erred in inventing a kingdom that the prophets had never promised. Therefore, they are so far from having the hand of God present to help their undertaking, that on the contrary, Christ leaves them. This was also the reason why under the Papacy, unhappy men wandered so long in gross darkness, as if God were absent, because they had dared to pollute all His worship with their inventions.

16. *His disciples went down.* Christ no doubt wanted to hide until the crowd dispersed. We know how difficult it is to calm a popular tumult. Now, if they had openly tried to do what they had intended the rumour of it would soon have spread and it would not have been so easy afterwards to wipe off the stain from Him. Meanwhile, He spent all that time in prayer, as the other Evangelists relate—perhaps that God His Father would correct the people's outburst. His crossing the lake miraculously is useful for His disciples, by strengthening their faith again. It had the further result that next day all the people could easily grasp that He had been brought there, not by a boat, but by His own power. For they blocked the shore from which He would have had to set out, and would hardly have been drawn away if they had not seen the disciples cross over.

17. *It was now dark.* John passes over many details which the others put in, such as their struggling against a head wind for several hours. For the storm probably got up immediately after night-fall, and they tell us that Christ did not appear to His disciples until the fourth watch. Those who conjecture they were still in the middle of the lake when Christ appeared to them, because John says that they had gone twenty-five or thirty furlongs, are led astray by thinking that they were sailing to the further or opposite shore. For Bethsaida, near to which Luke says the miracle was performed, and Capernaum to which the boat sailed, were situated in the same district. Pliny, in his fifth book, states that this lake was six miles across and sixteen long. Josephus, in the third book of the Jewish wars, puts it at one hundred furlongs long and forty wide. And since eight furlongs make a mile, we see easily how little the discrepancy is. So far as relates to this voyage, I surmise that they did not cover such a distance by a direct course, but by being driven to and fro. However that may be, the Evangelist wanted to convey that when Christ showed Himself to them they were in the utmost peril. It might seem strange that Christ's disciples were harassed like this when others had a calm voyage. But the Lord often exercises His people with serious dangers, that they may the better and more intimately recognize Him in their deliverance.

19. *They were afraid.* The other Evangelists explain as the cause of their fear that they thought it was a ghost. Now it is impossible not to be seized with consternation and dread when a ghost is presented be-

fore our eyes. We think either that Satan is deceiving us, or that God is presaging something. Besides, John here shows us, as in a mirror, what kind of knowledge of Christ we can conceive without the Word and what good it is. For if He reveals a bare example of His divinity, we immediately slip into imaginations, and every man fabricates an idol for himself in place of Christ. Hard upon these errors of the mind follow agitation and a confused terror of heart. But when He begins to speak, from His voice we receive clear and substantial knowledge, and joy and peace shine within our minds.

For there is great weight in the words: *It is I; be not afraid.* By them we are taught that only in Christ's presence have we strong enough grounds of confidence to be calm and at ease. But this pertains only to Christ's disciples; for later on we shall see that wicked men were struck down by the same words (18.6). The reason for the difference is that He is sent as Judge to the reprobate and unbelievers for their destruction; and therefore they cannot bear His presence without being engulfed. But the godly know that He is given to them as a propitiation; His name is a sure pledge to them of the love of God and their own salvation. And so when they hear it, they take heart as if they were raised from death to life, and so to say, blithely see fair weather, dwell safely on earth, and, victors over all ills, with His defence meet every danger. Nor does He only comfort and encourage them with His word, but also removes the cause of their fear by calming the tempest.

On the morrow the multitude which stood on the other side of the sea saw that there was none other boat there, save only that into which his disciples entered, and that Jesus entered not with his disciples into the boat, but that his disciples went away alone (howbeit there came boats from Tiberias nigh unto the place where they ate the bread after the Lord had given thanks): when the multitude therefore saw that Jesus was not there, neither his disciples, they themselves got into the boats, and came to Capernaum, seeking Jesus. And when they found him on the other side of the sea, they said unto him, Rabbi, when camest thou hither? (22-25)

22. *On the morrow.* Here the Evangelist relates the circumstances which would lead the crowd to think that Christ's crossing was divine. There was one ship. They saw it sail off without Christ. The next day ships came from other places and took them to Capernaum. And there they found Christ. It follows that He must have been carried across miraculously. There is an ἀνακόλουθον in the words, but their meaning is clear enough. In the first clause, John says there was only one boat, and it set sail from that shore and place in everyone's sight, and Christ was not on board. He adds that boats afterwards came from Tiberias and took the crowd across which had waited on the shore, blockading,

so to say, every landing place, so that Christ might not escape them.

23. *Nigh unto the place where they ate bread.* The meaning of the words is ambiguous. They can be explained either as Tiberias being near the place where they had been fed by Christ with five loaves, or that the boats reached the shore which was near and below that place. I prefer the latter explanation. Bethsaida, near which Luke says the miracle was performed, is halfway between Tiberias and Capernaum. Accordingly, ships that came down from there sailed along the shore where the multitude was standing. And no doubt they put in to take on passengers.

It is not an unnecessary repetition that John again mentions that Christ *gave thanks.* He means that Christ obtained by prayer that those few loaves sufficed to feed so many. And since we are so cold and lazy about prayer, he emphasizes the same thing again.

25. *On the other side of the sea.* We have said already that the city of Capernaum was not situated on the opposite shore. Tiberias stands on the broadest part of the lake; then comes Bethsaida; and Capernaum lies near the lowest part, not far from the mouth of the Jordan. Now, when John places it on the other side of the lake, we must not take him as meaning the district was directly opposite; but at the lower end the lake wound in and out, and because of the bay in between, the journey on foot could only be made by going all the way round. The Evangelist therefore says 'on the other side of the sea' in the common phrase, because the only direct and ordinary way was by boat.

Jesus answered them and said, Verily, verily, I say unto you, Ye seek me, not because ye saw signs, but because ye ate of the loaves, and were filled. Work not for the meat which perisheth, but for the meat which abideth unto eternal life, which the Son of man shall give unto you: for him the Father, even God, hath sealed. They said therefore unto him, What must we do, that we may work the works of God? Jesus answered and said unto them, This is the work of God, that ye believe on him whom he hath sent. (26-29)

26. *Jesus answered them.* Christ does not reply to their question to commend to them His power in the miracle; but rather chides them for rushing in thoughtlessly, for they were unaware of the true and real reason for His action, since they were seeking in Christ something other than Christ Himself. And so this fault is seen in them, that they seek Christ for the sake of the belly and not for the signs. And yet it is undeniable that they were mindful of the miracle. More; the Evangelist has already related that they were moved by the signs to follow Christ. But because they perverted the miracles to a different end, He deservedly reproaches them of having more regard for the belly than

for the signs—as if He were saying that they did not profit by the works of God as they should have done. For the true way to profit would have been to acknowledge Christ as Messiah in such a way as to submit to His teaching and government, and, led by Him, to make for the heavenly Kingdom of God. But all they look for in Him is to live happily and at ease in this world. This is to rob Christ of His principal power, for He was given by the Father and revealed Himself to men to re-form into the image of God those to whom He has given the Holy Spirit and to lead to eternal life those whom He has clothed with His righteousness.

It is very important, therefore, what we look at in Christ's miracles. For he who does not aspire to God's Kingdom but clings to the comforts of the present life, seeks only to fill his belly. Just as today many would eagerly embrace the Gospel if it were empty of the bitterness of the cross and only brought carnal delights. Indeed, we see many take Christ's side that they may live more merrily and freely. Some profess to be Christ's disciples from hope of gain, others from fear, others for the sake of those they want to please. Therefore the chief thing in seeking Christ is to despise the world and seek the Kingdom of God and His righteousness. Moreover, since most men persuade themselves they are seeking Christ excellently, when in fact they are prostituting all His power, Christ in His usual way, duplicates the word 'verily', as if by the oath He meant to bring out of the shadows the vice which is hidden under our hypocrisy.

27. *Work.* Here He teaches what He wants His people to be aiming at—eternal life. But because from the dullness of our understanding we are always devoted to earthly things, He corrects this innate disease before pointing out what we ought to do. The simple teaching would have been, 'Work for incorruptible food.' But He knows that men's senses are bound by earthly cares and so first bids them be loosed and freed from these fetters that they may rise to heaven. Not that He prohibits His people from labouring to get daily food. But He warns them that the heavenly life must be put before the earthly, for the only reason the godly have for living here is that, as pilgrims in the world, they may hasten to their heavenly homeland.

Next, we must see what the point of this is. For since Christ's power is defiled by those who are devoted to the belly and earthly things, He is discussing what we should seek in Him and why we should seek it. Moreover, He uses metaphors accordant with the situation. If food had not been mentioned, He would have said, without a metaphor, 'You must put aside the care of the world and strive after the heavenly life.' But because they run to their fodder like cattle, Christ frames His discourse metaphorically and calls everything pertaining to new-

ness of life 'food'. And we know that our souls are fed by the teaching
of the Gospel, when it is efficacious in us by the power of the Spirit.
Therefore, as faith is the life of the soul, all that nourishes and advances
faith is compared to food. This kind of food He calls incorruptible and
says that it abides unto eternal life, so that we may learn that our souls
are not fed for one day but are brought up in the hope of a blessed
immortality. For the Lord begins the work of our salvation that He
may perfect it until the day of Christ. We must receive the gifts of the
Spirit that they may be tickets and pledges of eternal life. Though the
reprobate taste this food and often spit it out, so that it does not stay
in them, yet believers feel that enduring power in their souls when
they perceive the continuing and never-failing power of the Spirit
in His gifts.

It is empty quibbling when some infer from the word 'work' that
we merit eternal life by works. For as we have said, Christ is exhorting
men to apply themselves to the meditation on the heavenly life instead
of cleaving to the world, as they are wont to do. And Christ Himself
removes every doubt, when He says that it is He who gives this food.
For what we receive as His gift, none provides by his own industry.
There is indeed an apparent contradiction in the words, but the two
statements readily agree—that the spiritual food of the soul is the free
gift of Christ, and that we must strive whole-heartedly to become
partakers of so great a blessing.

For him hath the Father sealed. He confirms the preceding statement;
for the Father ordained Him to us for this purpose. The old writers
have twisted this passage round to Christ's divine essence, as if He were
said to be sealed in that He is the stamp and express image of the
Father. Here He is not critically discussing his eternal essence, but says
what He has been commissioned and enjoined to do, what His office
is towards us and what we ought to seek and look for from Him.
Moreover, by an apt metaphor, He alludes to an ancient custom by
which they sealed with signet rings what they wanted to confirm by
their authority. And so Christ, that He may not seem to be taking
anything on Himself, declares that these duties had been placed on Him
by the Father, and that this decree of the Father was manifested by an
engraven seal. To summarize: Because it is not for everyone to feed
souls with incorruptible food, Christ comes forward and, pledging
Himself as the author of this great blessing, adds that He is approved
by God and has been sent to men with this mark of sealing.

Hence it follows that the desire of those who present their souls to
Christ for feeding, will not be disappointed. Let us know, then, that
life is set forth to us in Christ that each of us may aspire to it, not
casually, but sure of success. But at the same time we are taught that

all who give this praise to another than Christ are held guilty of false-hood before God. Hence it is plain that the Papists are altogether liars in every part of their teaching, for as often as they substitute other means of salvation in Christ's place they corrupt and, as it were, erase this unique and authentic seal of God with wicked presumption and base treachery. That we may not fall into such dreadful sin, let us learn to preserve unimpaired and undiminished in Christ all that is given Him by the Father.

28. *What must we do*, etc. The multitude understood well enough that Christ had exhorted them to strive higher than the comforts of the present life, and that those whom God calls elsewhere should not be preoccupied with the earth. But the people who ask this are partly mistaken in not understanding the kind of labour. They do not consider that God bestows on us whatever is necessary for spiritual life by the hand of His Son. First, they ask what they should do. Then, when they mention the works of God, they are wandering aimlessly about. Thus they betray their ignorance of God's grace. And yet here they seem to be grumbling superciliously against Christ, as if He accused them undeservedly: 'Do you think that we do not care about eternal life?' they ask; 'If so, why do you tell us to do what is beyond our power?' By *the works of God*, understand those which God demands and approves.

29. *This is the work of God.* They had spoken of works; Christ brings them back to one work, that is, faith. By this He means that whatever men undertake without faith is useless and vain, but that faith alone is enough, for God requires of us only that we believe. There is an implied contrast between faith and men's cares and efforts here, as if He were saying, 'Men are busied to no purpose when they try to please God without faith. It is as if they were running off the course and not keeping on towards the finishing post.' This is a remarkable passage and shows that even if men wear themselves out all their lives, they are only playing at work unless faith in Christ is the rule of their lives. They are mistaken who gather from this passage that faith is the gift of God, for Christ is not teaching what God produces in us but what He requires and wants of us.

But it seems absurd that God should approve nothing but faith only, for love should not be despised, nor should other godly practices lose their place and honour. Hence, although faith may hold the primacy, other works are not superfluous. The reply is easy. Faith excludes neither love nor any other good work, but contains them all within itself. Faith is called the only work of God because by it we possess Christ and become the sons of God, so that He governs us by His Spirit. Because, therefore, Christ does not separate its fruits from faith, it is not surprising if He makes it the be-all and end-all, as they say.

We have said in Chapter Three what the sense of the word 'believe' is. We must always remember that, to understand the power of faith, we must determine what Christ is in whom we believe and why He was given us by the Father. Besides, it is disgusting quibbling when some make use of this passage to assert that we are justified by works if faith justifies, since it is also called a work. First,[1] it is certain that Christ is not speaking precisely when He calls faith a work—just as Paul contrasts the law of faith to the law of works. Secondly, when we deny that men are justified by works, we mean works by whose merit men may win God's favour. Now, faith brings nothing to God. On the contrary, it sets man before God empty and poor, that he may be filled with Christ and His grace. It is therefore a passive work, so to say, to which no reward can be paid. And it bestows on man no other righteousness than what he receives from Christ.

They said therefore unto him, What then doest thou for a sign, that we may see and believe thee? What workest thou? Our fathers ate the manna in the wilderness; as it is written, He gave them bread out of heaven to eat. Jesus therefore said unto them, Verily, verily, I say unto you, It was not Moses that gave you the bread out of heaven; but my Father giveth you the true bread out of heaven. For the bread of God is that which cometh down out of heaven, and giveth life unto the world.

(30-33)

30. *What doest thou for a sign?* This wickedness abundantly proves the truth of what is said elsewhere, 'This wicked generation seeketh after a sign' (Matt. 12.39). They had been drawn to Christ at first by wonder at His signs; later, amazed by a new sign, they confessed that Christ was the Messiah and from this belief wanted to make Him a king. And now they demand a sign, as if He were unknown. Whence this sudden forgetfulness, save because they are ungrateful to God and are maliciously blind to the sight of His power? There is no doubt that they despise all the miracles they had already seen because Christ does not meet their wishes, and they do not find He is what they imagined. If He had offered hope of earthly happiness they would have praised Him continually, and would have undoubtedly hailed Him as a prophet and the Messiah and the Son of God. But because He blames them for being given up overmuch to the flesh, they decide not to listen to Him any more. How many there are like them today! At first, because they tell themselves that Christ will flatter their faults,

---

[1] The Latin text reads: ... *opus primum. Satis* ... The French: *appellee Oeuvre. Premierement il* ... It is clear from the 'Secondly' a few lines below that the French is the correct reading.

they eagerly snatch at the Gospel and do not ask for proof of it. But when they are called to deny the flesh and bear the cross, they begin to give up faith in Christ and ask where the Gospel came from. In fine, as soon as Christ does not correspond to their wishes, He ceases to be their Master

31. *Our fathers.* Christ put His finger on the sore when He said that they came like brute beasts to fill their bellies. They showed this gross attitude when they asked for a Messiah to feed them. And when they praise God's grace in the manna so highly, it is only a ruse to suppress the teaching of Christ when He condemned their immoderate desire for corruptible food. For they put forward in opposition to it the glorious title that adorned manna, in that it is called heavenly bread. But the Holy Spirit does not call manna the bread of heaven with the idea that God fed His people like a herd of swine and gave them nothing more valuable. Therefore, they have no excuse when they wickedly reject the spiritual food of the soul which God offers to them now.

32. *Verily, verily, I say unto you.* Christ seems to contradict their quotation from the Psalm; but He is only speaking comparatively. מָן (manna) is called the bread of heaven, though it is to feed the body. The bread which ought truly and properly to be reckoned heavenly is that which is the spiritual nourishment of the soul. Christ therefore here contrasts the world and heaven, because we ought to seek incorruptible life only in the Kingdom of Heaven. In this passage, truth is not contrasted to figures, as often elsewhere, but Christ is dealing with man's true life, that in which he differs from the brute beasts and by which he is pre-eminent among the creatures.

When He afterwards adds *My Father giveth you*, it is just as if He were saying, 'The manna that Moses gave your fathers did not bring heavenly life, but now the bread from heaven is indeed offered to you.' True, He calls the Father the Giver of the bread, but He means that it is given by His own hand. Thus the antithesis relates, not to Moses and God, but to Moses and Christ. Now, Christ says that His Father, rather than He Himself, is the Author of this gift, to gain more reverence—as if He were saying, 'Acknowledge Me as God's minister, by whose hand He wishes to feed your souls unto eternal life.' But again, this seems inconsistent with Paul's teaching, for in I Cor. 10.3 he calls manna spiritual food. I reply, Christ speaks on the level of those He is dealing with, and this is not uncommon in Scripture. We see how variously Paul himself writes about circumcision. When he is treating of the ordinance, he confesses it is the seal of faith; but when he has to contend with false apostles, he calls it a seal of cursing; and in that he was using their own ideas. Let us consider the objection made against Christ—that He did not prove Himself the Messiah unless He supplied His people with bodily food. Accordingly, He does not tell them openly what manna was the figure of, but denies that it was true bread that Moses fed their bellies with.

33. *For the bread of God is that.* Christ reasons negatively from the definition to the thing defined, in this way: 'The heavenly bread is that which comes down from heaven and gives life to the world. There was nothing like this in manna. Therefore, it was not the heavenly bread.' At the same time, He confirms what He had said before—that He was sent by the Father to feed men far better than Moses did. Manna certainly came down from the visible heaven, that is, from the sky, but not from the eternal Kingdom of God from which life flows to us. And the Jews, whom Christ is addressing, looked no higher than that in the wilderness their fathers' bellies were well stuffed and fattened.

What He had before called the bread of heaven, He now calls the bread of God. Not that the bread which sustains our present lives comes from any other than God, but because only that can be reckoned divine which quickens souls to blessed immortality. Moreover, this passage teaches us that the whole world is dead to God, save inasmuch as Christ quickens it, for life will be found only in Him.

Two things must be noted about the *coming down from heaven.* We have divine life in Christ, because He has come from God to be the Author of life to us. Secondly, heavenly life is near us, so that there is no need to fly above the clouds or cross the sea. For Christ descended to us because none could ascend to Him

They said therefore unto him, Lord, evermore give us this bread. Jesus said unto them, I am the bread of life: he that cometh to me shall not hunger, and he that believeth on me shall never thirst. But I said unto you, that ye have seen me, and yet believe not. All that the Father giveth me shall come unto me; and him that cometh to me I will in no wise cast out. For I am come down from heaven, not to do mine own will, but the will of him that sent me. And this is the will of the Father who hath sent me, that of all that he hath given me I should lose nothing, but should raise it up at the last day. For this is the will of him that sent me, that every one that beholdeth the Son, and believeth on him, should have eternal life; and I will raise him up at the last day. (34-40)

34. *Evermore give us.* They are doubtless speaking ironically, to accuse Christ of conceit, because He declared that He gives the bread of life. Thus unhappy men are not satisfied simply with the sin of rejecting God's promises, but throw the guilt of their unbelief on Christ.

35. *I am the bread of life.* First He tells them that the bread which they

asked for in mockery is before them. Then He reproves them. He begins with a lesson to show up their ingratitude. And there are two parts to the lesson: He shows whence we should seek life, and how we may possess it. We know that Christ used these metaphors because manna and daily food had been mentioned. And this figure is more suitable for touching the ignorant than a straightforward oration. When we eat bread for the nourishment of the body, both our own weakness and the power of divine grace are more apparent than if God were to impart a secret power to nourish the body without food. Thus the analogy from the body to the soul makes Christ's grace more clearly perceptible. For when we hear that Christ is the bread by which our souls must be fed, it sinks deeper into our minds than if Christ had simply said that He is our life.

But we must observe that the word *bread* does not express Christ's quickening power in such a way as we experience it. For bread does not begin life, but nourishes and sustains that which is already in existence. But by the kindness of Christ we not only keep life but also have its beginning, and therefore the comparison is partly inappropriate. Yet there is no absurdity in this, for Christ is suiting His style to the circumstances of His former discourse. The question had been raised as to which of the two was the more outstanding in feeding men, Moses or Christ. This is also why He calls it only bread, for it was the manna alone that they used as an objection to Him, and therefore He thought it sufficient to contrast to it another kind of bread. And the simple lesson is just this: Our souls do not live by what I may call an intrinsic power, but derive life from Christ.

He that cometh to me. Now He defines the manner of feeding—when we receive Him by faith. For it is of no avail to unbelievers that Christ is the bread of life, since they always remain empty. Christ becomes our bread when we come hungry to Him that He may fill us. 'To come to Christ' and 'to believe' mean the same thing here; but in the former word is expressed the effect of faith, namely, that we flee to Christ to seek life when we are compelled by a feeling of our hunger.

Moreover, those who infer from this passage that the eating of Christ is nothing but faith, do not reason carefully enough. I certainly acknowledge that we eat Christ in no other way than by believing. But the eating is the effect and fruit of faith rather than faith itself. For faith does not look at Christ merely from afar, but embraces Him, that He may become ours and dwell in us. It causes us to be united in His body, to have life in common with Him and, in short, to be one with Him. It is therefore true that we eat Christ by faith alone, so long as we grasp how faith unites us to him.

Shall never thirst. There seems no point in putting this in, for the

purpose of bread is not to quench thirst but to satisfy hunger. Christ
is therefore attributing more to bread than its nature permits. I have
already said that He uses the word bread alone, because the comparison
between manna and His heavenly power which sustains our souls in
life demanded it. At the same time, He uses the word bread generally
for all nourishment, according to the common usage of His nation.
For the Hebrews, by synecdoche, took 'to eat bread' for 'to dine' or
'to sup'; and when we ask from God our daily bread we include drink
and all other necessities of life. The meaning therefore is: Whoever
goes to Christ that he may have life from Him will lack nothing, but
will be fully satisfied with all that upholds life.

36. *But I said unto you.* He now chides them for maliciously rejecting
God's gift which is offered to them. And he who rejects what he knows
God has given him impiously despises God. Had Christ not made His
power known to them and plainly borne witness that He came from
God, the plea of ignorance could have lightened their guilt. But when
they reject the teaching of Him whom they had earlier confessed to be
the Lord's Messiah, it is an extreme insult. It is certainly true that men
never resist God purposely and deliberately as God; and Paul's saying
applies to this: They would never have crucified the Lord of glory if
they had known Him (I Cor. 2.8). But unbelievers shut their eyes to
the light of their own accord, and are justly said to see that which
immediately vanishes from their sight because Satan darkens their
minds. It is beyond doubt that when He said that *they saw*, it is not to be
taken of His bodily appearance, but rather that He is pointing to their
voluntary blindness, because they could have known what He was if
their malice had not stopped them.

37. *All that the Father giveth me.* That their unbelief may not detract
from His teaching, He says that the cause of their obstinacy is that they
are reprobate and outside God's flock. He here distinguishes between
the elect and the reprobate, so that the authority of His teaching may
stand firm even though many do not believe it. For not only do the
ungodly detract from the Word of God and despise it because they
are unmoved by reverence for it, but also many who are weak and
ignorant doubt whether what is rejected by a large part of the world
really is God's Word. Christ deals with this stumbling-block when
He denies that any unbelievers are His own; and there is no wonder if
the truth of God is distasteful to them but is embraced by all God's
children. In the first place He says that all whom the Father gives Him
come to Him. By these words He means that faith is not at men's
disposal, so that this man or that may believe indiscriminately and by
chance, but that God elects those whom He hands over, as it were, to
His Son. For when He says that whatever is given comes, we infer that

all are not given. Again, we deduce that God works in His elect by such an efficacy of the Spirit that none of them falls away. For the word *give* is equivalent to Christ's saying, 'Those whom the Father has elected, He regenerates and makes over to Me, to obey the Gospel.'

And him that cometh to me. This is added for the consolation of the godly, that they may be fully persuaded they have a clear way to Christ by faith, and that as soon as they commit themselves to His faithfulness and care, He will receive them kindly. Hence it follows that the teaching of the Gospel will be beneficial to all the godly, because none offers Himself as Christ's disciple who does not in return feel and experience Him to be a faithful and true teacher.

38. *For I am come down from heaven.* This confirms the preceding statement that we do not seek Christ in vain. For faith is God's work, by which He shows that we are His and appoints His Son to be the overseer of our salvation. But the Son's only purpose is to fulfil His Father's commands. Consequently, He will never turn away those sent by His Father. Finally, for this reason faith will never be in vain. The distinction that Christ makes between His own and His Father's will is an accommodation to His hearers because, since man's mind is prone to distrust, we are wont to invent something contrary that makes us doubtful. To take away all excuse for such wicked imaginings, Christ declares that He has been manifested to the world to confirm what the Father has decreed on our salvation by actually effecting it.

39. *And this is the will.* He now declares that the Father's purpose is that believers may find salvation secured in Christ. From which, again, it follows that all who do not profit by the teaching of the Gospel are reprobate. Therefore, if we see that it turns to the destruction of many, we have no cause to despair, since such men voluntarily bring the evil upon themselves. Let it suffice that the Gospel will always have the power to gather the elect to salvation.

I should lose nothing. That is, 'I should not let it be taken from me, or perish.' By this He means that He is not the guardian of our salvation for a day or two, but that He will care for it to the end, and bring us, so to say, from the starting point to the finishing post. This is why He mentions the final resurrection. And this promise is very necessary for those who labour wretchedly under the great weakness of the flesh, which every one of us is well aware of. At each moment, indeed, the salvation of the whole world might be overthrown did not believers, supported by Christ's hand, stretch forward boldly towards the day of resurrection. Let it, therefore, be fixed firmly in our minds that Christ has stretched out His hand to us and will not desert us in midcourse, but we may rely on His leading and boldly dare to raise our eyes to the last day.

He mentions the resurrection for another reason, too. While our life is hidden, we are like dead men. For how do believers differ from the ungodly, but that they are overwhelmed with miseries and, like sheep appointed for the slaughter, always have one foot in the grave? Yes, indeed, and are never far from being swallowed up by death? So the only prop for our faith and patience is to disregard the state of our present life and direct our minds and senses to the last day, and pass through the world's hindrances, until the fruit of our faith at last appears.

40. *And this is the will.* He had said that the Father had committed to Him the office of protecting our salvation. Now He also defines its mode. The way we obtain salvation is by obeying the Gospel of Christ. He has, indeed, glanced at this before, but now He expresses more clearly what He had said rather obscurely. And if God's will is that those whom He has elected shall be saved by faith, and He confirms and executes His eternal decree in this way, whoever is not satisfied with Christ but inquires curiously about eternal predestination desires, as far as lies in him, to be saved contrary to God's purpose. The election of God in itself is hidden and secret. The Lord manifests it by the calling with which He honours us.

Therefore, they are mad who seek their own or others' salvation in the labyrinth of predestination; for if God has elected us to the end that we may believe, take away faith and election will be imperfect. But it is wrong to break the unbroken and ordained order of beginning and end in God's counsel. Moreover, since the election of God carries His calling with it by an inseparable bond, so when God has effectually called us to faith in Christ it should have as much force with us as if He confirmed His decree concerning our salvation with an engraven seal. For the testimony of the Spirit is nothing but the sealing of our adoption. Therefore every man's faith is an abundant witness to the eternal predestination of God, so that it is sacrilege to inquire further; and whoever refuses to assent to the simple testimony of the Holy Spirit does Him a horrible injury.

He contrasts *behold* and *believe* with His earlier words of reproach to the Jews for not believing when they saw. Now, in regard to the sons of God, He joins the obedience of faith to their sense of the divine power in Christ. Moreover, these words show that faith flows from the knowledge of Christ. Not that it desires anything beyond the simple Word of God, but because if we trust in Christ we shall perceive what He is and what He brings us.

The Jews therefore murmured concerning him, because he said, I am the bread which came down out of heaven. And they said, Is not this Jesus, the son of Joseph, whose father and mother we know? How doth he now say, I am come down out of heaven? Jesus answered and said unto them, Murmur not among yourselves. No man can come to me, except the Father which sent me draw him: and I will raise him up in the last day. It is written in the prophets, And they shall all be taught of God. Every one that hath heard from the Father, and hath learned, cometh unto me.

(41-45)

41. *They murmured.* The Evangelist tells us that the murmuring arose from the Jews being put off by the lowliness of the flesh and therefore not seeing anything divine or heavenly in Christ. But he shows that their difficulty was twofold: one they had made up from a false idea, when they said, 'This is the son of Joseph, whose father and mother we know.' The other came from the perverted judgment that they did not reckon Christ to be the Son of God, since He descended to men clothed in their flesh. But we are very ill-disposed if we despise the Lord of glory because He emptied Himself and took the form of a servant for our sake. Rather was this the shining example of His boundless love toward us and of His wonderful grace. Besides, the divine majesty of Christ was not so concealed under the contemptible and lowly appearance of the flesh that it did not send forth beams of His manifold brightness. But those gross and stupid men lacked the eyes to see His manifest glory.

We, too, daily sin in both these ways. First, it is a great hindrance to us that we look at Christ only with carnal eyes and so see nothing sublime in Him. We pervert everything in Him and His teaching by our sinful outlook, such false interpreters are we. Secondly, not content with this we get hold of many falsehoods, which breed a contempt of the Gospel. Hence the world deliberately repels God's grace. The Evangelist expressly names the Jews, to let us know that the murmuring came from those who boasted that they had faith and were the Church, so that we all may learn to receive Christ reverently when He descends to us, and that the nearer He is to us, the more cheerfully we may approach Him, for Him to raise us to His heavenly glory.

43. *Murmur not.* He puts the blame for the murmuring on them, as if He said, 'There is nothing to cause offence in my teaching; but because you are reprobate, it irritates your poisoned souls, and you do not like it because your taste is distempered.'

44. *No man can,* etc. He does not merely accuse their perversity, but also tells them that the embracing of the doctrine which He proclaims is a peculiar gift of God. And He says this, lest their unbelief should upset the weak. For many are gripped by the foolishness of depending on the judgment of men in regard to the things of God, so that they distrust the Gospel as soon as they see it is not received by the world.

On the other side, unbelievers, who flatter themselves in their obstinacy, dare to condemn the Gospel because it does not please them. And so, in opposition to this, Christ says that although the teaching of the Gospel is preached to all indiscriminately, it cannot be understood by all, but that a new mind and a new attitude are necessary. Therefore faith is not at men's disposal but conferred by God.

Because *to come* to Christ is here used metaphorically for believing, the Evangelist, to relate the metaphor to the opposite clause, says that those are *drawn* whose minds God enlightens and whose hearts He bends and forms to the obedience of Christ. The sum of it is that we should not be surprised if many shrink from the Gospel, for none will ever be able to come to Christ of himself unless God prevents him by His Spirit. Hence it follows that not all are drawn, but that God honours with this grace those whom He has elected. As far as the manner of drawing goes, it is not violent so as to compel men by an external force; but yet it is an effectual movement of the Holy Spirit, turning men from being unwilling and reluctant into willing. Wherefore it is false and impious to say that only the willing are drawn, as if a man will yield obedience to God at his own motion. For when men follow God willingly it is what they already have from Him, who has formed their hearts to obey Him.

45. *It is written in the prophets.* From the testimony of Isaiah Christ confirms His saying that no man can come to Him unless he is drawn by the Father. He refers to prophets in the plural, because all their prophecies had been collected into one *corpus* and we can well think of the one book of all the prophets. The passage quoted here is to be found in Isa. 54.13 and Jer. 31.34, where, speaking of the restoration of the Church, he promises she shall have sons taught by the instruction of God. Hence we can easily deduce that the only way in which the Church can be restored is by God undertaking the office of schoolmaster, and bringing believers to Himself. The way of teaching which the prophet speaks of consists not only in the outward word but also in the secret operation of the Holy Spirit. In short, this teaching of God is the inward illumination of the heart.

When He says *all*, it must be limited to the elect, who alone are the true children of the Church. It is not difficult to see how Christ applies this prophecy to the present subject. Isaiah shows that the Church is only truly built up when her children are taught by God. Christ therefore justly concludes that men have no eyes to see the light of life until God has opened them. At the same time He emphasizes the general term, arguing from it that all who are taught by God are effectually drawn so that they come. And what He immediately adds pertains to this.

Every one that hath heard. The sum of this is that all who do not believe are reprobate and given over to destruction; for God makes all the sons of the Church and heirs of life His obedient disciples. From this it follows that none of God's elect shall be outside the faith of Christ. Again, as Christ earlier had denied that men are fitted for faith until they have been drawn, so He now declares that it is the effectual grace of the Spirit by which they are drawn, so that they necessarily believe.

The whole faculty of free will which the Papists dream about is utterly overturned by these two clauses. For if we begin to come to Christ only when the Father has drawn us, neither the beginning of faith, nor any preparation for it, lies in us. On the other hand, if all come whom the Father has taught, He gives them not only the freedom to believe but faith itself. When therefore we willingly obey the Spirit's guiding, it is a part and, as it were, sealing, of grace. For God would not draw us if He only stretched out His hand and left our will in a state of suspense. But He is properly said to draw us when He extends the power of His Spirit to the full completing of faith. They are said to hear God who willingly submit to God when He speaks within them, because the Spirit reigns in their hearts.

Cometh unto me. He shows the inseparable union that He has with the Father. The meaning is that it is impossible that any of God's disciples shall not submit to Christ, and that those who reject Christ will not be taught by God, since the only wisdom that all the elect learn in the school of God is to come to Christ. For the Father who sent Him cannot deny Himself.

Not that any man hath seen the Father, save he which is from God, he hath seen the Father. Verily, verily, I say unto you, He that believeth in me hath eternal life. I am the bread of life. Your fathers did eat the manna in the wilderness, and they died. This is the bread which cometh down out of heaven, that a man may eat thereof, and not die. I am the living bread which came down out of heaven: if any man eat of this bread, he shall live for ever; yea and the bread which I shall give is my flesh, which I shall give for the life of the word. (46-51)

46. *Not that any man.* So far, He has praised the grace of His Father. Now He earnestly calls believers to Himself alone. For these two things must be joined: there can be no knowledge of Christ until the Father enlightens by His Spirit those who are blind by nature; and yet it is useless to seek God unless Christ leads the way, for the majesty of God is higher than men's senses can reach. Nay, more! A supposed knowledge of God outside Christ will be a deadly abyss. When He says that He alone has known the Father, He means that this office

belongs peculiarly to Himself to manifest to men Him who would otherwise be hidden.

47. *He that believeth in Me.* This is an explanation of the foregoing statement, for it teaches us that God is made known to us when we believe in Christ. It is then that we begin to see the invisible God as in a mirror or a lively and express image. Accursed then be everything declared to us about God, unless it directs us to Christ! I have already explained what it is to believe in Christ; for we are not to imagine a confused and empty faith which despoils Christ of His power, as the Papists do, who believe of Christ just so much as they think fit. For we obtain life by faith because we are aware that all the parts of our life are contained in Christ. Some infer from this passage that to believe in Christ is equivalent to eating Christ or His flesh. But this is not well founded. For these two things differ as former and latter, just like coming to Christ and drinking Him. For the coming is first. I confess that Christ is eaten only by faith; but the reason is that we receive Him by faith that He may dwell in us, and that we may be made partakers of Him and thus one with Him. This eating is therefore the effect or work of faith.

48. *I am the bread of life.* Besides His earlier saying that He is the quickening bread by which our souls are nourished, He now, to explain it better, repeats the contrast between this bread and the ancient manna, as well as a comparison of the men concerned. *Your fathers,* He declares, *did eat the manna,* etc. He says that the manna was for their fathers a mortal food which did not exempt them from death. It follows, therefore, that only in Him will souls find that food by which they are fed unto eternal life. Besides, we must remember, as I have mentioned elsewhere, that this saying does not refer to the manna as a secret figure of Christ. For in that respect Paul calls it spiritual food. But we have said that Christ is here accommodating His discourse to the audience, who cared only about feeding their stomachs, and looked no higher in manna. Quite rightly, therefore, He declares that their fathers are dead—that is, those who were similarly devoted to the belly. And yet He invites them to eat, when He says that He is come *that any man may eat.* For this expression was as good as saying that He is ready for all who simply wish to eat of Him. That none of those who have once eaten Christ *shall die,* must be taken as meaning that the life He bestows on us is never extinguished, as we said in Chapter Five.

51. *I am the living bread.* He repeats the same thing often, for nothing is more necessary to be known; and everyone feels for himself how hard it is to believe it, and how quickly it passes away. We all desire life; but in seeking it we foolishly and perversely wander about in digressions; and even when it is set before us, the most part reject it

as distasteful. For who does not invent for himself a life outside Christ? And how many are satisfied with Christ alone? It is no superfluous repetition, then, for Christ to state so frequently that He alone suffices to give life. For He claims the title of bread for Himself to tear from our hearts all fictitious hopes of living. He now calls Himself the living bread in the same sense as He has said before that He is the bread of life; that is, life-giving bread.

He often speaks of His coming down from heaven, for spiritual and incorruptible life will not be found in this world, whose form passes away and vanishes, but only in the heavenly Kingdom of God.

Whenever He uses the word *eat* He is exhorting us to faith, which alone makes us enjoy this bread unto life. Nor is this in vain, for few deign to stretch out their hand to put this bread into their mouths. Even when the Lord puts it right up to their mouths, few taste it; some are filled with wind and others, Tantalus-like, are starving through their own folly with the food close beside them.

The bread which I will give. Since this secret power of bestowing life of which He is speaking might be referred to His divine essence, He now comes to the second step and tells them that this life resides in His flesh so that it may be drawn from it. It is a wonderful purpose of God that He has set life before us in that flesh, where before there had only been the material of death. And thus He provides for our weakness, for He does not call us above the clouds to enjoy life, but exhibits it on earth just as if He were exalting us to the mysteries of His Kingdom. And yet while correcting the pride of our mind, He tests the humility and obedience of our faith by commanding those who would seek life to rely on His flesh, which in its appearance is contemptible.

But it is objected that the flesh of Christ cannot give life, since it was liable to death and even now is not in itself immortal; and again, that it is not the property of flesh at all to give life to souls. I reply, although this power comes from another source than the flesh, this is no reason why this office may not accord with it. For as the eternal Word of God is the fountain of life, so His Flesh is a channel to pour out to us the life which resides intrinsically, as they say, in His divinity. In this sense it is called life-giving, because it communicates to us a life that it borrows from elsewhere. This will not be at all obscure if we consider what is the reason for life, namely, righteousness. Although righteousness flows from God alone, we shall not have the full manifestation of it anywhere else than in Christ's flesh. For in His flesh was accomplished man's redemption; in it a sacrifice was offered to atone for sins, and an obedience yielded to God to reconcile Him to us; it was also filled with the sanctification of the Spirit; finally, having overcome death, it was received into the heavenly glory. Therefore it follows that in it are placed all the parts of life, so that none can rightly complain that He is deprived of life because it is hidden and far off.

Which I will give for the life of the world. The word 'give' is used in various ways. The first giving, which He mentioned earlier, is made daily, as often as Christ offers Himself to us. In the second place, it denotes that unique giving which was made on the cross when He offered Himself to the Father as a sacrifice. Then He delivered up Himself for the life of men; and now He invites us to receive the fruit of His death. For it would be no use to us that the sacrifice was once offered, if we did not now feed upon that sacred feast. It should also be noted that Christ claims to Himself the office of sacrificing His flesh. This shows up the wicked sacrilege that the Papists defile themselves with when in the Mass they usurp to themselves what belonged exclusively to that one High Priest.

The Jews therefore strove one with another, saying, How can this man give us his flesh to eat? Jesus therefore said unto them, Verily, verily, I say unto you, Except ye eat the flesh of the Son of man and drink his blood, ye have not life in yourselves. He that eateth my flesh and drinketh my blood hath eternal life; and I will raise him up at the last day. For my flesh is meat indeed, and my blood is drink indeed. He that eateth my flesh and drinketh my blood abideth in me, and I in him. As the living Father sent me, and I live because of the Father; so he that eateth me, he also shall live because of me. This is the bread which came down out of heaven: not as the fathers did eat manna, and died: he that eateth this bread shall live for ever. (52-58)

52. *The Jews therefore strove.* He again mentions the Jews, not to honour them, but to accuse them of unbelief, because they do not receive the teaching, well-known to them, of eternal life; or at least, do not search it out modestly, if it is still obscure and doubtful. For when He says that they strove, it is a sign of their obstinacy and contempt. And indeed, those who dispute so pugnaciously block their own way to the knowledge of the truth. But they are not censured simply for inquiring into the manner; for the same blame would fall on Abraham and the Blessed Virgin. They are therefore either led astray through ignorance, or are lacking in frankness, who overlook the passion and eagerness for quarrelling, which is all that the Evangelist condemns, and attack the one word *how*, as if it were unlawful for the Jews to ask about the mode of eating. If we knowingly and willingly leave in their tangle those knotty difficulties which are untied for us by the Word of the Lord, it is rather to be imputed to sloth than to the obedience of faith. Not only is it lawful, therefore, to inquire into the mode of eating the flesh of Christ, but it is also very important for us

to grasp it, so far as it is explained in the Scriptures. Away then with that most obstinate pretence of humility, 'For my part, I am content with the Word of Christ alone, when He says that His flesh is meat indeed;' to all the rest I gladly shut my eyes.' As if heretics would not have the same excuse when they are willingly ignorant that Christ was conceived by the Holy Spirit, because they believe that He was of the seed of Abraham and inquire no further. Only, we must keep such a moderation about the secret works of God, as not to desire to know more than He determines by His Word.

53. *Verily, verily, I say unto you.* This oath was wrung from Christ when He saw His grace rejected with such proud contempt. He does not now use straightforward teaching, but mingles threats with it to terrify them. He pronounces eternal perdition against all who refuse to seek life from His flesh, as if He were saying, 'If My flesh is despicable to you, rest assured that no other hope of life remains for you.' For all who despise Christ's grace there remains the vengeance that they and their pride will miserably perish. And they must be urged with abrupt severity, so that they may not go on flattering themselves. For if we threaten sick people who will not take medicines that they will die, what are we to do with the ungodly, when they strive, so far as they can, to destroy life itself?

When He says *the flesh of the Son of man*, He is emphasizing it. For He reproves their contempt, which came from their seeing that He was like other men. So the meaning is: 'Despise me if you like for the low and despicable appearance of my flesh; yet within that despicable flesh is life; and if you lack that, nowhere else will you find anything to give you life.'

The ancients made a bad mistake in supposing that little children were deprived of eternal life if they were not given the Eucharist. This sermon does not refer to the Lord's Supper, but to the continual communication which we have apart from the reception of the Lord's Supper. Nor were the Hussites in the right, when they proved from this passage that the cup should be given to all indiscriminately. As far as young children are concerned, Christ's ordinance forbids them to participate in the Lord's Supper, because they cannot yet try themselves or celebrate the remembrance of the death of Christ. The same ordinance makes the cup common to all as well as the bread, for it commands us all to drink of it.

54. *He that eateth my flesh.* This is a repetition, but it is not superfluous, for it confirms what was hard to believe—that souls feed on His flesh and blood in precisely the same way that the body is sustained by eating and drinking. Therefore, as He had just declared that only death awaits all who seek life elsewhere than in His flesh, so now He stirs up

the godly to a good hope, when He promises them life in the same flesh.

Notice how often He connects the resurrection with eternal life, because our salvation will be hidden until that day. Hence none can feel what Christ bestows on us save he who rises above the world and places the final resurrection before his eyes. From these words it is plain that it is wrong to expound this whole passage as applying to the Lord's Supper. For if it were true that all who come to the Lord's holy Table are made partakers of His flesh and blood, all alike will obtain life. But we know that many of them fall into perdition. And indeed, it would have been inept and unseasonable to preach about the Lord's Supper before He had instituted it. So it is certain that He is now treating of the perpetual eating of faith. At the same time, I confess that there is nothing said here that is not figured and actually presented to believers in the Lord's Supper. Indeed, we might say that Christ intended the holy Supper to be a seal of this discourse. This is also the reason why John makes no mention of the Lord's Supper. And therefore Augustine follows the proper order when, in expounding this chapter, he does not touch on the Lord's Supper until he comes to the end. And then he shows that this mystery is represented in a symbol whenever the Churches celebrate the sacred Supper, in some places daily, in others only on the Lord's day.

55. *For my flesh is meat indeed.* He confirms it in other words, 'As the body is weakened and exhausted by fasting, so the soul will soon perish with hunger if it is not refreshed with heavenly bread.' For when He states that His flesh is meat indeed, He means that souls are starved if they lack that food. You will only find life in Christ when you seek the substance of life in His flesh. Thus we should glory with Paul in I Cor. 2.2 that we regard nothing as excellent but Christ crucified; for as soon as we depart from the sacrifice of His death, we encounter nothing but death. Nor does any other way but His death and resurrection lead us to a sense of His divine power. Embrace Christ, therefore, as the Servant of the Father, that He may show Himself to you as the Prince of life. For by His emptying Himself, we were enriched with the abundance of all blessings; His humiliation and descent raised us up to heaven; by bearing the curse of the cross He set up a noble banner of righteousness. Consequently, they are false interpreters[1] who lead souls away from Christ's flesh.

But why does Christ mention His blood separately, when it is contained under flesh? I reply, He did so in respect to our weakness. For when He distinctly mentions food and drink, He says that the life which He bestows is complete in every part, so that we may not imagine some semi- or imperfect life. It is as if He said that no part of

---

[1] i.e. of the Eucharist; French: *expositeurs du mystere de la Cene.*

life shall be lacking to us, provided we eat His flesh and drink His blood. Thus also, in the Lord's Supper, which corresponds to this teaching, He is not content with the symbol of the bread alone, but adds also the cup, so that, having a twofold token of life in Him, we may learn to be satisfied with Him alone. For only the man who has complete and perfect life in Christ will find a part of life in Him.

56. *He that eateth my flesh.* Here is another confirmation. Since He alone has life in Himself, He tells us how we may enjoy it—by eating His flesh. As if He affirmed that there is no other way for Him to become ours than by our faith being directed to His flesh. For none will ever come to Christ-God who neglects the man. Wherefore, if you want to have anything in common with Christ you must especially take care not to despise His flesh.

When He says that He *abideth*, it is just as if He had said that the one bond of union, and the way in which He becomes one with us, is when our faith rests on His death. Moreover, we may infer from this that He is not speaking of the outward symbol, which many unbelievers receive indiscriminately and yet remain outside Christ. By this is also refuted the mad idea that Judas received the body of Christ no less than the others when Christ gave the bread to all. For as it is ignorant to limit this teaching to the outward sign, so we should remember what I said before, that the teaching which we have here is sealed there. Now it is certain that Judas never was a member of Christ; secondly, it is more than absurd to imagine the flesh of Christ dead and empty of the Spirit; and lastly, those who dream of any eating of the flesh of Christ without faith are ridiculous, since faith alone is, so to say, the mouth and the stomach of the soul.

57. *As the living Father sent me.* Christ has explained hitherto how we are to become partakers of life. Now He turns to the principal cause, since the first source of life is in the Father. He forestalls an objection; for it might seem as if He were taking away from God what belonged to Him, when He made Himself the Cause of life. Therefore He claims to be the Author of life in such a way as to acknowledge that what He administers to others was also given to Him by another. Let us observe that this sermon is also accommodated to the capacity of Christ's audience; for He compares Himself to the Father only in respect to the flesh. For although the Father is the beginning of life, the eternal Word is also properly life. But the eternal divinity of Christ is not under discussion here; for He shows Himself as He was manifested to the world, clothed in our flesh.

Therefore, when He says that He lives because of the Father, it does not apply to His naked divinity, nor does it belong to His human nature simply and in itself; but it is a description of the Son of God manifested in the flesh. Besides, we know that it is not unusual for Christ to ascribe to the Father everything divine in Himself. But it must be noted that He here enumerates three degrees of life. In the first place is the living Father, who is the source, but remote and hidden. Then follows the Son, whom we have exhibited to us as a fountain and through whom life flows to us. The third is the life we derive from Him. Now we see the heart of the matter: God the Father, in whom life dwells, is far removed from us; and Christ, placed between us, is the second Cause of life, that what would otherwise be concealed in God may reach us from Him.

58. *This is the bread.* He returns to the comparison between manna and His flesh which He had started out from; for the necessary end to the sermon was, 'You have no cause to prefer Moses to me because he fed your fathers in the wilderness. I supply you with far better food, for I bear heavenly life with me.' For as I said before, the bread is said to have come down from heaven because it has no savour of the earth or corruptibility, but breathes the immortality of the Kingdom of God. They who thought only of feeding the belly did not find this power in manna. For although manna had a twofold use, the Jews whom Christ is disputing with saw in it nothing but bodily food. But the life of the soul is not transitory, but increases more and more until the whole man is renewed.

These things said he in the synagogue, as he taught in Capernaum. Many therefore of his disciples, when they heard this, said, This is a hard saying; who can hear it? But Jesus knowing in himself that his disciples murmured at this, said unto them, Doth this cause you to stumble? What then if ye should behold the Son of man ascending where he was before? It is the spirit that quickeneth; the flesh profiteth nothing: the words that I have spoken unto you are Spirit, and are life. But there are some of you that believe not. For Jesus knew from the beginning who they were that believed not, and who it was that should betray him. (59-64)

59. *These things said he in the synagogue.* John mentions the place to show that many were present, and likewise that a sermon was preached on a weighty and important subject. But it at once goes on, that of such a great multitude there were hardly even a few who profited from it. Indeed, it caused many professed disciples of Christ to fall away. If the Evangelist had said that only some of them were offended we should think it terrible. But when they rise up in crowds and conspire together, what shall we call it? Let this story, then, sink deep into our minds, that we may never murmur against Christ when He speaks. And if we see anything like this in others today, we must not let their pride disturb our faith.

60. *This is a hard saying.* On the contrary, the hardness was in their hearts and not in the saying. But the reprobate are wont to gather together stones out of the Word of God to dash themselves against; and when in their hard obstinacy they rush against Christ, they complain that His saying is hard, which really ought to have softened them. For whoever submits humbly to Christ's teaching will find nothing hard or rough in it. To unbelievers, however, who obstinately oppose it, it will be a hammer breaking the rocks in pieces, as the prophet puts it in Jer. 23.29. But the same hardness is inborn in all of us, and if we judge of Christ's teaching from our feelings, His words will just be so many paradoxes. Therefore nothing remains but for everyone to commit himself to the guidance of the Spirit, that He may inscribe on our hearts what otherwise would never even have entered into our ears.

Who can hear it? Here we see how malicious unbelief is. Those who wickedly and profanely reject the teaching of salvation are not content to excuse themselves, but blatantly make the Son of God guilty in their place and say that He does not deserve to be heard. Thus today the Papists not only boldly reject the Gospel, but also bring out their fearful blasphemies, lest they should seem to be repelling God without reason. And indeed, since they want darkness, it is not surprising if Satan deceives them with fictitious portents. But what in their immoderation they cannot bear, will not be merely bearable to the moderate and teachable, but will support and comfort them. Nevertheless, the reprobate by their obstinate outcries will simply bring a worse destruction on themselves.

61. *But Jesus knowing.* Christ certainly knew that the offence taken by the reprobate was irremovable; for His teaching does not wound them so much as uncover the internal putrid ulcer which they nourished within their hearts. But He wished by every method to find out if any of those who were offended might not still be curable, and to stop the mouths of the rest. By asking this question, He means that they have no cause for offence, or at least that the substance of offence does not lie in the teaching itself. This is how we should restrain the wickedness of those who are excited only by a currish madness to slander the Word of God, and chastise the folly of those who rashly attack the truth.

He says that Jesus knew in Himself, because they had not yet openly said what was upsetting them, but were quietly grumbling among themselves. So He forestalls their open complaints. If anyone objects that their nature was not obscure, since they rejected Christ's doctrine in plain words, I acknowledge that the words which John related earlier are clear enough, but at the same time I say that they muttered and grumbled quietly among themselves like enemies. Had they spoken to Christ there would have been far more hope, because a way would have been opened up for teaching them. But when they are murmuring to themselves, they shut the road of learning against themselves. Therefore, when we do not follow the Lord's meaning at once, the best thing to do is to go straight to Him for Him to settle all these problems for us.

Doth this cause you to stumble? Here Christ seems to augment the offence instead of removing it. But if anyone examines the cause of offence more closely, the following statement contained enough to satisfy their minds. The lowly and despicable condition of Christ which they actually saw when, clothed in flesh, He did not differ from the common man, prevented them giving His divine power a chance. But now, drawing back a veil, as it were, He calls them to look at His heavenly glory; as if He were saying, 'Because I live without honour among men, you despise me, and recognize nothing divine in Me. But soon it will come to pass that God will adorn Me with great power and raise Me from the contemptible state of this mortal life above the heavens.' For in Christ's resurrection appeared such a power of the Holy Spirit as plainly showed Christ to be the Son of God, as Paul also teaches in Rom. 1.4. And when Ps. 2.7 says, 'Thou art my son; this day have I begotten thee,' the resurrection is established as a proof for the acknowledgment of Christ's glory, and His ascension into heaven was the complement of that glory. His saying that He was in heaven before does not strictly accord with His humanity, though He speaks of the Son of man. But since the two natures in Christ constitute one person, it is not an unusual way of speaking, to transfer what is proper to one nature to the other.

63. *It is the Spirit that quickeneth.* By these words Christ tells us that the Jews did not benefit by His teaching, because it is spiritual and quickening, and did not encounter ears well prepared. But since this passage has been expounded in various ways, it is important first to grasp the real meaning of the words and then Christ's purpose will easily appear. Chrysostom, wrongly to my mind, refers His statement that the flesh profits nothing to the Jews, who were carnal. I acknowledge, indeed, that in heavenly mysteries the whole power of the human mind disappears and fails. But Christ's words do not have that meaning without being violently twisted. Equally forced is the opinion about the antithesis—that it is the illumination of the Spirit that quickens. Nor are they right who say that the flesh of Christ profits inasmuch as He was crucified, but that when it is eaten it is of no advantage to us. On the contrary, it is necessary to eat the crucified flesh for it to benefit us. Augustine thinks that we should supply the word 'only' or 'by itself', because it must be joined with the Spirit. This fits in well with the argument, for Christ is referring simply to

the manner of eating. He does not exclude every kind of usefulness, as if none at all could be obtained from His flesh, but says that it will be useless if separated from the Spirit. For where does the flesh get its quickening power, but because it is spiritual? Therefore whoever stops short at the earthly nature of the flesh will find in it nothing but what is dead. But those who raise their eyes to the power of the Spirit with which the flesh is imbued, will feel from the effect itself and the experience of faith that quickening is no empty word.

We now understand how the flesh is meat indeed and yet profits nothing. It is meat in that, by it, life is procured for us, in it God is reconciled to us, and in it we have all the parts of salvation accomplished. It profits nothing if considered in its origin and nature; for the seed of Abraham, which in itself is subject to death, does not give life, but receives its power of feeding us from the Spirit. Therefore we also must bring the spiritual mouth of faith that we may be truly nourished by it.

The sentence was cut short, probably because Christ saw that He had to act like this towards unbelievers. So He broke off the sermon with this clause, because they did not deserve Him to speak to them any more. But He did not neglect the godly and teachable, for they have here in a few words enough to satisfy them abundantly.

The words that I have spoken. This is an allusion to the preceding sentence, for He now uses the word Spirit in a different sense. He had spoken of the secret power of the Spirit and now neatly applies it to His teaching, since it is spiritual. For the word *Spirit* has to be made into an adjective. Now, that Word is called spiritual which calls us upward to seek Christ in His heavenly glory through the guidance of the Spirit, by faith and not by our carnal perception. For we know that what was said can only be understood by faith. And it is also worth noticing that He connects life with the Spirit. He calls His Word life from its effect; as if He had called it quickening; but says that it will only be quickening to those who receive it spiritually, and others will derive death from it. For the godly this is a most delightful commendation of the Gospel, because they are assured that it is appointed for their eternal salvation. Yet at the same time they are warned to take care to show themselves genuine disciples.

64. *But there are some of you.* He again blames them. They are empty of the Spirit, and corrupt and pervert His teaching wickedly, and thus turn it to their destruction. Otherwise they could have objected, 'You claim that what you speak is quickening, but we experience nothing of the sort.' He therefore says that they are hindering themselves; for unbelief is always proud and will never comprehend anything in Christ's words, which it despises and disdains. Therefore,

if we desire to profit at all under this Master, let us bring minds well disposed to listen to Him. For if the entrance to His teaching is not opened up by humility and reverence, our understandings are harder than stones and will not admit any part of sound doctrine. Therefore, when in our own day we see so few in the world profiting from the Gospel, let us remember this comes from men's depravity. For how many deny themselves and truly devote themselves to Christ? As to His saying merely that there were some unbelievers when the accusation fitted almost all of them, He seems to have done it lest any who were yet curable should be thrown into despair.

For he knew from the beginning. The Evangelist added this in case any should think that Christ formed a hasty opinion of His hearers. Many professed to be of His flock, but their sudden apostasy laid bare their hypocrisy. But the Evangelist says that Christ knew their treachery, even when it was hidden from others. And this is said, not so much on His account, as to teach us not to form a judgment until we know the truth of the matter. That Christ knew them from the beginning was peculiar to His divinity. It is different with us. Because we do not know the hearts, we ought to suspend judgment until ungodliness shows itself in outward signs, and thus the tree may be judged by its fruits.

> *And he said, For this cause have I said unto you, that no man can come unto me, except it be given unto him of the Father. Upon this many of his disciples went back and walked no more with him. Jesus said therefore unto the twelve, Would ye also go away? Simon Peter answered him, Lord, to whom shall we go? thou hast the words of eternal life. And we have believed and know that thou art the Christ, the Son of the living God. Jesus answered them, Did not I choose you the twelve, and one of you is a devil? Now he spake of Judas the son of Simon Iscariot, for it was he that should betray him, being one of the twelve. (65-71)*

65. *For this cause have I said unto you.* He again says that faith is a rare and special gift of God's Spirit, so that we may not be surprised if the Gospel is not received everywhere and by all. For we misunderstand things badly and think less highly of the Gospel if the whole world does not assent to it. The thought comes into our minds, 'How can it be that the greater number of men deliberately reject their salvation?' Christ therefore gives a reason why there are so few believers—because none reaches faith by his own intuition; for all are blind until they are enlightened by the Spirit of God, and therefore only they partake of this great blessing whom the Father honours with participation in it. If this grace were for all indiscriminately, it would have been inopportune and inappropriate to mention it in this passage;

for we must grasp Christ's aim, that not many believe the Gospel, since faith proceeds only from the secret revelation of the Spirit.

He now uses the word *give* instead of *draw*, which He used before. By this He means that the only reason why God draws is because He freely befriends us. For what we obtain from the gift and grace of God, none procures for himself by his own industry.

66. *Upon this many of his disciples went back.* The Evangelist now relates how much disturbance that sermon caused. And it is dreadful and monstrous that so kind and friendly an invitation of Christ should have alienated the minds of many, especially of those who had earlier been on His side and were even His close disciples. But this example is put before us as a mirror to see how great is the world's depravity and ingratitude, which heaps up material to stumble over even on the smooth way of life, that it may not come to Christ. Many might say that it would have been better that such a sermon had never been preached which caused many to fall away. But we ought to look at it very differently. For it was necessary then, and is now daily necessary, that what had been foretold about Christ should be seen in His teaching, namely, that He is the stone of stumbling (Isa. 8.14).

We ought, of course, to moderate our preaching so that none will be offended through our fault. As far as possible, we ought to keep all men. And in short we ought to take care that we do not, by unconsidered talking, upset ignorant or weak minds. But it will never be possible to be so careful that Christ's teaching will not be a cause of offence to many. For the reprobate, who are given up to destruction, suck poison from the most wholesome food and gall from honey. The Son of God undoubtedly knew best what was useful; and yet we see that He does not escape offending many of His own. Therefore, although many dislike pure doctrine, we are not at liberty to suppress it. But let the teachers of the Church remember Paul's admonition that the Word of God ought to be rightly divided (II Tim. 2.15), and then let them advance boldly through every kind of offence. And if it happens that many fall away, let us not blame the Word of God because it does not please the reprobate. For they are too dainty and soft who are so shaken by the apostasy of some, that as soon as such fall away, they are discouraged.

When the Evangelist adds *and walked no more with him*, he means that it was not a complete apostasy, but that they only withdrew from close companionship with Christ; and yet he does condemn them as apostates. From this we should learn that we cannot retreat one step without the jeopardy of falling into a treacherous denial.

67. *Jesus said therefore unto the twelve.* Since the apostles' faith might be seriously shaken when they saw that they, only a few, remained of

a great multitude, Christ turns His discourse to them and tells them there is no cause for them to let themselves be carried away by the lightness and fickleness of the others. When He asks them whether they also want to go away, He does it to confirm their faith. For by setting Himself before them as the one they may remain with, He also exhorts them not to become the companions of apostates. And indeed, if faith is to be founded on Christ, it will not depend on men and will never waver though it should see heaven and earth in disorder. We should also notice that, when Christ is deprived of nearly all His disciples, He keeps the twelve only; in the same way as Isaiah had been commanded to bind the testimony and seal the law among the disciples (Isa. 8.16). By examples like these, every believer is taught to follow God, even though he had no companions.

68. *Simon Peter answered him.* Here as elsewhere, Peter replies in the name of all, since they were all of the same mind—except that there was no sincerity in Judas. This reply contains two clauses: first Peter says why he and his brethren gladly remain with Christ—because they see that His teaching is wholesome and quickening; and secondly, he confesses that if they left Him, nothing but death awaited them, whoever they went to.

When he says *the words of life*, he uses the genitive for an adjective, which is common among the Hebrews. Now, it is a remarkable commendation of the Gospel that it administers eternal life to us; just as Paul testifies that it is the power of God unto salvation to all who believe (Rom. 1.16). The Law does, indeed, also contain life; but because it pronounces the sentence of eternal death against transgressors, it can do nothing but kill. Far otherwise is life offered to us in the Gospel, when God reconciles us to Himself freely, not imputing our sins. Moreover, Peter is saying no ordinary thing about Christ when he declares that He has *the words of eternal life*. But he ascribes this to Him as peculiar to Him alone. Hence follows the second statement, which I pointed to above, that as soon as they have gone away from Christ, nothing remains for them but death, wherever they go. Certain destruction awaits all who are not satisfied with that Master, but fly away to men's inventions.

69. *And we have believed.* The verbs are in the past tense, but they can be changed into the present; it makes little difference to the meaning. In these words Peter gives a short summary of faith. But the confession seems unrelated to the matter in hand, for the question concerned the eating of the flesh of Christ. I reply, although the twelve did not at once understand all that Christ was teaching, it was enough for them, according to the measure of their faith, to confess Him as the author of their salvation and submit to Him in everything.

The word *believe* is put first, because the obedience of faith is the beginning of true understanding; or rather, faith is itself truly the eye of the mind. But at once knowledge is added, which distinguishes faith from erroneous and false opinions. For Turks and Jews and Papists believe, but without knowing or understanding anything. Knowledge is joined to faith, because we have a sure and undoubted conviction of God's truth, not in the same way as human sciences are apprehended, but when the Spirit seals it in our hearts.

70. *Jesus answered them.* In that Christ replied to them all, we may infer that all spoke by the mouth of Peter. And now Christ prepares and arms the eleven apostles against a fresh offence which was already threatening. It was a powerful instrument of Satan to shake their faith, that they were already reduced to such a small number. But the fall of Judas might discourage them altogether. For since Christ had chosen that sacred number, who would ever have thought that any of its completeness could be torn away? Therefore Christ's admonition may be interpreted thus: 'Out of a large company you twelve alone are left. If your faith has not been shaken by the unbelief of many, prepare for a new trial. This band, small as it is, will be diminished still further by one man.'

When Christ says that He has chosen *twelve*, He is not referring to the eternal purpose of God. For it is impossible that any of those who have been predestinated to life will fall away. But they, who had been chosen to the apostolic office, ought to have surpassed all others in godliness and holiness. Therefore, He used the word *chosen* for those who were selected and separated from the common rank.

And one of you is a devil. There is no doubt that, by this name, He wanted to make Judas utterly abominable. For they are mistaken who extenuate the awfulness of the word. We cannot execrate enough those who dishonour such a sacred office. Teachers who faithfully discharge their office are called angels (Mal. 2.7). He is justly accounted a devil, therefore, who falls away by his treachery and wickedness when he has been admitted to so honourable an order. There is another reason too; for God allows more power and liberty to Satan over wicked and ungodly ministers than over other more ordinary men. And therefore, if those who were chosen to be pastors are driven by such devilish madness that they are like wild and monstrous beasts, we should not despise the dignity of their order, but rather honour it the more when its profanation is followed by such fearful punishment.

71. *Now he spake of Judas.* Although Judas had a bad conscience, we do not read that he was moved. So numbed are hypocrites that they do not feel their own wounds, and before men they are so hardened that they do not scruple to prefer themselves to the very best of men.

CHAPTER SEVEN

And after these things Jesus walked in Galilee: for he would not walk in Judaea, because the Jews sought to kill him. Now the feast of the Jews, the feast of the tabernacles, was at hand. His brethren therefore said unto him, Depart hence, and go into Judaea, that thy disciples also may behold thy works which thou doest. For no man doeth anything in secret, and himself seeketh to be known openly. It thou doest these things, manifest thyself to the world. For even his brethren did not believe on him. Jesus therefore saith unto them, My time is not yet come; but your time is alway ready. The world cannot hate you; but me it hateth, because I testify of it, that its works are evil. Go ye unto the feast: I go not up yet unto this feast; because my time is not yet fulfilled. (1-8)

1. *Jesus walked in Galilee.* The Evangelist does not seem to be composing a continuous narrative but to select events worth relating from what occurred at different times. He says that Christ lived in Galilee for a time, because nowhere among the Jews was safe for Him. If anyone thinks it strange that Christ sought a hiding place, when at His will He could break and incapacitate all the efforts of His enemies, the solution is easy. He remembered the commission given Him by the Father and wanted to confine Himself within the limits of humanity. For He took the form of a servant and emptied Himself until the Father exalted Him, and thus in a human manner He fled from danger.

If it be objected that He knew that the time of His death was foreordained and therefore had no reason for avoiding it, the same solution applies here also, for He behaved as a man who was at the mercy of danger, and it was not right for Him to rush headlong into danger. In meeting perils, it is not for us to ask what God has determined about us, but what He commands and enjoins on us, what our office requires and demands, and what is the proper way to order our life. Besides, although Christ avoided dangers, He did not turn aside a hair's-breadth from the course of His duty. For what is the point of a safe life except to serve the Lord? We must always beware that we do not for the sake of life lose the purpose for living. When a despised corner of Galilee gives a lodging to Christ whom Judaea cannot endure, we learn that piety and the fear of God are not always outstanding in the chief places of the Church.

2. *Now the feast of the Jews was at hand.* Although I do not assert it definitely, this probably happened in the second year after Christ's

Baptism. We need not say much at present about this feast day that the Evangelist mentions. Moses teaches for what purpose and use it was commanded, in Lev. 23.33ff. It was that by this annual ceremony the Jews might remember how their fathers had lived forty years in tabernacles when they had no houses, that they might in this way praise the grace of their deliverance. We have said above that Christ came to Jerusalem at this feast for two reasons. One was that as He was subject to the Law to redeem us all from its bondage, He did not want to omit any part of its observation. The other was that He had a better opportunity to spread the Gospel in a crowd and unusual assembly. But now the Evangelist relates that Christ stayed quietly in Galilee as if He were not going to Jerusalem.

3. *His brethren therefore said unto him.* Under this name the Jews embraced all kindred and blood relations, to whatever degree. He says that they mocked Christ because He fled from the public eye and hid in the obscure and despised district of Galilee.[1] They were without doubt impelled by ambition to desire that Christ should become famous. But granting this, it is still plain that they despise and ridicule Him because they think He is acting unwisely and injudiciously. They even reproach Him for folly as wishing to be something but lacking the self-confidence to appear openly among men. When they say *that thy disciples also may behold*, they mean not only His inner circle of disciples but all those He wanted to win out of the whole nation; for they add, 'You want to be known by all, and yet you hide yourself away.'

4. *If thou doest these things.* That is, if you aspire to such greatness that all talk of you, bring it to pass that all shall look to you. And they contrast the world to those few among whom He was living without honour. Another meaning can also be drawn from it: If you do these things—i.e. you have the power to win fame by miracles—do not waste them; for everything that God has given you you are wasting here where there are none to witness and esteem you as you deserve. Here we see how lazy men are in considering the works of God. For Christ's kinsmen would never have spoken like this if they had not trampled under foot, as it were, the shining proofs of His divine power which they ought to have seen and revered with the highest admiration. What we hear about Christ happens daily. The children of God suffer worse annoyance from their relations than from outsiders, for they are Satan's instruments to tempt either to ambition or to avarice those who desire to serve God purely and faithfully. But Christ repels such Satans sharply and warns us by His example not to yield to the foolish wishes of our brethren.

[1] The text has *Judaea*, but Calvin's comment on 7.1 above suggests that *Galilee* is intended.

5. *For even his brethren.* From this we infer how worthless is carnal relationship, for the Spirit brands Christ's relations with an everlasting mark of infamy, because even when they were proved wrong by the witness of so many works they did not believe. Therefore whoever would be reckoned to be in Christ, as Paul says, let him be a new creature (II Cor. 5.17; Gal. 6.15); for those who give themselves entirely to God are placed in the position of father and mother and brethren to Christ, but others He utterly disavows. The more ridiculous is the Papist's superstition in disregarding everything else in the Virgin Mary and giving her only the honour of relationship; as if Christ Himself had not reproved the woman who called out from the crowd, 'Blessed is the womb that bare thee, and the breasts which thou didst suck,' by replying, 'Yea, rather, blessed are they that hear the word of God' (Luke 11.27-28).

6. *My time is not yet come.* Some interpret this as the time of His death, but erroneously, for it means the time of His setting out on His journey. He is telling them that in this He is different from His relations. They may freely and safely go about at all hours before the world, because the world is friendly and on their side. But He rightly fears for Himself, because the world hates Him. By these words He means that they are wrong to give advice on something they do not understand. When He says that the world cannot hate them, He is reproving their utter carnality. For peace with the world can only be bought by an ungodly assent to vices and every kind of evil.

7. *But me it hateth because I testify.* The world is here to be taken as men who are not born again but retain their own nature. Therefore Christ says that all who have not yet been regenerated by the Spirit are His enemies. And why? Because He condemns their works. And if we agree with Christ's decision, we must acknowledge that the whole nature of man is so corrupt and perverse that nothing right, nothing sincere, nothing good can proceed from it. It is just for this reason that we are all pleased with ourselves so long as we remain of that mind.

Christ now says that He is hated because He has testified to the world that its works are evil. He means that the Gospel cannot be preached aright without summoning the whole world as guilty to the judgment seat of God, that flesh and blood may thus be crushed and reduced to nothing according to the saying, 'When the Spirit shall come, he will reprove the world of sin' (John 16.8). We learn from it that so great is man's natural pride, that he flatters and applauds himself in his vices. For men would not flare up at reproof were they not blinded by too much self-love, and so flatter themselves in their own sins. Among all the vices of men, the chief and most destructive is haughtiness and arrogance. The Spirit alone softens us to bear reproofs patiently and so to offer ourselves willingly to be slain by the sword of the Gospel.

And having said these things unto them, he abode still in Galilee. But when his brethren were gone up unto the feast, then went he also up, not publicly, but as it were in secret. The Jews therefore sought him at the feast, and said, Where is he? And there was much murmuring among the multitudes concerning him: some said, He is a good man; others said, Not so, but he leadeth the multitude astray. Howbeit no man spake openly of him for fear of the Jews. (9-13)

9. *He abode still in Galilee.* The Evangelist here sets before our eyes, on the one hand Christ's relations who, in the usual way, pretend to worship God but yet are friendly with unbelievers and so walk in safety, and, on the other hand, Christ Himself, who was hated by the world and comes secretly into the city until the necessity of His office compels Him to show Himself openly. But if there is nothing worse than being estranged from Christ, cursed be that costly peace which makes us renounce Christ.

11. *The Jews therefore sought him.* Here we ought to consider what was the state of the Church. For at that time the Jews gaped for the promised redemption like hungry men. Yet when Christ appears to them they remain doubtful. Hence that confused murmuring and variety of opinions. That they whisper secretly is an indication of the tyranny that the priests and scribes took to themselves. It is indeed a fearful example that this Church—at that time the only Church on earth—is here represented as a confused and shapeless chaos. Those who rule, instead of being shepherds, hold down the people in fear and terror, and throughout the whole body there is a shameful desolation and a sad scattering. By *the Jews* he means the common people, who for two years had been used to hearing Christ and now seek Him because He does not appear according to His custom. For when they say, *Where is he?* they are speaking of someone they knew; and yet the word shows that they had not yet been seriously moved and always remained in doubt.

12. *And there was much murmuring.* He means that they were holding private conservations about Christ in the manner of people gathered in large crowds. The dissension related here proves that it is no new evil for men to differ in their opinions about Christ, even in the very bosom of the Church. And although we may not hesitate to receive Christ who was once condemned by the most part of His own people, yet we should be armed with the same kind of shield, lest these everyday dissensions should disturb us. Again, we can see how great is men's rashness in divine affairs. In some unimportant matter they would not have been so arbitrary, but where the Son of God and His most holy

doctrine is concerned, they immediately rush at a judgment. We should observe the greater moderation, that we may not condemn our life by the eternal truth of God. And if the world regards us as impostors, let us remember that these are the marks of Christ, so long as we show at the same time that we are genuine. Moreover, this passage shows that in a great multitude, even when the mass of it is confused, there are always some right-thinking ones. But the few well-disposed are swallowed up by the many who are unsound.

13. *Howbeit no man spake openly.* Here by the Jews he means the ruling classes who had the government in their hands. They burned with such hatred against Christ that they did not allow a single word on either side. Not that they disliked Him being slandered with any sort of calumny, but because they saw it was best if His name could be buried in oblivion. Thus, when the enemies of the truth find that they gain nothing by their savagery, their great desire is to suppress the remembrance of it and this alone they strive after. That all were silent and subdued by *fear* was a proof of utter tyranny, as I have already said. For just as unbridled licence has no place in a well regulated Church, so when all liberty is kept suppressed by fear so that no one dares utter a word, it is the most wretched condition. But the power of Christ shone forth more clearly and wonderfully when He gained a hearing for Himself among armed foes and their furious hatred and under a repressive government, and asserted the truth with an open mouth, as they say.

But when it was now the midst of the feast Jesus went up into the temple and taught. The Jews therefore marvelled, saying, How knoweth this man letters, having never learned? Jesus therefore answered them, and said, My teaching is not mine, but his that sent me. If any man willeth to do his will, he shall know of the teaching, whether it be of God, or whether I speak for myself. He that speaketh from himself seeketh his own glory: but he that seeketh the glory of him that sent him, the same is true, and no unrighteousness is in him. Did not Moses give you the law, and yet none of you doeth the law? Why seek ye to kill me?

(14-19)

14. *He went up into the temple.* We now see that Christ was not so afraid as to fail in His duty, for the reason for His delay was to preach to a very big crowd. We may sometimes, therefore, retire from danger, but we should never neglect or omit any opportunity of doing good. As to His teaching in the Temple: He does so according to the ancient order and custom. For although God had commanded so many ceremonies, He did not want His people to be occupied with cold and empty spectacles. For their purpose to be understood, they

had to be accompanied by teaching. In this way external rites are lively images of spiritual things when they take their form from the Word of God. But because the priests were then almost dumb and the scribes adulterated pure doctrine with their leaven and false inventions, Christ undertook the teaching office. And this justly, for He was the High Priest—He affirms shortly afterwards that He undertakes nothing but by the command of the Father.

15. *The Jews therefore marvelled.* They are at fault who think that Christ's word was so welcomed that it was esteemed and honoured. For the Jews' marvelling meant that they made it a cause of contempt. For the ingratitude of men lies in always deliberately finding an occasion for erring when they judge of God's works. If God acts by the usual means and in the ordinary way, as they say, those visible means are like veils which prevent us perceiving the divine hand, so that we only acknowledge the human in them. But if an unusual power of God shines out above the order of nature and the generally known means, we are paralysed, and what ought to have deeply affected all our senses vanishes like a dream. For such is our pride that we take no account of anything whose cause is hidden.

It was a wonderful proof of God's power and grace that Christ, untaught by any master, was yet exceptionally powerful in His understanding of the Scriptures, that He who had never been a pupil should be a most excellent Teacher and Master. For the Jews despise the grace of God, simply because it exceeds their grasp. Let us be warned by their example, therefore, and learn to exercise greater reverence for God than we usually do in considering His works.

16. *My teaching is not mine.* Christ tells the Jews that what was an offence to them should rather have been a ladder for them to rise higher, to perceive God's glory; as if He had said, 'When you see a teacher untrained in the schools of men, confess that he has been taught by God.' For the reason why the heavenly Father determined that His Son should come out of an artisan's workshop instead of from the schools of the scribes, was to make the origin of the Gospel stand out the more, so that none should think it had been made up on earth or imagine that any man was its author. For the same reason Christ chose ignorant and uneducated men to be His apostles and let them remain in gross ignorance for three years, that when He had taught them for one moment He might put them forth as new men, and even as angels come down from heaven.

Meanwhile, Christ shows where we should look for the authority of spiritual teaching—from God alone. And when He asserts that the doctrine of His Father is not His, He is thinking of the capacity of His hearers, who had no higher opinion of Him than that He was a man.

So by way of concession He lets Himself be reckoned different from His Father, yet so as to bring forward nothing but what He had commanded. The sum of it is that what He teaches in the name of His Father is not of men and did not proceed from men, so that it could be despised with impunity. We see the argument by which He procures authority for His teaching. He refers it to God as its author. We see also by what right and for what reason He demands to be heard. It is because the Father sent Him to teach. Both these should be possessed by every man who takes up the office of a teacher and wants to be believed.

17. *If any man willeth.* He anticipates objections to the contrary. He had many adversaries there, and one of them might have been ready to grumble, 'Why do you boast to us of the name of God? We do not acknowledge that you have come from Him. So why do you put to us as a principle (which we do not at all admit) that you teach nothing but by His command?' Christ therefore replies that right judgment flows from the fear and reverence of God; so that if our minds are disposed to the fear of God they will easily see whether what He preaches is true or not. At the same time He rebukes them indirectly; for how is it that they cannot distinguish but because they lack the first necessity for a sound understanding, namely, godliness and an earnest desire to obey God?

This statement is very noteworthy. Satan continually lies in wait for us and everywhere spreads his nets, to catch us with his tricks. Here Christ gives us an excellent warning to beware of laying ourselves open to any of his impostures—that if we are ready to obey God He will never fail to illuminate us by the light of His Spirit, so that we shall be able to distinguish between truth and falsehood. There is nothing to stop us judging aright but our unteachableness and obstinacy, and whenever Satan deceives us we are justly punished for our hypocrisy. Thus Moses tells us that when false prophets arise, we are tried and proved by God, for they will never be deceived whose hearts are upright (Deut. 13.3). Hence it is evident how wickedly and foolishly many in our own day, fearing the danger of erring, smother all desire for learning by that very fear—as if it were said in vain, 'Knock, and it shall be opened unto you' (Matt. 7.7).

But let us, on the contrary, not doubt that God will give us the Spirit of discernment to be our continual Guide and Director if we are entirely given up to His obedience. If others like to waver, they will find at last how empty are the excuses for their ignorance. And indeed, we shall see that all who now hesitate and would rather nurse their doubt than inquire seriously by reading and hearing where the truth of God is, are bold enough to defy God in general prinicples. One will say that he prays for the dead because he distrusts his own judgment and will not dare condemn what perverse men have invented about purgatory—and yet he will freely let himself commit fornication. Another will say that he is not clever enough to distinguish between Christ's pure doctrine and the spurious inventions of men—but he will be clever enough to steal or perjure himself. In short, all the sceptics, hiding behind a veil of doubt in our present day controversies, show an open contempt of God in matters that are not at all obscure. So there is no need to be surprised that the teaching of the Gospel is received by very few today, since the fear of God is so rare in the world. These words of Christ also contain a definition of true religion —it is when we are heartily ready to follow the will of God; and only he can do this who has renounced his own point of view.

Or whether I speak from myself. We must notice how Christ wants us to form judgments on any doctrine. He wants us to receive without argument what is from God, but lets us reject freely whatever is of man. For this is the only mark He sets out for us to distinguish doctrines by.

18. *He that speaketh from himself.* Hitherto He has shown that the only cause of men's blindness lies in their not being ruled by the fear of God. He now sets a mark on the doctrine itself by which it may be known whether it is of God or of man. Everything that displays God's glory is holy and divine; but everything that serves men's ambition and so obscures God's glory by exalting them, not only does not deserve to be believed but ought to be rejected outright. He who makes God's glory his object will never go wrong, and he who decides and tests by this touchstone what is put forward in the name of God will never be deceived by a semblance of right. It also warns us that none can discharge the office of teacher in the Church faithfully, save he who is devoid of ambition and undertakes as his one activity and with all his might the promotion of the glory of God. When He says that *no unrighteousness is in him,* He means that there is nothing wicked or false, but that He acts as becomes an upright and sincere minister of God.

19. *Did not Moses?* The Evangelist does not relate Christ's sermon completely, but only selects the principle topics which furnish a summary of the whole. The priests and the scribes had flared up in anger against Him because He had healed the paralytic, and they said it was because they were zealous for the Law. To refute their hypocrisy He reasons, not from the subject but from their characters. For they all unrestrainedly indulged in their vices as if they had never known any law. Therefore He takes it that they are untouched by any love or care for the Law. This argument would not, indeed, have been

sufficient to prove His case, for although we must allow that they covered their wicked and unjust hatred under a false motive, it does not follow that Christ acted rightly if He did anything against the command of the Law. For we must not try to extenuate our own guilt by the sins of others.

In fact, Christ joins up two clauses here. In the former He appeals to His enemies' consciences, and since they proudly boasted they were the guardians of the Law He tears this mask off them by rebuking them for allowing themselves to break the Law as often as they liked and so caring nothing for the Law. Then He comes to the question itself, as we shall see later. Hence His defence is complete and strong in all respects. And the sum of this clause is that there is no zeal for the Law in those who despise it. Christ therefore infers that the great rage of the Jews in wanting to kill Him has another source. This is the way we should drag the wicked from their hiding places when they fight against God and sound doctrine and pretend to act from godly motives.

Those who are today the fiercest enemies of the Gospel and the most vigorous defenders of the Papacy have nothing more laudable on their side than a burning zeal. But if their lives are investigated they are all seen to conceal ugly shame, so that they openly mock God. Who does not know that gross Epicureanism reigns in the Papal Court? And have bishops and abbots enough modesty to hide their filthiness, so that even a semblance of religion may be apparent? Are not monks, also, and such brawlers, given up to all wickedness, lust, avarice and every kind of unnatural crime, so that their life cries aloud that they have forgotten God? And if they are not at all ashamed to boast of their zeal for God and the Church, ought they not to be curbed by this reply of Christ?

The multitude answered, Thou hast a devil: who seeketh to kill thee? Jesus answered and said unto them, I did one work, and ye all marvel. Therefore hath Moses given you circumcision (not that it is of Moses, but of the fathers); and on the sabbath ye circumcise a man. If a man receiveth circumcision on the sabbath, that the law of Moses may not be broken; are ye wroth with me, because I made a man every whit whole on the sabbath? Judge not according to appearance, but judge righteous judgement. (20-24)

20. *Thou hast a devil.* This is as much as to say, You are mad. It was a common phrase among the Jews, who had been brought up to believe that when men are impelled by rage or have lost their minds and reason, they are disturbed by the devil. And indeed, as gentle and moderate chastisements are God's fatherly rods, so when He treats us with greater harshness and severity He does not seem to strike us with

His own hand but rather to use the devil as the executioner and minister of His wrath. And the multitude in its simplicity reproaches Christ, for the common people were ignorant of the priest's intentions. These foolish men therefore call it madness when Christ complains that they were seeking to kill Him. We learn from this that we should be very careful not to make up our minds about unknown subjects; and if we are ever condemned thoughtlessly by the ignorant we should, after Christ's example, mildly swallow the insult.

21. *I did one work.* Now He leaves their characters and begins to speak about the matter. He proves that the miracle He did is in no way contrary to God's Law. When He says that He did one work He means that He is held guilty of one crime or is blamed only for the one work of healing a man on the sabbath, whereas they do many works of the same or a similar kind on the sabbath without reckoning them wrong—for not a sabbath passed but what many infants were circumcised in Judaea. He defends His action by this example, although He does not merely argue from what is similar, but compares the greater with the less. Circumcision and the healing of the paralytic were similar in that each was a divine work. But Christ maintains that the latter is the more excellent, since its benefit extends to the whole man. Now, if He had merely healed the man's physical disease, the comparison would have been invalid; for circumcision would have been more excellent as pertaining to the health of the soul. Christ is therefore connecting the spiritual result of the miracle to the outward benefit granted to the body. And so He rightly prefers the entire healing of a man to circumcision.

There might also be another reason for the comparison—that the Sacraments are not always attended by power and efficacy, whereas Christ worked efficaciously in healing the paralytic. But I prefer the former exposition, that the Jews are maliciously and slanderously blaming a work in which God's grace shines more brightly than in circumcision, which they honour so much that they think the sabbath is not broken by it. The marvelling of which He speaks means the murmur called forth by what Christ had done, because they thought He dared to do more than was lawful.

22. *Therefore Moses.* The introductory particle seems unsuitable. And so some take διὰ τοῦτο as διὰ τό; but the Greek construction is against this opinion. I explain it more simply—that circumcision was commanded in such a way that the practice of that sign was necessary even on the sabbath. 'Therefore,' He says. As if He were saying that now it has been sufficiently shown that the worship of the sabbath is not broken by the works of God. It is thus that Christ accommodates the example of circumcision to the present case. He at once makes a

correction when He says that Moses was not the first minister of
circumcision. But it was enough that Moses, who so strictly insisted
on the sabbath, should have commanded infants to be circumcised on
the eighth day, even though it coincided with the sabbath.

24. *Judge not.* Having ended His defence He rebukes them for being
carried away by their perverse dispositions and not forming a judgment
from the facts of the case. They rightly revered circumcision, and when
it was performed on the Sabbath they knew that the Law was not
broken, because God's works agree with one another. Why do they
not think the same of Christ's work, save because their minds are full
of a preconceived judgment against His person? Judgment will never
be right unless it is formed from the truth of the reality. For as soon as
personality comes into it, eyes and senses are focused on that and the
truth immediately disappears. This warning should be observed in
all cases and affairs; but it is especially necessary where heavenly
doctrine is concerned. For there is nothing we are more prone to than
being put off that doctrine by hatred or contempt of men.

*Some therefore of them of Jerusalem said, Is not this he whom they seek
to kill? And lo, he speaketh openly, and they say nothing unto him.
Can it be that the rulers indeed know that this is the Christ? Howbeit
we know this man whence he is: but when the Christ cometh, no one
knoweth whence he is. Jesus therefore cried in the temple, teaching and
saying, Ye both know me, and know whence I am; and I am not come
of myself, but he that sent me is true, whom ye know not. I know him:
because I am from him, and he sent me. They sought therefore to take
him: and no man laid his hand on him, because his hour was not yet
come. (25-30)*

25. *Some of them of Jerusalem;* that is, some who knew the plots of
the rulers and how much Christ was hated; for the common people,
as we saw above, regarded this as a dream or madness. And those who
knew how heartily the rulers of their nation hated Christ have reason
to be surprised that, while Christ not only openly walks in the Temple
but preaches freely, they leave Him be. But they are wrong in that
they do not take into account the providence of God in such a divine
miracle. Whenever carnal men see any unusual work of God, they do
indeed wonder, but no thought of God's power ever enters into their
mind. It is our duty, however, to ponder the works of God more
wisely. In particular, when the ungodly do not hinder the progress of
the Gospel as they would wish, we ought to be sure that their efforts
are ineffective because God has set His hand against them and scattered
them.

27. *Howbeit we know this man whence he is.* We see here not only

how great men's blindness is in judging divine things, but that they have the almost innate vice of being clever at building obstacles that will stop them arriving at the knowledge of the truth. Offences often arise from the craft of Satan and alienate many from Christ. But even were the road plain and smooth, everyone would make a stumbling-block for himself. So long as the rulers were against Christ their unbelief alone would have hindered this multitude. Now that that obstacle has been taken away, they invent for themselves a new reason for not coming to the faith. And even though it was right for them to be influenced by their rulers' example, they are so far from following the right path that of their own accord they stumble at the first step. Thus men who began well often soon fall away unless the Lord directs their course to the end.

The argument by which they hinder themselves is as follows: The prophets bore witness that Christ's origin should be unknown. But we know where this man comes from. Therefore, He cannot be regarded as the Christ. By this we are reminded how dangerous a thing it is to mangle the Scriptures, and, what is more, Christ Himself, estimating Him by only a half of Himself. God promised a Redeemer from the seed of David; but always He claims this office as His own. Therefore, He must have been God manifested in the flesh to be the Redeemer of His Church. Thus Micah points out the place where Christ should be born—'Out of thee, Bethlehem,' he says, 'shall come a prince to govern my people' (5.2). But immediately afterwards he speaks of another going forth which is far higher and therefore hidden and secret. Yet when those unhappy men only saw in Christ what was contemptible, they unthinkingly concluded that He was not the promised one. Therefore, let us learn to look on Christ's lowliness as to the flesh in such a way that this humility, despised by the wicked, may raise us to His heavenly glory. Thus Bethlehem, where the man had to be born, will be a door for us to go in unto the eternal God.

28. *Jesus therefore cried.* He attacks them with bitter words for their rashness, because they arrogantly flattered themselves in a false opinion and shut themselves off from the knowledge of the truth; as if He said, 'You know everything and yet you know nothing.' And indeed there is no worse plague than when men are so drunk with their belief in their little learning that they boldly reject everything contrary to their opinion.

He speaks ironically when He says *Ye both know me, and whence I am; and I am not come of myself.* Against the false opinion they had formed He contrasts the truth—as if He were saying, 'You have your eyes fixed on the earth and you think you see the whole of me; and therefore you despise me as a lowly son of the earth. But God will bear

witness that I am come from heaven; and though I may be rejected
by you, God will confess that I am truly His.'

He calls God *true* in the same sense that Paul calls Him faithful. 'If
we are faithless,' he says, 'he abideth faithful: for he cannot deny
himself' (II Tim. 2.13). For His argument is that the faith of the Gospel
is not at all diminished by all the world's efforts to overthrow it;
although the wicked may take from Christ what belonged to Him, yet
He remains complete, because the truth of God is firm and remains
always like itself. Christ sees that He is despised. But so far is He from
yielding that, on the contrary, He splendidly triumphs over the mad
arrogance of those who thought nothing of Him. All believers ought
to be endued with a like unconquerable and heroic greatness; nay, our
faith will never be stable and firm unless it derides the presumption of
the wicked when they rise up against Christ. And above all, godly
teachers ought to rely on this support, to persevere in upholding sound
doctrine even though the whole world resist it. Thus Jeremiah appeals
to God as his surety and guardian when he is condemned as an impos-
tor: 'O Lord, thou hast deceived me, and I was deceived,' he says (20.7).
Thus Isaiah, overwhelmed on all sides by slanders and reproaches, flies
to the refuge that God will approve his cause (50.8). Thus Paul, when
he is oppressed by unjust judgments, appeals against them all to the
day of the Lord (I Cor. 4.5), reckoning it enough to have God alone
to set against the whole raging world.

Whom ye know not. He means that it is not surprising if the Jews do
not know Him, when they do not know God; for the beginning of
true wisdom is to look to God. When He says that He knows God,
He means that He is not carried away thoughtlessly to such great
confidence; and by His example He warns us not to take the name of
God lightly and boast of Him as the patron and defender of our cause.
For many are too presumptuous in boasting they have God's authority.
Indeed, no greater readiness and boldness in rejecting the judgments of
all men can be imagined than that of the fanatics who claim that their
own inventions are the oracles of God. But these words of Christ
teach us to beware especially of puffed up and foolish confidence, and
to resist men bravely only after we have discovered the truth of God.
He who is fully aware that God is on his side has no reason to fear the
accusation of arrogance in trampling down all the world's haughtiness.

Because I am from him. Some distinguish these two clauses so as to
refer the former to the divine essence of Christ, and the latter to the
office laid on Him by the Father, to execute which He assumed flesh
and human nature. Although I do not go so far as to reject this, I am
not sure that Christ wanted to speak so subtly. I acknowledge indeed
that Christ's heavenly descent may be inferred from it, but it would

not be a firm enough proof of His eternal divinity against the Arians.

30. *They sought therefore to take him.* They did not lack the will to hurt Him. They even made the attempt, and they had the power to do it. Why then, with so much enthusiasm, are they paralysed, as if their hands and feet were bound? The Evangelist replies that Christ's hour was not yet come—by which he means that Christ was guarded against their violence and furious attacks by God's protection. At the same time he anticipates the offence of the cross; for we have no cause to be upset when we hear that Christ was dragged to death, not at the desire of men, but because He was appointed to be such a sacrifice by the decree of the Father. From this a general doctrine must be gathered; for though we live unto the day, the hour of everyman's death has nevertheless been fixed by God. It is difficult to believe that, subject as we are to so many accidents, exposed to so many injuries and dangers from man and beast, and liable to so many diseases, we are safe from all dangers until God wishes to call us away. But we must fight against our own mistrust. And first we should hold to the doctrine taught here and next to its object and the exhortation drawn from it—namely, that each of us should cast his cares on God and serve in his own calling and not be led away from his duty by any fears. Yet no man must go beyond his own limits. Confidence in the providence of God must go no further than God Himself commands.

But of the multitude many believed on him; and they said, When the Christ shall come, will he do more signs than those which this man hath done? The Pharisees heard the multitude murmuring these things concerning him; and the chief priests and the Pharisees sent officers to take him. Jesus therefore said, Yet a little while am I with you, and I go unto him that sent me. Ye shall seek me and shall not find me: and where I am, ye cannot come. The Jews therefore said among themselves, Whither will this man go that we shall not find him? will he go unto the Dispersion among the Greeks, and teach the Greeks? What is this word that he said, Ye shall seek me, and shall not find me: and where I am, ye cannot come? (31-36)

31. *But of the multitude many.* It might seem as if Christ were preaching to the deaf and utterly obstinate; and yet the Evangelist says that some fruit followed. And therefore, though some may grumble, others smile and others slander, and though many differences may arise, the preaching of the Gospel will not be without effect. So we must sow the seed and then wait patiently, until in course of time the fruit appears. The word *believe* is here used imprecisely, for they depended more on miracles than on teaching, and were not convinced that Jesus was the Christ; but as they were ready to listen to Him and

gave themselves teachably to Him as their Master, such a preparation for faith is called faith. Therefore when the Holy Spirit gives to a small spark of the right attitude such an honourable title, it should encourage us not to doubt that faith, however small, will be accepted by God.

32. *The Pharisees heard.* It is clear from this that the Pharisees were on the watch and always set on preventing Christ from being known. In the first instance the Evangelist names them alone, but then he joins to them the priests of whom they were a section. There is no doubt that, because they wanted to be thought the most zealous enthusiasts for the Law, they opposed Christ more bitterly than all the rest. But alone they were not equal to putting Christ down, and so they delegated the affair to the whole priestly order. Thus those who differed in other respects, now conspire together with one consent under the guidance of Satan against the Son of God. For the rest, since the Pharisees were so zealous and careful to defend their tyranny and the corrupt state of the Church, how much more fervent ought we to be in maintaining the Kingdom of Christ! The Papists' desire to extinguish the Gospel nowadays is no less furious. But it is terrible that our earnestness is not at least whetted by their example to labour more courageously in the defence of true and sound doctrine.

33. *Yet a little while.* Some think that this sermon was addressed to the present assembly; others, that it was addressed to the officers sent to arrest Christ. For my part, I do not doubt that Christ is speaking especially to His enemies, who had made plans to destroy Him. He ridicules their efforts, for they will all labour in vain until the time decreed by the Father is come. And He also rebukes their obstinacy in not only rejecting, but furiously opposing the grace that is offered to them; and at the same time He threatens that it will shortly be taken from them.

When He says *I am with you*, He is rebuking their ingratitude; for although He had been given to them by the Father, although He had come down to them from His heavenly glory, although by lovingly inviting them to Him, He desired nothing more than to be present with them, yet only a few received Him. When He says, 'Yet a short time', He is warning them that God will not long endure that His grace should be exposed to such shameful contempt. He also means that neither His life nor His death is placed in their power, but that a time has been fixed by His Father which must be fulfilled.

I go unto him that sent me. In these words He declares that He will not be annihilated by death, but will, when He shall have put off His mortal body, be declared the Son of God by the magnificent victory of His resurrection. It was as if He said, 'Work as hard as you can, you will never stop my Father receiving Me into His heavenly glory when I have discharged the embassy committed to me. Thus not only will My state remain entire after My death, but a far more excellent one is then provided for Me.' A general admonition is also to be drawn from this; for Christ is present with us so often as He calls us to the hope of salvation by the preaching of the Gospel. It is not without reason that the preaching of the Gospel is called a descent of Christ to us in Eph. 2.17. If we take the hand that He holds out, He will lead us to the Father. And as long as we have to sojourn in the world, He will not only show Himself to be near us but will continually dwell in us. If we disregard His presence, He will lose nothing; but if He departs from us, He will leave us utter strangers to God and life.

34. *Ye shall seek me.* They sought Christ to put Him to death. Christ here plays on the ambiguous meaning of the word, for they are soon going to seek Him in another way—namely, to find some help and comfort in their wretchedness and lost state. It was as if He had said, 'My presence, now so irksome and unbearable to you, is but for a short time, and soon you will seek Me in vain; for I shall be far away from you, not only physically, but also in power, and from heaven I shall behold your destruction.' But here it may be asked of what nature this seeking of Christ was. For it is plain enough that Christ is speaking of the reprobate, who were obstinate to the extreme in rejecting the Gospel. Some refer it to teaching, in that the Jews, by wrongly pursuing the righteousness of works, did not obtain what they desired. Many take it of the person of the Messiah, in that the Jews in vain begged for a Redeemer when they were reduced to extremities. But I simply explain it as denoting the distressed groans of the wicked when they are by necessity forced to look in some sense to God.

But even in seeking Him they do not really seek Him, for unbelief and obstinacy shut up their hearts, as it were, and so alienate them from God. They certainly want God to be present as their Redeemer, but by impenitence and hardness of heart they obstruct their path. We have an example in Esau who, when his birthright is snatched from him, is not only filled with grief but groans and gnashes his teeth and bursts out into furious indignation (Gen. 27.38; Heb. 12.17). But he is so far from the right way of seeking the blessing, that he even then makes himself quite unworthy of it. Thus is God wont to avenge contempt for His grace among the reprobate, so that, afflicted by severe punishments or oppressed by a conviction of their misery, or shut up in other straits, they complain and cry and howl, but all to no purpose, for, because they are always like themselves, they nourish inwardly the same cruelty as before and are not brought to God, but rather wish, since they cannot destroy Him, that He were different. Let us learn from this that Christ must be received without delay while He is still present with us, lest the opportunity for enjoying Him should pass away from us. For if the door be once shut, it will be useless for us to try to enter. 'Seek ye the Lord', says Isaiah, 'while he may be found, call ye upon him while he is near' (Isa. 55.6). We must therefore be diligent to go to God while it is 'the acceptable time', as the same prophet says (59.8), for we do not know how long God will bear with our laziness. In the words 'where I am, you cannot come', He uses the present tense instead of the future.

35. *Whither will this man go?* The Evangelist added this expressly to show how great was the people's stupidity. The ungodly are not only deaf to God's teaching, but even pass over dreadful threatenings in mockery, as if they were listening to a fable. Christ spoke of the Father by name, but they stay fixed on the earth and only think of a journey to distant lands. It is well known that the Jews called overseas nations Greeks. But they do not mean that Christ will go to the un-circumcised, but to the Jews dispersed throughout the various regions of the world. For the word *Dispersion* would not apply to the natives of the place who inhabit their native soil, but fits the Jews who were fugitives and exiles. Thus Peter inscribes his first epistle παρεπιδήμοις διασπορᾶς of Pontus, Galatia, etc. (I Pet. 1.1), and James salutes the twelve tribes ἐν τῇ διασπορᾷ, an expression taken from Moses and the prophets. The words therefore mean, 'Will He cross the sea and go to the Jews who dwell in a land unknown to us?' Perhaps they wanted to vex Christ with this mockery. 'If this man is the Messiah, will He set up the throne of His Kingdom in Greece, when God has made over to Him the land of Canaan as His habitation?' But however that may be, we see that they were not at all affected by Christ's severe threaten-ing.

Now on the last day, the great day of the feast, Jesus stood and cried, saying, If any man thirst, let him come unto me, and drink. He that believeth on me, as the scripture hath said, out of his belly shall flow rivers of living water. But this spake he of the Spirit, which they that believed on him were to receive: for the Spirit was not yet; because Jesus was not yet glorified. (37-39)

37. *On the last day.* The first thing to be noticed here is that none of His enemies' plots or intrigues frightened Christ off doing His duty. On the contrary, His courage rose with danger and He went on the more bravely. This is shown by the circumstances—the time, the assembly of the people, and His freedom in calling out when He knew

that hands were ready on every side to arrest Him, for the officers were probably then ready to execute their commission.

Next we must notice that, relying on nothing but God's protection, He could stand firm against the violent efforts of those who had everything in their power. For what other reason can be given for Christ preaching on the great day in the midst of the Temple which they ruled completely and after they had got ready a band of officers, but because God restrained their rage? Yet it is very useful to us that the Evangelist should introduce Christ crying aloud, 'All who thirst may come to me.' For we infer that not just one or two were invited in a low and gentle whisper, but that the doctrine is proclaimed to all, in such a way that it is hidden from none but those who shut their ears deliberately and will not hear this loud and resounding cry.

If any man thirst. In this clause He exhorts all to partake of His blessings, so long as they are aware of their own poverty and want to be helped. For we are indeed all poor and empty and destitute of all blessings, though the sense of their poverty does not excite all to seek the remedy. Hence many do not stir a foot, but waste away in a wretched decline; and there are even very many who are not affected by their emptiness until the Spirit of God with His own fire kindles hunger and thirst in their hearts. It is the office of the Spirit, therefore, to give us an appetite for His grace.

As to the present passage, the first thing to be grasped is that none is called to obtain the riches of the Spirit but he who burns with a desire for them. We know how acute the pain of thirst is, so that the very strongest men, who can endure any amount of toil, are made faint by thirst. He invites the thirsty rather than the hungry so as to follow up the metaphor which He later uses in the words water and drink, so that all the parts of His discourse may be consistent. And I do not doubt that He is alluding to the passage in Isaiah, 'Everyone that thirsteth, come ye to the waters' (55.1). For what the prophet there attributes to God had at length to be fulfilled in Christ. Again, it is like the song of the blessed Virgin, that 'the rich and full he hath sent empty away' (Luke 1.53). He therefore tells us to come direct to Himself, as if He said that only He can fully satisfy the thirst of all, and that all who seek even the slightest alleviation of their thirst elsewhere are cheated and labour in vain.

And drink. A promise is added to the exhortation. For although the word is an exhortation, it contains a promise within itself. Christ declares that He is not a dry and empty cistern but an inexhaustible fountain plentifully and abundantly supplying drink to all. Hence it follows that if we ask from Him what we want, our desire will not be disappointed.

38. *He that believeth on me.* Here the manner of coming is shown.
It is not an approach on foot but by faith. Or rather, to come is simply
to believe—that is, if you define the word 'believe' properly. As we
have already said, we believe in Christ when we embrace Him as He
is set before us in the Gospel, full of power, wisdom, righteousness,
purity, life and all the gifts of the Spirit. Moreover, He confirms here
more plainly and fully the promise we have just mentioned; for He
says that He possesses a rich abundance with which He will fully
satisfy us.

At first sight the metaphor that rivers of living water shall flow out
of the bellies of believers seems uncouth, no doubt. But the meaning
is perfectly clear: those who believe shall lack no spiritual blessings.
He calls it *living water,* whose spring never grows dry and whose flow
never ceases. *Rivers* in the plural I interpret as the multiple graces of
the Spirit, which are necessary for the spiritual life of the soul. In
short, there is here promised to us the perpetuity and the abundance of
the gifts of the Spirit. Some understand waters flowing *out of the belly*
of believers to mean, that he to whom the Spirit has been given diverts
a part to his brethren, since there should be a mutual communication
between us. But the meaning seems simpler to me, that whoever
believes in Christ will have a fountain of life springing up in himself,
as it were; as Christ said in Chapter Four, 'whosoever drinketh of this
water shall never thirst'. For whereas ordinary drinking quenches
thirst only for a short time, Christ says that by faith we draw in the
Spirit, who is a fountain of water springing up into everlasting life.

Yet He does not tell us that believers are so filled with Christ on the
first day that they neither hunger nor thirst afterwards; but rather that
the enjoyment of Christ kindles a new desire for Him. The meaning
is that the Holy Spirit is like a living and ever-flowing fountain in
believers—just as Paul says in Rom. 8.10 that He is life in us although
we still carry about the cause of death in the remnants of sin. And
indeed, inasmuch as everyone partakes of the gifts of the Spirit according to the measure of his faith, there can be no perfect fulness of them
in this life. But as believers advance in faith, they continually aspire to
new increases of the Spirit, so that the firstfruits with which they are
imbued suffice for the continuance of eternal life. But this also warns
us how small is the capacity of our faith, since the graces of the Spirit
scarcely come to us by drops, which would flow like rivers if we gave
due place to Christ, that is, if faith made us capable of Him.

As the scripture hath said. Some restrict this to the former clause,
others to the latter. I extend it to cover the whole trend of the discourse. Moreover, in my opinion, Christ is not pointing to any particular passage of Scripture, but takes a testimony from the common

teaching of the prophets. For whenever, in promising an abundance of His Spirit, the Lord compares it to living waters, He refers chiefly to Christ's Kingdom and directs the minds of believers to that. All the predictions of living waters, therefore, have their fulfilment in Christ; for He alone has opened and revealed God's hidden treasures. The graces of the Spirit are poured out on Him so that we may all draw from His fulness. Wherefore those who are so kindly and graciously called by Christ, and yet wander off in every direction, deserve to perish miserably.

But this spake he of the Spirit. The word water is sometimes applied to the Spirit because of its purity; for it is His office to cleanse away our pollutions. But in this and similar passages the expression has a different meaning. This is, that we are destitute of all the sap and moisture of life save when the Spirit of God quickens us and waters us, as it were, by a secret power. This is synecdoche, for under the one word water He comprehends all the parts of life. From this we also infer that all who have not been regenerated by Christ's Spirit are to be regarded as dead, whatever mask of life they may put up.

For the Spirit was not yet. The Spirit is eternal, as we know. But the Evangelist is saying that, so long as Christ dwelt in the world in the lowly form of a Servant, that grace of the Spirit which was poured out on men after the resurrection of Christ, had not come forth openly. And indeed he is speaking comparatively, as when the New Testament is compared to the Old. God promises His Spirit to believers as if He had never given Him to the Fathers. At that time the disciples had undoubtedly already received the firstfruits of the Spirit. For where does faith come from if not from the Spirit? The Evangelist then does not simply deny that the grace of the Spirit was revealed to believers before the death of Christ, but that it was not yet so bright and clear as it would be afterwards. For the chief glory of Christ's Kingdom is that He governs the Church by His Spirit. But He entered into the lawful and, as it were, ceremonial possession of His Kingdom when He was exalted to the right hand of the Father. So there is nothing surprising in His delaying the full manifestation of the Spirit until then.

But one question still remains. Does He mean here the visible graces of the Spirit, or regeneration, which is the fruit of adoption? I answer: the Spirit, who had been promised at the coming of Christ, appeared in those visible gifts as in mirrors. But here He is referring strictly to the power of the Spirit, by which we are born again in Christ and become new creatures. That we lie on earth poor and famished and almost destitute of spiritual blessings, while Christ sits in glory at the right hand of the Father, clothed with the highest majesty of empire, must be imputed to our slothfulness and the narrowness of our faith.

Some of the multitude therefore, when they heard these words, said,
This is of a truth the prophet. Others said, This is the Christ. But
some said, What, doth the Christ come out of Galilee? Hath not the
scripture said that the Christ cometh of the seed of David, and from
Bethlehem, the village where David was? So there arose a division
in the multitude because of him. And some of them would have taken him;
but no man laid hands on him. (40-44)

40. *Some of the multitude therefore.* The Evangelist now relates the
result of this latest discourse—the different opinions gave rise to a
division among the people. It should be noted that John is not speaking
of the professed enemies of Christ, or of those who were already filled
with hatred against sound doctrine, but of the common people, among
whom there should have been greater integrity. He enumerates three
classes:

The first acknowledged that Jesus really was a prophet. From this
we conclude that they did not dislike His doctrine. But on the other
hand, the lightness and carelessness of this confession is plain from the
fact that, although they approve of the teacher, they neither understand
nor relish what He means and says. They could not truly embrace
Christ as a prophet, without also confessing Him to be the Son of God
and the Author of their salvation. Yet there is this much to be said for
them, that they see something divine in Christ, which leads them to
reverence Him; for there could be an easy passage from this teachableness to faith.

More correct are the second, who plainly confess that He is the
Christ. But the others rise up against them, and hence comes the
division. We are warned by this example not to think it strange if in
our own day men are divided by various controversies. We learn that
Christ's sermon produced a schism, not among Gentiles outside the
faith, but in the midst of the Church of Christ and even in the capital
of the Church. Is Christ's teaching to be blamed for this as the cause
of the disturbances? No; though the whole world were in tumult,
the Word of God is so precious that we should want it to be received
by a few at any rate. So there is no reason for our consciences to be
worried when we see those who wish to be reckoned among God's
people disputing and arguing with each other.

Yet we must also notice that divisions do not really have their origins
in the Gospel. For there can be no firm agreement among men except
in certain truth. The peace that is cultivated by those who do not
know God comes from stupidity rather than true agreement. In short,
the cause and seed of all the differences that spring up when the Gospel
is preached, is already latent in men. When these are, so to say,

awakened out of sleep, they start to move; just as mists are produced by something other than the sun, but do not show until the sun rises.

Doth the Christ come out of Galilee? They arm themselves with the testimony of Scripture lest they should seem to reject Christ thoughtlessly. And though they twist it against Christ, they have a certain semblance of truth. They are wrong only in making Christ a Galilaean. But what is the cause of this ignorance but contempt? If it had not been too much trouble to inquire, they would have seen that Christ was adorned with both titles; that He was born in Bethlehem and was the son of David. But such is our nature: in small things we are ashamed of laziness, whereas in the mysteries of the Kingdom of Heaven we snore at our ease. It is also noteworthy that they are diligent and industrious in seeking an excuse to turn from Christ but are surprisingly slow and dull to receive sound doctrine. Men often construct obstacles for themselves like this against coming to Christ out of the very Scriptures which lead us to Christ by the hand.

43. *And some of them.* The Evangelist means by these words that they not only despised Christ, but that their wicked rejection of Him was joined with cruelty and a lust to hurt Him; for superstition is always cruel. The ineffectiveness of their efforts must be put down to the providence of God. For as was said earlier, since Christ's hour was not yet come, He relied on and was guarded by His Father's protection and so surmounted all dangers.

> *The officers therefore came to the chief priests and Pharisees; and they said unto them, Why did ye not bring him? The officers answered, Never man so spake. The Pharisees therefore answered them, Are ye also led astray? Hath any of the rulers believed on him, or of the Pharisees? But this multitude which knoweth not the law are accursed. Nicodemus saith unto them (he that came to him by night, being one of them), Doth our law judge a man, except it first hear from himself and know what he doeth? They answered and said unto him, Art thou also of Galilee? Search, and see that out of Galilee ariseth no prophet. And they went every man unto his own house. (45–53)*

45. *The officers therefore came.* Here we can see how blind is the arrogance of the ungodly. They so admire and worship their greatness in the world that they do not hesitate to trample down human and divine law. If anything happens against their wishes they willingly throw everything into confusion. When these wicked priests ask why Christ was not brought to them they magnify their power as if nothing should oppose their command.

46. *Never man so spake.* The men confess that they are overcome and tamed by Christ's Word alone; and yet it does not make them

repent or give due honour to that Word. If it is true that man never so spake, why did not the divine power which they were forced to feel so touch their hearts as to bring them to devote themselves wholly to God? But Isaiah's words had to be fulfilled in this way: 'he shall smite the wicked with the breath of his mouth' (11.4). More, we shall see later on how those who were seeking His death fell backwards as if they had been knocked down with a hammer, overcome simply by the voice of Christ. Let us therefore learn that Christ's doctrine has such power as even to terrify the wicked; but as this turns to their destruction, let us take care to be softened rather than broken. Even today we see many who are very like those officers. They are reluctantly drawn to admire the teaching of the Gospel, and yet are so far from yielding to Christ that they remain in the enemy's camp. Some are still worse, and to curry favour with the wicked defame that teaching with all the slander they can find, even though they are inwardly convinced it is from God.

47. *Are ye also led astray?* They reprove their officers in such a way as to keep them obedient. They mean by these words that it would be unreasonable and out of place for them to be unsteady, even if the whole people fell away. But we must look at the grounds of their argument when they insult Christ haughtily. 'Only the common people and the ignorant', they say, 'are on His side. The rulers and notables are against Him.' They name the Pharisees in particular, because they had a higher reputation than others, both for learning and holiness, and were like the princes of the rulers. This objection seems quite plausible, for if the rulers and governors of the Church do not retain their authority, nothing can possibly ever be well-ordered, nor can the Church long continue in a well-ordered condition. We know the passions of the common people, and the most anarchical disorder that must soon follow when every man is allowed to do as he likes. The authority of rulers is therefore a bridle necessary to maintain order in the Church, and it was accordingly provided by the Law of God that, if any question or controversy arose, the inquiry into it should rest with the high priest (Deut. 17.8). Their sin lies in their being unwilling to submit to God, and claiming for themselves the highest authority. It is true that God delegated the decision to the high priest, but He only intended him to decide in accordance with the Law.

Whatever authority pastors have, therefore, is subject to God's Word so that all may be kept in their own order, from the highest to lowest, and God alone exalted. If pastors who honestly and sincerely do their duty claim authority for themselves, it is a holy and legitimate claim. But when the mere authority of men is exalted apart from God's Word, it is vain and useless boasting. It often happens, however, that the wicked dominate the Church, and therefore we must beware of attributing anything to men when once they depart from the Word of God.

We see that nearly all the prophets were worried by this nuisance, for, to bury their doctrine, men continually opposed to them the lofty titles of princes and priests and the Church. The Papists today, armed with the same weapons, are no less fierce than were the opponents of Christ and the prophets. It is indeed a fearful blindness when a mortal man is not ashamed to set himself against God. Yet this is the madness that Satan drives those into, who love their own ambition better than the truth of God. But we, for our part, must so revere the Word of God that all the splendour of the world is extinguished and its empty mists scattered. For we should be in a bad way if our salvation depended on the will of princes, and our faith would be most unstable if it were to stand or fall at their pleasure.

49. *But this multitude.* The first part of their pride was to rely on the title of priest and want to tyrannize over everybody. The next is that they despise the rest as worthless—for those who are over-pleased with themselves are always contemptuous of others, and disdain of the brethren always follows love of ourselves. They pronounce all the masses accursed; and why? They certainly allege ignorance of the Law, but they kept the other reason quiet—that they thought there was no holiness except in their own order. Likewise the Papist priests in our own day claim that they alone are the Church, and they despise the laity as they call them, as if they were heathen. But God throws down such arrogant madness by preferring the lowly and despised to the highest and most powerful. It should be noticed that the knowledge of the Law they are boasting of here is not that which teaches men religion and the fear of God, but such as they possessed when, with professorial superciliousness, they gave their replies as if they alone were the proper interpreters of the Law. It is certainly true that all who have not been taught in the Law of God are accursed, inasmuch as by the knowledge of it we are truly sanctified. But this knowledge is not confined to a few, so that, swollen with perverted confidence, they may exclude themselves from the ranks of the rest; it belongs to all the children of God in common, so that all, from the least to the greatest, may be gathered together in the same obedience of faith.

50. *Nicodemus saith unto them.* The Evangelist describes Nicodemus as neutral and not venturing on a serious defence of godly doctrine, and yet that he cannot bear to have the truth oppressed. When he says *he that came by night* it is partly to his praise, partly to his shame. If he had not loved Christ's teaching, he would never have dared go against the rage of the ungodly, for he knew that if anyone only opened his

mouth he would at once be exposed to their dislike and to danger. When therefore he ventures to say one word, however feeble, it is a small spark of godliness shining from his heart. That he does not defend Christ more freely comes from his over-timidity. So the Evangelist means that he still has a hankering for the concealment of night and is not a true disciple of Christ. He says that he once came to Christ by night, but remained in open among the enemy, and kept his place in their camp.

This is the more carefully to be observed in that there are many today who pretend that they are like Nicodemus, and hope to mock God unpunished by putting on this mask. Granting their point that there is no difference between them and Nicodemus, how, pray, does such an example help them? Nicodemus says that Christ should not be condemned unheard. Precisely the same might be said of a robber or murderer; for it is well known and famous that it is better to acquit the guilty than to condemn the innocent. Moreover, in his desire to clear Christ's character, he leaves and abandons the teaching itself. What can we find here worthy of a godly and believing man? Thus the seed of the Gospel, which afterwards bore fruit, still lay choked in him. It will be far more profitable if we apply this example to another end— that the Lord often makes the doctrine which seemed to have perished gradually take root secretly and after a long time put forth some buds, at first apparently abortively, but then with life and vigour. In this way, the faith of Nicodemus received a new and sudden vigour from the death of Christ.

52. *Art thou also of Galilee?* They say that all who favour Christ are of Galilee; and this is spoken reproachfully, as if He could not have anyone on His side except from the lowly corner of Galilee. Their violence against Nicodemus shows with what a furious hatred they burned against Christ; for he had not openly undertaken to defend Christ, but had only said that He should not be condemned unheard. Thus among the Papists today no man can show the slightest sign of impartiality about the oppression of the Gospel, without the enemy at once flying into a passion and calling him a heretic.

53. *And they went every man unto his own house.* Now follows an astonishing close to the scene. If anyone considers the way the priests ruled and their rage and the power at their command, with, on the other side, Christ bare and unarmed without an armed bodyguard, He was bound to be finished. When so formidable a conspiracy dissolved of its own accord and all these men break themselves with their own violence like waves of the sea, who will not acknowledge that they are scattered by God's hand? But God abides ever like Himself. There- fore, He will, whenever He pleases, break up all the efforts of His

enemies; so that when they have everything in their power, and are ready and prepared to carry out their plans, they will depart without doing their work. And we have often found, that whatever schemes the enemy has made to extinguish the Gospel, they soon failed by the amazing grace of God.

CHAPTER EIGHT

But Jesus went unto the mount of Olives. And early in the morning he came again into the temple, and all the people came unto him; and he sat down, and taught them. And the scribes and the Pharisees bring a woman taken in adultery; and having set her in the midst, they say unto him, Master, this woman hath been taken in adultery, in the very act. Now in the law Moses commanded us to stone such: what then sayest thou of her? And this they said, tempting him, that they might have whereof to accuse him. But Jesus cast down his eyes,[1] and with his finger wrote on the ground. But when they continued asking him, he lifted up his eyes,[2] and said unto them, He that is without sin among you, let him first cast a stone at her. And again he stooped down, and with his finger wrote on the ground. And they, when they heard it, were reproved by their conscience and went out one by one, beginning from the eldest, even unto the last: and Jesus was left alone, and the woman, where she was, in the midst. And Jesus lifted up himself, and said unto her, Woman, where are they? did no man condemn thee? And she said, No man, Lord. And Jesus said, Neither do I condemn thee: go thy way; from henceforth sin no more. (1-11)

3. *And the scribes and the Pharisees bring to him.* It is quite clear that this story was unknown to the ancient Greek Churches. Hence some conjecture that it was inserted from another place. But it has always been received by the Latin Churches and is found in many Greek manuscripts, and contains nothing unworthy of an apostolic spirit; so there is no reason why we should refuse to make use of it. When the Evangelist says that the scribes brought a woman to Him, he means that they were acting in concert to lay a trap for Christ. He mentions the Pharisees in particular because they were paramount in the order of the scribes. They were extremely wicked to adopt this pretext for slander; and their very words gave them away, for they do not disguise the fact that they have a clear commandment of the Law. Hence it follows that they act maliciously in asking a question as if it were doubtful. But their intention was to force Christ to give up His office of preaching grace, so that He might seem fickle and unsteady. They say plainly that adulteresses are condemned by Moses, to hold Christ bound by the decision of the Law, for it was not right to acquit those

---

[1] French: *s'enclinant en bas*: stooping down.
[2] *il se dressa*: he lifted up himself.

whom the Law condemned. But if He consented to the Law, He might seem somewhat unlike Himself.

6. *But Jesus cast down his eyes.* By this gesture He showed that He despised them. Those who suppose that He wrote something or other are mistaken, in my opinion. Nor do I approve the ingenuity of Augustine, who thinks that in this way the distinction between the Law and the Gospel is indicated, in that Christ wrote, not on tables of stone, but on man who is dust and earth. Rather, Christ intended, by doing nothing, to show that they were not worth listening to. Just as if anyone, while another was speaking to him, were to trace lines on the wall with his finger, or turn his back or show by some other sign that he was not attending to what was being said. Thus today, when Satan tries in various ways to draw us aside from the right path of the Gospel we ought contemptuously to pass by the many things he sets against us. The Papists worry us as much as they can with many trifling cavils, like clouds scattered in the air. If godly teachers laboriously examine each one of their cavils, they will be starting on a Penelope's web. Therefore hindrances of this kind, which merely impede the progress of the Gospel, are wisely disregarded.

7. *He that is without sin among you.* He said this according to the custom of the Law. For God commanded that the witnesses should put malefactors and evildoers to death with their own hands, so that very great scrupulousness might be shown in bearing witness (Deut. 17.7). There are many who rush thoughtlessly into overwhelming their brother with perjury, because they do not reflect that they inflict a deadly wound with their tongue. And this argument had weight with those slanderers, wicked as they were; and when it is put to them, they lay aside the fierce passions which animated them when they came. Yet Christ's words are different from the command of the Law, in that then God merely warned them not to condemn a man with words except him whom they were allowed to put to death with their own hands, but here Christ is demanding perfect innocence from the witnesses, so that no man may take it upon him to avenge a crime in another, unless he himself be pure and free from all guilt. Now what He then said to a few we ought to take as spoken to all, so that whoever accuses another should impose on himself a law of innocence. Otherwise, we are not attacking wicked deeds but are against men's persons.

In this way, however, He seems to be removing justice from the world, so that none will dare to say that he punishes crimes. Is there one single judge who is not conscious of something wrong in himself? Can a single witness be brought forward who is not guilty of some fault? So He seems to be driving all witnesses away from the witness box and all judges from their bench. I reply, this is not an absolute and simple prohibition, in which Christ forbids sinners to do their duty in correcting the sins of others. But by this word, He only reproves hypocrites, who gently flatter themselves and their own vices, but are excessively severe and even savage judges of others. None, then, must let his own sins stop him correcting the sins of others and even punishing them when necessary, so long as he hates, both in himself and in others, what is to be condemned. More, every man should begin by interrogating his own conscience and be both witness and judge against himself before he comes to others. In this way we shall wage war on sins without hating men.

9. *And being reproved by their conscience.* Here we see the great power of an evil conscience. Though these wicked hypocrites meant to get the better of Christ with their cavils, their shame puts them to flight as soon as He pierces their consciences with a single word. This is the hammer to break the pride of hypocrites with—they must be summoned to the judgment seat of God. It may be, however, that their shame before men had more influence over them than the fear of God. Yet it is much that of their own accord they confess they are guilty and flee away confounded. The detail is to be noticed that their conviction of guilt went in proportion to their status. Would that our present day scribes who sell their work to the Pope to oppose Christ had at least as much shame. But they are so shameless that, notorious for all wickedness, they glory that they can be shameless with impunity. We should also observe how much this feeling of sin with which the scribes were touched, differs from true penitence. For we ought to be so affected by the judgment of God that we shall not look for hiding places to flee from the presence of the Judge, but shall go straight to Him to ask His forgiveness.

Jesus was left alone. The Spirit of wisdom brought it to pass that those wicked men went away when they had tempted Christ in vain. And there is no reason to doubt that we shall be superior to all the schemes of our enemies if only we will let ourselves be ruled by the same Spirit. But it often happens that they overthrow us because we do not notice their shares and do not trouble to take advice, or, trusting in our own wisdom, do not think how much we need the government of the Holy Spirit. He says that Christ remained alone; not that the people whom He had been teaching had left Him, but because all the scribes who had brought the adulteress troubled Him no more. When it is said that *the woman* remained with Christ, let this example teach us that there is nothing better for us than to be brought guilty to His judgment, so long as we submit ourselves calmly and obediently to it.

11. *Neither do I condemn thee.* It is not related that Christ simply absolved the woman, but that He let her go free. And this is not

surprising, for He did not wish to undertake anything that did not belong to His office. He had been sent by the Father to gather the lost sheep, and so, mindful of His calling, He exhorts the woman to repentance and comforts her with a promise of grace. Those who deduce from this that adultery should not be punished by death must, on the same reasoning, admit that inheritances should not be divided, since Christ refused to arbitrate between two brothers. Indeed, every crime will be exempt from the penalties of the law if the punishment of adultery is remitted, for the door will then be thrown open to any kind of treachery and to poisoning, murder and robbery. Moreover, when an adulteress brings an illegitimate child into a family, she not only steals the family name, but robs the legitimate issue of the right of inheritance and transfers it to strangers. But the chief evil is that the wife disgraces the husband to whom she had been joined, by prostituting herself to a shameful deed, and violates the sacred covenant of God, without which no sound holiness can continue to exist in the world.

Yet the Popish theology is that in this passage Christ has brought in the law of grace, by which adulterers may be freed from punishment. And though they try by every means to efface from men's minds the grace of Christ (such grace as is everywhere declared to us by the preaching of the Gospel) at this one point they loudly preach the law of grace! Why is this, but that they may pollute with unbridled lust nearly every marriage bed with impunity? This is the result of that diabolical celibacy, that those who are not allowed to have a lawful wife may fornicate indiscriminately. But let us hold that, although Christ remits men's sins, He does not subvert the social order or abolish legal sentences and punishments.

Sin no more. From this we gather the aim of the grace of Christ. It is that when the sinner is reconciled to God, he may honour the Author of his salvation by a godly and holy life. In short, the same Word of God that offers us pardon calls us at the same time to repentance. Besides, although this exhortation looks forward to the future, it nevertheless humbles sinners with the memory of their past life.

Again therefore Jesus spake unto them, saying, I am the light of the world: he that followeth me shall not walk in the darkness, but shall have the light of life. The Pharisees therefore said unto him, Thou bearest witness of thyself; thy witness is not true. Jesus answered and said unto them, Even if I bear witness of myself, my witness is true; for I know whence I came, and whither I go; but ye know not whence I come, or whither I go. (12-14)

12. *I am the light of the world.* Those who omit the foregoing narrative join this discourse of Christ to the sermon He preached on

the last day of the assembly. It is a most beautiful title of Christ when He is called the light of the world. We are all blind by nature, but a remedy is offered to rescue and free us from darkness and make us partakers of the true light. And this blessing is not offered just to one here or there, for Christ says that He is the light of the whole world. By this general statement He wanted to remove the distinction both between Jews and Gentiles, and the learned and ignorant, and gentle-folk and the common people.

But we must first see the need for seeking this light. For none will ever present themselves to Christ to be enlightened save those who have known both that this world is darkness and that they themselves are altogether blind. Let us know, then, that when the means of obtaining light is shown us in Christ, we are all condemned of blindness and everything that we think is light is compared to darkness and thick night. For Christ is not speaking of what He has in common with others, but claims it as uniquely His own. Hence it follows, that outside Him there is not even a spark of true light. There may be some semblance of brightness, but it is like lightning, which only dazzles the eyes. We must also notice that the power and function of enlightening is not confined to the physical presence of Christ, for although He is far from us bodily, He nevertheless daily sheds His light upon us in the teaching of the Gospel and by the secret power of His Spirit. But we do not have a full definition of this light until we learn that we are enlightened by the Gospel and the Spirit of Christ, so that we may know that the fountain of all knowledge and wisdom is hidden in Him.

He that followeth me. To the teaching He adds an exhortation, which He immediately confirms with a promise. For when we hear that all who let themselves be ruled by Christ are out of danger of straying, we ought to be stirred up to follow Him; and indeed, He draws us to Him with outstretched hand, as it were. So great and magnificent a promise must also be full of power, so that those who look to Christ are certain that they will have a sure way even through the midst of darkness, and that not for a little while but until they have reached their goal. For that is the significance of the words being put in the future tense, *he shall not walk in the darkness, but shall have the light of life.* This is also the meaning of the latter clause, which expressly states the perpetuity of light. We must not be afraid, then, that it will fail in the middle of our journey, for it leads us right to life. The genitive is used, in the Hebrew manner, instead of the adjective, to denote the effect—as if He had said, 'the life-giving light'. There is no wonder that such gross darkness of errors and superstitions reigns in the world when so few look to Christ.

13. *The Pharisees therefore said.* They object the common saying that no one is to be trusted in his own cause. *A true witness* is put for what is lawful and worthy of belief. In short, they mean that His words are idle, unless He brings proof from elsewhere.

14. *Even if I bear witness.* Christ replies that His witness has sufficient credit and authority because He is not a private person among the great mass of men but holds a very different rank. For when He says that He knows whence He came and whither He goes, He is excluding Himself from the common number of men. The meaning is therefore that every man is suspect in his own cause, and the laws provide that none is to be believed when he speaks to his own advantage. This does not apply to the Son of God, however, who stands above the whole world. For He is not reckoned as belonging to the rank of men, but has been adorned by His Father with the privilege of bringing all men to order by His Word alone.

I know whence I came. By these words He declares that His origin is not from the world, but that He proceeded from God. Hence it would be unjust and unreasonable for His teaching, which is divine, to be subjected to men's laws. But because they despised Him who was then clothed with the form of a servant for the lowliness of the flesh, He recalls them to the future glory of His resurrection, which was a clear proof of His hitherto hidden and unknown divinity. Therefore that intermediate state ought not to have prevented the Jews from submitting to God's only ambassador, who had been promised beforehand to them in the Law.

When He says that He knows but they do not, He means that His glory is not at all diminished by their unbelief. And as He has given us the same testimony, our faith ought to despise all the contradictions and murmurings of the ungodly; for, if it is founded upon God, it will be far above the highest loftiness of the world. But in order that His majesty in the Gospel may stand firm in us, we must always be set on the heavenly glory of Christ and hear Him speaking in the world, so that we remember where He came from and what authority He has now that He has performed His embassy. As He humbled Himself for a season, so He now sits at the right hand of the Father, that every knee may bow to Him.

Ye judge after the flesh; I judge no man. Yea and if I judge, my judgement is true; for I am not alone, but I and the Father that sent me. Yea and in your law it is written, that the witness of two men is true. I am he that beareth witness of myself, and the Father that sent me beareth witness of me. They said therefore unto him, Where is thy Father? Jesus answered, Ye know neither me, nor my Father: if ye knew me, ye

*would know my Father also. These words spake he in the treasury, as
he taught in the temple: and no man took him; because his hour was not
yet come.* (15-20)

15. *Ye judge after the flesh.* This can be expounded in two ways—
either that they judge according to the depraved point of view of the
flesh or from the appearance of the person. For *the flesh* is sometimes
used of the outward appearance of a man. Both meanings fit in well
with this passage, since neither truth nor justice has any place where
the attitude of the flesh prevails or a respect for persons overrules the
judgment. But it seems to me that the meaning will be more certain
if you contrast the flesh to the Spirit, so that He denies they are lawful
and competent judges, because they are not guided by the Spirit.

I judge no man. Commentators differ here also. Some make the
distinction that He does not judge as man. Others refer it to the time,
that He had not yet undertaken the office of judge while He was on
earth. Augustine gives both expositions, but does not come to a
decision. But the former distinction does not apply at all. The sentence
contains two clauses—that Christ does not judge, and that if He judges,
His judgment is firm and authoritative because divine. And so I
restrict the former clause, in which He says that He does not judge, to
the circumstances of the present passage. For, to convict His enemies
more deeply of pride, He makes use of the comparison that they
irregularly assume the licence to judge, and yet cannot condemn Him
when He only teaches and refrains from executing the office of judge.

Yea and if I judge. He adds this correction, lest He should seem to be
giving up His right entirely. If I judge, my judgment is true, He says;
that is, it deserves authority. Now the authority arises from His doing
nothing that is not in accord with His Father's commandment.

The phrase *I am not alone* comes to the affirmation that He is not one
in the ordinary number of men, but must be looked at with the office
placed upon Him by the Father. But why does He not assert His
divinity expressly, as He might truly and fairly have done? Because,
as His divinity was hidden under the veil of the flesh, He sets before
them His Father, in whom it was more conspicuous. Nevertheless, the
tenor of the discourse is that all He does and teaches should be accounted
divine.

17. *Yea and in your law.* At first sight the argument might seem
weak, in that no man is accepted as witness in his own case. But we
must remember what I have already said, that Christ is to be excluded
from the ordinary number of men, since He is neither a private man,
nor transacts His own private business. By distinguishing Himself
from the Father He accommodates Himself to the capacity of His

hearers. He does this for the sake of His office; for at that time He was the Father's minister, and so He asserts that the Father is the Author of all His doctrine.

19. *Where is thy Father.* Without doubt they inquired about His Father in mockery. For they not only with their usual pride treat what He said about the Father contemptuously, but also ridicule Him for highly exalting His Father, as if He Himself traced His origin from heaven. Hence by these words, they affirm that they do not value Christ's Father so highly as to ascribe to His Son anything on His account. And the reason why there is such bold contempt of Christ everywhere today is that few consider that He was sent by God.

Ye know neither me. He does not condescend to give them a straight answer, but curtly reproaches the ignorance within which they flattered themselves. They asked about the Father, and yet with the Son present before their eyes, seeing they did not see. It was therefore a just punishment of their pride and wicked ingratitude that those who despised the Son of God exhibited so closely to them, never approached the Father. For how can any mortal man ascend to the height of God unless He is raised on high by His hand? God in Christ descended to the lowliness of men to stretch out His hand to them. So do not those who reject God when He approaches them like this deserve to be excluded from heaven?

Let us know that the same thing is addressed to us all. Whoever aspires to know God without beginning at Christ must wander in a labyrinth, so to say; for it is not for nothing that He is called the image of the Father, as has been said already. Again, because everyone is deprived of all right knowledge of God who leaves Christ and strives Titan-like after heaven, so whoever directs his mind and all his senses to Christ will be led straight to the Father. For the Apostle truly declares that by the mirror of the Gospel we clearly behold God in the person of Christ, (II Cor. 3.18). And it is indeed an incomparable reward for the obedience of faith that he who humbles himself before Christ penetrates above all the heavens, even unto those mysteries which the angels behold and adore.

20. *These words spake he,* etc. The treasury was the part of the Temple where the sacred offerings were stored. It was much frequented, and so we infer that Christ preached this sermon to a large assembly of men, and that the people had the less excuse. The Evangelist also shows us the astonishing power of God, in that they were constrained to endure Christ's openly teaching in the Temple, even though, shortly before, they had sought to put Him to death. For their rule in the Temple was undisputed, so that they domineered there with a tyrannical fierceness and could have banished Christ at a word. When

He dared to take upon Himself the office of teacher, why did they not at once lay hands on Him violently? So we see that God made them hear Him, and guarded Him by His protection, so that those savage beasts did not touch him, though their jaws were open for Him. He again mentions His hour, to teach us that it is not by men's will, but God's, that we live and die.

He said therefore again unto them, I go away, and ye shall seek me, and shall die in your sin: whither I go, ye cannot come. The Jews therefore said, Will he kill himself, that he saith, Whither I go, ye cannot come? And he said unto them, Ye are from beneath; I am from above; ye are of this world; I am not of this world. I said therefore unto you, that ye shall die in your sins: for except ye believe that I am, ye shall die in your sins. (21-24)

21. *I go away.* When He sees that He is doing no good among these obstinate men, He threatens their destruction. And this is the end of all who reject the Gospel, for it is not sown uselessly in the air but must breathe forth the odour either of life or death. The sum of the words however is this: In the end, the wicked will feel how great an evil it was that they rejected Christ when He freely offered Himself to them. But it will be too late, and there will be no more room for repentance. And to frighten them still more by the nearness of their judgment, He first says that He will soon go away, meaning that the Gospel is preached to them only for a little while, and if they let this opportunity slip, the accepted time and days of salvation will not last for ever. Thus also today, we must go at once to meet Christ when He knocks at our door, lest He get tired at our laziness and go away from us. And indeed it is well known from many experiences in all ages, how greatly this departure of Christ is to be feared.

But we must first discover how these people now spoken of sought Christ. For if there had been a real change, they would not have sought Him in vain, since He has truly promised that as soon as a sinner mourns, He will be present to help. Therefore, Christ did not mean that they sought Him by the right way of faith, but were like men in extreme trouble and looking everywhere for help. For unbelievers would like God to be reconciled to them, but do not cease to fly from Him. God calls them. The way to Him is by faith and repentance. But they oppose God by hardness of heart and when they are over-whelmed by despair they fret against Him. In short, they are so far from aspiring to God that they do not give Him an opportunity to help them, unless He deny Himself, which He will never do.

In this way, however wicked the scribes were, they would gladly have applied to themselves the redemption promised by the hand of the Messiah, if only Christ had transfigured Himself according to their inclination. Therefore, by these words Christ threatens and denounces against all unbelievers that, when they have despised the teaching of the Gospel, they will be brought to such straits that they will be forced to cry to God; but their howling will be useless, because as we have already said, seeking, they do not seek. And this is expressed plainly enough in the next clause, where He says, *Ye shall die in your sin.* For He is telling them that the cause of their destruction will be their disobedience and rebellion against God to the very end. The nature of their sin we shall see shortly.

22. *Will he kill himself?* The scribes continue not only in their bold scorn, but also in impudence; for they ridicule His saying that they cannot follow whither He is going. It is as if they said, 'We acknowledge that we cannot accompany Him if He kills Himself, for we do not choose to do so.' For they think nothing of Christ's absence and imagine that they will beat Him in every respect; and so they tell Him to go where He likes. Shocking stupidity! But this is how Satan bewitches the reprobate, so that drunk with worse than madness they may throw themselves into the midst of the flame of God's wrath. Do not we today see the same rage in many who stupefy their consciences, and with their jests and insolent jeering mock at everything they hear about the dreadful judgment of God? Yet this is certainly a sardonic smile, for inwardly they are pierced with unseen wounds; but of a sudden, as if bereft of their senses, they burst out into furious guffaws.

23. *Ye are from beneath.* Since they did not deserve Him to teach them, He only wanted to strike them with curt reproofs. So in this passage He says that they do not receive His teaching because the Kingdom of God is utterly abhorrent to them. He includes under *world* and *beneath*, all that men have by nature, and thus indicates the difference between His Gospel and the acuteness and perspicacity of the human mind; for the Gospel is heavenly wisdom, but our mind crouches to the earth. Therefore, only he whom Christ has formed by His Spirit will ever be a proper disciple. And this is why faith is so rare in the world, because the whole human race is naturally opposed and averse to Christ—except for those whom He raises on high by the special grace of His Spirit.

24. *Ye shall die in your sins.* First He had used the singular and now He puts it in the plural, though with the same meaning, except that in the former passage He wanted to point out that unbelief is the fountain and cause of all evils. Not that unbelief alone is sin, or that it alone makes us guilty of eternal death before God, as some say too extravagantly. But it alienates us from Christ and deprives us of His grace,

from which we should seek deliverance from all our sins. The deadly
ill of the Jews is that they reject the medicine with obstinate malice.
Hence also the slaves of Satan do not cease to heap up sin upon sin and
continually to bring fresh guilt upon themselves. And therefore he
at once adds

Except ye believe that I am. For there is no other way for the lost to
recover salvation than by flying to Christ. The emphasis is on the
phrase *that I am.* We must understand by it all that the Scripture
ascribes to the Messiah and all that it tells us to expect from Him. But
the sum and substance is the restoration of the Church, of which the
beginning is the light of faith, from which spring righteousness and a
new life. Some of the ancients have misapplied this to the divine
essence of Christ. He is in fact speaking of His office towards us. The
statement is noteworthy, for men never sufficiently consider the evils
in which they are plunged; and although they are constrained to
acknowledge their destruction, they neglect Christ and look around
them to useless remedies. Hence, we must believe that until the grace
of Christ is manifested to save us, there reigns a boundless mixture of
all evils.

They said therefore unto him, Who art thou? Jesus said unto them,
From the beginning, because I also speak to you. I have many things to
speak and to judge concerning you: howbeit he that sent me is true; and
the things which I heard from him, these speak I unto the world. They
perceived not that he spake to them of the Father. Jesus therefore said,
When ye have lifted up the Son of man, then shall ye know that I am he,
and that I do nothing of myself, but as the Father taught me, I speak
these things. And he that sent me is with me; he hath not left me alone;
for I do always the things that are pleasing to him. (25-29)

25. *From the beginning.* They are very mistaken who take 'beginning' in the nominative as if Christ were here asserting His eternal
divinity. There can be no ambiguity of the sort in Greek, but the
Greek commentators also differ among themselves. They are, indeed,
all agreed that a preposition is to be supplied, but many expound it as
an adverb, as if Christ were saying, 'This is the first thing to be observed.' Some too, like Chrysostom, make it read continuously: 'The
beginning, which also speak to you, I have many things to say and
judge of you.' This sense has been put into verse by Nonnus. But a
different reading is more generally adopted and seems the true one to
me. I interpret τὴν ἀρχήν 'from the beginning'; so that, to my mind,
the meaning is this: 'I did not arise suddenly but I now come forth
publicly just as I was formerly promised.'

He adds *Because I also speak to you.* By this He means that He is declaring plainly enough who He is if only they had ears for it. The causal particle ὅτι is not used merely to give a reason, as if Christ wanted to prove that He was from the beginning because He is now speaking. Rather He asserts that the agreement between His doctrine and the eternity He has spoken of is such that it ought to be taken as an undoubted confirmation of it. The words may be explained thus: 'According to the beginning, that is He whom I confirmed in time past as I now do anew,' or 'And indeed what I now speak is in accord with the prophecies of all ages as a sure proof of them.'

In short this reply consists of two clauses. In the word *beginning* He includes a continuous series of ages, from when God made His Covenant with the fathers. When He says that He also speaks, He joins His present teaching to the ancient prophecies and shows that it depends on them. It follows that the only reason for the ignorance of the Jews was that they believed neither the prophets nor the Gospel, for it is the same Christ exhibited in them all. They pretended to be the prophets' disciples and to look to the eternal Covenant of God, but yet they rejected Christ, who had been promised from the beginning and presented Himself before them.

26. *I have many things.* Seeing that He is preaching to the deaf, He does not go on with His sermon, but only declares that God will vindicate that doctrine of which He is the Author and which they despise. 'If I wanted to accuse you,' He says, 'your malice and wickedness give Me ample substance. But I leave you for the present. My Father, who has committed to Me the office of teaching, will not neglect His part. He will always justify His Word against the ungodly and sacrilegious contempt of men.' This saying of Christ's means much the same as Paul's, 'If we deny him, he abideth faithful; for he cannot deny himself' (II Tim. 2.13). In short, He threatens the judgment of God against unbelievers, who refuse to believe His Word, because God must necessarily defend His truth. Now, this is the true stability of our faith, when we believe that God is sufficient of Himself to establish the authority of His doctrine, though the whole world should reject it. All who rely on this doctrine, and serve Christ faithfully, may fearlessly accuse the whole world of falsehood.

And the things which I heard. He says that He is putting forward nothing that He has not received from the Father. And the sole confirmation of teaching is when the minister shows that what he speaks has come from God. Now we know that Christ undertook then the part of a minister; and therefore it is not surprising if He demands a hearing, since He brings God's commands to men. Moreover, by His example He lays down a general law for the whole Church: that no man is to be heard unless he speaks from the mouth of God. But while He casts down the perverse arrogance of those who put themselves forward without the Word of God, faithful teachers, who are well aware of their calling, are fortified and armed by Him with unconquerable firmness, that they may, under God's guidance, boldly defy all mortals.

27. *They perceived not.* From this it appears how stupid are those whose minds are possessed by Satan. Nothing could be plainer than that they were summoned to the judgment seat of God; but they are altogether blind to this, just as other enemies of the Gospel are every day. And their blindness should teach us to fear.

28. *When ye have lifted up.* Displeased at the dullness that the Evangelist has described, Christ again declares that they are unworthy to hear any more from Him. 'All your senses', He says, 'are, as it were, bewitched, and therefore you understand nothing that I say. But the time will yet come when you will realize that a prophet of God has lived among you and spoken to you.' This is the way we should deal with the ungodly; we ought to summon them positively to the judgment-seat of the supreme Judge. But the knowledge that Christ speaks of comes too late when the ungodly are dragged to punishment and reluctantly confess that the God they ought calmly to have revered is their Judge. For He does not promise them repentance, but says that, when they have been struck with new and unexpected horror at God's wrath, they will be aroused from that numbness in which they now rest. Thus were Adam's eyes opened, so that he was overwhelmed with shame, and sought in vain for hiding places, and at last saw that he was lost. Yet this knowledge of Adam, useless in itself, turned to his advantage through the grace of God. But when the reprobate are overwhelmed with despair, their eyes are only opened to see their destruction. And God leads them to this kind of knowledge in a variety of ways. Often, they are forced by afflictions to realize that God is angry with them. Sometimes, He tortures them inwardly without any outward punishment. And, sometimes, He lets them go on sleeping until He calls them out of this world.

By the word *lift up* Christ indicates His own death. He mentions His death to warn them that they will gain nothing by destroying Him after the flesh. It is as if He said, 'You now haughtily mock My speaking. But your wickedness will soon go further, even to killing Me. Then you will triumph, as if your wish had come true; but it will not be long before you feel, to your utter ruin, how little My death is My destruction.' He uses the word *lift up* to prick them the deeper. They wanted to plunge Christ down to the lowest depths. He tells them they will be completely disappointed and that the outcome will be just the opposite. It may be, indeed, that He was alluding to the outward form of His death, that He was to be lifted up on the cross. But He was chiefly looking to its glorious result, which followed soon after, contrary to all expectation. It is true that even in the cross He triumphed magnificently over Satan before God and the angels, blotting out the handwriting of sin and cancelling the condemnation of death. But it was only after the Gospel had been preached that this triumph began to be apparent to men. The same thing that happened soon after—that Christ rose from the grave and ascended to heaven—is what we ought to expect daily; for however the ungodly may scheme to oppress Christ in His teaching and His Church, He will not only rise above them, but will turn their wicked efforts to the greater advance of His Kingdom.

That I am. I have already said that this does not refer to Christ's divine essence, but to His office. This appears still more clearly from the context, where He affirms that He does nothing but at the command of His Father. For this was as good as saying that He was sent by God and performs His office faithfully.

I do nothing of myself. That is, I do not put myself forward and undertake anything rashly. The word *speak* refers to the same thing, that is, the teaching office. For when Christ wants to prove that He does nothing without the Father's command, He says that He speaks as He has been taught by Him. And so the sum of the words is: 'In all my activity, which you condemn, no part is my own; I am simply executing what God has commanded Me. The words you hear from My mouth are His and My calling is governed by Him alone who is its Author.' But we must remember that these words are, as I have mentioned before now, accommodated to the capacity of the hearers. Since they regarded Christ merely as one among the common rank of men, He asserts that whatever in Him is divine is not His own—as if He were saying, that it is not of man or by man, because the Father teaches us by Him and appoints Him to be the only Teacher in the Church. This is why He says that He has been taught by the Father.

29. *And he that sent me.* He again proclaims that God, under whose guidance and authority He does all things, will help Him, and therefore He will not labour in vain and uselessly. It is as if He said that the power of God's Spirit is joined to His ministry. All faithful teachers should have the same confidence and not doubt that the hand of God will be near them when they fulfil the ministry that He demands with a clear conscience. For God does not equip them with His Word to strike the air with a cold and empty sound. He gives success to His Word by the secret efficacy of His Spirit, and at the same time guards them under His protection, so that their enemies may be vanquished and they left standing invincible against the whole world. If they judge of

themselves and their own powers, they must be overthrown every
moment. Therefore, the only way for them to stand is for them to be
convinced that they are upheld by the hand of God.

But we must notice the reason why Christ says that God is on His
side and He will never be without His help. It is because He depends
entirely on His will and serves Him sincerely. For this is what the
adverb *always* means—that He does not just partially obey God but is
entirely and without exception devoted to His obedience. Hence, if
we want to enjoy this same presence of God, our whole reason must
be subjected to His rule. For if our senses hold any part of the government, all our endeavours will be fruitless, since the blessing of God will
be absent. And though for a time, a happy appearance of success may
please us, the final result will be unhappy.

When Christ says *he hath not left me alone*, He is indirectly bewailing
the treachery of His nation, where He found hardly any to support
Him. Yet He shows that it is quite enough for Him to have God to
protect Him. This is the spirit we ought to have today, so that we may
not be discouraged by the scantiness of believers. For even if the whole
world is opposed to our teaching, we are not alone. Hence also, the
boasting of the Papists is plain. They overlook God and boast of their
vast numbers.

*As he spake these things, many believed on him. Jesus therefore said to
those Jews which had believed him, If ye abide in my word, then are ye
truly my disciples; and ye shall know the truth, and the truth shall make
you free. They answered unto him, We be Abraham's seed, and have
never yet been in bondage to any man; how sayest thou, Ye shall be made
free? Jesus answered them, Verily, verily, I say unto you, Every one
that committeth sin is the bondservant of sin. And the bondservant
abideth not in the house for ever: the son abideth for ever. If therefore
the Son shall make you free, ye shall be free indeed. I know that ye are
Abraham's seed; yet ye seek to kill me, because my word hath not free
course in you. I speak the things which I have seen with my Father:
and ye also do the things which ye have seen with your father.* (30-38)

30. *As he spake these things.* Although the Jews were then not unlike
a dry and barren soil, God did not allow the seed of His Word to be
lost completely. Against all hope and amid many obstructions, some
fruit appears. But the Evangelist imprecisely calls faith what was only
a sort of preparation for faith. For he is saying nothing better about
them than that they were disposed to receive the teaching of Christ.
And the next warning also refers to this.

31. *If ye abide in my word.* Here Christ first warns them that it is
not enough for anyone to begin well if he does not correspondingly

progress to the end. And this is why He exhorts those who have tasted His doctrine to persevere in the faith, when He says that those who are so firmly rooted in His Word that they continue in it will truly be His disciples. He means that many profess to be disciples who are not really and do not deserve to be accounted such. He distinguishes His followers from hypocrites by the mark that those who falsely proclaimed they believed, give way from the very start, or at least in the middle of the race, whereas believers persevere to the winning-post. Therefore, if Christ is to account us as His disciples, we must endeavour to persevere.

32. *And ye shall know the truth.* He says that those who have attained some knowledge of it shall know the truth. It is true that those whom Christ was addressing were as yet uneducated and hardly in the first lessons, so that it is not surprising if He promises them a fuller understanding of His doctrine. But the statement is general. Whatever progress any of us has made in the Gospel, let him know that he needs fresh additions. The reward that Christ bestows on their perseverence is to make them more familiar with Himself. But by doing so, He merely adds another gift to the former, so that no man may think that he is repaid anything by way of reward. For He who puts His Word in our hearts by His Spirit is the same who daily chases from our minds the clouds of ignorance which obscure the brightness of the Gospel. That the truth may be fully revealed to us, we should strive after it sincerely and earnestly. It is the same unvarying truth which Christ teaches His own from first to last; but first He enlightens them with small sparks, as it were, and finally pours out a full light upon them. Thus, until they have been fully confirmed, believers are in a sense ignorant of what they know. Yet this knowledge of faith is not so small and obscure that it is not efficacious for salvation.

The truth shall make you free. He commends the knowledge of the Gospel from the fruit we receive from it or, which is just the same, from its effect; namely, it restores us to freedom. This is an incomparable blessing. Hence it follows that there is nothing more excellent or desirable than the knowledge of the Gospel. All feel and acknowledge that slavery is a most wretched thing. Since the Gospel delivers us from this, it follows that the treasure of the blessed life comes from the Gospel.

We must now ascertain what kind of liberty Christ is describing here. It is that which sets us free from the tyranny of Satan, sin and death. And if we obtain it by means of the Gospel, it is clear that by nature we are the slaves of sin. Next, we must find out the method of our deliverance, for so long as we are ruled by our own sense and nature, we are in bondage to sin. But when the Lord regenerates us by His Spirit He also makes us free, so that we are released from the snares of Satan and willingly obey righteousness. But regeneration comes from faith. Hence it is evident that freedom is from the Gospel.

Now let Papists go and proudly boast about their free will. But let us who are aware of our own slavery glory in none but Christ our Liberator. For the reason why we must regard the Gospel as having achieved our deliverance is that it offers and gives us to Christ to be freed from the yoke of sin. Lastly, we should observe that freedom has its degrees according to the measure of faith. This is why Paul, although already set free, still groans and sighs for perfect freedom.

33. *We be Abraham's seed.* It is uncertain whether the Evangelist is here introducing the same people speaking or others. I think they replied to Christ confusedly, as usually happens in a mixed crowd, and that they were despisers rather than believers. It is a customary mode of expression in Scripture, when a body of people is mentioned, to ascribe generally to all what belongs only to a part.

Now those who object that they are Abraham's seed and have always been free, easily gathered from Christ's words that freedom was promised to them as slaves. But they cannot bear being called slaves, they who are a holy and elect people. For what was the use of the adoption and the Covenant, by which they were separated from other nations, unless they were accounted the children of God? So they think they are being insulted when freedom is exhibited to them as a blessing foreign to them. But it might be thought strange that they should deny they were ever enslaved, when they had been so often oppressed by various tyrants and were even then subject to the Roman yoke and groaned under the heaviest burden of slavery. From this we can easily see how foolish their boasting was. Yet they had a certain excuse, in that the unjust domination of their enemies did not hinder them from continuing to be free by right. But they were wrong, first, in not considering that the right of adoption was founded on the Mediator alone. For how is it that Abraham's seed is free, but because by the unique grace of the Redeemer it is exempted from the bondage common to the human race? But there was another and less tolerable error. Although they were altogether degenerate, they wanted to be reckoned among Abraham's children and did not consider that it is only the regeneration of the Spirit that makes them legitimate children of Abraham.

And indeed, it has been a vice too common in almost all ages to refer the extraordinary gifts of God to a carnal origin and to ascribe to nature those remedies that God bestows for correcting nature. Moreover, we see how all who are swollen with a false confidence, and flatter themselves on their state, drive away the grace of Christ. Yet this pride is spread over the whole world, so that there is hardly one in a hundred who feels he needs the grace of God.

34. *Every one that committeth sin*, etc. This is arguing from opposites. They boasted that they were free. He proves that they are the slaves of sin because, enslaved by the desires of the flesh, they continually sin. It is astonishing how men are not convinced by their own experience and learn to be humble and put away their pride. And this is more than common today; the greater the mass of vices anyone is buried under, the more fiercely and bombastically does he extol free will.

It seems as if Christ is saying nothing more here than was earlier discussed by the philosophers: that they who are devoted to their lusts are in the worst bondage. But there is a deeper and more hidden meaning. He is not only speaking of the evil that men bring on themselves, but of the state of human nature. The philosophers thought that any man by his own choice becomes a slave and returns to freedom. But here Christ declares that all who are not freed by Him are in slavery, and that all who derive the contagion of sin from corrupted nature are slaves from birth. We must grasp this comparison between grace and nature which Christ emphasizes here, and from which we can easily see that men are despoiled of freedom unless they recover it from elsewhere. Yet this slavery is voluntary, so that those who sin of necessity are not forced to sin.

35. *And the bondservant*, etc. He adds a simile from common and civil law (*a legibus et iure politico*). A slave, though he has power for a while, is not the heir of the house. From this He deduces that there is no perfect and permanent freedom but what is obtained through the Son. In this way He accuses the Jews of vanity, in that they present a mask in place of the reality. For as Abraham's offspring they were nothing but a mask. They occupied a place in the Church of God; but such a place as Ishmael the slave, triumphing over his free-born brother, usurped for a little while. The conclusion is that all who boast of being Abraham's children have nothing but a false and transient appearance.

36. *If therefore the Son shall make you free.* By these words He means that the right of freedom belongs to Himself alone, and that all others are born slaves and can be delivered only by His grace. For what He has of His own nature He communicates to us by adoption, when we are engrafted by faith into His body and made His members. Therefore we should remember what I said before—that He sets us free by the signed deed of liberation. Hence, our freedom is a benefit of Christ, but we obtain it by faith, through which Christ also regenerates us by His Spirit.

When He says that they *shall be free indeed*, the emphasis is on the word *indeed*. We must supply the contrast to the foolish persuasion with which the Jews were swollen; just as a good part of the world imagine they possess a kingdom, when they are in the most wretched slavery.

37. *I know that ye are Abraham's seed.* I expound this as a concession. Yet at the same time He laughs at their folly in glorying in such a worthless title, as if He said, 'Even allowing the thing you flatter yourselves on so much, what is the use of those being called the children of Abraham who rage against God and His ministers, and are moved by such wicked and horrible hatred of the truth that they rush headlong into shedding innocent blood?' Hence it follows that nothing is less like the truth than what they wanted to be called, for they have no resemblance to Abraham.

Ye seek to kill me. When He says that they seek to kill Him because His Word has no place in them, He means that they are not merely murderers, but are impelled to such rage by a hatred of God and His truth; and this is far worse, for the outrage is not merely against men but also dishonours God. He says *that they cannot receive his words*, for their minds are blocked by malice, and they cannot let in anything wholesome.

38. *The things which I have seen with my Father.* He had already mentioned His Father frequently, and now, by an argument from opposites, He infers that they are enemies to God and children of the devil, because they oppose His teaching. 'I bring forward nothing,' He says, 'but what I have learned from my Father. Why is it then that the Word of God exasperates you so, except that you have an opposite father?' He says that He *speaks* and they *do* because He performed the office of teacher, whereas they worked hard to extinguish His teaching. At the same time, He frees the Gospel from contempt, for it is not surprising if it is opposed by the devil's children. Some render it *do you*, as if Christ were saying, 'Come now, show that you are the children of the devil by opposing Me, for I speak nothing but what God has commanded Me.'

They answered and said unto him, Our father is Abraham. Jesus saith unto them, If ye were Abraham's children, ye would do the works of Abraham. But now ye seek to kill me, a man that hath told you the truth, which I heard from God: this did not Abraham. Ye do the works of your father. They said unto him, We were not born of fornication; we have one Father, even God. Jesus said unto them, If God were your Father, ye would love me: for I came forth and am come from God; for neither have I come of myself, but he sent me. (39-42)

39. *Our father is Abraham.* This dispute shows quite plainly how proudly and fiercely they despised all Christ's reproofs. They con-

tinually claim that they are Abraham's children, and they do not mean that they are just descendants born of Abraham, but that they are a holy race, the heritage of God and the children of God. And yet they are only relying on the confidence of the flesh. But carnal descent without faith is a mere mask. We now understand what it was that blinded them so and made Christ of no interest to them, armed though He was with deadly thunder. In the same way, the Word of God, which should move stones, is in our day ridiculed by the Papists as if it were a fable, and fiercely persecuted by sword and fire—and this only because they rely on their false title of the Church and hope to be able to deceive both God and men. In short, as soon as hypocrites have got a plausible pretext they oppose God with iron obstinacy, as if He could not pierce into their hearts.

If ye were Abraham's children. Christ now differentiates more clearly between the degenerate and the legitimate children of Abraham and takes away the name from all who are unlike Abraham. True, it often happens that children do not reflect in their conduct the father from whom they are sprung. But Christ is not discussing carnal descent here, but only affirming that those who do not by faith keep the grace of adoption are not to be reckoned among Abraham's children before God. For, since the Lord promised to the seed of Abraham that He would be their God, all unbelievers abdicate from Abraham's family by rejecting the promise.

The position therefore is this: Should those who reject the blessing offered to them in the Word be accounted Abraham's children and therefore a holy nation, the peculiar people of God and a royal priesthood? Christ denies it, and justly. For those who are the children of the promise must be born again by the Spirit and all who wish to obtain a place in God's Kingdom must be new creatures. Fleshly descent from Abraham was not indeed useless and unimportant so long as the truth was added to it. Election resides in the seed of Abraham, but it is free, so that those are accounted heirs of life whom God sanctifies with His Spirit.

40. *But now ye seek.* He demonstrates from the effect that they are not, as they boasted, the children of Abraham, since they opposed God. For what is more praiseworthy in Abraham than the obedience of faith? And this is the distinguishing mark whenever we have to differentiate his children from strangers. For empty titles, however much they may be esteemed by the world, are nothing to God. Christ therefore again concludes that they are the children of the devil, because they are deadly enemies of true and sound doctrine.

41. *We were not born of fornication.* They claim no more for themselves than before. For it meant the same thing to them to be Abra-

ham's children or God's. But they were greatly at fault in imagining
that God was bound to the whole seed of Abraham. They reason like
this: 'God adopted the family of Abraham to Himself. Therefore,
because we are Abraham's descendants, we must be the children of
God.' We now see that they thought they had holiness from the womb,
because they were sprung of a holy root. In short, they maintain that
they are the Church of God because they trace their origin from the
holy patriarchs. A continual succession from the fathers puffs up the
Papists today and makes them swollen-headed. Satan deceives them
with tricks like this, so that they separate God from His Word, the
Church from faith and the Kingdom of Heaven from the Spirit.

Let us know, then, that those who have corrupted the seed of life
are anything but children of God, even though, after the flesh, they
are not illegitimate but make a plausible claim to being the Church.
For let them beat about the bush as much as they like, they can never
avoid the fact that their only boast is, 'We have succeeded the holy
fathers; therefore we are the Church.' And if Christ's reply was enough
to refute the Jews, it is no less so now to expose the Papists. Hypocrites
will always falsely claim the name of God with a most wicked boldness.
But the false grounds of boasting which they babble, will never fail to
be ridiculous to all who abide by the decision of Christ. ·

42. *If God were your Father.* Christ's argument is this: 'Everyone
who is a son of God will acknowledge and love His first-born Son.
But you hate me. Therefore you have no reason to claim that you are
the sons of God.' We should pay careful heed to this passage, for
where Christ is rejected there is no piety or fear of God. Feigned
religion certainly hides boldly behind God; but what agreement can
they have with the Father who disagree with His only Son? What
kind of knowledge of God is it, where His lively image is rejected?

And this is what Christ means when He declares that *he came from
the Father*; for He means that all that He has is divine, and that therefore
it is most inconsistent that true worshippers of God should flee from
His truth and righteousness. He says: 'I did not come of Myself. You
cannot discover anything in Me that is against God. In short, you will
find nothing earthly or human in My teaching or in the whole of My
ministry.' For He is not speaking of His essence but of His office.

*Why do ye not understand my language? Even because ye cannot hear
my word. Ye are of your father the devil, and the lusts of your father it
is your will to do. He was a murderer from the beginning, and stood not
in the truth, because there is no truth in him. When he speaketh a lie,
he speaketh of his own: for he is a liar, and the father thereof. But
because I say the truth, ye believe me not.* (43-45)

43. *Why do ye not understand my language?* In this passage He reproves the obstinacy of the Jews, which was so great that they could not bear even to hear Him speaking. From this He infers that they are motivated and carried away by a devilish rage. Some distinguish here between language and speech, in that it is more to say than to speak; but I do not see it. And it would not fit in for the lesser word to be put first. Many divide this verse so as to make the question end with the word *language*, as if it consisted only of the words, 'Why do you not understand my language?' And then the reason is given at once, 'Because you cannot hear my word.' But I think it ought to be read in one sequence, as if He said, 'For what reason is My speech barbarous and unknown to you, so that I do no good by speaking to you, and you do not even trouble to open your ears to what I say?' In the first clause He rebukes their stupidity; in the second, their obstinate and unbridled hatred of His teaching. Afterwards He gives a reason for both, by saying that they are sprung from the devil. For by questioning them, He wanted to take away their continual boast that they were led by reason and judgment to oppose Him.

44. *Ye are of your father the devil.* He now expresses more fully what He had twice said obscurely, that they are the children of the devil. We have to supply the antithesis, that they could not hate the Son of God so much were it not that their father was the perpetual enemy of God. Moreover, He calls them children of the devil, not only because they imitate him, but because they are led by his prompting to fight against Christ. We are called the children of God, not only because we are like Him, but because He governs us by His Spirit, and Christ lives and is vigorous in us, conforming us to the image of His Father. Similarly on the other hand, the devil is said to be the father of those whose minds he blinds, whose hearts he stirs up to all unrighteousness and, in short, on whom he acts powerfully and exercises his tyranny (II Cor. 4.4, Eph. 2.2, and other places).

The Manichees vainly and foolishly misused this passage to prove their madness. When Scripture calls us the children of God, it is not referring to the transmission or origin of substance, but to the grace of the Spirit regenerating us to newness of life. Thus this saying of Christ is not concerned with transmission of substance but with the corruption of nature, of which man's fall was the cause and origin. Therefore that men are born the children of the devil is not to be imputed to creation, but to the vitiation of sin. And Christ proves this from the effect, in that they willingly and of their own accord are disposed to follow the devil.

He was a murderer. He explains what those desires are, and mentions two instances, cruelty and falsehood, in which the Jews greatly resembled Satan. When He says that he was a murderer, He means that he schemed man's destruction. For as soon as man was created, Satan was impelled by a wicked desire to hurt, and directed his strength to destroying him. Again, Christ does not mean the beginning of the creation, as if it were God who had planted in him a desire to hurt; but He is condemning in Satan the faultiness of nature which he brought upon himself.

This comes out more clearly in the second clause, where He says *he stood not in the truth.* For although those who imagine the devil was wicked by nature try to get out of this, these words plainly express a change for the worse and say that Satan was a liar, in that he deserted from the truth. His being a liar does not arise from his nature having always been against the truth, but from his defection by a voluntary fall. This description of Satan is very useful to us, so that everyone may take care to beware of his snares and also to repel his power and force. 'For he goeth about as a roaring lion, seeking whom he may devour' (I Pet. 5.8), and is furnished with a thousand tricks to deceive. So much the more should believers be armed with spiritual weapons for the fight, and so much the more earnestly should they watch with vigilance and prudence. Now if Satan cannot put off this disposition, we must not be troubled at it, as if it were a new and uncommon thing for various errors to spring up. For Satan stirs up his followers like agitators to distract the world with their impostures. And it is not surprising that Satan tries so hard to extinguish the light of truth, for it is the only life of the soul. Hence the chief and most deadly weapon for killing the soul is falsehood. As anybody with eyes can see such a picture of Satan in the Papacy today, they ought first of all to consider the enemy they are fighting against, and next to take refuge in the command of Christ their captain, under whose banner they fight.

What follows, *because there is no truth in him,* is a confirmation from the effect, *a posteriori* as they say. For Satan hates the truth and cannot bear it, but is utterly filled with falsehoods. Hence Christ infers that he is entirely fallen and turned away from the truth. Let us not be surprised, therefore, if he daily shows the fruits of his apostasy.

When he speaketh a lie. These words are commonly explained as referring to Christ's denial that the blame for lies belongs to God, who is the Author of nature, and His affirmation that it proceeds rather from corruption. But I expound it more simply; that it is customary for the devil to lie and that he thinks of nothing but the contriving of frauds, deceits and tricks. And yet we properly infer from these words that the devil has this vice from himself and that it is peculiar to him in such a way as at the same time to be accidental. For although Christ calls the devil the maker of lying, He plainly separates him from God, nay, declares him contrary to God. The word *father* which He now adds has the same scope. For Satan is said to be the father of lies because he is estranged from God, in whom alone dwells the truth and from whom it flows as a unique fountain.

45. *But because I say the truth.* He confirms the above statement; for since they have no other reason for opposing Him than that the truth is hateful and unbearable to them, they show openly that they are the children of Satan.

> *Which of you convicteth me of sin? If I say truth, why do ye not believe me? He that is of God heareth the words of God: for this cause ye hear them not, because ye are not of God. The Jews answered and said unto him, Say we not well that thou art a Samaritan, and hast a devil? Jesus answered, I have not a devil; but I honour my Father, and ye dishonour me. But I seek not mine own glory: there is one that seeketh and judgeth.* (46-50)

46. *Which of you?* This question comes from perfect confidence. For he knows that He was innocent of any blame, and glories over His enemies as the victor. And yet He does not say that He was free from their slanders; for although there was no substance in their reproach, they did not cease to attack Christ with their abuse. But He means that there is no fault in Him. And this is the significance of the word ἐλέγχειν or, as the Latin would say, *coarguere (to prove guilty)* when a man is held convicted of the accusation. But those who think that Christ is here asserting His perfect innocence, in that He alone was perfect among men, inasmuch as He was the Son of God, are mistaken. For His defence must be limited to the circumstances of the passage; so that He was claiming that nothing could be adduced to show that He was not a faithful minister of God. Likewise Paul also glories that he is not aware of anything against himself (I Cor. 4.4). This does not cover his whole life, but is only a defence of his doctrine and apostleship. It is therefore irrelevant to speculate, as some do, about the perfection of righteousness which belongs to the Son of God alone; for His only object is to gain credit for His ministry, as comes out more clearly in what follows, when He again adds at once *If I say truth*, etc. From which we may infer that Christ is defending His teaching rather than His person.

47. *He that is of God.* He has a right to take it for granted that He is the ambassador of His heavenly Father and that He is faithfully executing the office committed to Him. Therefore He inveighs against them more vehemently, for their ungodliness was no longer hidden now that they were so obstinate in rejecting the Word of God. He had shown that they could not bring forward anything which He had taught

as not coming from God's mouth. And so He concludes that they
have nothing in common with God, because they do not hear Him;
and without saying anything about Himself He accuses them of fighting against God. Moreover, we are taught in this passage that there is
no plainer sign of a reprobate mind than when a man cannot bear the
teaching of Christ, even though in other respects he shines outwardly
with an angelic sanctity. Just as, if we embrace it cheerfully, we have,
as it were, a visible seal of our election. For he who has the Word
enjoys God Himself; but he who rejects it deprives himself of righteousness and life. And there is nothing we should fear more than falling
under that awful sentence.

48. *Say we not well?* They show more and more how much they
are stupefied by Satan. For although they are quite convicted, they
are not ashamed to rush into the midst of despair. Moreover, though
they bring a twofold reproach against Christ, all they want to do is to say
in a few words that He is a man to be execrated and is motivated by an
evil spirit. Because the Jews regarded the Samaritans as apostates and
corrupters of the Law, they called a man a Samaritan when they wanted
to vilify him. Therefore, not having a worse accusation to reproach
Christ with, they seize at random and uncritically this vulgar one. To
put it briefly, we see that they curse Him as men usually do when they
are infuriated like mad dogs and cannot find anything to say.

49. *I have not a devil.* That He passes over the first charge and clears
Himself only of the second, some impute to His overlooking the insult
to His person and undertaking only the defence of His teaching. But
in my judgment they are mistaken; for it is not likely that the Jews
would be so subtle in distinguishing between His life and teaching.
Besides, the dislike of this name arose, as we have said, from the fact
that the Samaritans, who observed the Law perversely and degener-
ately, had debased it with many superstitions and corruptions, and had
polluted the whole worship of God with alien inventions. Augustine
takes refuge in allegory, and says that Christ did not refuse to be called
a Samaritan because He is a true guardian of His flock. But it seems
to me that Christ's meaning was different. The two reproaches cast
on Him had the same object, and by refuting one He refutes the other.
And indeed, if we think about it carefully, the insult of Samaritan was
worse than that of demoniac. But as I have said, Christ is content with
a simple refutation, drawn from the opposite, asserting that He studies
the honour of His Father. For he who duly and sincerely honours Him,
must be guided by the Spirit of God and be His faithful servant.

Ye dishonour me. This clause may be expounded as if Christ were
complaining that He does not receive the honour due to Him who
promotes the glory of God. But I think He is looking higher and

connecting God's glory with His own, as if He said, 'I claim for Myself nothing that does not turn to the glory of the Father. His majesty shines in Me; His power and authority dwell in Me. When therefore I am received so unworthily by you, you insult God Himself.' So He at once adds that God will avenge this insult. For they might have accused Him of ambition had He not said that He was not worried personally or humanly about the honour or contempt shown to Him, but inasmuch as the honour or contempt of God was concerned. And though we are far removed from Christ, let everyone be fully convinced that if he sincerely desires to seek God's glory, abundant praise will be laid up for him with God. For we shall always find the saying true, 'Them that honour me, I will honour' (I Sam. 2.30). Should men not only despise him but load him with reproaches, let him with a calm mind wait for the day of the Lord to dawn.

Verily, verily, I say unto you, If a man keep my word, he shall never see death. The Jews said unto him, Now we know that thou hast a devil. Abraham is dead, and the prophets; and thou sayest, If a man keep my word, he shall never taste of death. Art thou greater than our father Abraham, which is dead? and the prophets are dead: whom makest thou thyself? Jesus answered, If I glorify myself, my glory is nothing: it is my Father that glorifieth me; of whom ye say, that he is your God; and ye have not known him: but I know him; and if I should say, I know him not, I shall be like unto you, a liar: but I know him, and keep his word. (51-55)

51. *Verily, verily, I say unto you.* Christ undoubtedly knew that some in that multitude were curable and that others were not hostile to His teaching. For this reason, He wanted to terrify the desperately malicious wicked, but yet so as to leave grounds of consolation for the good or draw to Him those who were not yet lost. However much the greater part may abhor God's Word, the godly teacher must not give all his time to reproving the wicked but should also impart the teaching of salvation to the children of God, and try to bring to a sound mind any who are not absolutely incurable. Therefore in this passage, Christ promises eternal life to His disciples, but demands disciples who will not merely nod their assents like donkeys, or profess with the tongue that they approve His teaching, but who will keep it as a precious treasure. He says that *they shall never see death*; for when faith quickens a man's soul, the sting of death is already blunted and its poison wiped off, and so it cannot inflict a deadly wound.

52. *Now we know.* The reprobate persist in their stupidity and are as untouched by promises as by threats, so that they can neither be led nor drawn to Christ. Some think that they slanderously twist His

words because they say, 'taste of death', which Christ did not say. But this seems groundless to me. I think that the phrases 'to taste of death' and 'to see death' were synonymous in Hebrew and meant 'to die'. But they are false interpreters, in that they transfer the spiritual teaching of Christ to the body. No believers will see death, because, having been born again of incorruptible seed, they live even when they die; because they are united to Christ their Head and cannot be extinguished by death; because death is for them a passing into the heavenly Kingdom; because the Spirit who dwells in them is life on account of righteousness, until He shall swallow up the residue of death. But these men are carnal and know of no deliverance from death unless it appears openly in the body. And it is a too common disease in the world that most men care almost nothing for the grace of Christ, since they judge of it only by their carnal perception. Lest the same thing should happen to us, we must arouse our minds to discern spiritual life in the midst of death.

53. *Than our father Abraham.* Here is another fault. They try to darken Christ's glory by the splendour of Abraham and the saints. But just as the brightness of the sun obscures all the stars, so all the glory that is to be found in the saints must fade away before the immeasurable brightness of Christ. They are acting unjustly and absurdly, then, to contrast the servants with the Lord. And they even do an injury to Abraham and the prophets by misusing their name against Christ. But this wickedness has prevailed in almost every age and has spread to our own day, that the ungodly tear the works of God and make Him seem contrary to Himself. God illuminated His name through the apostles and martyrs. The Papists make the apostles and martyrs idols for themselves, to take the place of God. In so doing, are they not manufacturing armaments from the very kindnesses of God to destroy His power? How little remains for God or for Christ if the saints possess what the Papists so prodigally bestow on them! Therefore, we must know that the whole order of God's Kingdom is confounded unless prophets, apostles and all real saints are placed far below Christ, that He alone may be exalted. And indeed, we cannot give the saints a greater honour than by subjecting them to Christ. But the Papists, though they may deceive the ignorant by boasting that they are honest worshippers of the saints, do an injury both to God and to them; for by raising them on high, they reduce Christ to their level. And indeed they are doubly wrong, because they prefer the saints to Christ in teaching, and because by clothing them with what they have taken from Christ, they strip Him of almost all His power.

54. *If I glorify myself.* Before replying to the unfair comparison, He begins by saying that He does not seek His own glory, and thus meets

their slander. If any object that Christ also glorified Himself, the answer is easy. He did so, not as man, but by the direction and authority of God. For here, as in many other passages, He makes a concession to them by distinguishing between Himself and God. In short, He says that He desires no glory save what had been given Him by the Father. These words teach us that when God glorifies His Son, He will not allow the world to despise Him with impunity.

Those words of God sound from heaven: 'Kiss the Son'; 'Let all the angels worship Him'; 'Let every knee bow to Him'; 'Hear ye him'; 'Let the Gentiles seek him'; and 'Let all flesh be humbled', should greatly encourage believers to worship Christ. We are also reminded by these words that all the glory men gain for themselves is trivial and worthless. How blind ambition is, working so hard for nothing! Let us always keep before our eyes Paul's saying: 'Not he that commendeth himself is approved, but whom God commendeth' (II Cor. 10.18). Moreover, as we are all destitute of God's glory, let us learn to glory in Christ alone, inasmuch as by His grace He makes us partakers of His glory.

Of whom ye say. He snatches from them the false pretence of the name of God which they were wont to take. 'I know how audaciously you boast that you are God's people,' He says, 'but it is a false claim, for you do not know God.' From this we also learn the genuine profession of faith as that which comes from true knowledge. And where does that knowledge arise, but from the Word? Hence all who boast of the name of God without the Word of God are nothing but liars. But Christ encounters their impudence with the assurance of His conscience. And so all God's servants should be prepared in their hearts to be satisfied with having God alone on their side, even if the whole world rose against Him. Thus of old, the prophets and apostles had an invincible greatness of soul, and stood fast against the fearful assaults of all the world, because they knew who had sent them. But when this substantial knowledge of God is lacking, we have nothing to uphold us.

And if I should say. By this phrase Christ declares that the needs of His office force Him to speak and silence would be a betrayal of the truth. This statement is noteworthy that God reveals Himself to us, so that we may profess with our mouths before men the faith of our hearts. For it should strike us with powerful terror that those who dissimulate to please men and either deny God's truth or disfigure it with ungodly inventions, are not just reproved lightly but banished to be the children of the devil.

Your father Abraham rejoiced to see my day; and he saw it, and was

glad. The Jews therefore said unto him, Thou art not yet fifty years old,
and hast thou seen Abraham? Jesus said unto them, Verily, verily, I
say unto you, Before Abraham was, I am. They took up stones therefore
to cast at him: but Jesus hid himself, and went out of the temple. (56-59)

56. *Your father Abraham.* He grants them, though only in word,
what He had earlier refused them; that Abraham was their father. But
He shows them how weak the objection from Abraham's name is.
'The only object he set himself during his whole life,' He says, 'was to
see My kingdom flourish. He desired Me when I was absent; you
spurn Me when I am present.' What Christ here says of Abraham
applies to all the saints; but this teaching has more weight in regard to
Abraham, in that he is the father of the whole Church. Whoever then
wishes to be numbered among the godly, let him, as he should, receive
with joy the presence of Christ, for which Abraham ardently longed.
For the word *rejoice* intimates a vehement and ardent affection.

We must now supply the contrast. Although the knowledge of
Christ was still so obscure, Abraham was inflamed by such a strong
desire, that he prized its consummation above all good things. How
disgusting then is the ingratitude of those who despise and even reject
Him when He is openly revealed to them! The word *day* does not
denote eternity in this passage as Augustine thought, but the time of
Christ's Kingdom, when He appeared in the world, clothed in flesh,
to fulfil the office of Redeemer.

But the question now arises, How, even with the eyes of faith, did
Abraham see the revelation of Christ? It does not seem to fit in with
another of Christ's statements: 'Many prophets and kings desired to see
the things which ye see, and saw them not' (Luke 10.24). I reply, faith
has its degrees of seeing Christ. The ancient prophets beheld Christ
afar off, as He had been promised to them, and yet were not permitted
to behold Him present, as He made Himself intimately and completely
visible when He came down to men from heaven.

Moreover, we are taught by these words that just as God did not
disappoint Abraham's desire, so now He will not let anyone aspire to
Christ in vain, but will satisfy his godly desire. The reason why He
does not grant the enjoyment of Himself to many is because of men's
malignity, for few desire Him. Abraham's rejoicing testifies that he
looked upon the knowledge of Christ's Kingdom as an incomparable treasure; and we are told that he rejoiced to see the day of Christ
that we may know there was nothing he valued more. But all the
godly receive from their faith the fruit that they are satisfied with
Christ alone and in Him are fully and completely blessed and happy,
their consciences calm and cheerful. And indeed, none knows Christ

aright save he who gives Him the honour of resting entirely in Him.

Others expound it that after Abraham was dead he felt the presence of Christ when He appeared in the world; and so they make a difference between the time of desiring and seeing. And it is certainly true that the coming of Christ was revealed to the spirits of the saints after death, when they had been held in expectation of it all through their lives. But I do not know if such a refined exposition accords with Christ's words.

57. *Fifty years old.* They try to refute Christ's saying as impossible, in that He who was not yet fifty years old makes himself on a par with Abraham, who had died centuries before. Christ was not even thirty-four years old; but they allow Him to be somewhat older so as not to seem too stiff and precise in dealing with Him—as if they said, 'You certainly cannot make yourself as old as that, even if you were to claim to be already fifty years old.' Accordingly, they who conjecture that His face was more worn than His years suggested, or that the years mentioned in the passage are not solar years, labour to no purpose. The notion of Papias, who handed it down that Christ lived more than forty years, cannot be admitted at all.

58. *Before Abraham was.* Unbelievers judge only from the appearance of the flesh; and therefore Christ reminds them that He possesses something greater and higher than human appearance, which is hidden from the senses of the flesh and seen only by the eyes of faith; and that in this way He might be seen by the holy fathers before He appeared openly in the flesh. But He uses different verbs: Before Abraham was born, I am. By these words He excludes Himself from the ordinary number of men and claims for Himself a heavenly and divine power, the perception of which was diffused from the beginning of the world throughout all ages.

But the words may be explained in two ways. Some think that it simply applies to Christ's eternal divinity, and compare it to that passage of Moses, 'I am that I am' (Exod. 3.14). But I extend it much further, in that Christ's power and grace, inasmuch as He is the Redeemer of the world, were common to all ages. It therefore fits in with the saying of the apostle, 'Christ yesterday, and today, and for ever' (Heb. 13.8). For the context seems to demand this interpretation. He had earlier said that Abraham longed with a burning desire for His day. As this seemed unbelievable to the Jews, He adds that He Himself also was then. The reason given will not seem strong enough if we do not grasp that He was even then acknowledged as the Mediator by whom God was to be appeased. Yet that the grace of the Mediator flourished in all ages depended on His eternal divinity. And this saying of Christ contains a remarkable statement of His divine essence.

We should also notice the solemn form of an oath, *Verily, verily.*

And I do not disapprove of Chrysostom's opinion that there is great weight in the present tense of the verb; for He does not say 'I used to be' or 'I was', but *I am*, signifying a condition uniformly the same from the beginning to the end. And He does not say, 'Before Abraham was', but 'Before Abraham became', thus attributing a beginning to him.

59. *They took up stones therefore.* It is possible that they did this as thinking that Christ had to be stoned according to the command of the Law. Hence we infer the great madness of thoughtless zeal. They have no ears to learn the real state of the case, but they have hands ready for murder. I do not doubt that Christ delivered Himself by His secret power, though under the appearance of a lowly condition, for He did not want to display His divinity plainly without leaving room for human weakness. Some copies have the words, *And went through the midst of them*; which Erasmus judiciously considers to have been borrowed from Luke 4. It also deserves notice that the wicked priests and scribes retain possession of the outward Temple when they have banished Christ in whom dwelleth all the fulness of the Godhead. But they are very deceived in thinking that they have a Temple, when it is empty of God. Thus the Pope and his followers today, when they have driven Christ away, and so profaned the Church, foolishly glory in the false mask of a Church.

CHAPTER NINE

And as he passed by, he saw a man blind from his birth. And his disciples asked him, saying, Rabbi, who did sin, this man, or his parents, that he should be born blind? Jesus answered, Neither did this man sin, nor his parents: but that the works of God should be made manifest in him. I must work the works of him that sent me, while it is day: the night cometh, when no man can work. While I am in the world, I am the light of the world. (1-5)

1. *He saw a man blind.* In this chapter, the Evangelist describes the enlightening of the blind man, at the same time mingling teaching with it, which proclaims the fruit of the miracle. *From his birth.* This detail amplifies Christ's power, for a blindness which he had brought from his mother's womb and had endured until he reached manhood, could not be cured by human remedies. And this was the cause of the disciples' asking the question, Whose sin was this the punishment of? In the first place, since Scripture declares that all the troubles to which the human race is liable come from sin, whenever we see anyone in a bad state, we cannot stop the thought at once coming to our minds that the distresses which press upon him are punishments inflicted by God's hand. But here we generally err in three ways:

Since everyone is a bitter censor of others, few apply the same severity to themselves as they should do. If things go badly with my brother, I at once acknowledge the judgment of God. But if God chastises me with a heavier stroke, I overlook my sins. In considering punishments, every man should begin with himself and spare none less than himself. And so, if we want to be fair judges in this matter, let us learn to be perspicacious in our own evils rather than in those of others.

The second error lies in immoderate severity. No sooner is a man touched by the hand of God than we interpret it as deadly hatred, and make crimes out of faults, and almost despair of his salvation. On the other hand, we extenuate our sins, and are hardly conscious of faults when we have committed most serious crimes.

Thirdly, we are wrong to put under condemnation all without any exception whom God exercises with the cross. What we have said just now is undoubtedly true, that all our distresses arise from sin. But God afflicts His people for various reasons. Just as there are some whose crimes He does not avenge in this world, but whose punishment He delays to the future life, to try them the harder, so He often treats His faithful more severely; not because they have sinned more, but that He may mortify the sins of the flesh for the future. Sometimes, too, He is not concerned with their sins, but only testing their obedience or training them to patience. As we see that holy man Job unfortunate beyond all others, and yet he is not beset on account of his sins; but God's purpose was quite different—that his godliness might be the more fully testified in adversity. They are false interpreters, therefore, who attribute all afflictions without distinction to sins; as if the measure of punishments were equal, or as if God regarded nothing else in punishing men than what every man deserves.

There are therefore two things to be observed here: judgment begins, for the most part, at the house of God (I Pet. 4.17); and consequently, whereas He passes by the ungodly, He punishes His own people severely when they have sinned, and in correcting the sinful actions of the Church His stripes are far more severe. Secondly, there are various reasons why He afflicts men, for He gave Peter and Paul to the executioner no less than the most wicked robbers. Hence we infer that we cannot always put our finger on the causes of men's punishments.

When the disciples follow the common opinion and ask what kind of sin it was that God in heaven punished as soon as he was born, they do not speak so absurdly as when they ask whether he sinned before he was born. Yet this silly question was derived from a common and prevalent opinion. For it is quite plain from other passages of Scripture that they believed in the μετεμψύχωσις which Pythagoras dreamed about. From this we see what a deep labyrinth is men's curiosity, especially when presumption is added to it. They say that some were born lame, some cross-eyed, some entirely blind, and some with a deformed body. But instead of revering the hidden judgments of God, as they should have done, they wanted to have a clear reason for His works. Through their rashness they fell into those childish fooleries of thinking that when a soul has finished one life it migrates into a new body and there undergoes the punishments due to the past life. Nor are the Jews today ashamed to proclaim this foolish dream in their synagogues as a revelation from heaven.

We are taught by this example that we ought to beware lest our mind's wandering and erring should hurry and plunge us into dreadful abysses, if we inquire into God's judgments beyond the measure of sobriety. It was truly monstrous that such a gross error should have found a place among the elect people of God, in whom the light of heavenly wisdom had been kindled by the Law and the Prophets. But if God avenged their presumption so severely, the best thing for us in considering the works of God is such a modesty that when their reason escapes us, our minds shall burst out in admiration and our tongues shall forthwith cry, 'Righteous art thou, O Lord, and righteous are thy judgments, even though they are incomprehensible.'

The disciples' question about the sin of the parents is not irrelevant. For although the innocent son is not punished for his father's fault, and 'the soul that sinneth it shall die' (Ezek. 18.20), yet it is not an empty threat that the Lord casts the parents' crimes into the bosoms of the children and is the avenger to the third and fourth generation (Exod. 20.5). Thus the anger of God often rests upon one house for many generations; and as He blesses the children of believers for their sake, so He also rejects an ungodly offspring, determining the children to the same ruin as their fathers, by a just punishment. And none can complain that in this way he is unfairly punished for the sin of another. For where the grace of the Spirit is lacking, from bad crows there must come bad eggs. This was the cause of the apostles wondering whether the Lord punished in the son some crime of the parents.

3. *Neither did this man sin*. Christ does not free the blind man and his parents absolutely from all blame, but says that the cause of the blindness was not to be sought in sin. And this is what I have already said, that God sometimes has another purpose than punishing men's sins when He sends them afflictions. Consequently, when the causes of afflictions are hidden, our curiosity must be restrained so that we may neither injure God nor be malicious to our brethren.

And so Christ adduces another reason why this man was born blind: *that the works of God should be made manifest in him*. He does not say one work, but works in the plural; for so long as he was blind, there was exhibited in him an example of the divine severity, from which others might learn to fear and to humble themselves. It was followed by the benefit of his deliverance, in which the wonderful goodness of God was reflected. So Christ intended by these words to stir His disciples up to expect a miracle. But at the same time He reminds them in general that this cause must be abundantly seen as true and lawful in the theatre of the world when God glorifies His name. Nor have men any right to argue with God when He makes them the instruments of His glory in both ways, whether He appears as merciful or severe.

4. *I must work*. He now testifies that He has been sent to manifest the grace of God in enlightening the blind. He also makes use of a comparison from ordinary life. When the sun is risen, man rises to his labour; but the night is given for rest, as Ps. 104.22 says. He therefore calls the time fixed by the Father *the day*, in which He must finish the work commanded Him. Just as every man called to some public office has to be employed in his daily task to do what the nature of his office demands. From this we should also deduce a universal rule, that the course of a man's life is as it were his day. Therefore, as the shortness

of daylight stirs labourers to industry and toil, that they may not be overtaken by the darkness of night in the middle of their work, so when we see that a short time of life is allotted to us we should be ashamed of lazing in idleness. In short, as soon as God enlightens us by calling us, we must not delay, lest the opportunity be lost.

5. *While I am in the world.* I interpret this as having been added by way of anticipation. For it might have seemed absurd that Christ should fix in advance His time of working, as if there were danger that He, like others, would be overtaken by the night. Thus He makes such a distinction between Himself and others as to say that His time of working also is limited. For He compares Himself with the sun, which lightens the earth with its brightness, but when it sets, takes the day away with it. Thus He means that His death will be like the setting of the sun; not that it will extinguish or obscure His light, but that it takes away the sight of it from the world. At the same time He shows that when He was brought forth in the flesh, it was then truly the daylight of the world. For though God enlightened all ages, yet Christ brought forth a new and unwonted brightness by His coming. Hence He infers that this was a very fit and proper time, the brightest day, so to say, for making clear the Father's glory, when God wanted to show Himself more plainly in His wonderful works.

But here arises a problem; after Christ's death, a greater power of God shone forth, both in the fruit of the teaching and in miracles. And Paul applies this rightly to the time of his own preaching: 'God, who from the beginning of the world commanded the light to shine out of darkness, at that time shone in the face of Jesus Christ by the Gospel' (II Cor. 4.6). And Christ irradiates the world no less now than when He lived among men. I reply, when Christ had fulfilled the course of His office, He laboured no less powerfully through His ministers than He had through Himself when He was in the world. This I confess to be true; but first, it is not inconsistent with His being bound to perform through Himself what had been commanded Him by the Father when He was manifested in the flesh for that purpose. Secondly, it is not inconsistent with His bodily presence being the true and wonderful day of the world, whose brightness was spread over all ages. For whence came light and day to the holy fathers in old times or to us now, but because the manifestation of Christ always sent forth its rays afar, so as to form one continual day? From this it follows that all who have not Christ for their guide grope in the dark like the blind and wander in confusion and disorder. Yet this meaning must be grasped, that as the sun discovers to our eyes the most beautiful theatre of earth and heaven and the whole order of nature, so God has visibly displayed the chief glory of His work in His Son.

When he had thus spoken, he spat on the ground, and made clay of the spittle, and anointed the eyes of the blind with clay, and said unto him, Go, wash in the pool of Siloam (which is by interpretation, Sent). He went away therefore, and washed, and came seeing. The neighbours therefore, and they which saw him aforetime, that he was a beggar, said, Is not this he that sat and begged? Others said, It is he: others said, No, but he is like him. He said, I am he. They said therefore unto him, How then were thine eyes opened? He answered, The man that is called Jesus made clay, and anointed mine eyes, and said unto me, Go to Siloam, and wash: so I went away and washed, and I received sight. And they said unto him, Where is he? He saith, I know not. (6-12)

6. *He spat on the ground.* Christ's purpose was to restore sight to the blind man; but he starts the work in what seems a very absurd way; for by anointing his eyes with clay He so to say doubles the blindness. Anyone would have thought He was mocking the poor man or carrying on senseless fooleries like a madman. But by doing this, He meant to try the faith and obedience of the blind man, that he might be an example to all. It was certainly no common proof of faith that the blind man embraces His bare Word and is quite convinced that his sight will be restored, and with this trust hastens to go where he was told. It is also a wonderful commendation of his obedience that he simply obeys Christ, though many things swayed him against it. And it is the test of true faith when the godly mind is satisfied with the simple Word of God, and is confident in advance of what otherwise appears incredible. A readiness to obey instantly follows faith, so that whoever is convinced that God will be his faithful Guide, calmly yields himself to His ruling. There can be no doubt that a suspicion and fear that he was being mocked crossed the blind man's mind. But he found it easy to break through every obstruction when he decided it was safe to follow Christ. If any object that the blind man did not know what Christ was and could not give Him the honour due to Him as the Son of God, I acknowledge that this is so; but since he believed that Christ had been sent by God, he submitted to Him and, without doubting that He was true, beheld in Him nothing but the divine. Moreover, his faith deserves the more praise, because with such little knowledge, he devoted himself completely to Christ.

7. *Wash in the pool of Siloam.* There was certainly no virtue for healing the eyes either in *the clay* or in *the water of Siloam*, but Christ freely and often adorned the outward symbols with His miracles, either to accustom believers to the use of signs, or to show that all things were under His will, or to testify that there is just so much power in each of His creatures as He chooses to give. But some ask what the

clay, made of dust and spittle, signifies, and explain it as a figure of Christ, in that the dust denotes the earthly nature of His flesh, and the spittle, coming from His mouth, the divine essence of the Word. But I put this allegory aside as more ingenious than solid, and am content with the simple view that, just as man was at first made of clay, so Christ used clay in restoring his eyes, to show that He had the same power over a part of the body that the Father had exercised in creating the whole man. Or perhaps He wanted by this sign to declare that it was no more difficult for Him to remove the obstruction and open the blind man's eyes than for anyone to wash the clay away. And on the other hand that it was in His power to control the man's sight as much as it was for another to bedaub his eyes with clay. I prefer this latter interpretation.

He ordered him to wash in the pool of Siloam, perhaps to show the Jews that it was their own fault that they could not discern the present power of God. Just as Isaiah reproaches his contemporaries that they 'despise the waters of Siloam, that go softly' (Isa. 8.5). This, I think, was also why Elisha ordered Naaman the Syrian to wash in Jordan. If we may believe Jerome, the pool was formed by waters welling at certain hours out of Mount Zion.

The Evangelist deliberately adds the interpretation of the word *Siloam*. For the fountain, which was near the Temple, daily reminded the Jews of the Christ who was to come, yet whom they despised when He was exhibited to them. So the Evangelist is commending Christ's grace, since He alone lightens our darkness and restores sight to the blind. In the case of this one man there is depicted the state of our nature —we are all from the womb deprived of light and understanding and should seek the cure for this ill in Christ alone.

Observe that, even though Christ was then present, He did not wish to neglect symbols for reproving the dulness of the nation which abolished the substance and kept only the empty shadow of the signs. Moreover, the wonderful goodness of Christ shines in His coming of His own accord to heal the blind without waiting for his prayers to give help. And indeed, since by nature we are turned away from Him, unless He meets us before we call upon Him and in His mercy prevents us who are drowned in forgetfulness of the light and life, it is all up with us.

8. *The neighbours therefore, and they which saw him.* The blind man was known not only to the neighbours but to all the inhabitants of the city, since he used to sit and beg at the gate of the Temple, and the common people take more notice of such as him. This knowledge of the man spread the fame of the miracle to many. But ungodliness is clever at obscuring the works of God and so many thought it was not

the same man, since a new power of God appeared in him. The brighter the majesty of God in His works, the less credit do they obtain among men. But their doubts helped to prove the miracle, for they made the blind man praise Christ's grace the more by his testimony. So the Evangelist collects all the details which showed up the truth of the miracle more clearly.

11. *So I went away and washed.* Such a happy outcome of obedience summons us to surmount all obstacles and proceed courageously wherever the Lord calls us, and not even doubt that whatever we undertake at His leading and authority will turn out well.

They bring to the Pharisees him that aforetime was blind. Now it was the sabbath on the day when Jesus made the clay, and opened his eyes. Again therefore the Pharisees also asked him how he received his sight. And he said unto them, He put clay upon mine eyes, and I washed, and do see. Some therefore of the Pharisees said, This man is not from God, because he keepeth not the sabbath. But others said, How can a man that is a sinner do such signs? And there was a division among them. They say therefore unto the blind man, What sayest thou of him, in that he opened thine eyes? And he said, He is a prophet. (13-17)

13. *They bring him,* etc. The narrative which follows shows that the ungodly are so far from profiting by the works of God that the more they are pressed by their power, the more they discharge the poison conceived within them. The restoration of sight to the blind should have softened even minds of stone. Or the Pharisees ought to have been struck with the novelty and greatness of the miracle, so as at least to have hesitated for a little, while they inquired into whether it was a divine work. But hatred of Christ drives them headlong into such unreasonableness that out of hand they condemn what they hear He has done.

The Evangelist names the Pharisees; not that the other parties were on Christ's side, but because this sect was more zealous than the others to maintain the *status quo.* Hypocrisy is ever cruel and proud. Therefore, swollen with a false idea of their own holiness, they were chiefly wounded by the teaching of the Gospel, which condemned all their fake righteousnesses. Above all, they are fighting for their power and kingdom under pretence of defending the Law.

When the Evangelist says that the multitude brought the blind man to the Pharisees, their attitude and purpose are uncertain. Hardly one of them but knew how much the Pharisees hated Christ; and it is therefore possible that many flatterers, to curry favour with them, deliberately tried to hide the glory of the miracle. But I think that the greater part, as usually happens, wanted to make their rulers the arbiters and judges. But being wilfully blind in the sunlight, they bring on themselves a darkness which obscures its light. The common people have a perverted religion. Under the cloak of reverence to God, they adore the ungodly tyrants of the Church and despise God Himself in His Word and works, or at least, do not trouble to consider Him.

14. *Now it was the sabbath.* Christ purposely chose a sabbath day, which would give cause of offence to the Jews. He had already found, in regard to the paralytic, that even this work was open to misrepresentation. Why then does He not avoid the offence, as He could easily have done, save because the malignant reaction of His enemies would magnify the power of God? The sabbath day is like a whet-stone that sharpens them to inquire more eagerly into the whole affair. And yet what good does a careful and earnest examination of the question do, but that the truth of the miracle shines more brightly. Moreover, we are taught by this example that if we want to follow Christ, we have to exasperate the enemies of the Gospel, and that those who compromise between the world and Christ, so as to condemn every kind of scandal, are utterly mad, since Christ, on the contrary, knowingly and deliberately provoked the ungodly. So we should pay heed to the rule that He lays down elsewhere, that the blind and the leaders of the blind are to be disregarded (Matt. 15.14).

15. *The Pharisees also asked him.* The people had heard this confession from the mouth of the blind man already. Now the Pharisees become witnesses to it, who might have objected that a baseless rumour had been thoughtlessly circulated by the common people and as thoughtlessly believed. First of all, leaving aside the question as to the fact, as they say, they argue only about the law of the case. They do not deny that Christ restored sight to the blind man, but they find a crime in the time it was done, and deny it was a work of God, since it broke the sabbath. But the first inquiry ought to be whether a divine work was a violation of the sabbath. What hinders them from seeing this but that they are blinded by a depraved attitude and malice and see nothing? Besides they had already been abundantly taught by Christ that the benefits which God gives to men are no more contrary to observance of the sabbath than circumcision is. For the words of the Law command men to rest only from their own works and not from the works of God. That they take for granted an error that had been so powerfully refuted must be put down to obstinate malice. Or at least, there is no other reason why they err than because they are pleased to err.

In the same way, the Papists never cease with hardened impudence to bring forward their empty and foolish slanders which have been

answered a hundred times. So what are we to do with them? When
the opportunity arises, so far as is in us, we must oppose the wickedness
of those who reproach and slander the Gospel out of a false prejudice.
And if no defence, however just, silences them, we have no need to be
discouraged but should trample down with a great and bold spirit that
obstinate eagerness to slander by which they wish to oppress us. We
readily grant their principles that we ought not to listen to those who
secede from the Church and break the unity of the faith. But they
cunningly pass over what ought to be the chief topic of discussion and
which we have explained clearly in a thousand places: that nothing
could be less like the Church than the Pope and his gang; that a hotch-
potch of corrupt inventions infected by so many superstitious fictions
is far from the genuine faith. But with all their furious impudence they
will never stop the truth, which we have so often and firmly maintained, from prevailing in the end. Similarly the Pharisees accused
Christ with the plausible axiom that he who breaks the sabbath is not
from God. But they were unjust and wrong in asserting that the work
of God is a violation of the sabbath.

16. *How can a man that is a sinner?* As in many other places, 'sinner'
is used here for someone grossly wicked and a despiser of God. 'Why
does your master eat with publicans and sinners?' (Mark 2.16), that is,
with ungodly and wicked men whose badness is notorious. For His
enemies inferred from His breaking the sabbath that He was a heathen
man and irreligious. Those who are neutral and judge more fairly,
however, decide that He is a godly and religious man, who is equipped
with a remarkable power of God to work miracles. And yet the
argument does not seem strong enough. For God sometimes allows
false prophets to perform miracles, and we know that Satan like an ape
imitates the works of God to deceive the unwary.

Tranquillus (alias Suetonius) relates that when Vespasian was in
Alexandria and was on his judgment seat to dispense justice in the open
court, he was asked by a blind man to anoint his eyes with spittle, this
remedy having been shown him in a dream by Serapis. Vespasian was
unwilling to expose himself to contempt and was reluctant and slow
to agree. But when his friends all around him urged him, he granted
the blind man's request, and in this way his eyes were at once opened.
Who would number Vespasian among the servants of God for this
reason or adorn him with praise for piety? I reply, among good men
and god-fearers, miracles are undoubted pledges of the power of the
Holy Spirit; but by a just judgment of God it happens that Satan
deceives unbelievers with false miracles as by witchery. I do not think
that what I have just quoted from Suetonius is fabulous, but ascribe it
to the righteous vengeance of God, that the Jews, who had despised so

many clear miracles of Christ were at last dismissed to Satan as they deserved. They should have been profited in the pure worship of God by Christ's miracles; they should have been confirmed in the teaching of the Law and should have risen to the Messiah who was the end of the Law. There is no doubt that by giving sight to the blind Christ had clearly proved that He was the Messiah.

Now, although these men act uprightly in that they speak with reverence of the miracles in which God's power is displayed, they do not advance a valid reason why Christ should not be reckoned a prophet of God. Nor did the Evangelist mean that their answer should be taken as an oracle. He is only showing the ungodly obstinacy of Christ's enemies in maliciously carping at the manifest works of God, and not even stopping for a little when they are warned.

And there was a division among them. Schism is the worst and most harmful evil in the Church of God. Why then does Christ sow cause for discord among the very teachers of the Church? The answer is easy. Christ's only aim was to bring with outstretched hand, as it were, all men to God the Father. The division arose from the malice of those who had no wish to go to God. Therefore it is those who will not be obedient to the truth of God who tear the Church by schism. Yet, better that men should disagree, than that they should all with one consent secede from godliness. Therefore, whenever differences arise we should always consider their origin.

17. *They say therefore unto the blind man again.* The more diligently they inquire, the more powerfully does God's truth appear. for they act like someone trying to blow out a flame with his breath. So when we see the wicked endeavouring in every way to overwhelm the truth of God, we need not be afraid or over anxious about the result, for in this way they will only make it burn more fiercely.

Moreover, when they ask the blind man for his opinion, it is not because they want to abide by his judgment, or think it has the slightest value, but because they hope the man will be frightened and give them the answer they want. In this the Lord disappoints them—for when a poor man disregards their threats and boldly maintains that Christ is a prophet, we must ascribe it to God's grace. So this confidence is another miracle. And if he, who did not yet know that Christ was the Son of God, courageously and freely confessed He was a prophet, how shameful is the treachery of those who out of fear either deny Him or are silent, though they know that He sits at the right hand of the Father and from thence will come to be the judge of the whole earth! If this blind man did not quench his tiny spark of knowledge, we should endeavour that a frank and full confession should blaze forth from the full brightness which has shone in our hearts.

The Jews therefore did not believe concerning him, that he had been blind, and had received his sight, until they called the parents of him that had received his sight, and asked them, saying, Is this your son, who ye say was born blind? how then doth he now see? His parents answered and said, We know that this is our son, and that he was born blind: but how he now seeth, we know not; or who opened his eyes, we know not: ask him; he is of age; he shall speak for himself. These things said his parents, because they feared the Jews: for the Jews had agreed already, that if any man should confess him to be Christ, he should be put out of the synagogue. Therefore said his parents, He is of age; ask him. (18-23)

18. *They did not believe.* There are two things to be noticed here. They do not believe a miracle has been performed; and because they are wilfully blinded by a perverse hatred of Christ, they do not see what is plain. The Evangelist relates that they did not believe. If the reason is asked, there is no doubt that their blindness was voluntary. What stops them seeing a clear work of God set before their eyes? Or when they have been completely refuted, what prevents them believing what they already know, save that the inward malice of their hearts keeps their eyes shut? Paul tells us that the same thing happens in the preaching of the Gospel. He says that it is veiled and hidden only to the reprobate, 'whose minds the god of this world hath blinded' (II Cor. 4.3, 4). Let us be warned by such examples not to put obstacles in our own way, which keep us from the faith. By synecdoche the Evangelist calls them Jews who were the rulers of the people.

19. *Is this your son?* Having failed at their first attempt, they now try another way. But the Lord not only upsets their efforts in a wonderful manner, but even turns them to an opposite purpose. They do not simply ask one straightforward question, but cunningly wrap up several all together, to prevent a reply. But out of this entangled and captious interrogation, the parents of the blind man select only a half to reply to. They say he is their son and he was blind from the womb. Hence it follows that he does not see naturally, but that his eyes have been opened by a miracle. But they pass over this latter point, since it was unacceptable. By this silence they show their ingratitude. For when they had received such a shining gift of God, they should have burned to celebrate His name. But they are terror-struck and bury the grace of God, so far as lies in them; except that they put their son in their place as witness to explain the whole affair as it happened, with less ill-will and more credit. But though they prudently avoid danger by taking this middle path of testifying indirectly to Christ by the mouth of their son, it does not prevent the Spirit condemning their cowardice by the mouth of the Evangelist, because they failed in their

duty. How much less excuse will they have, who by treacherous denial completely hide Christ with His teaching. His miracles and His power and grace?

22. *The Jews had agreed.* This passage shows that the custom of excommunication is ancient and has been exercised in all ages. For excommunication was not newly invented then, but was a punishment which had been used in ancient times against apostates and despisers of the Law and was used against Christ's disciples. So we learn that the rite of excommunication arose out of the most ancient discipline of the Church. Also, that the vice is not of recent origin and is not confined to one age whereby ungodly men corrupt the holy ordinances of God by their sacrilege. God determined from the beginning that there should be some form of correction to restrain rebels. The priests and scribes not only misused this power tyrannically to harass the innocent, but at last impiously attacked God Himself and His doctrine. Christ's truth was so powerful that they could not resist it with laws and regulations, and therefore they brandished the thunders of excommunication to crush it.

The same thing has been done to Christian people. It is impossible to express the barbarous tyranny which the pseudo-bishops have exercised in subduing the people, so that none dared to whisper. And now we see how cruelly they turn this weapon of excommunication against all who worship God. But we ought to hold that when excommunication is applied to a different end by men's passions, it can safely be treated with contempt. For when God committed the right to excommunicate to His Church, He was not arming tyrants with a sword or executioners to murder poor souls, but was laying down a rule for governing His people, and that moreover, on the condition that He should hold supreme rule and have men for His ministers. Let the pseudo-bishops thunder as they like. They will not terrify any with their empty noises, except those who wander about in uncertainty and doubt, not yet taught by the voice of the Good Shepherd what is the true fold.

In short, nothing is more certain than that those whom we see insubordinate to Christ are deprived of the lawful power of excommunicating. Nor should we fear to be shut out of their assembly, from which Christ our life and salvation is also banished. We have no reason at all to dread being thrown out. On the contrary, if we want to be united to Christ, we must withdraw from the synagogues of the Pope of our own accord. Yet although the ordinance of excommunication was so wickedly corrupted in the ancient Church, Christ did not mean it to be abolished by His coming, but restored it to purity, so that it might soundly flourish among us. Although a filthy profanation of this holy discipline prevails in the Papacy today, we should, instead of abolishing it, rather use the utmost diligence to restore it to its former integrity. Things will never be so well ordered in the world but that even the holiest laws of God will degenerate into corruption through men's vice. It would certainly give too much power to Satan, could he annihilate everything he corrupts. We should then have no Baptism, no Lord's Supper and, in short, no religion; for he has left no part of it untouched by his pollutions.

So they called a second time the man that was blind, and said unto him, Give glory to God: we know that this man is a sinner. He therefore answered, Whether he be a sinner, I know not: one thing I know, that, whereas I was blind, now I see. They said therefore unto him, What did he to thee? how opened he thine eyes? He answered them, I told you even now, and ye did not hear: wherefore would ye hear it again? would ye also become his disciples? And they reviled him, and said, Thou art his disciple; but we are disciples of Moses. We know that God hath spoken unto Moses: but as for this man, we know not whence he is. The man answered and said unto them, Why, herein is the marvel, that ye know not whence he is, and yet he opened mine eyes. We know that God heareth not sinners: but if any man be a worshipper of God, and do his will, him he heareth. Since the world began it was never heard that any one opened the eyes of a man born blind. If this man were not from God, he could do nothing. (24-33)

24. *So they called a second time.* It was without doubt shame that made them call the blind man, whom they had at first found too firm and steadfast. And so the more they struggle against God, the more nooses do they wind round themselves and the faster they tie themselves up. Moreover, they interrogate him in such a way as to try to make him say what they want. It is a specious start, indeed, when they tell him to give the glory to God. Immediately, they strictly forbid him to reply according to his convictions. Hence, by claiming the authority of God, they demand a servile obedience from him.

Give glory to God. This exhortation can be referred to the circumstances of the case, in that the blind man was not to obscure God's glory by ascribing to man the benefit he had received. But I rather agree with the opinion of those who think it was a solemn formula which was used when an oath was demanded of anyone. For Joshua adjures Achan with the same words when he wants him to confess honestly to having taken the accursed thing (Joshua 7.19). And with these words they were reminding him that no light insult is offered to God if a man lies in His name. And indeed, if we are required to take an oath, we should remember this preface, so that the truth may be no less precious to us than God's glory. If this were done, the sacredness of an oath would be looked at very differently. Now the greater number thoughtlessly and contemptuously rush into swearing without thinking that they deny God when they invoke His name to maintain a falsehood, and so everywhere is full of perjuries. And also we can see how hypocrites pretend to have the greatest reverence for God, but are not only deceitful, but also mock Him insolently. For at the same time they add that the blind man should irreligiously swear what they want, and so openly insult God. Thus God drags their wicked plans into the light, however much they try to put a plausible complexion on them, or hide them behind a smoke-screen of pretence.

25. *Whether he be a sinner, I know not.* The blind man does not seem to have been turned aside from his frank witness by fear. For it is improbable that he had any doubts about Christ, as his words seem to imply. I think that he was speaking ironically to prick them more deeply. He had confessed that Christ was a prophet a little earlier. Seeing that he is no farther forward, he suspends judgment about the man, and puts forward the fact itself. Therefore his concession is not without mockery.

26. *They said therefore unto him.* When we see the ungodly so busy with their own depraved actions, we should be ashamed of our laziness, in acting with such coolness in the business of Christ. Although they hunt out material for slander to obscure the miracle, the Lord defeats their efforts remarkably by the unshaken firmness of the blind man. Not only does he persist in his opinion, but freely and severely reproaches them for trying to bury the truth with their continual investigations after they had learned and known it well enough. He also accuses them of a perverted hatred of Christ, when he says, 'Do you also want to become His disciples?' He means that if they are refuted a hundred times they will never give way, so seized are they by a malicious and hostile attitude. It is indeed a wonderful liberty that a lowly and obscure man, one almost shameful because of his begging, fearlessly provokes the rage of all the priests against himself. If nothing more than a slight preparation for faith made him so confident when he came to the struggle, what excuse can be put forward for those who are great preachers of the Church when they are out of range of the darts, but are silent in danger? Moreover, this question is ironical. He means that they are motivated by malevolence and not for a sincere desire for the truth, to press this question so urgently.

28. *And they reviled him.* They probably called him everything that in the violence of their fury they could lay their tongues to. But in particular, they called him an apostate from the Law. To their mind

he could not be Christ's disciple without defection from the Law of
Moses. And they expressly represent these two things as contraries.
And it seems a most beautiful excuse, that they are afraid of falling
away from the teaching of Moses. For a true rule of godliness is that
we should listen to the prophets, by whom it is certain that God spoke,
so that our faith may not be carried about by any ideas of men. They
deduce their certainty as to the Law of Moses from this true principle.
Where they lie is that they say they are Moses' disciples, for they had
turned aside from the end of the Law. This is how hypocrites are
accustomed to tear God asunder when they want to shelter under His
name. If Christ is the soul of the Law, as Paul teaches in Rom. 10.4,
how can the Law be anything but a dead body when it is separated
from Him? By this example we are taught that only he truly hears
God so as to understand what He wishes and says, who listens atten-
tively to His voice.

When they say *we know not whence Christ is*, they are not referring
to His country or birthplace, but to the prophetical office. They claim
that they have no knowledge of His calling, so that they should receive
Him as having come from God.

30. *Why, herein is the marvel.* He reproves them indirectly that they
are quite unmoved by such a striking miracle, and that they pretend
they were unaware of Christ's calling; as if he were saying that it was
altogether wrong that such an example of divine power should be
regarded as nothing and that Christ's calling, proved and testified by it,
should gain no credit among them. And to show up their stupidity or
malice the more clearly, he magnifies the excellence of the miracle,
from the fact that from men's earliest remembrance it had never been
heard that such a deed had been done by a man. From this it follows,
that those who deliberately shut their eyes to a manifest work of God
are malicious and ungrateful. Hence he infers that He was sent from
God, since He is endued with the mighty power of God's Spirit and
so wins credit for Himself and His teaching.

31. *We know that God heareth not sinners.* Those who think the man
spoke this in line with the common opinion are mistaken. Here, as a
little before, 'sinner' means an ungodly and immoral man. It is the
continual teaching of Scripture that God listens only to those who call
upon Him with a true and sincere heart. For since faith alone opens to
us the door to God, it is certain that all the ungodly are debarred from
approaching Him. He even says that He detests their prayers and
abhors their sacrifices. It is a unique privilege that He invites His
children to Him; and it is the Spirit of adoption alone that cries in our
hearts, 'Abba, Father' (Rom. 8.15). In short, none is properly prepared
to pray to God, unless His heart is purified by faith. But because

251

wicked men profane God's sacred name by their prayers, they deserve
to be punished for the sacrilege rather than obtain anything for salvation. Consequently, the blind man does not reason badly that Christ
has come from God because He is favourable to His prayers.

They answered and said unto him, Thou wast altogether born in
sins, and dost thou teach us? And they cast him out. Jesus heard
that they had cast him out; and finding him, he said, Dost thou believe
on the Son of God? He answered and said, And who is he, Lord,
that I may believe on him? Jesus said unto him, Thou hast both seen
him, and he it is that speaketh with thee. And he said, Lord, I believe.
And he worshipped him. And Jesus said, For judgement came I into
this world, that they which see not may see; and that they which see
may become blind. Those of the Pharisees which were with him heard
these things, and said unto him, Are we also blind? Jesus said unto them,
If ye were blind, ye would have no sin: but now ye say, We see: your
sin remaineth. (34-41)

34. *Thou wast altogether born in sins.* I do not doubt that they were
referring to his blindness, in the way the proud have of worrying the
unhappy and unfortunate. They insult him as if he had been born with
the mark of his sins. For all the scribes were persuaded in their hearts
that when souls had finished one life they migrated into new bodies
and there suffered the punishment of their former sins. Hence they
conclude that he who was born blind was even then defiled and polluted by his sins.

This perverted blame should teach us to be very careful in not
always measuring anyone's sins by the chastisements of God. For, as
we have seen already, the Lord has various aims in inflicting calamities
on men. But those hypocrites not only insult the unhappy man, but
also reject his holy and good warnings. It is very common that people
cannot bear being taught by a man they despise. Now, since God must
always be listened to, whoever He talks to us by, let us learn not to
despise any man, so that God may find us ever teachable and submissive
even though He uses a man utterly contemptible and of no account to
teach us. For there is no worse plague than when pride stops our ears
and we do not trouble to hear those who warn us for our good. God
often selects worthless and base men to teach and warn us, that He may
cast down our loftiness.

And they cast him out. Though it is possible that they cast him out of
the Temple with physical violence, it seems to me that the Evangelist
actually means that they excommunicated him, and thus his casting
out would have the appearance of legality. This also agrees better with
the context, for if they had only cast him out physically, it would not

have been important enough to have come to Christ's ears. But from the fact that Christ heard of it, I conjecture that they did it as if they were enacting a solemn rite of great moment. This example teaches us how trivial and little to be feared are the anathemas of Christ's enemies. If we are cast out from the assembly where Christ reigns, it is a dreadful judgment executed against us that we are delivered over to Satan, since we are banished from the Kingdom of the Son of God. But from that place where Christ does not rule by His Word and Spirit, we ought of our own accord to flee if none expels us. We certainly have no cause to fear that tyrannical judgment by which the ungodly insult Christ's servants.

And finding him. If he had been kept in the synagogue, he would have run the danger of becoming gradually alienated from Christ and plunged into the same destruction as the ungodly. Christ now meets him wandering about outside the Temple and embraces him who is cast out by the priests, raises him who is fallen and offers life to him who had been sentenced to death. We have known the same thing in our own time. For when Luther, and others like him, were beginning to reprove the grosser abuses of the Pope, they had scarcely the slightest taste for pure Christianity. But after the Pope had fulminated against them and cast them out of the Roman synagogue by terrifying bulls, Christ stretched out His hand and made Himself fully known to them. So there is nothing better for us than to be far away from the enemies of the Gospel so that He may come near to us.

Dost thou believe in the Son of God? He is speaking to a Jew, who had been instructed in the teaching of the Law from his childhood and had learned that God had promised the Messiah. Therefore this question is equivalent to Christ's exhorting him to follow the Messiah and give himself up to Him. He uses, however, a more honourable name than was then customary, for the Messiah was regarded only as the Son of David.

36. *And who is he, that I may believe on him?* From the blind man's reply, it is plain that although he did not yet know anything certain or clear about Christ, he was nevertheless ready and teachable. For these words mean, 'I am ready to embrace Him as soon as He is pointed out to me.' But it should be noted that the blind man wants to be taught by Christ as a prophet. He was already convinced that Christ had been sent by God, and therefore he is not thoughtlessly putting his trust in His teaching.

37. *Thou hast seen him.* These words of Christ would not carry the blind man higher than to a cold and small fragment of faith. For Christ does not mention His power, or the reason why He was sent by the Father, or what He brought to men. But the chief thing in faith is to

know that our sins are purged by the sacrifice of His death and we are reconciled to God; that His resurrection was a victory over vanquished death; that we are renewed by His Spirit so that, dead to the flesh and sin, we may live unto righteousness; that He is the only Mediator; that the Spirit is the earnest of our adoption; in short, that in Him are all the parts of eternal life. But the Evangelist either does not relate the whole of Christ's conversation with him, or he merely means that the blind man joined Christ's side, so as to begin to be one of His disciples. I have no doubt at all that Jesus wanted to be acknowledged by Him as the Christ, so that from this beginning of faith He might lead him onward to a fuller knowledge of Himself.

38. *And he worshipped him.* It may be asked whether he gave divine honour to Christ. The word which the Evangelist uses simply means to show respect and veneration by bending the knee, or by other signs. I myself certainly think it signifies something rare and unusual; in fact that the blind man gave far more honour to Christ than to an ordinary man or a prophet. But I do not think that at that time he had progressed so far as to know that Christ was God manifested in the flesh. What does 'worship' mean then? The blind man was convinced that Jesus was the Son of God and prostrated himself before Him, carried away in wonder as if he were out of his mind.

39. *For judgement came I.* The word judgment cannot be taken in this passage simply as the punishment inflicted on the ungodly and despisers of God, for it is extended to the grace of illumination. Christ calls it judgment, in that He restores to its true order what was confused and disordered. But He means that this is done by a wonderful plan of God and contrary to the ordinary opinions of men. And indeed human reason regards nothing as more unreasonable than that they who see should be blinded by the light of the world. Therefore this is one of the secret judgments of God, by which He casts down men's pride. Moreover, it should be noticed that the blindness mentioned here proceeds rather from the fault of men than from Christ. By its own nature it does not properly blind any man. But since the strongest desire of the reprobate is to extinguish its light, the eyes of their minds, which are sick of malice and depravity, must be dazzled by the light shown to them. In short, since Christ is by nature the light of the world, it is accidental that some are made blind by His coming.

But again it may be asked, since all are accused universally of blindness, who are these that see? I reply, this is said ironically in concession, because although unbelievers are blind, they think that they are very acute and perspicacious; and puffed up by this confidence, they will not trouble to listen to God. Moreover, outside Christ, the wisdom of the flesh looks very fine, because the world does not understand what it is to be truly wise. So then, Christ says that they see who, deceiving themselves by a foolish confidence of wisdom, are guided by their own opinion and think their empty imaginings are wisdom. As soon as Christ appears in the brightness of His Gospel, they are blinded; not only in that their foolishness, which had been hidden in the darkness of unbelief, is now uncovered, but because they are plunged into a deeper darkness by God's righteous vengeance, and lose that small remnant of I know not what light which had been theirs.

We are indeed all born blind, but yet amid the darkness of corrupted and vitiated nature some sparks still shine, so that men are different from the brute beasts. Now if any man is puffed up by proud confidence in his own reason and refuses to submit to God, he may seem, apart from Christ, to be wise, but Christ's brightness will make him foolish. For the vanity of the human mind only begins to appear when heavenly wisdom is brought into view. But as I have already said, Christ meant to express something more by these words. For before Christ shines, hypocrites do not resist God so obstinately. But as soon as the light is brought near them, they rise against God in open war. Because of this depravity and ingratitude they become doubly blind, and God, in righteous vengenace, puts out their eyes completely, which were formerly destitute of the true light.

We now see the sum of this passage—that Christ came into the world to enlighten the blind and to drive to madness those who think they are wise. In the first place He mentions enlightening, which is properly the cause for His coming. For He did not come to judge the world, but rather to save that which was lost. Thus when Paul declares that he has vengeance prepared against all rebels, he adds at the same time that this punishment will take place after the obedience of the godly shall have been fulfilled (II Cor. 10.6). And this vengeance should not be limited to Christ's physical presence (*ad Christi personam*), as if He did not perform the same thing daily through the ministers of His Gospel.

We ought all to be the more careful that we do not bring this dreadful punishment on ourselves through a foolish opinion of our own wisdom. Experience teaches us how true this statement of Christ is. For we see many mad with dizziness and rage simply because they cannot endure the rising of the Sun of righteousness. Adam lived and was endowed with the true light of understanding; but he lost that divine blessing by wanting to see more than was lawful. Now if, when we are plunged in blindness and are humbled by the Lord, we are still pleased with ourselves in our darkness and set our mad ideas against the heavenly wisdom, we must not be surprised if the vengeance of God falls heavily upon us and we are made doubly blind. In earlier times this same punishment was inflicted on the ungodly under the Law. For Isaiah is sent for the blinding of the ancient people, that seeing they may not see: blind the heart of this people, and shut their ears (Isa. 6.9). But the brightness of the divine light is displayed more fully in Christ than in the prophets. And therefore this example of blindness must have been shown and seen more obviously. Just as today the noon-tide light of the Gospel drives hypocrites into extreme rage.

40. *Those of the Pharisees heard.* They felt at once that they were wounded by Christ's saying; but they do not seem to have been among the worst, for Christ's open enemies abhorred Him so much that they had nothing to do with Him. Those men, however, submitted to listen to Christ, though it did them no good; for none is a fit disciple of Christ until he has put off himself—and they were very far from that.

Moreover, their question arose out of indignation. They considered they were insulted by being classed among the blind. It also shows a proud and derisive contempt of Christ's grace, as if they were saying, 'You cannot become famous without our disgrace. Are we going to put up with you getting honour from our shame? As for your promise to give new light to the blind—clear out and take your blessing with you. We do not want to be enlightened by you at the price of admitting that we have been blind.' Thus we see that hypocrisy has ever been full of pride and venom. Their pride is in self-satisfaction and a refusal to part with anything; and their venom lies in their rage with Christ, so that they argue with Him as if He had seriously wounded them when He pointed out their sickness. Hence their contempt of Christ and the grace He offered them.

The emphasis is on the word *also*. It means that even if all the rest were blind, they ought not to be numbered among the common rank. Those who hold superior positions are far too often drunk with pride and almost forget they are men.

41. *If ye were blind.* These words can be taken in two ways. Either that ignorance would extenuate their guilt to some extent, if they were not quite set in their ways and were not deliberately fighting against the truth; or that their disease of ignorance would be curable if only they would acknowledge it. The former is confirmed by Christ's words, which we shall have in Chapter Fifteen, 'If I had not come and spoken unto them, they had not had sin,' etc. But as in this passage it is added *but now ye say, We see,* it seems more consistent if you explain it that he is blind who is aware of his blindness and seeks a remedy for his disease. Like this, the contrasts correspond to each other. Thus the

meaning will be, 'If you acknowledged your disease, it would not be entirely uncurable. But because you think you are healthy, you remain in a desperate state.' When He says that those who are blind have no sin, it does not excuse their ignorance as being harmless and inculpable. He only means that the disease can be cured easily when it is really felt; for when a blind man desires deliverance, God is ready to help him. But those who are insensible of their diseases and despise God's grace are incurable.

CHAPTER TEN

Verily, verily, I say unto you, He that entereth not by the door into the
fold of the sheep, but climbeth up some other way, the same is a thief and
a robber. But he that entereth in by the door is the shepherd of the sheep.
To him the porter openeth; and the sheep hear his voice: and he calleth
his own sheep by name, and leadeth them out. When he hath put forth
all his own, he goeth before them, and the sheep follow him: for they know
his voice. And a stranger will they not follow, but will flee from him:
for they know not the voice of strangers. This parable spake Jesus unto
them: but they understood not what things they were which he spake
unto them. (1-6)

1. *Verily, verily, I say unto you.* Christ was dealing with scribes and
priests, who were regarded as the shepherds of the Church. He had
therefore to take the honour of this title away from them, if He wanted
His teaching to be received. The small number of believers might also
lessen the authority of His teaching. He therefore insists that we must
not reckon as shepherds or sheep all who outwardly claim a place in
the Church. The mark to distinguish lawful shepherds from the
reprobate, and true sheep from the false, is if He Himself is the object
and beginning and end of all.

This warning has been very useful in every age. Today it is especially
necessary. There is no plague more destructive to the Church than
when wolves go about under the mask of shepherds. We know what
a grievous offence it is when bastard or degenerate Israelites claim to
be the sons of the Church and triumph over believers. Throughout
almost all ages the Church has been subject to both these evils. But
today there is nothing which alarms the ignorant and weak more than
seeing the Sanctuary of God occupied by the Church's greatest enemies.
For it is not easy to make them understand that it is the teaching of
Christ which the shepherds of the Church resist so fiercely. Moreover,
since the most part are led into errors by false teaching, each man looks
and waits for others and hardly anyone lets himself be led into the
right path.

Therefore, if we do not want of our own accord to lay ourselves
open to wolves and thieves, we must particularly guard against being
deceived by false shepherds or sheep. The name 'Church' is honourable
and rightly so; but the greater the reverence it deserves, the more
careful and attentive should we be in observing the distinction between

the true Church and the false. Christ here says plainly that we are not to regard as shepherds all who claim the title, nor reckon as sheep all who boast the outward marks. He is speaking of the Jewish Church, but ours is not unlike it in this respect. We should also consider the purpose of what He said, so that weak consciences may not be alarmed or discouraged when they see that those who rule in the Church in the place of shepherds are hostile and opposed to the Gospel. And they must not secede from the faith because among those who are called Christians they have few fellow-disciples in listening to the teaching of Christ.

He that entereth not. In my opinion, those who scrutinize every part of this parable very closely are wasting their time. Let us be content with the general view that Christ likens the Church to a sheepfold in which God assembles His people, and compares Himself to the door, since He is the only entrance into the Church. It follows from this that they alone are good shepherds who lead men straight to Christ; and that they are truly gathered into God's fold and reckoned His flock who give themselves up to Christ alone.

But all this refers to teaching. For since 'all the treasures of wisdom and knowledge are hidden in Christ' (Col. 2.3), he who turns aside from Him to go elsewhere neither keeps to the way nor enters by the door. Now the man who does not despise Christ as his teacher will easily get rid of the hesitation which perplexes so many, as to what the Church is and who are to be listened to as shepherds. For if the so-called shepherds try to lead us away from Christ, we should flee from them, as Christ tells us, as if they were wolves or thieves; and we ought not to join or to stay in any society save that which is agreed in the pure faith of the Gospel. This is why Christ exhorts His disciples to separate from the unbelieving multitude of the whole nation, and not let themselves be ruled by ungodly priests or be imposed upon by proud but empty names.

3. *To him the porter openeth.* If anyone wants to understand this as being God, I do not object. Christ even seems to be expressly contrasting God's judgment with men's false opinions in approving of shepherds; as if He were saying, 'There are some whom the world in general applauds and willingly honours. But God, who holds the reins of government, acknowledges and approves only those who lead the sheep in this path.'

When He says that the sheep are called *by name*, I refer it to the mutual consent of faith. The disciple and the teacher are united by the one Spirit of God, so that the one goes before and the other follows. Some think that it expresses the intimate knowledge which a shepherd ought to have of each sheep, but I do not know if this is strong enough.

4. *For they know his voice.* Although He is here speaking of ministers, He wants not so much them, as God speaking through them, to be heard. For we must notice the exception He has laid down, that he alone is the faithful shepherd of the Church who governs his sheep under the guiding and authority of Christ. We should observe the reason given why the sheep *follow.* It is because they can distinguish the shepherds from wolves by the voice. This is the spirit of discernment, by which the elect discriminate between the truth of God and men's false inventions. Hence in Christ's sheep there is first a knowledge of the truth, and then an earnest desire to obey; so that they not only understand what is true but receive it heartily. Nor does He commend the obedience of faith only because the sheep come submissively at the shepherd's voice, but also because they do not heed the voice of strangers, and do not scatter when anyone shouts at them.

6. *This parable.* This is why, proud of their own wisdom, they rejected Christ's light. For in quite an obvious matter they are very dull. There are variant readings in the Greek for the words *but they understood not what things they were,* etc. Some MSS have, 'they did not understand what he said'. Another, which I have followed, is fuller, though it comes to the same thing. A third is that 'they did not know that he who spoke of himself was the Son of God'; but this is not much received.

Jesus therefore said unto them again, Verily, verily, I say unto you, I am the door of the sheep. All that came before me are thieves and robbers: but the sheep did not hear them. I am the door: by me if any man enter in, he shall be saved, and shall go in and go out, and shall find pasture. The thief cometh not, but that he may steal, and kill, and destroy: I came that they may have life, and may have it abundantly. (7-10)

7. *I am the door.* Unless this explanation had been given, the whole discourse would have been allegorical. But He now expounds more clearly the chief part of the parable by declaring that He is the door. The sum of it is that the head of all spiritual teaching, which souls are fed on, consists in Him. Hence also Paul, one of the shepherds, says, 'I thought nothing worth knowing save Jesus Christ' (I Cor. 2.12). And this expression is equivalent to Christ saying that it is to Him alone that we must all be gathered together. He therefore invites and exhorts all who desire salvation, to come to Himself. By these words He means that those who have left Him and still strive after God, wander about in vain, since only one door lies open and every other approach is barred.

8. *All that came before me.* Literally, 'all, as many as'. Those who restrict it to Judas the Galilean and his like are far from Christ's meaning, in my opinion; for He is contrasting all false teaching in general

to the Gospel and all false prophets to faithful teachers. It would not, in fact, be unreasonable to extend the statement to the Gentiles, in that all who from the beginning of the world have professed to be teachers, without trying to gather sheep for Christ, have abused their title to the destroying of souls. But this does not at all apply to Moses and the prophets. They had no other purpose than to establish Christ's Kingdom. We must observe that the words of Christ are contrasted to their opposites. But we cannot find any contradiction between the Law and the teaching of the Gospel, for the Law is nothing but a preparation for the Gospel. In short, Christ says that all the doctrines which have led the world away from Him are deadly plagues, since apart from Him is nothing but destruction and a horrible scattering. We can also see how much importance antiquity has with God and should have with us when it enters, so to say, into contest with Christ. Lest anyone should be swayed by the fact that there have in all ages been teachers who cared nothing about directing men to Christ, He Himself expressly declares that it does not matter how many such there have been or how early they began to appear. What should be considered is that there is only one door and that those who by-pass it and make openings or breaches in the walls are thieves.

But the sheep did not hear them. He now confirms with greater clarity what He had already said more obscurely and in allegory: that those who were led astray by impostors did not belong to the Church of God. He said this, first, lest when we see a great multitude going astray we should decide to follow their example, and perish; and next, lest we should waver when God lets impostors loose to deceive many. For it is a great comfort and ground of confidence when we know that Christ has always guarded His sheep under His faithful protection, amid the manifold attacks and devices of wolves and robbers, so that none should leave Him.

But here a question arises. When does a man begin to belong to the flock of Christ? We see many straying and wandering through the deserts for the most of their life and then at last gathered into Christ's fold. I reply, the word *sheep* is here taken in two ways. When Christ says afterwards that He has other sheep, He comprehends all the elect of God who were at that time nothing like His sheep. Here He means sheep branded with the shepherd's mark. By nature we are not His sheep at all. Rather, we are born bears and lions and tigers until Christ's Spirit tames us, and out of wild and savage beasts forms us into a meek flock. According to the secret election of God, we are already 'sheep' in His heart, before we are born; and we begin to be 'sheep' in ourselves, through the calling by which He gathers us into His fold. Christ says that those who are called into the order of believers cleave to Him too firmly to wander or be carried about by any wind of new doctrine.

If any object that even those who had given themselves to Christ sometimes go astray and that this is proved by frequent experience, and that Ezekiel is right to ascribe it to a good shepherd that he gathers the scattered sheep (Ezek. 34.12), I readily admit that it is not a rare occurrence for those who were of the household of faith to be estranged for a time. But this does not contradict Christ's statement, for inasmuch as they go astray, they cease in a sense to be 'sheep'. Christ simply means that all God's elect, even though they were tempted into numerous errors, were kept in the obedience of pure faith and not exposed as a prey to Satan and his ministers. But this work of God is no less wonderful when He brings again the sheep which had wandered for a little, than if they had all along been kept in the fold. It is always and without exception true, that 'they who go out from us were not of us, but they who were of us remain with us to the end' (I John 2.19).

This passage should make us deeply ashamed. First, because we are so unused to the voice of our Shepherd, that hardly any listen to it without indifference. And then, because we are so slow and lazy to follow Him. I am speaking of the good, or at least of the passable; for the greater part of those who claim they are Christ's disciples openly kick against Him. Lastly, as soon as we hear the voice of any stranger, we are carried unstably hither and thither, and this unsteadiness and levity shows well enough how little we have so far advanced in the faith. But although the number of believers is less than we should wish, and many of this small number default continually, faithful teachers have the consolation of knowing that they are heard by the elect of God, who are Christ's sheep. It is for us to work hard and strive in every way to bring if possible the whole world to agree in the unity of the faith. Meanwhile let us be satisfied with our number.

9. *By me if any man enter in.* It is a rare comfort for the godly, that they hear they are out of danger when once they have embraced Christ. For Christ promises them salvation and a happy state. He afterwards expresses in two parts that they shall go in safety wherever they need to go, and that they shall be fed to the full. By *going in and out*, Scripture often intends all the activities of life; as in French we use *aller et venir* for 'to dwell'. According to these words therefore, the Gospel is of service to us in two ways: in it our souls find nourishment, which otherwise languish with hunger and are fed only with wind; and also He will be a faithful protector and defence against the attacks of wolves and robbers.

10. *The thief cometh not.* By this saying, Christ as it were pulls our ear, lest Satan's ministers should come round us when we are sleepy

and careless; for our great unconcern lays us open on all sides to false teaching. For whence such credulity that those who should have stayed in Christ fly about through a multitude of errors, except that they have not a sufficient fear and defence against the many false teachers? And not only that, but our ungovernable curiosity is so pleased with the novel and strange inventions of men that we rush headlong to meet thieves and wolves of our own accord. It is not without reason that Christ says that false teachers, however smoothly they may insinuate themselves, carry round a deadly poison; so that we must be the more careful to drive them away. Paul's warning is similar, 'Take heed lest any man make spoil of you through vain philosophy etc.' (Col. 2.8).

I came. Another comparison. Christ had earlier called Himself the door, and said that those who bring sheep to this door are true shepherds. Now He Himself assumes the role of Shepherd, and, indeed, affirms that He is the only Shepherd, for to no one else does this honour and title properly belong. Because it is He who raises up faithful shepherds for the Church, equips them with the necessary gifts, governs them by His Spirit and works by them, they do not stop Him from being the only Governor of His Church or from ruling as the only Shepherd. For although He makes use of their ministry, He does not cease to fulfil and discharge the office of a Shepherd by His own power. And they are masters and teachers in such a way as not to derogate from His Mastership. In short, when the word shepherd is applied to men, it is used, as they say, in a subordinate sense; and Christ so communicates His honour to His ministers that He still remains the only Shepherd of them and of the whole flock.

Now, when He says that He came that the sheep might have life, He means that it is only those who do not submit to His shepherd's crook who are exposed to the attacks of wolves and thieves; and, to give them added confidence, He says that life is continually increased and strengthened in those who do not depart from Him. And indeed the more any man advances in faith, the closer does he approach to fulness of life, because the Spirit, who is life, increases in him.

I am the good shepherd: the good shepherd layeth down his life for the sheep. He that is a hireling, and not a shepherd, whose own the sheep are not, beholdeth the wolf coming, and leaveth the sheep, and fleeth, and the wolf snatcheth them, and scattereth them: he fleeth because he is a hireling, and careth not for the sheep. I am the good shepherd; and I know my sheep, and mine own know me, even as the Father knoweth me, and I know the Father; and I lay down my life for the sheep. (11-15)

11. *The good shepherd layeth down his life.* From His unique love for

263

the sheep, He shows that He really acts as a shepherd towards them, for He is so anxious for their salvation that He does not even spare His own life. It follows from this that those who reject the guardianship of such a kind and lovable Shepherd are quite ungrateful and deserve to perish a hundred times, and are open to every kind of injury. What Augustine says is very true, that we are here shown what we should desire, and what avoid, and what endure, in the government of the Church. Nothing is more to be wished than that the Church should be governed by good and diligent shepherds. Christ says that He is the one good Shepherd, who keeps His Church safe and sound, by Himself in the first place, and then also by His instruments. Whenever there is good order and fit men rule, Christ acts as the Shepherd in fact. But there are many wolves and thieves who, under the mask of shepherds, wickedly scatter the Church. Christ denounces them as men to be avoided, whatever name they may assume. If the Church could be purged of hirelings, so much the better, but because the Lord exercises the patience of believers in this way, and also because we are unworthy of such a wonderful blessing as Christ appearing to us in true shepherds, they are to be tolerated, however much they may be disapproved and disliked.

Understand by hirelings those who keep the pure doctrine but proclaim the truth, as Paul says, as time-servers rather than from pure zeal. Such men, though they do not serve Christ faithfully, ought to be heard. For just as Christ wanted the Pharisees to be heard because they sat in Moses' seat, we should also give such honour to the Gospel as not to despise its less good ministers. And since even the least little offences make the Gospel distasteful to us, we must always remember, as I hinted earlier, that if Christ's Spirit does not work so powerfully in ministers as to show plainly in them that He is their shepherd, we are suffering the punishment of our sins and also our obedience is being tested.

He that is a hireling, and not the shepherd. Although Christ claims the name of Shepherd for Himself alone, He tacitly grants that in a certain sense He has it in common with the instruments by whom He acts. We know how many there have been since the time of Christ who have not hesitated to shed their blood for the salvation of the Church. Even the prophets before His coming did not spare their own lives. But in Himself He offers a perfect example to serve as a model for His ministers. For how vile and shameful our laziness is, when our lives are more dear to us than the salvation of the Church, which Christ put before His own life!

What is said here about laying down His life for the sheep is the chief and sure mark of fatherly love. Christ wanted first to testify to

the remarkable example of His love towards us which He showed in
His death; and then to stir up all His ministers to imitate His example.
Yet we must notice the difference between Him and them. He laid
down His life as the payment of satisfaction, shed His blood to cleanse
our souls and offered His body as a propitiatory sacrifice to reconcile
the Father to us. There can be none of this in the ministers of the
Gospel, who all need cleansing and receive atonement and reconciliation to God by His unique sacrifice. But Christ is not discussing the
efficacy or fruit of His death and comparing Himself with others, but
proving what manner of love He had towards us and inviting others
to follow His example. In short, inasmuch as it is peculiar to Christ to
win for us life by His death and to execute all that is in the Gospel, so
it is the common duty of all pastors to defend the doctrine which they
proclaim, even to the laying down of their lives and the sealing of the
teaching of the Gospel with their blood, to testify that it is not in vain
that Christ has won salvation for themselves and for others.

But here a question can be put. Should we regard as a hireling the
man who for any reason shrinks from encountering the wolves? In
olden days this was a burning question, when tyrants raged cruelly
against the Church. Tertullian and his like were, in my opinion, too
rigorist on this point. I much prefer Augustine's moderation. He
allows pastors to flee, on condition that by doing so they rather contribute to the public safety than betray the flock committed to their
charge by forsaking it. He shows that this is the case where the Church
is not deprived of proper ministers, and when the life of the pastor
personally is so eagerly sought by the enemy that his absence mitigates
their rage. But if the danger is common to all and there is reason to
believe that the pastor is fleeing more from a fear of death than from a
desire for the common good, he contends that this is not at all lawful,
since the example of his flight will do more harm than his life can do
good in the future. This may be read in the epistle to Bishop Honoratus
(Ep. 108). For this reason it was lawful for Cyprian to flee, who was
so far from fearing death that he bravely refused life offered at the
price of a treacherous denial of his Master. Only we must hold that a
shepherd should put his flock or even a single sheep before his own life.

Whose own the sheep are not. Christ here seems to make all, without
exception, apart from Himself, to be hirelings. For, since He alone is
the Shepherd, none of us has a right to call the sheep he feeds his own.
But let us remember that those who are guided by God's Spirit look
upon what belongs to their Head as their own; not to claim power for
themselves, but faithfully to look after what has been committed to
their charge. For he who is really united to Christ will never regard as
alien to him that which was so dear to Him. This is what He says next:

13. *The hireling fleeth.* Because he cares not for the sheep; i.e. because he is not touched by the scattering of the flock, since he thinks it does not belong to him. For he who looks to the wages, and not to the flock, may deceive when the Church is at peace, but when the fight is on he will soon afford evidence of his treachery.

14. *And I know my sheep.* In the first clause He commends His love towards us again; for knowledge is born of love and is accompanied by care. But it also means that He thinks nothing of those who do not obey the Gospel; for in the second clause He repeats and confirms what He had said before—that He is also known by the sheep in return.

15. *Even as the Father knoweth me.* It is unnecessary and inexpedient to enter into the thorny speculations as to how the Father knows His Wisdom. Christ simply says that, inasmuch as He is the bond of our union with God, He is set between Him and us. It is as if He said, that it is no more possible for Him to be oblivious of us than for the Father to reject or neglect Him. At the same time He demands a duty from us on our side. As He uses for our protection all the power He has received from the Father, so He wants us to be obedient and devoted to Him, just as He wholly is to the Father and refers all things to Him.

And other sheep I have, which are not of this fold: them also I must bring, and they shall hear my voice; and they shall become one flock, one shepherd. Therefore doth the Father love me, because I lay down my life, that I may take it again. No one taketh it away from me, but I lay it down of myself. I have power to lay it down, and I have power to take it again. This commandment received I from my Father. (16-18)

16. *And other sheep I have.* Although some refer this indiscriminately to all, whether Jews or Gentiles, who were not yet Christ's disciples, I have no doubt that He was thinking of the calling of the Gentiles. For He calls the congregation of the ancient people *the fold* in which they were separated from the other nations of the world, and united into one body as the heritage of God. God had adopted the Jews in such a way as to surround them with, as it were, boundaries of rites and ceremonies, that they might not be confused with unbelievers; yet the door of the fold was the gracious Covenant of eternal life confirmed in Christ. This is why He called them other sheep; they had not the same mark, but were of a different kind. In short, the meaning is that Christ's office as a Shepherd is not restricted to the confines of Judaea, but is far wider.

Augustine's observation on this passage is indeed true. Even as there are many wolves within the Church, so there are many sheep without. But it is not entirely applicable to this passage, which refers to the outward aspect of the Church, in that the Gentiles, who had been temporarily strangers, were afterwards taken into the Kingdom of God along with the Jews. Yet I admit that it applies in the sense that Christ calls unbelievers 'sheep' who in themselves could not be regarded as sheep at all. And by this word He not only shows what they will be, but, even more, refers it to the secret election of God, in that we are already God's sheep before we are aware that He is our Shepherd; just as elsewhere we are called enemies, even when He loved us (Rom. 5.10) and this is also why Paul says that we were known of God before we knew Him (Gal. 4.9).

Them also I must bring. He means that God's election will be sure and nothing will perish that He wishes to be saved. For the secret purpose of God by which men were ordained to life is at length manifested in His own time by the calling. And that calling is effectual, for He regenerates to Himself as sons by His Spirit those who were born of flesh and blood.

But it may be asked how the Gentiles were brought to be allied with the Jews. For the Jews did not have to reject the Covenant that God made with their fathers, before they could become Christ's disciples. Nor did the Gentiles on their side have to submit to the yoke of the Law, to be engrafted into Christ and allied with the Jews. Here we must keep to the distinction between the substance of the Covenant and its outward appurtenances. The Gentiles could only consent to the faith of Christ by embracing that everlasting Covenant on which the salvation of the world was founded. Thus the prophecies were fulfilled: 'Strangers shall speak the language of Canaan' (Isa. 19.18). Again, 'Seven men of the Gentiles shall take hold of the cloak of one Jew, and say, We will go with you' (Zech. 8.23). Again, 'They shall come from afar, and ascend into mount Sion.' Abraham was also called a father of many nations, because 'they shall come from the east and the west, and shall sit down with him in the kingdom of God' (Matt. 8.11). As for the ceremonies, they are the middle wall which Paul tells us has been thrown down (Eph. 2.14). Thus we have been joined with the Jews in the unity of the faith as to the substance. But the ceremonies were abolished, so that nothing might stop them from stretching out their hand to us.

And there shall be one flock. That is, so that all the children of God may be gathered into one body, even as we confess that there is one holy catholic Church and there must be one body with one Head. Paul says that there is one God, one faith, and one baptism; so that we ought to be one, even as we are called into one hope (Eph. 4.4-5). Now although the flock seems to be divided into different folds, yet believers who are scattered throughout the world are enclosed within common bounds, in that the same Word is preached to all and the same Sacraments are used, they have the same order of prayer and everything necessary for the profession of faith.

Observe the way in which the flock of God is collected. It is when there is one Shepherd of all and His voice is heard. These words mean that only when the Church submits to Christ alone, obeys His commands and hears His teaching, is she in a well-ordered condition. If Papists can show us anything like this among them, they can enjoy the sitle of Church which they boast so much about. But if Christ is tilent there, His majesty trodden under foot and His sacred ordinances ridiculed, what is their unity but a devilish conspiracy, worse and far more abhorrent than any scattering? Let us remember, therefore, that our starting point must always be at the Head. In this way the prophets, in describing the restoration of the Church, always join King David to God, as if they were saying that there is no Church if God does not reign there, and no Kingdom of God but where the title of shepherd is allowed to Christ.

17. *Therefore doth the Father love me.* There is, of course, another higher reason why the Father loves the Son. For the voice from heaven was not meaningless. 'This is the beloved Son, in whom dwells the good pleasure of God' (Matt. 3.17). But as He became man for our sakes and the Father loved Him to the end that He might reconcile us to Himself, it is not surprising that He says that He is loved, since our salvation is dearer to Him than His own life. Here is a wonderful commendation of the divine goodness to us which should ravish our whole souls into admiration, that God not only extends to us the love due to the only-begotten, but ascribes it to us as the final cause. And indeed there was no need for Christ to put on our flesh, in which He was beloved, except that it might be the pledge of His fatherly mercy in redeeming us.

That I may take it again. Because the death of Christ would give the disciples great sorrow when they heard of it and their faith might even be gravely shaken, He comforts them with the hope of His resurrection, soon to take place. As if He said that He would not die to be swallowed up by death, but speedily to rise again as Conqueror. And we today should so contemplate Christ's death that we remember at the same time the glory of His resurrection. So we know that He is life because He has conquered magnificently in His conflict with death and achieved a noble triumph.

18. *No one taketh it away from me.* Here is another consolation to encourage the disciples at the death of Christ; He is not forced to die, but offers Himself willingly for the salvation of His flock. Not only does He deny that men have power to kill Him without His permission, but He declares that He is free from all violence of necessity.

It is different with us. We are under a necessity of dying, because of our sins. Christ Himself was certainly born a mortal man; but it was a voluntary submission and not a bondage imposed by another.

Christ wanted to fortify His disciples, lest they should be broken-hearted when they saw Him soon afterwards being dragged to death as if He were overcome by His enemies. He wanted them to know that it came about by the wonderful providence of God that He should die for His flock. And this doctrine is useful continually, that Christ's death is an expiation for our sins, in that it was a voluntary sacrifice; as Paul said, 'Through the obedience of the one shall the many be made righteous' (Rom. 5.19).

But I lay it down of myself. These words can be expounded in two ways. Either, that Christ divests Himself of life, but still remains complete, just as a man puts off a garment from his body; or, that He dies by His own choice.

This commandment. He recalls us to the eternal counsel of the Father, to teach us that He was so careful for our salvation that He gave over to us His only begotten Son, great as He is. Christ Himself, who came into the world to be completely obedient to His Father, confirms that in everything His only aim is to think of us.

There arose a division again among the Jews because of these words. And many of them said, He hath a devil, and is mad; why hear ye him? Others said, These are not the sayings of one possessed with a devil. Can a devil open the eyes of the blind? And it was the feast of the dedication at Jerusalem: it was winter; and Jesus was walking in the temple in Solomon's porch. The Jews therefore came round about him, and said unto him, How long dost thou hold us in suspense? If thou art the Christ, tell us plainly. Jesus answered them, I told you, and ye believe not: the works that I do in my Father's name, these bear witness of me. But ye believe not, because ye are not of my sheep. My sheep hear my voice, and I know them, and they follow me: and I give unto them eternal life; and they shall never perish, and no one shall snatch them out of my hand. My Father, which hath given them unto me, is greater than all; and no one is able to snatch them out of the Father's hand. I and the Father are one. (19-30)

19. *There arose a division.* Christ's sermon had the result of winning Him some disciples. But because His teaching also has many enemies, a division arises, so that those who had hitherto seemed to be the one body of the Church, now split up. For with one consent, they all professed to worship the God of Abraham and to follow the Law of Moses. Now when Christ comes forward, He causes them to start differing. If their profession had been genuine, Christ would not have

broken up their agreement, for He is the strongest bond of love and His office is to gather together the things that are scattered. But by the light of His Gospel He uncovers the hypocrisy of many who claimed to be the people of God but had only a false pretence.

Thus the wickedness of many today is the reason why the Church is troubled by divisions and why controversies are started. Yet those who disturb the peace blame us for it and call us schismatics—for the chief accusation that the Papists bring against us is that our teaching has upset the peace of the Church. But if they would yield quietly to Christ and uphold the truth, all the commotions would be settled at once. When they murmur and brawl against Christ and will not let us be at rest on any other condition than that God's truth is extinguished and Christ banished from His Kingdom, they have no right to accuse us of schism. Everyone can see that it ought to be laid to their charge. We should be very grieved that the Church is torn by internal divisions. But it is better that some shall separate themselves from the ungodly and be united to Christ their Head, than that all should agree in despising God. And so, in regard to schism, the thing to notice is who are the ones who revolt from God and His pure doctrine.

20. *He hath a devil.* They slander Christ with the most offensive reproach they can think of, so that all may be afraid to hear Him. Lest they should be forced to yield to God, the ungodly shut their eyes and burst out furiously into a proud vilifying of Him and excite others to the same rage, so that not a word of Christ is heard in silence. But Christ's teaching has enough power in it to defend it against slanders. And this is what the believers mean by their reply when they say, *These are not the sayings of one possessed with a devil.* It is as if they are demanding that men should judge from the fact itself. For the truth, as has been said, can look after itself well enough. And the one thing that upholds our faith is, that the ungodly will never be able to prevent God's power and wisdom shining in the Gospel.

22. *And it was the feast of the dedication.* That is to say, 'renewals'. For the Temple, which had been polluted, was reconsecrated at the command of Judas Maccabaeus, and it was then determined that the new dedication should be an annual feast and celebration to call to remembrance the grace of God which had put an end to the tyranny of Antiochus. At that season Christ appeared in the Temple as usual, so that His preaching might be more fruitful among a large assembly.

23. *In Solomon's porch.* The Evangelist calls it the Temple, but it was only an annex to the Temple and not the Sanctuary itself. And he does not mean the old porch built by Solomon, which had been completely destroyed by the Chaldaeans; but that which the Jews, perhaps immediately after their return from the Babylonian captivity,

built on the pattern of the old porch and called by the same name to give it more honour. Herod afterwards built the new Temple.

24. *The Jews therefore came round about Him.* There is no doubt that at least the authors of the scheme were cunningly attacking Christ. For the common people might quite sincerely want Jesus to manifest Himself openly as the one sent by God to be a liberator. But just the few were captious and crafty, and wanted to extract this word from Him in the crowd, so that He might be lynched in a disturbance or arrested by the Romans.

By complaining that they were *kept in suspense,* they pretend that they are so ardent for the promised redemption that their minds are incessantly taken up with the desire for Christ. It is indeed the genuine attitude of godliness to find in Christ alone what will satisfy our minds or truly quieten them—as He Himself says, 'Come unto me, all ye that labour and are heavy laden, and I will refresh you, and ye shall find rest unto your souls '(Matt. 11.28-29). Therefore those who come to Christ should be prepared in the same sort of way as these men pretended to be. But they accuse Christ unfairly, as if He had not hitherto established their faith; for it was entirely their own fault that they had not a full and perfect knowledge of Him. But it is always the case with unbelievers that they would rather fluctuate in doubt than be founded on the sure Word of God. Today we see that many voluntarily shut their eyes and spread out the mists of their doubt to obscure the clear light of the Gospel. We also see many flighty spirits fluttering about in idle speculations and never finding in all their life a fixed position.

When they demand that Christ shall declare Himself plainly or *freely* and confidently, they mean that He shall no longer hint indirectly and evasively. And so they accuse His teaching of obscurity, when it was abundantly plain and distinct but for falling on deaf ears. Now this story warns us that we cannot escape the tricks and slanders of the wicked if we are called to preach the Gospel. Therefore we should be on our guard, and not let it take us by surprise if the same thing happens to us as to our Master.

25. *I told you.* The Lord does not conceal that He is the Christ; but nor does He teach them as if they were ready to learn. Rather, He reproaches them with their obstinate malice, in that, although they had been instructed by the Word and works of God, it had not done them any good. Hence He says it is their own fault that they do not know Him; as if He said, 'My teaching is easily understood in itself, and it is you who are to blame, because you malignantly resist God.'

He then speaks of His *works,* to convict them of a double obstinacy. They had, as well as the teaching, a striking testimony in His miracles, if they had not been ungrateful to God. He twice says that they do not *believe*, to prove that they were deaf to teaching and blind to works of their own accord. This was a sign of extreme and desperate malice. He says that He did *the works* in His Father's name, because His aim was to testify the power of God in them, from which it might become plain that He was from God.

26. *Because ye are not of my sheep.* He gives a profounder reason for their not believing either in His miracles or His teaching—it is because they are reprobate. We must notice Christ's aim. Since they boasted that they were the Church of God, He affirms that believing is a special gift, lest their unbelief should detract at all from the Gospel. And indeed, that men may know God, they must first be known by Him, as Paul says (Gal. 4.9). On the other hand, those for whom God has no regard, must of necessity always remain turned away from Him. If anyone murmurs at this that the cause of unbelief lies in God, because it is for Him alone to make 'sheep'; I reply, He is free from all blame, for it is only by their voluntary malice that men reject His grace. God does everything necessary to bring about faith in Himself, but wild beasts will never be tamed till they are changed into 'sheep' by God's Spirit. Those who are wild try in vain to throw the blame for their wildness on God, for it belongs to their own nature. In short, Christ means that it is not surprising if only a few obey His Gospel, because all whom the Spirit of God does not subdue to the obedience of faith are fierce and untameable beasts. So much the more intolerable and unreasonable is it that the authority of the Gospel should depend on the assent (*fide*) of men. Believers should rather reckon that they are the more strongly bound to God because while others remain in blindness they are drawn to Christ by the enlightening of the Spirit. This also is a comfort to ministers of the Gospel if their labour is not profitable to all.

27. *My sheep.* He proves by an argument from contraries that they are not sheep, because they do not obey the Gospel. For God effectually calls those whom He has elected, so that Christ's sheep are proved by their faith. And indeed, believers are called sheep because they surrender themselves to God to be ruled by the hand of the head Shepherd, and putting aside their first fierceness, become leadable and meek. It is no small consolation to godly teachers that, although the larger part of the world does not listen to Christ, He has His sheep whom He knows and by whom He is also known. They must do their utmost to bring the whole world into Christ's fold, but when they do not succeed as they would wish, they must be satisfied with the single thought that those who are sheep will be collected together by their work. The rest has been expounded already.

28. *And they shall never perish.* It is the incomparable fruit of faith that Christ bids us be sure and untroubled when we are brought by faith into His fold. But we must also see what basis this assurance rests on. It is that He will be the faithful guardian of our salvation, for He says that it is *in His hand.* And as if this were not enough, He says that they will be safely protected by His Father's power. This is a remarkable passage, teaching us that the salvation of all the elect is as certain as God's power is invincible. And Christ was not just tossing this Word thoughtlessly into the air, but giving a promise which should remain deeply fixed in their minds. Therefore we infer that Christ's saying indicates that the elect are firmly certain of their salvation. We are surrounded by powerful enemies, and so great is our weakness that we are not far from death every moment. But He who keeps what we have committed unto Him is *greater* and more powerful *than all*; and so we have nothing to be afraid of, as if our life were in danger.

From this, too, we see how mad is the confidence of the Papists, relying on free will, their own strength and the merits of their works. Christ teaches His followers, very differently from this, to remember that in this world they are, so to say, in the middle of a forest among innumerable robbers; and what is more, are not only unarmed and exposed as a prey, but know that the cause of death lies within themselves, so that they can only walk safely when relying on the protection of God. In short, our salvation is certain because it is in the hand of God. Our faith is weak, and we are given to wavering; but God has taken us in His hand and is powerful enough to scatter with a breath all the efforts of our enemies. It is very important for us to look at this, so that fear of temptations may not dismay us. For Christ also meant to show how the sheep live quietly in the midst of wolves.

And no one is able to snatch them out of the Father's hand. The copula is used instead of the particle *therefore* in this passage. For from the invincible power of God, Christ deduces that the salvation of the godly is not exposed to their enemies' desires, because God, who has taken them under the protection of His hand, would first have to be overcome.

30. *I and the Father are one.* He wanted to meet the jeers of the ungodly; for they might have objected that God's power did not belong to Him, so that He could promise His disciples its certain aid. He therefore declares that His affairs are so much one with the Father's that the Father's help will never be lacking to Himself and His sheep. The ancients misused this passage to prove that Christ is ὁμοούσιος with the Father. Christ is not discussing the unity of substance, but the concord He has with the Father; so that whatever Christ does will be confirmed by His Father's power.

The Jews took up stones again to stone him. Jesus answered them, Many good works have I shewed you from the Father; for which of those works do ye stone me? The Jews answered him, For a good work we stone thee not, but for blasphemy; and because that thou, being a man, makest thyself God. Jesus answered them, Is it not written in your law, I said, Ye are gods? If he called them gods, unto whom the word of God came (and the scripture cannot be broken), say ye of him, whom the Father sanctified and sent into the world, Thou blasphemest; because I said, I am the Son of God? (31-36)

31. *They took up stones again.* When godliness upholds God's glory, it burns with a zeal directed by the Spirit of God. In the same way, unbelief is the mother of fury, and the devil so stirs up the ungodly that they breathe out slaughter. The result shows their motive in putting the question to Christ, for His open confession, which they pretended to want, at once drives them to madness. And yet though they are carried away with such violence to oppress Christ, there is no doubt that they hid behind a colour of legality, as if they were acting according to the command of the Law by which God commands false prophets to be stoned (Deut. 13.5).

32. *Many good works.* Here Christ is saying that they not only have no cause for their cruelty, but also accuses them of ingratitude in repaying God's blessings so inequitably. He does not say that He has deserved well of them by one or two works, but that He has been kind to them in many ways. Then He reproves them for being ungrateful, not only to Himself, but rather to God; for He says that He is the Father's Minister, openly manifesting His power to make it known and witness it to them. For when He says *from the Father*, He means that God was their Author. The sum of it is this: 'God wanted to make known to you by me the excellent benefits bestowed on you by my hand. Examine me as you wish, I have done nothing among you but what deserves praise and thanks. Therefore, you must needs want to persecute in me the gifts of God.' But put as a question it has greater force to pierce their consciences than if He had said it straight-forwardly.

33. *For a good work we stone thee not.* Although the ungodly wage open war on God, they never want to sin without a semblance of honesty. Therefore, when they rage against the Son of God, they are not satisfied with this cruelty but accuse Him without provocation and make themselves advocates and avengers of the glory of God. A good conscience should be like a wall of brass to us, to repel boldly the reproaches and slanders with which we are attacked. For however plausibly their malice may be tricked up, and whatever ignominy they may bring upon us for a time, if we are fighting for the cause of God,

He will not refuse to uphold His truth. But the ungodly never lack excuses for oppressing God's servants and they have such hardened impudence that they do not stop reviling even when they are overcome. Therefore we need patience and meekness to support us to the end. The word *blasphemy*, which secular authors use generally for any kind of reproach, the Scriptures apply to God when His majesty is wounded and insulted.

Because that thou, being a man. There are two kinds of blasphemy. The one is when God is despoiled of His due honour. The other when anything unworthy of or foreign to His nature is ascribed to Him. They contend therefore that Christ is a blasphemer and sacrilegious, because as a mortal man He usurps divine honour. And this would be a true definition of blasphemy if Christ were nothing more than a man. Where they go wrong is in not troubling to contemplate His divinity, which was conspicuous in His miracles.

34. *Is it not written in your law?* He clears Himself of the fault charged against Him, not by denying He is the Son of God but by maintaining that He had been right to say He was. Yet He fits His reply to the persons instead of explaining the matter fully, for He regarded it as sufficient at present to refute their malice. He hints indirectly, rather than expresses plainly, the sense in which He called Himself the Son of God. The argument He uses is taken, not from things equal, but from the less to the greater.

Scripture calls 'gods' those on whom God has laid an honourable office. But He whom God separated to be eminent above all others is far more worthy of this noble title. Whence it follows that they are malignant and false expositors who admit the first but are offended at the second. The passage which Christ quotes comes in Ps. 82.6, where God expostulates with the kings and judges of the earth, who tyrannically abuse their authority and power for their own passions and oppressing the poor and every kind of evil. He reproaches them for being unmindful of the one from whom they received so much honour and profaning the name of God. Christ applies this to the present case. They are adorned with the name of gods, because they are God's ministers to govern the world. Scripture calls the angels 'gods' for the same reason, in that through them God's glory shines forth upon the world. Let us note the phrase:

35. *To whom the word of God was addressed.* Christ means that they were furnished with a definite command from God. From this we infer that empires did not spring up by chance or from men's mistakes but were appointed by the will of God, who wishes political order to flourish among men and that we should be governed by right and law. This is why Paul says that all who resist the power are rebels against

God, because there is no power but what is ordained of God (Rom. 13.1-2). If any object that other callings are also from God and are approved by Him, and yet that we do not call farmers or cowherds or cobblers 'gods', I reply, this declaration is not general, that all who are called by God to any particular way of life are called 'gods'. Christ is speaking of kings, whom God has raised to a higher rank that they may rule and be above the rest. In short, let us know that magistrates are called 'gods' because God has committed the rule to them. Under the word *law* Christ embraces the whole teaching by which God governed His ancient people. For since the prophets were simply expounders of the Law, the Psalms were also regarded as an appendage to the Law. *The scripture cannot be broken* means that the doctrine of Scripture is inviolable.

36. *Whom the Father sanctified.* There is a sanctification that is common to all the godly. But here Christ is claiming something far better for Himself; namely, that He was separated from all others that the power of the Spirit and the majesty of God might be displayed in Him. As He had said earlier, He was sealed by God the Father (6.27). But this refers properly to the person of Christ as He is manifested in the flesh. Therefore, these two things are joined, that He was sanctified and that He was sent into the world. But we must also understand for what reason and on what condition He was sent. It was to bring salvation from God and prove and show Himself in every way to be the Son of God.

Say ye, Thou blasphemest? The Arians twisted this passage to prove that Christ is not God by nature, but has a kind of secondary (*precarius*) divinity. But this error is easily refuted, for Christ is not now discussing what He is in Himself, but what we should acknowledge Him to be from His miracles in human flesh. For we can never apprehend His eternal divinity until we embrace Him as the Redeemer revealed to us by the Father. Moreover, we should remember what I suggested before, that in this passage Christ is not openly and distinctly explaining what He is, as He would have done to His disciples. He is rather concentrating on refuting the slander of His enemies.

If I do not the works of my Father, believe me not. But if I do them, though ye believe not me, believe the works: that ye may know and believe that the Father is in me, and I in the Father. They sought again to take him: and he went forth out of their hand. And he went away again beyond Jordan into the place where John was at the first baptizing; and there he abode. And many came unto him; and they said, John indeed did no sign: but all things whatsoever John spake of this man were true. And many believed on him there. (37-42)

37. *If I do not the works.* He again emphasizes His miracles, lest the Jews should reply that He was boasting of sanctification and all that depended on it in vain; for they were plain enough proof of His divinity. This is in the form of a concession, as if He were saying, 'I do not want you to feel bound to believe in me for any other reason than that the fact itself appears plainly. You can reject me with impunity if God has not given open testimony to me.' He calls them *the works of my Father* because they were truly divine, and a greater power shone in them than could be ascribed to man.

38. *But if I do.* He shows that they are obviously guilty of ungodly and sacrilegious contempt because they give no honour to the manifest works of God. It is a second concession when He says, 'Although I were to let you doubt my teaching, you cannot deny, at any rate, that the miracles I have done are from God. You are therefore openly rejecting God and not a man.'

Although He puts faith after knowledge, as if it were inferior, He does so because He is dealing with unbelieving and perverse men, who will never yield to God until they are overcome and forced by experience. For rebels want to know before they believe. And yet God indulges us so far as to prepare us for faith by a knowledge of His works. But the knowledge of God and of His secret wisdom follows faith in order, because the obedience of faith opens to us the door of the Kingdom of Heaven.

That the Father is in me. He repeats the same thing as He had earlier said in other words, 'I and the Father are one.' It all comes to this, that in the conduct of His ministry there is nothing contrary to His Father. 'The Father is in me,' He says. That is, divine power is manifested in Me. 'And I am in my Father.' That is, I do nothing but by God's authority, so that there is a mutual connexion between Me and my Father. For this saying does not refer to the unity of essence, but to the manifestation of divine power in the person of Christ, which showed that He was sent from God.

39. *They sought again to take him.* This was undoubtedly that they might drag Him out of the Temple and stone Him. For their rage was in no way appeased by Christ's words. As to its saying that *he slipped out of their hand,* this could only have been accomplished by the wonderful power of God. It reminds us that we are not exposed to the passions of the wicked, which God restrains by His bridle whenever He wishes.

40. *He went away again beyond Jordan.* Christ passed beyond Jordan so that He should not have to be always fighting without much advantage. He has therefore taught us by His example to make use of convenient opportunities. On the place of His retreat, see 1.28.

41. *And many came unto Him*. The large assembly shows that Christ was not seeking solitude to neglect His duty, but to set up a Sanctuary to God in the wilderness when His own place, Jerusalem, had obstinately driven Him out. And this was assuredly a dreadful vengeance of God, that when the Temple chosen by God was a den of thieves, God's Church was gathered together in a despised place.

John indeed. They infer that Christ is more excellent than John because His miracles were so remarkable, whereas John did not perform any miracles. Not that we should always judge from miracles; but when they are joined with teaching, they have no small weight, as has been frequently said already. Moreover, their argument is defective. They compare Christ with John, but express only one part of it. And they take it for granted that John was an outstanding prophet of God and endued with a unique grace of the Spirit. They sensibly reason, therefore, that Christ is to be preferred to John because it was only by the certain providence of God that John, who in other respects was a very great prophet, was not given the honour of performing a miracle. Hence they conclude that this happened for Christ's sake, that He might be more highly esteemed.

But all things whatsoever he spake. It seems that this was not said by them, but added by the Evangelist to show that they were induced to believe in Christ by a twofold argument. They saw that the witness which John had borne to Him was true, and that the miracles procured Him greater honour.